S0-FQX-813

SOCIOLOGICAL METHODOLOGY

2001

SOCIOLOGICAL METHODOLOGY 2001

VOLUME 31

An official publication by Blackwell Publishers for

THE AMERICAN SOCIOLOGICAL ASSOCIATION

FELICE LEVINE, *Executive Officer*

Library of Congress Catalog Card Information
Sociological Methodology, 1969–85

San Francisco, Jossey-Bass. 15 v. illus. 24 cm. annual. (Jossey-Bass behavioral science series)

Editor: 1969, 1970: E. F. Borgatta; 1971, 1972, 1973–74: H. L. Costner; 1975, 1976, 1977: D. R. Heise; 1978, 1979, 1980: K. F. Schuessler; 1981, 1982, 1983–84: S. Leinhardt; 1985: N. B. Tuma

Sociological Methodology, 1986–88

Washington, DC, American Sociological Association. 3 v. illus. 24 cm. annual.

Editor: 1986: N. B. Tuma; 1987, 1988: C. C. Clogg

Sociological Methodology, 1989–1992

Oxford, Basil Blackwell. 4 v. illus. 24 cm. annual.

Editor: 1989, 1990: C. C. Clogg; 1991, 1992: P. V. Marsden

"An official publication of the American Sociological Association."

1. Sociology—Methodology—Year books. I. American Sociological Association. II. Borgatta, Edgar F., 1924– ed.

HM24.S55 301′.01′8 68-54940
rev.
Library of Congress [r71h2]

British Cataloguing in Publication Data
Sociological Methodology. Vol. 30

1. Sociology. Methodology
301′.01′8

ISBN 0-631-23219-2
ISSN 0081-1750

REVIEWERS

Kenneth A. Bollen
Anne Boomsma
Babette Brumback
Michael Chernew
Marcel A. Croon
Nan Dirk de Graaf
Aimée R. Dechter
Scott Eliason
David Firth
Noah Friedkin
John C. Gower
Martin Karlberg
Steven Kou
Barry Markovsky
Peter Marsden
Abt Mooijaart
Susan A. Murphy
Philippa Pattison
Marc Scott
Tom A. B. Snijders
Hal Stern
Ross M. Stolzenberg
Clem Stone
Peter G.M. van der Heijden
Jeroen K. Vermunt
Stanley Wasserman
David Weakliem
Christopher Winship
Kazuo Yamaguchi
Yu Xie

CONTENTS

Reviewers v

Contributors ix

Information for Authors xi

In This Volume xiii

1. Statistics in Sociology, 1950–2000: A Selective Review 1
Adrian E. Raftery

2. A Framework for the Study of Individual Behavior and Social Interactions 47
Steven N. Durlauf
Discussion:
Comment on Steven Durlauf's "A Framework for the Study of Individual Behavior and Social Interactions" 89
Samuel Bowles
Modeling Social Interdependence: Is It in the Structure or in Our Hearts? 97
Lin Tao and Christopher Winship
Comment: Potential Applications and Extensions for a Choice-Based Social Interaction Framework 107
Aimée R. Dechter
Rejoinder: 123
Steven N. Durlauf

3. Analysis of Categorical Response Profiles by Informative Summaries 129
Zvi Gilula and Shelby J. Haberman

4. Statistical methods and Graphical Displays for Analyzing How the Association Between Two Qualitative Variables Differs Among Countries, Among Groups, or Over Time. Part II: Some Exploratory Techniques, Simple Models, and Simple Examples 189
Leo A. Goodman and Michael Hout

5. Latent Class Factor and Cluster Models, Bi-Plots and Related Graphical Displays 223
Jay Magidson and Jeroen K. Vermunt

6. Covariance Models for Latent Structure in Longitudinal Data 265
Marc A. Scott and Mark S. Handcock

7. The Cohesiveness of Blocks in Social Networks: Connectivity and Conditional Density 305
Douglas White and Frank Harary

8. The Statistical Evaluation of Social Network Dynamics 361
Tom A.B. Snijders

CONTRIBUTORS

Samuel Bowles, Department of Economics, University of Massachusetts

Aimée Dechter, Department of Sociology, University of Wisconsin, Madison

Steven N. Durlauf, Department of Economics, University of Wisconsin, Madison

Zvi Gilula, Department of Statistics, Hebrew University, Jerusalem, Israel

Leo A. Goodman, Department of Sociology, University of California, Berkeley

Shelby J. Haberman, Department of Statistics, Northwestern University

Mark S. Handcock, Departments of Statistics and Sociology, University of Washington

Frank Harary, Computer Science Department, New Mexico State University

Michael Hout, Department of Sociology, University of California, Berkeley

Jay Magidson, Statistical Innovations, Belmont, Massachusetts

Adrian E. Raftery, Departments of Statistics and Sociology, University of Washington

Marc A. Scott, Department of Humanities and Social Sciences, Steinhardt School of Education, New York University

Tom A.B. Snidjers ICS, Department of Statistics and Measurement Theory, University of Groningen, The Netherlands

Lin Tao, Department of Sociology, Harvard University

Jeroen K. Vermunt, Department of Methodology, Faculty of Social and Behavioral Sciences, Tilburg University, the Netherlands

Douglas R. White, Department of Anthropology, University of California, Irvine

Christopher Winship, Department of Sociology, Harvard University

SUBMISSION INFORMATION FOR AUTHORS

Sociological Methodology is an annual volume on methods of research in the social sciences. Sponsored by the American Sociological Association, its mission is to disseminate material that advances empirical research in sociology and related disciplines. Chapters present original methodological contributions, expository statements on and illustrations of recently developed techniques, and critical discussions of research practice.

Sociological Methodology seeks contributions that address the full range of problems confronted by empirical work in the contemporary social sciences, including conceptualization and modeling, research design, data collection, measurement, and data analysis. Work on the methodological problems involved in any approach to empirical social science is appropriate for *Sociological Methodology*.

The content of each annual volume of *Sociological Methodology* is driven by submissions initiated by authors; the volumes do not have specific themes. Editorial decisions about manuscripts submitted are based on the advice of expert referees. Criteria include originality, breadth of interest and applicability, and expository clarity. Discussions of implications for research practice are vital, and authors are urged to include empirical illustrations of the methods they discuss.

Authors should submit five copies of manuscripts to

Ross M. Stolzenberg, Editor
Sociological Methodology
Department of Sociology
307 Social Science Building
1126 East 59th Street
Chicago, Illinois 60637

Manuscripts should include an informative abstract of not more than one double-spaced page, and should not identify the author within the text. Submission of a manuscript for review by *Sociological Methodology* implies that it has not been published previously and that it is not under review elsewhere.

Inquiries concerning the appropriateness of material and/or other aspects of editorial policies and procedures are welcome; prospective authors should correspond with the editor by E-mail at r-stolzenberg@uchicago.edu.

IN THIS VOLUME

FOREWORD

The eight chapters in this volume of *Sociological Methodology* touch on both long-standing and more recent themes in social statistics. In one way or another, all these themes (as well as others) are discussed at greater length in Chapter 1, "Statistics in Sociology, 1950–2000: A Selective Review." Dividing this period into three generations based on the type of data structure most typically featured, Adrian Raftery first reviews the analysis of cross-tabulations, a theme reflected here in the papers by Haberman and Gilula, Goodman and Hout, and Magidson and Vermunt. Next, he reviews statistical methods developed to analyze survey data on individuals—for example, structural equation models and survival (event-history) models. Scott and Handcock, who propose new methods for modeling longitudinal data, nicely combine a number of themes that have emerged primarily during this second generation. Finally, Raftery turns his attention to the future, discussing limitations of some current work and outlining some developments he thinks important for social statistics during the years ahead. One of the topics discussed is social networks, a theme reflected directly in the article by White and Harary and the piece by Snijders on the analysis of longitudinal network data. Raftery also discusses recent work in spatial statistics, noting that approaches based on random fields have proved productive; Durlauf uses random fields to study social interactions. Raftery also outlines the need for further advances in the analysis of textual and qualitative (not tabular) data, narrative and sequence analysis, and the need for putting simulation modeling on a firmer inferential footing, going so far as to make specific types of proposals on the types of advances and how these might be achieved. Social statistics will blossom if the many leads identified by Raftery are followed, and the next generation of social statisticians should be grateful to him for seeing so clearly some of the steps ahead.

Steven Durlauf's outstanding and forward-looking work on what is perhaps the most important issue in sociology—the interdependence between group and individual—is just the kind of advance Raftery would appreciate (even if it is not anticipated in his essay). Although economists have long recognized the interdependence of preferences, such considerations have not been incorporated into standard economic models of individual decision making (in part because it is hard to do). Sociologists, who often use these models, nevertheless complain that economists treat individuals as atomized actors. If ever such complaints were legitimate, Durlauf's paper amply evidences that it is time to cease and desist. To be sure, one might not like the way Durlauf incorporates social interactions into the models he proposes or think that this is the only productive way to do so. The point, however, is that Durlauf has put forth a coherent framework in which such objections can be raised, and the models improved and extended, both in directions Durlauf might imagine and in directions he might not. Furthermore, Durlauf's framework is not merely theoretical. The models he proposes can be estimated and used to inform important sociological issues, such as decisions to have (not have) a child or to move (not move) neighborhoods, or how many years of education to obtain. Use of this framework should also lead future workers to use more interesting and informative data structures than those routinely used in current work.

Due to the potential importance and novelty of Durlauf's work, we believed that further discussion of his paper would be most interesting and useful for *Sociological Methodology* readers. We are grateful to Samuel Bowles, Lin Tao and Christopher Winship, and Aimée Dechter, for agreeing to serve as discussants and for contributing to this volume. We also thank Steven Durlauf for graciously consenting to this discussion and for responding to the discussants.

Chapters 3 through 5 discuss the modeling of categorical data. Haberman and Gilula consider estimation and description of a vector of dependent categorical variables (for example, binary responses on ten items) using as predictors one or more covariates. When there are many dependent variables and/or categories of the dependent variables and large samples, no nontrivial log-linear model typically fits the data using χ^2 tests; furthermore, such tests might not always be appropriate. Nevertheless, one wants to know how much the covariates help in predicting the response. This paper discusses appropriate estimation methods for fitting log-linear models in this case and using them to describe the resulting predictive power of the model and compare competing sets of predictors. Goodman and Hout take up several special cases of the model for comparing differences in association across a third variable that they proposed in their 1998 *Sociological Methodology* paper. Magidson and Vermunt discuss exploratory latent class models and their relationship to latent class factor models, arguing that the latter often have interpretive and empirical advantages over the former. They also propose using "bi-plots" to graphically display the results from fitting these models.

Longitudinal data analysis is now a large area of interest, and many different types of models and modeling strategies have been proposed, as nicely documented in the paper by Scott and Handcock. Readers of *Sociological Methodology* are most likely to be familiar with methods designed to describe the mean of a population (population average analysis) or subpopulation or methods designed to describe the mean of given persons—for example, random coefficient models. In the former case, the covariance is a nuisance parameter and one wants to be able to model the mean structure properly without worrying about modeling the covariance structure correctly. In the second case, it is usual to endow individuals with unobserved components that reflect individual differences. Other approaches to modeling longitudinal data discussed in this paper include latent curve modeling and latent class models, in which individuals belong to latent classes with different trajectories. However, these methods do not yield a population average analysis of variation, which is what one would need to assess dispersion in wage profiles, a subject of great interest to labor economists. Scott and Handcock propose new models (proto-spline models) that combine features of the approaches above, enabling them to address such issues.

Chapters 7 and 8 take up themes in network analysis. In the first of these, White and Harary take up the topic of cohesion, which they regard as one component of solidarity (the other being adhesion), arguing that connectivity and conditional density are two measures of cohesion. In Chapter 8, Snijders proposes a continuous-time Markov chain model for studying the evolution of a network of actors on which a directed relationship is defined. The dynamics are generated by actors maximizing objective functions (which include a random term) by adding new relations and/or dropping old ones. The model is estimated using MCMC methods.

ACKNOWLEDGMENTS

The chapters in this volume represent a number of different themes, ranging far beyond our expertise. We are especially grateful to our expert reviewers for their excellent and thoughtful advice and for giving so generously of their time. The reviews we received were of exceptional quality and we (not to mention the authors of submitted papers) learned a great deal by paying careful attention to them.

Our editorial term ends with the production of this volume. We have learned a great deal from this experience, and it has been our privilege to serve the intellectual community. Editors often quickly learn who can be counted on for thoughtful and timely reviews and then proceed to repeatedly call on these individuals for help. We have been no different in this regard, and we at least want to especially thank those persons who reviewed for us time and time again without ever objecting to the undue burden we placed upon them. Their contributions to the journal far outweigh any that we have made as editors. We are also grateful to Carson Hicks, managing editor, who has kept the journal functioning and whose organizational abilities far exceed our own. It has truly been our pleasure to work with her. We also thank Stephanie Argeros-Magean for her excellent work as copy editor these past years. Karen Edwards has been our contact person at the American Sociological Association and we are grateful to her for assistance in all official matters.

1

STATISTICS IN SOCIOLOGY, 1950–2000: A SELECTIVE REVIEW

*Adrian E. Raftery**

Statistical methods have had a successful half-century in sociology, contributing to a greatly improved standard of scientific rigor in the discipline. I identify three overlapping postwar generations of statistical methods in sociology, based on the kinds of data they address. The first generation, which started in the late 1940s, deals with cross-tabulations and focuses on measures of association and log-linear models, perhaps the area of statistics to which sociology has contributed the most. The second generation, which began in the 1960s, deals with unit-level survey data and focuses on LISREL-type causal models and event-history analysis. The third generation, starting to emerge in the late 1980s, deals with data that do not fall easily into either of these categories, either because they have a different form, such as texts or narratives, or because dependence is a crucial aspect, as with spatial or social network data. There are many new challenges, and the area is ripe for statistical research; several major institutions have recently launched new initiatives in statistics and the social sciences.

1. INTRODUCTION

To mark the year 2000, the *Journal of the American Statistical Association* published a series of about 50 short vignettes, each about some aspect of statistical development in the century that was ending. The idea was to

I am very grateful to Mark Becker, Mark Handcock, Don Rubin, Tom Snijders, Rob Warren, Yu Xie, and Kazuo Yamaguchi for extremely helpful comments that greatly improved the manuscript.

*University of Washington

summarize some of the best work and to highlight potentially fruitful areas of future research. I wrote the vignette about statistics in sociology (Raftery 2000). Other vignettes of possible interest to *Sociological Methodology* readers include the ones on contingency tables and log-linear models (Fienberg 2000), causal inference in the social sciences (Sobel 2000), demography (Xie 2000), political methodology (Beck 2000), psychometrics (Browne 2000), and empirical methods in legal science (Eisenberg 2000).

Many colleagues sent me comments on the first draft, quite a few of them correctly pointing out important developments that I had missed. It was impossible to rectify this given the small amount of space allocated by JASA, but *Sociological Methodology* editors Michael Sobel and Mark Becker invited me to submit an expanded version that would provide more appropriate coverage of this dynamic field.

The roots of sociology go back to the mid-nineteenth century and to seminal work by Auguste Comte (who invented the word "sociology"), Karl Marx, Max Weber, and Emile Durkheim on the kind of society then newly emerging from the Industrial Revolution. Sociology has used quantitative methods and data from the beginning. Comte, who launched the discipline, was quite explicit about its grounding in statistical data. Durkheim's (1897) *Le Suicide*, for example, made extensive use of statistical data.

However, prior to World War II, the data tended to be fragmentary, often bordering on the anecdotal, and the statistical methods simple and descriptive. Camic and Wilson (1994) identified Franklin H. Giddings as the father of quantitative sociology in America. Giddings, who was appointed professor of sociology at Columbia in 1894 and died in 1931, defined sociology as a field that studies social phenomena at the aggregate level. He held that statistical analysis in sociology consists largely of counting the individuals in each of several categories and finding average characteristics of each category. From a modern statistical perspective, a striking feature of his work was his relative lack of concern with variation.

Since then, the data available have grown in complexity, and statistical methods have been developed to deal with them. Much of this statistical development has been due to sociologists rather than statisticians; Clogg (1992) and the discussants of his article made this point emphatically, and documented it well. This partly reflects the fact that the number of statisticians working on sociological problems has always been relatively small. Statisticians have tended to work in greater numbers on problems emerging from medicine, engineering and the biological sciences; this probably reflects the balance of available funding in the latter half of the twentieth century. There are some signs recently that this situation is changing, which I will mention at the end of the article.

The overall trend in sociology in the past 50 years has been toward more rigorous formulation of hypotheses, larger and more detailed data sets, statistical models growing in complexity to match the data, and a higher level of statistical analysis in the major sociological journals. Statistical methods have had a successful half-century in sociology, contributing to a greatly improved standard of scientific rigor in the discipline.

Sociology has made extensive use of a wide variety of statistical methods and models. I will focus here on the ones developed by sociologists, those whose development was directly motivated by sociological problems, and those that were first published in sociological journals. Many other methods, such as those for limited dependent variables (logistic regression springs to mind), have been used extensively in sociology, but they were primarily developed in other disciplines in response to other problems. Important though they are for sociology, I will mention these areas more briefly.

A major omission from this article is any in-depth discussion of statistical methods that have come to sociology from econometrics rather than from statistics; this would merit a separate review article in its own right. Econometrics has been very influential in sociological methodology, some would argue as much or more as statistics itself, but here I do not review this important influence except incidentally.

At the risk of controversy, I will classify statistical methods in sociology by the kind of data that they address, rather than by the method itself. I will distinguish three postwar generations of statistical methods in sociology, each defined by the kind of data to which they are most often applied: (1) cross-tabulations, (2) unit-level survey data, and (3) newer data forms. Like real generations, these intellectual generations overlap and the boundaries between them are not clear-cut; they all remain active today, albeit at different levels of maturity, and even their starting points are not uniquely defined.

In the period starting after World War II, much of the data that sociologists had to work with came in the form of cross-tabulations of counts from surveys and censuses. The first generation of methods I will discuss deals with data of this kind. Typically these cross-classifications involved only a small number of variables such as sex, age group and occupational category; social mobility tables provided the canonical example for much of the methodological work. This is perhaps the area of statistics to which sociologists have contributed the most; indeed, it could be argued that sociologists have dominated this subfield and that the methods they have developed have been diffusing out from sociology into other disciplines. Schuessler (1980) is a survey that largely reflects this first-generation work.

By the early 1960s, sociologists no longer had to rely on cross-tabulations of counts, and unit-level data from surveys that measured many variables were becoming available. Computing power was also developing to the point where it could handle such data fairly easily. The second generation of methods was developed to deal with data of this kind. This generation of methods was galvanized by Blau and Duncan's (1967) highly influential book, *The American Occupational Structure*, and also by the establishment of *Sociological Methodology* in 1969, and that of *Sociological Methods and Research* in 1972 as publication outlets. Edgar Borgatta established both of these publications, the second when it became rapidly apparent that there was both the supply and demand for more articles than could be published by *Sociological Methodology* alone. These developments marked the coming of age of research on quantitative methodology in sociology.

By the late 1980s, sociologists had conceived the ambition of analyzing data that do not fit easily into the standard straitjackets of cross-tabulations or data matrices (although they can sometimes be forced into it). These include texts or narratives, and data in which dependence is a crucial aspect, such as social network data and data in which spatial referencing is a crucial aspect. They also include data sets that combine multiple types of data, such as satellite images, ethnographic accounts, and quantitative measurements. The third generation of methods is being developed to address data such as these. As befits its youth, so far it is a lively and exciting grab bag of ideas and developments, not having yet achieved the well-organized maturity of the first two generations.

My classification of statistical methods in sociology into generations defined by the kind of data addressed, rather than the kind of method used, does not reflect the usual organization of graduate training, and it is bound to be somewhat controversial. Perhaps for reasons of convenience and efficiency in training, the major methods of sociology have tended to be grouped together under categories such as regression models, limited dependent variable models, log-linear models, structural equation models, event-history analysis, and so on. However, I have found it easier to attempt to discern past trends and to think about future developments by focusing on the types of data that motivate the development of the methods in the first place.

We have come a long way in the past 50 years. Today, much sociological research is based on the reanalysis of large high-quality survey sample data sets, often collected with public funds and publicly available to researchers, with typical sample sizes in the range 5,000 to 20,000, or greater. This has opened the way to easy replication of results and has helped to produce standards of scientific rigor in sociology comparable to and greater than those in many of the natural and medical sciences. Perhaps in part because of this, social statistics has recently started a rapid expansion as a research area, and several major institutions have launched initiatives in this area in the past few years.

2. THE FIRST GENERATION: CROSS-TABULATIONS

2.1. *Categorical Data Analysis*

Initially, much of the data that quantitative sociologists had to work with came in the form of cross-classified tables, and so it is not surprising that this is perhaps the area of statistics to which sociology has contributed the most. A canonical example has been the analysis of social mobility tables, usually in the form of two-way tables of father's against respondent's occupational category; typically the number of categories used is between 5 and 17.

At first the focus was on measures of association, or mobility indices as they were called in the social mobility context (Glass 1954; Rogoff 1953), but these indices failed to do the job of separating structural mobility from exchange (or circulation) mobility. The solution to this key problem in the analysis of mobility tables turned out to require explicit probability models for the tables. Birch (1963) proposed the log-linear model for the observed counts $\{x_{ij}\}$, given by

$$\log(E[x_{ij}]) = u + u_{1(i)} + u_{2(j)} + u_{12(ij)}, \tag{1}$$

where i indexes rows and j columns, $u_{1(i)}$ and $u_{2(j)}$ are the main effects for the rows and columns, and $u_{12(ij)}$ is the interaction term, measuring departures from independence. This provided the overall framework needed for the rigorous analysis of mobility and similar tables. However, the difficulty with model (1) in its original form for social mobility and similar tables is that the number of parameters is too large for inference and interpretation. For example, in the U.S. data sets 17 categories were used, so the interaction term involves $16^2 = 256$ parameters.

To make progress, it was necessary to model the interaction term parsimoniously (i.e., with few parameters), but in a way that fits the data. A successful general approach to doing this is the association model of Duncan (1979) and Goodman (1979):

$$u_{12(ij)} = \sum_{m=1}^{M} \gamma_m \alpha_i^{(m)} \beta_j^{(m)} + \phi_i \delta(i,j), \tag{2}$$

where $\delta(i,j) = 1$ if $i = j$ and 0 otherwise. In (2), $\alpha_i^{(m)}$ is the score for the ith row on the kth scoring dimension, and $\beta_j^{(m)}$ is the corresponding score for the jth column; these can be either specified in advance or estimated from the data. The last term allows a different strength of association on the diagonal. (The model [2] is unidentified as written; various identifying constraints are possible.) This is often called the RC(M) model. In most applications to date, $M = 1$; the first genuine substantive application of the model in sociology with $M > 1$ was to labor market experiences and outcomes by Clogg, Eliason, and Wahl (1990).

Goodman (1979) initially derived this model as a way of describing association in terms of local odds ratios. Goodman (1985) has shown that this model is closely related to canonical correlations and to correspondence analysis (Benzécri 1976), and provides an inferential framework for these methodologies. When the categories are ordered, the uniform association model with $\alpha_i = \beta_i = i$ is a useful starting point (Haberman 1979). In this model, the odds ratios in all 2×2 subtables are equal, so this can be viewed as a discrete analog to the bivariate normal distribution, with $\gamma \equiv \gamma_k$ specifying the correlation.

Table 1 shows the actual counts for a reduced version of the most extensive U.S. social mobility study, and the fitted values from an association model; the model accounts for 99.6 percent of the association in the table and its success is evident. Hout (1984) extended the range of application of these models by modeling the scores and diagonal terms in (2) as sums or products of covariates, such as characteristics of the occupational categories in question; this is an extension of Birch's (1965) linear-by-linear interaction model.

TABLE 1
Observed Counts from the Largest U.S. Social Mobility Study and Expected Values from a Goodman Association Model with Four Degrees of Freedom.*

Father's Occupation	Son's Occupation									
	Upper Nonmanual		Lower Nonmanual		Upper Manual		Lower Manual		Farm	
	Obs.	Exp.	Obs.	Exp.	Obs.	Exp.	Obs.	Exp.	Obs.	Exp.
Upper nonmanual	1414	*1414*	521	*534*	302	*278*	643	*652*	40	*42*
Lower nonmanual	724	*716*	524	*524*	254	*272*	703	*698*	48	*43*
Upper manual	798	*790*	648	*662*	856	*856*	1676	*1666*	108	*112*
Lower manual	756	*794*	914	*835*	771	*813*	3325	*3325*	237	*236*
Farm	409	*386*	357	*409*	441	*405*	1611	*1617*	1832	*1832*

*Sample size is 19,912.
Source: Hout (1983).

This methodology has also made it feasible to model relatively high-dimensional tables with large numbers of categories in a parsimonious and interpretable way. This has led to important discoveries, including Hout's (1988) finding that social mobility has been increasing in the United States. This is a subtle result because of the complex nature of the data underlying it, and it would have been hard to discover it without using the association model methodology. This substantive result was confirmed and refined in Ganzeboom, Luijkx, and Treiman's (1989) discovery, based on several hundred social mobility tables from different countries at different time points, that social mobility has been increasing by about 1 percent a year in industrialized countries in the second half of the twentieth century.

Biblarz and Raftery (1993) and Biblarz, Raftery and Bucur (1997) adapted the models to higher dimensional tables to study social mobility in nonintact families. The tables they used had up to about 7,000 cells and five dimensions: (1) father's occupation, (2) offspring's occupation, (3) gender, (4) race, and (5) period. Thus standard log-linear models would not have revealed anything, but association modeling, extending the models mentioned earlier, did provide interpretable results, parameter estimates, and conclusions. They showed that occupational resemblance is weaker in nonintact families than in intact ones, that offspring raised by working single mothers succeed much better on average than those from other nonintact families, and that these patterns have remained essentially constant from the 1960s through the 1990s, in spite of the many changes in family structure and occupational distribution as well as the relationship between gender, race, and occupational and labor force status. Other important applications of log-linear and related models include the analysis of sex segregation (Charles and Grusky 1995), and assortative mating (Kalmijn 1991). From sociology, the use of association models has diffused to other disciplines, such as epidemiology (Becker 1989).

One common reason for analyzing tables with more than two dimensions is to assess how two-way associations vary across a third (or several other) dimension(s). Yamaguchi (1987) and Xie (1992) have proposed specific forms of the higher-dimensional association model that are adapted for this purpose, and these were unified and extended by Goodman and Hout (1998). A particularly appealing aspect of the latter approach is the availability of a range of graphical displays that facilitate the interpretation of the rather complex data and model parameters that arise in this setting.

These models are for situations with discrete independent variables. Perhaps the most successful models for the dependence of cross-classifications on *continuous* independent variables are Sobel's (1981, 1985) diagonal mobility models. These have been applied in a variety of settings, for example to marital fertility (Sorensen 1989), cultural consumption (De Graaf 1991), and voting behavior (Weakliem 1992).

An intuitive alternative formulation of the basic ideas underlying (1) and (2) is in terms of marginal *distributions* rather than the main effects in (1). The resulting marginal models specify a model for the marginal distributions and a model for the odds ratios, and this implies a model for the joint distribution that is not log linear (Lang and Agresti 1994; Becker 1994; Becker and Yang 1998). The first substantive application of these models in sociology was to modeling social mobility (Sobel, Becker, and Minick 1998).

2.2. *Latent Class Models*

An alternative approach that answers different questions is the latent class model (Lazarsfeld 1950; Lazarsfeld and Henry 1968; Goodman 1974a,b). In its basic form, this represents the distribution of counts as a finite mixture of distributions within each of which the different variables are independent. The model was introduced to account for observed associations in multivariate discrete data, the original motivation being somewhat akin to that for factor analysis for multivariate continuous data.

Hagenaars (1988, 1990) has extended the latent class model to the situation where each component in the mixture can exhibit dependence. Clogg (1995) gives a survey of this area. There have been many applications of this model. One interesting recent application to criminology is by Roeder, Lynch, and Nagin (1999).

This basic model has been formulated and used in other contexts. Chickering and Heckerman (1997) formulated it as a Bayesian graphical model with one hidden node. This formulation facilitates estimation of latent class models with many variables, and also makes it easier to estimate the model when there are missing data for some individuals, and to make inference about the missing data. Celeux and Govaert (1991) used the same basic model for clustering multivariate discrete observations, again potentially with large numbers of variables.

2.3. *Hypothesis Testing and Model Selection*

Sociologists often have sample sizes in the thousands, and so they come up early and hard against the problem that standard P-values can indicate rejection of null hypotheses in large samples, even when the null model seems reasonable theoretically and inspection of the data fails to reveal any striking discrepancies with it. The problem is compounded by the fact that there are often many models rather than just the two envisaged by significance tests, and by the need to use stepwise or other multiple comparison methods for model selection (e.g., Goodman 1971). By the early 1980s, some sociologists were dealing with this problem by ignoring the results of P-value-based tests when they seemed counterintuitive and by basing model selection instead on theoretical considerations and informal assessment of discrepancies between model and data (e.g., Fienberg and Mason 1979; Hout 1983, 1984; Grusky and Hauser 1984).

It was soon pointed out that this problem could be alleviated by basing model selection instead on Bayes factors (Raftery 1986a), and that this could be simply approximated for log-linear models by preferring a model if BIC—defined by BIC = Deviance − (Degrees of freedom) $\log(n)$—is smaller (Schwarz 1978; Raftery 1986b). For nested hypotheses, this can be viewed as defining a significance level for a test that decreases automatically with sample size. Since then, this approach has been used in many sociological applications of log-linear models. Kass and Wasserman (1995) showed that the approximation is quite accurate if the Bayesian prior used for the model parameters is a unit information prior—i.e. a prior distribution that contains about the same amount of information as a single "typical" observation. Raftery (1995) indicated how the methodology can be extended to a range of other models.

Weakliem (1999) criticized the use of BIC on the grounds that the unit information prior to which it corresponds may be too diffuse in practice, leading BIC to tend to favor the null hypothesis too often. However, Raftery (1999) pointed out that the unit information prior does provide a reasonable representation of the prior knowledge of investigators who have some advance information, but not a great deal, about the parameter values for the model they are estimating. It can thus be viewed as approximating the situation where there is little prior information. A more knowledgeable investigator would have a tighter prior distribution, and thus might have a basis for rejecting a null hypothesis when BIC does not, but this would be based on prior information rather than on data, and this should be made explicit in any report that does so. BIC provides a conservative assessment of evidence: one can be quite confident of the reality of any "effect," evidence of whose existence is favored strongly by BIC. Weakliem's arguments can be viewed as implying that if real prior information is indeed available it should be used, and I would agree with this. This points toward using Bayes factors based on priors that reflect the actual information available; this is easy to do for log-linear and other generalized linear models (Raftery 1996).

3. THE SECOND GENERATION: UNIT-LEVEL SURVEY DATA

The second generation of statistical models responded to the availability of unit-level survey data in the form of large data matrices of independent cases. The methods that have proved successful for answering questions about such data have mostly been based on the linear regression model and its extensions to path models, structural equation models, generalized linear models and event-history models. For questions about the *distribution* of variables rather about than their predicted value, however, nonparametric methods have proved useful (Morris, Bernhardt, and Handcock 1994; Bernhardt, Morris, and Handcock 1995; Handcock and Morris 1998, 1999). We start by reviewing the development of the measurement of occupational status, which provided a major impetus for the growth of the second generation of methods.

3.1. *Measuring Occupational Status*

Occupational status is an important concept in sociology, and developing a useful continuous measure of it was a signal achievement of the field. It was important for the development of statistical methods in sociology because, starting in the early 1960s, it encouraged greater use of regression analysis and related methods among scholars with an interest in the sources and consequences of job-holding. These methodological approaches diffused rapidly into other areas of the discipline.

Initially, the status of an occupation was equated with its perceived prestige, as measured in national surveys beginning in the 1940s. However, surveys could measure the prestige of only a small number of the several hundred occupations identified in each decennial Census classification. To fill in missing prestige scores for the 1960 Census classification, Duncan (1961) regressed the prestige scores for the 45 occupations for which they were available on measures of the proportion of occupational incumbents who had completed high school and the proportion of incumbents who earned more than \$10,000. He found that the predictions were very good ($R^2 = 0.91$) and that the two predictors were about equally weighted. Based on this, he created a predicted prestige score for all occupations in the 1960 classification, which became known as the Duncan Socioeconomic Index (SEI); the SEI later turned out to be a better predictor of various social outcomes than the prestige scores themselves. Duncan's initial work has been updated several times for subsequent Census classifications (Featherman and Stevens 1982; Nakao and Treas 1994; Hauser and Warren 1997), but it has recently been critiqued on conceptual and empirical grounds (Hauser and Warren 1997; Warren, Sheridan, and Hauser 1998).

In much social research, particularly in economics, current income is used as a predictor of social outcomes, but there are good reasons to prefer occupational status. It has proved to be a good predictor of many social outcomes. Jobs and occupations can be measured accurately, in contrast to income or wealth, whose measurement is plagued by problems of refusal, recall, and reliability. Also, occupational status is more stable over time than income, both within careers and between generations. This suggests that occupational status may actually be a better indicator of long-term or permanent income than (current) income itself. The status of occupations tends to be fairly constant both in time and across countries (Treiman 1977).

3.2. *The Many Uses of Structural Equation Models*

Figure 1 shows the basic path model of occupational attainment at the heart of Blau and Duncan (1967); see Duncan (1966). Wright (1921) introduced path analysis, and Blalock (1961) gave it a causal interpretation in a social science context. One of the important uses and motivations of structural equation models was to decompose a total effect into direct and indirect effects. Alwin and Hauser (1975) played an important role in showing how to do this for sociological data. See Freedman (1987) and Sobel (1998) for critiques, and Section 3.8 below for more discussion of causality in the social sciences.

Often, variables of interest in a causal model are not observed directly, but other variables are observed that can be viewed as measurements of the variables, or "constructs" of interest, such as prejudice, alienation, conservatism, self-esteem, discrimination, motivation or ability. Jöreskog (1973) dealt with this by maximum likelihood estimation of a structural equation model with latent variables; this is sometimes called a

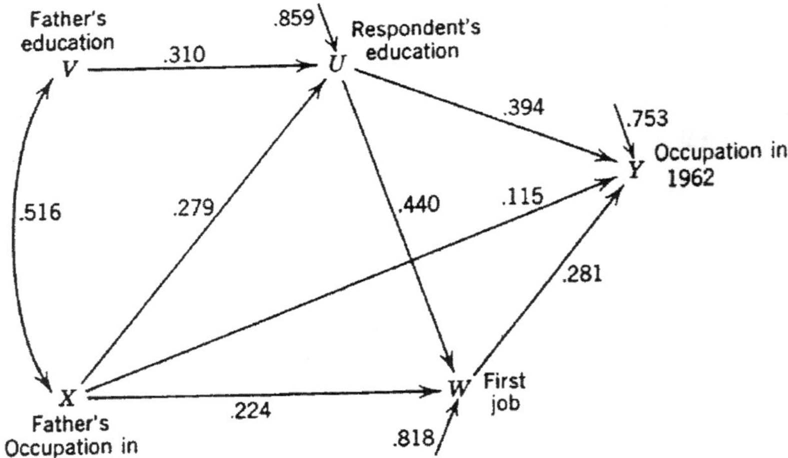

FIGURE 1. A Famous Path Model: The Process of Stratification, U.S. 1962. The numbers on the arrows from one variable to another are regression coefficients, 0.516 is the correlation between V and X, and the numbers on the arrows with no sources are residual standard deviations. All the variables have been centered and scaled.
Source: Blau and Duncan (1967).

LISREL model, from the name of Joreskog's software. Duncan (1975) played a big role in introducing these ideas into sociology, and Long (1984a,b) and Bollen (1989) provide well-written and accessible accounts geared to sociologists. A typical model of this kind is shown in Figure 2; the goal of the analysis is testing and estimating the strength of the relationship between the unobserved latent variables represented by the thick arrow. Diagrams such as Figures 1 and 2 have proved useful to sociologists for specifying theories and hypotheses and for building causal models.

The LISREL framework has been extended and used ingeniously for purposes beyond those for which it was originally intended. Muthén (1983) extended it to categorical variables, and Muthén (1997) showed how it can be used to represent longitudinal data, growth curve models, and multilevel data. Kuo and Hauser (1996) used data on siblings to control for unobserved family effects on socioeconomic outcomes, and cast the resulting random effects model in a LISREL framework.

The advent of graphical Markov models (Spiegelhalter et al. 1993), specified by conditional independencies rather than by regression-like relationships, is important for the analysis of multivariate dependencies, although they can seem less interpretable to sociologists. They have been particularly useful for propagating information about some variables through a system of dependent variables, to yield information about other, unobserved variables, as is needed, for example, in the construction of expert systems for medical diagnosis and other applications. They have been less used so far for inference and modeling in social research, per-

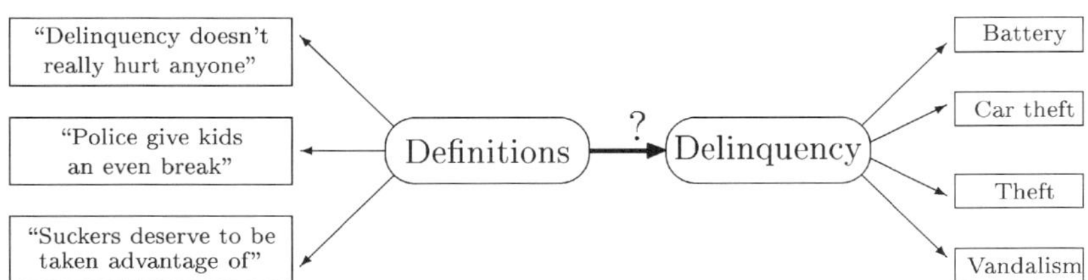

FIGURE 2. Part of a structural equation model to assess the hypothesis that learned definitions of delinquency cause delinquent behavior. The key goal is testing and estimating the relationship represented by the thick arrow. The constructs of interest, "Definitions" and "Delinquency," are not measured directly. The variables inside the rectangles are measured.
Source: Matsueda and Heimer (1987).

haps because sociological hypotheses tend to be formulated more often in terms of regression or causal relationships than in terms of conditional independencies between variables.

The relationship between graphical Markov models and structural equation models has begun to be understood (Koster 1996; Spirtes et al. 1998). Also, the LISREL model seems ideally suited to Gibbs sampling and Markov chain Monte Carlo (MCMC) methods (Gilks et al. 1996), and this is likely to permit useful extensions of the framework (Raftery 1991; Arminger 1998; Scheines, Hoijtink, and Boomsma 1999).

3.3. *Event-History Analysis*

Unit-level survey data often include or allow the reconstruction of life histories. These include the times of crucial events such as marriages, divorces, births, commitals to and releases from prison, job changes, or going on or off welfare.

Prior to 1972, two approaches were available for the analysis of the distribution of the time to a single event such as death, and of the factors influencing it. One was life table analysis from demography, but this did not allow easy analysis of the factors influencing time to an event. The other was regression analysis of the observed times to the event, but this was plagued by censoring, and by the often extreme nonnormality of the response.

This field was revolutionized by the introduction of the Cox (1972) proportional hazards model, which brought together these two approaches. Tuma (1976) and Tuma and Hannan (1984) generalized this approach to allow for repeated events, for multiple types of events, such as marriages and divorces, and for events consisting of movement between different types of states, such as different job categories. Yamaguchi (1991) and Petersen (1991) have provided accessible accounts of the methodology, emphasizing sociological applications, and Mayer and Tuma (1990) described a collection of case studies from social science. One important area of application of hazard rate models has been organizational birth and death processes; this is unique to sociology. Petersen (1995) extended the basic model further to multiple types of events where the events are interdependent—i.e. where the occurrence or nonoccurrence of one type of event affects the probability that the other type of event happens. An example is the relationship between becoming unemployed and getting divorced. Xie (2000) has discussed the roots of event-history analysis in demography and life table analysis.

Uses of the Cox model in medicine have tended to treat the baseline hazard nonparametrically, but in social science it has sometimes been found useful to model it parametrically. For example, Yamaguchi (1992) analyzed permanent employment in Japan where the surviving fraction (those who never change jobs) and its determinants are of key interest; he found that covariates were associated both with the timing of job change and with the surviving fraction. Yamaguchi and Ferguson (1995) provide another application of this idea to the stopping and spacing of child births.

Social science event-history data are often recorded in discrete time—for example, by year—either because events tend to happen at particular times of year (e.g., graduation), or because of measurement constraints. As a result, discrete-time event-history models have been popular (Allison 1982, 1984; Xie 1994), and in some ways are easier to handle than their continuous-time analogs. Ways of dealing with multilevel event-history data, smoothly time-varying covariates, and other complications have been introduced in this context (e.g., Raftery, Lewis, and Aghajanian 1995; Fahrmeir and Knorr-Held 1997).

This basic framework has also been found useful to model a different kind of phenomenon: that of diffusion of innovations and social influence. Burt (1987) provided a theoretical framework for this work, and the extended event-history framework proposed for modeling it was developed by Marsden and Podolny (1990), Strang (1991), and Strang and Tuma (1993). A different approach, using accelerated failure-time models rather than proportional hazards models, was developed by Diekmann (1989) and Yamaguchi (1994).

One problem with social science event-history data is that dropping out can be related to the event of interest. For example, people may tend to leave a study shortly before a divorce, which will play havoc with estimation of divorce rates. The problem seems almost insoluble at first sight, but Hill (1997) produced an elegant solution using the Shared Unmeasured Risk Factor (SURF) model of Hill, Axinn, and Thornton (1993). The basic trick is to observe that, although one does not know which of the people who dropped out actually got divorced soon afterward, one can estimate which ones were most at risk of divorcing. One can then use this information to adjust the empirical divorce rates in the study by modeling divorce and dropout simultaneously.

3.4. *Binary Dependent Variables*

The term "limited dependent variable" is usually used to refer to a scalar dependent variable in a regression model, the set of whose possible values is restricted in a way that violates the assumptions of normal linear regression too severely for it to be used. The canonical example is binary dependent variables; others include nominal, ordinal, and compositional variables, and, in some contexts, variables that are constrained to be positive.

Limited dependent variables, especially binary variables, arise frequently in social research, and many articles in leading sociological journals use models and methods specifically developed for this situation. Nevertheless, much of the methodological development in this area has come from disciplines other than sociology. However, sociologists have played a major role in expositing, adapting, and synthesizing these methods; for example, see the books by Long (1997) and Xie and Powers (2000).

For binary responses, the method of choice in sociology in the past 20 years has been logistic regression. Much of the early development was for medical applications (Cornfield 1951, 1962; Truett et al. 1967), and the monograph by Cox (1970) helped to introduce the methods to a wide audience. The advent of generalized linear models (Nelder and Wedderburn 1972), and the recognition that logistic regression is a special case, as well as the development of the associated GLIM software (Baker and Nelder 1977), helped to make logistic regression a standard tool in many disciplines, particularly in the social and health sciences. Some version or descendant of the GLIM software is now included in most major commercial statistical packages.

Logistic regression is not the only possible model for regression with binary responses. Ordinary linear regression gives similar results if most of the probabilities are far enough from 0 and 1 (say between 0.1 and 0.9). Logistic regression is more "correct" than linear regression since, for example, it constrains fitted probabilities to lie between 0 and 1. Nevertheless, in the 1970s and 1980s there was a debate about whether logistic regression is really needed, given that it is more complex to estimate and needs more computer time than linear regression. The subsequent increase in computer speed made the additional computer time negligible, and the debate was settled in favor of logistic regression.

Another alternative is probit regression, in which the dependent variable is assumed to arise by truncating an unobserved normal random variable whose expectation depends linearly on the independent variables. This is soundly based and easy to estimate, because it is also a generalized linear model and so can be estimated using GLIM; it tends to give results that are very similar to those from logistic regression. However, in sociology, as in many other disciplines, it has lost out to logistic regression, perhaps because of the appealing interpretation of the logistic regression coefficients as odds ratios. There has been a revival of interest in probit regression recently among statisticians. This is because it is defined in terms of latent variables, and so can be included relatively easily as a component in more complex Bayesian models that are estimated using Markov chain Monte Carlo methods (e.g., Albert and Chib 1993).

A further alternative is complementary log-log regression, in which $\log(-\log(p))$ is assumed to be a linear combination of independent variables, where p is the conditional probability of the event of interest, given the independent variables. This is also a generalized linear model and so is easy to estimate. It can fit much better than logistic regression, and often gives quite different predicted probabilities, particularly for more extreme values of the independent variables. One example of this is the Irish educational transition data discussed by Raftery and Hout (1985); see Kass and Raftery (1995).

The introduction of two-sided logit models by Logan (1996, 1997) was an important development. This recognizes that in many situations in social life where individuals choose between different outcomes, there are two types of force in play: the preferences and attributes of the individual, and those of the possible choices. For example, in the labor market, which job an individual ends up in depends not only on his or her own attributes and preferences or utilities, but also on those of the other candidates in the job market, and those of the available employers and jobs. Logan's approach is to model both of these processes explicitly and simultaneously, and to explain the final labor market outcomes in terms of the interaction between them. The model can be estimated using either individual-level data or data aggregated into a cross-classification.

3.5. *Other Limited Dependent Variables*

Logistic regression has been extended to nominal dependent variables with more than two categories; for example, see Hosmer and Lemeshow

(1989). Maximum-likelihood estimation of the resulting multinomial logistic regression model is relatively straightforward, and software to do it is available. Begg and Gray (1984) have shown that this can be very well approximated by an appropriately set up (binary) logistic regression; see also Hosmer and Lemeshow (1989). Logistic regression has also been extended to ordinal dependent variables; for example, see McCullagh and Nelder (1989) and Agresti (1990).

Another important kind of limited dependent variable arises when the variable is positive, but has a nonnegligible probability of being exactly equal to zero. One example is income from work: Some people are out of the labor force or unemployed and have zero income from work, while all others have positive income. Data of this kind have often been analyzed using the Tobit model of Tobin (1958). In this model, it is assumed that those with zero income actually have an unobserved negative income, and the true income (now assumed to be capable of taking all positive and negative values) is modeled using ordinary linear regression.

The Tobit model in its original form seems rather unsatisfactory. For one thing, the postulated unobserved value does not exist: those who have zero income actually do have zero income (ignoring measurement error), not some unobserved negative income. Also, and perhaps more seriously, the model assumes that the mechanism determining whether or not someone has income from work is essentially the same as the one that determines how much he or she earns. It could easily be the case, however, that the mechanism that determines whether or not individuals are in the labor force is quite different from the mechanism that determines how much they earn if they are in the labor force, and with the Tobit model it is hard to make this distinction.

The Tobit model was developed before the widespread availability of specific methods for binary dependent variables. Now, however, there is a simple alternative approach that avoids the problems with the Tobit model. One simply models the data in two steps. In the first step, the dependent variable is whether or not the dependent variable is zero, and this is modeled using probit regression. Then in the second step, the dependent variable is the amount earned and only individuals with positive earnings are included. This is the standard sample selection model, which led to the development of the Heckman (1979) two-stage estimator. Amemiya (1985) calls this the Type II Tobit model. Winship and Mare (1992) review subsequent developments in this area.

A further kind of limited dependent variable arises in the analysis of compositional data. Here the dependent variable is a vector of positive values that sum up to one and consist of proportions. An example is the analysis of household budgets: the response is a vector, each element of which is the proportion of total household expenditure spent on some category, such as rent, food, utilities, education, and so on. One's first idea might be to model each proportion separately using regression, or perhaps to use a multivariate regression method that takes account of the correlation between the different responses. These methods do not work, however, because of the constraint that the responses add up to one, and so standard distributional assumptions do not apply. The observations lie on a *simplex*, the high-dimensional analog of the triangle, not on the full Euclidean space. A literature studying this situation has been summarized in part by Aitchison (1986); his main recommendation is to first transform the p-dimensional vector of proportions to a $(p-1)$-dimensional vector on the full Euclidean space using the multivariate logistic transform, and then to proceed using standard methods.

3.6. *Multilevel Models*

Multilevel models extend the regression models and their generalizations to situations where individual-level outcomes depend not just on individual-level covariates but also on social context. Much of the development in the social sciences has been in the context of education. A canonical example is where the individual-level outcomes are grades or test scores, and the contexts are the class, the school, the school district, the state, or some subset of these.

Often there is interest in the situation where the effect of an individual-level attribute, such as household income, depends on the context. For example, it might be hypothesized that in some schools the effects on test scores of inequalities due to differences in household income would be less than in other schools. The simplest approach to modeling such situations, with a view to estimating and testing the hypothesized effects, is via a fixed effects multilevel model. Suppose that y_i is the outcome for student i who attends school $s(i)$, where there are S schools represented in the data, and that x_i is his or her family income. Then a simple fixed effects model is

$$y_i = \alpha + \beta_{s(i)} x_i + \varepsilon_i, \tag{3}$$

where $\beta_{s(i)}$ is the effect of household income on test score in student i's school, and $\varepsilon_i \stackrel{\text{iid}}{\sim} N(0, \sigma_\varepsilon^2)$. There is a different regression coefficient β_j for each school j. This model can be estimated by ordinary least squares regression; for example, see Boyd and Iversen (1979) and Blalock (1984).

There are several difficulties with this model. One is that the number of parameters to be estimated, equal to $(S + 2)$, is large if there are many contexts (schools) involved, and so the model is hard both to estimate accurately and to interpret. Another is that, if the number of students from a particular school is small, and the estimated regression coefficient for that school is extreme relative to the estimates for the other schools, the resulting estimate is likely to be poor. This can be a problem, as it is often precisely these more extreme estimates that are of most interest.

There has been a great deal of work on overcoming these difficulties, and analogous ones in more complex and realistic multilevel situations, using random-effects models. In a simple formulation, (3) is supplemented by

$$\beta_j = \psi + \delta_j, \tag{4}$$

where $\delta_j \stackrel{\text{iid}}{\sim} N(0, \sigma_\delta^2)$. Combining (3) and (4) we get

$$y_i = \alpha + \psi x_i + u_i, \tag{5}$$

where

$$u_i \stackrel{\text{indep}}{\sim} N(0, \sigma_\varepsilon^2 + \sigma_\delta^2 x_i^2).$$

Equation (5) differs from (3) in having only four parameters to be estimated, instead of $(S + 2)$, and also in that the error variances differ, and depend on the value of the independent variable. One consequence is that the estimated "school effects" tend to be less extreme. It has been shown in several contexts that less extreme "shrunken" estimates such as those tend to be better on average (e.g., Morris 1983).

The basic idea of random-effects multilevel models goes back at least to Lindley and Smith (1972), who introduced the idea in a Bayesian context. Many different names have been used for the general class of models, including multilevel models, hierarchical models, random-effects models, variance component models, contextual models, random-coefficient models, and parametric empirical Bayes models. The area has benefited from a superb level of expository writing; for example, see Bock

(1989), Bryk and Raudenbush (1992), Longford (1993), DiPrete and Forristal (1994), Goldstein (1995), and Snijders and Bosker (1999). It has also spawned easy to use software, including HLM, MLn and VARCL, which has helped to spread the ideas.

Many of the applications have been in education, but there have been important applications in other areas of sociology. One successful application that helped to spread the methodology arose in demography, to modeling fertility decline (Mason et al. 1983; Entwisle et al. 1985, 1986, 1989; Wong and Mason 1985). Another fruitful area of application is meta-analysis—i.e., the pooling of results from different studies (Hedges and Olkin 1985; Goldstein et al. 2000).

The model can be estimated by maximum likelihood using the EM algorithm, viewing the random effects as "missing data" (Dempster, Laird, and Rubin 1977). The Bayesian formulation has proved useful in recent years, particularly for going beyond the hierarchical linear model, of which (5) is an example, to other more complex situations, such as multilevel models with limited dependent variables, event-history outcomes, multivariate outcomes, and so on. This has proved quite amenable to estimation using Markov chain Monte Carlo methods (e.g., Gelman et al. 1995; Daniels and Gatsonis 1999). Recent social science applications include Bradlow and Zaslavksy (1999), Boatwright et al. (1999), Datta et al. (1999), and Elliott and Little (2000). This seems to be a fruitful area for future research.

3.7. *Missing Data*

Missing data are pervasive in social science. By far the most common approach to dealing with the problem has been listwise deletion, in which cases with missing data on any of the relevant variables are removed from the analysis. Sometimes variables with a great deal of missing data are removed from the analysis as well. This works well as long as it does not lead to too many cases being removed: unbiased parameter estimators remain unbiased given that the missing data are missing at random, and the main problem is the loss of precision due to the reduction in the amount of data.

However, this approach starts to break down if the number of variables is considerable and the amount of missing data significant, as then much of the data can end up being removed. Various ways around this problem have been tried. One of these, mean imputation, in which the missing value is replaced by the mean of the variable over the cases for which it is observed, can lead to biased estimates and is not to be recommended; unfortunately, it is frequently used, and it is even available in some widely distributed commercial software. Single imputation, also called regression imputation, consists of replacing the missing value by its conditional expectation given the values of the other variables for the case, estimated by regression. This gives unbiased estimates but tends to underestimate standard errors and other measures of uncertainty, to an extent that increases with the amount of missing information.

A consensus seems to be building that the method of choice for missing data is multiple imputation (Rubin 1977). This consists of simulating several replicates of the missing data from an approximate conditional or posterior distribution of the missing data given the observed data. These can then be combined to provide a composite inference that takes into account uncertainty about the missing data, does not discard any data, and is relatively easy to use (Little and Rubin 1987; Rubin 1987, 1996). This consensus is not a total one, and multiple imputation has been criticized and alternative suggestions made (e.g. Fay 1996; Rao 1996). It is possible, but more complicated, to specify a model for the missing data, and to compute maximum-likelihood estimates for the model (regression) parameters using the EM algorithm, taking account of the missing data and of uncertainty about them (Little and Rubin 1989; Little 1992).

The motivation for multiple imputation was Bayesian, and the resulting inferences are approximately Bayesian. Recently, a more exact Bayesian approach to this problem has been developed using Markov chain Monte Carlo (e.g. Schafer 1997). This extends multiple imputation by allowing one to simulate values of the missing data and of the parameters at the same time, to yield a sample from a posterior distribution of the parameters that takes full account of the missingness. This yields more accurate estimates and statements of uncertainty than Rubin's original version of multiple imputation, but it is also more cumbersome to implement.

Multiple imputation relies for its validity on the assumption that whether or not a particular value is missing is in some sense random and independent of the other data. The technical term *missing completely at random (MCAR)* was coined to denote the situation in which missingness is statistically independent of all the data, observed and unobserved. It turns out, fortunately, that this rather demanding assumption does not have to be met for multiple imputation to be valid. Instead, the missingness needs only to be conditionally independent of the unobserved data given the observed data, a condition technically referred to as *missing at random (MAR)*. This latter condition holds, at least approximately, in many situations. It does not hold, however, if the missingness is related to the missing data themselves (e.g., if people with higher incomes are more likely to refuse to say what their income is). We have previously discussed one approach to this more difficult problem of "nonignorable missingness" in the specific case of event-history data, using the SURF model.

3.8. *Causality*

The goal of much of the regression and other statistical modeling that we have been discussing is, at least implicitly, to make statements about the mechanisms that underlie social life, social behavior, and social structure. In other words, to make causal statements. Statisticians, on the other hand, have tended to avoid the language of causality, cautioning that statistical models can show association between variables but cannot prove that the association is causal in origin.

The regression approach to causality has loomed large in social science because it seems to fit well with how empirical social researchers proceed. Much of (social) science proceeds by a researcher positing a causal theory of how and why a phenomenon occurs, implying that the presence of some attribute *X* causes an outcome *Y*. Data on observed values of *X* and *Y* are then collected. If a correlation between *X* and *Y* is observed, it provides some support for the causal theory but does not demonstrate it because there are other possible explanations of the correlation, notably: (a) *Y* might be causing *X* instead of the other way round, or (b) some third (set of) attribute(s) *Z* might be causing both *X* and *Y*.

The most common approach in these circumstances is to collect time-ordered or longitudinal data on *X* and *Y* to try to exclude (a), and to collect data on as many hypothesized common causes *Z* as possible to try to render (b) less plausible. This is done by "controlling" for *Z*—i.e., by assessing whether *X* and *Y* remain correlated when cases with each value of *Z* are considered separately. If *Z* can take many possible values (e.g., because it consists of several variables, or of variables that can take many values), this will not be feasible, and instead a regression model is built that represents the relationships in a more parsimonious way. If the "effect" of *X* on *Y* remains significant after controlling for *Z*, that is taken as evidence for the posited causal theory. It does not provide a conclusive demonstration of X causing Y, however. For example, there might be other Z variables that we could not measure or did not think of.

When there is some additional causal information—such as the presence of an independent variable that is known to be causally related to one of X and Y but not to the other—causal inferences can sometimes be made. The basic approach is instrumental variables estimation, and this is a major topic in econometrics, but I will not discuss it further here.

Several scientists have been trying to make the case that one *can* infer causation from observational data in the absence of additional causal information, describing methods for doing so, and giving examples of its being done. This contention remains controversial. Two primary approaches to this task have been taken: the structural equation or graphical model approach and the counterfactual approach.

The first of these traditions of causal inference is that of structural equation modeling, or, more recently, graphical models. This tradition is motivated by the effort to infer causal structure from the multivariate (perhaps simply cross-sectional) structure of data. Perhaps the boldest claims about the possibility of doing this were made by Spirtes, Glymour, and Scheines (1993), drawing in part on work by Blalock (1961) and Costner (1969). They argued there that while the saying "correlation does not imply causation" is clearly true for two variables, it is not necessarily true for three or more variables. As the simplest example, they considered the case where the correlation structure of three variables, X, Y, and Z, is of the form $X - Y - Z$—i.e., X and Z are both correlated with Y but uncorrelated with each other. They pointed out that in this case, most people would agree that the causal structure of the data is of the form $X \rightarrow Y \leftarrow Z$, and they gave conditions under which this inference would be correct.

Extending this work, Spirtes et al. (1998) considered linear structural equation models, and asked several questions that arise. If there is a causal model that fits the data well, are there other equivalent models that imply the same covariance structure but a different path diagram, and if so, how many are there? Given that there are equivalent models, is it possible to extract the features common to all of them? When does a nonzero partial regression coefficient correspond to a nonzero coefficient in a structural equation? They provided answers to some of these questions using the key property of *d-separation*, defined by Verma and Pearl (1988). This can be viewed as a generalization of the concept of conditional independence. This makes it possible to read causal relations off the graph.

The second major current approach to causal inference is the counterfactual one. This starts from the idea that the randomized experiment with perfect compliance and no missing data is the gold standard for estimating the causal effects of treatment interventions. In social science, randomized experiments are sometimes done to estimate treatment effects—e.g., the effects of social programs. However, unlike randomized experiments in some other areas of science, such experiments suffer from the problem of noncompliance—some subjects refuse the treatment to which they are assigned. These experiments also tend to suffer from missing data.

The counterfactual approach to estimating causal effects from such experiments was first proposed by Rubin (1974) in the context of what later became known as the Rubin causal model. An accessible description of this framework was provided by Holland (1986); see also Manski (1993, 1995), Manski and Nagin (1998), and Heckman and Hotz (1989). This approach was illustrated by Barnard et al. (1998), who described methods for dealing with both noncompliance and missing data in this framework, illustrating their points with issues from the analysis of the Milwaukee Parental Choice Program, a natural randomized experiment.

Sobel (1990, 1994, 1995, 1997, 1998) has investigated the application of the counterfactual framework to observational data, which is more common in sociology than the (imperfect) randomized experiments that Rubin and his collaborators have considered. Sobel argues that when using data from observational studies, sociologists should attempt to identify causes, and then think about the covariates that would justify invoking the assumption of conditional random assignment, and attempt to measure these in the study. In Sobel (1998) he applied his reasoning to an attainment model of Featherman and Hauser (1976), concluding that the "effects" of family background on educational attainment and occupational achievement should not be viewed as causal. Sobel's conclusion in what would often be regarded as a rather clear-cut case of a causal effect suggests that few observational studies in sociology would meet his criteria for causal inference to be possible. Simplistically put, this is because one can rarely be sure that there is no unmeasured common cause out there. This is a useful caveat, as is his detailed description of the relatively rare cases when causal inference from observational studies will be possible.

However, much of sociology is about marshaling evidence for *competing* causal explanations, and observational studies *can* allow one to do this, regardless of whether or not they allow one to show any causal explanation to be correct in an absolute sense. Such studies do provide a basis for saying which of the current causal theories is best supported by the data. The most common way of doing this is by testing one or several coefficients in a regression-type model for significance. This has the limitation that it can be used only to compare pairs of theories that correspond to nested statistical models. Often, however, competing theories do not neatly fit inside one another in this way, but instead correspond to quite different ways of explaining a phenomenon, and so do not correspond to nested hypotheses. In this case, standard statistical significance testing becomes difficult. However, Bayes factors can still be used to make these comparisons (Kass and Raftery 1995; Raftery 1995).

The search for causal explanation, although widely accepted as the basis for much social research, is not uncontroversial. For example, Abbott (1998) argued that the regression model of causality, although dominant in American sociology, is too narrow and needs to be expanded to include broader concepts of explanation and to reinstate the central role of description. He put forward the historical narrative-based approach as one way of achieving a more compelling and interesting account of social life. He mentioned nonstatistical simulation models and cluster analysis as potentially useful methods in this context, allowing one to describe relational and spatial aspects of social life, as well as temporal ones. This kind of "noncausal" or "postcausal" thinking is an important ingredient in the development of the third generation of methods, to which we now turn.

4. THE THIRD GENERATION: NEW DATA, NEW CHALLENGES, NEW METHODS

4.1. *Social Networks and Spatial Data*

Social networks consist of sets of pairwise connections, such as friendships between adolescents (Udry and Bearman 1998), sexual relationships between adults (Laumann et al. 1994), or patterns of marriage exchange and political alliance across social groups (White 1963; Bearman 1997; Padgett and Ansell 1993). The analysis of data about such networks has a long history (Wasserman and Faust 1994). Frank and Strauss (1986) developed formal statistical models for such networks related to the Markov random field models used in Bayesian image analysis, and derived using the Hammersley-Clifford theorem (Besag 1974). This has led to the promising "p^*" class of models for social networks (Wasserman and Pattison 1996). An alternative approach to formal statistical modeling of social networks based on Goodman-type association models is due to Yamaguchi (1990).

Methods for the analysis of social networks have focused mostly on small data sets with complete data. In practical applications, however, such as the effect of sexual network patterns on the spread of sexually transmitted diseases (Morris 1997), the data tend to be large and very incomplete, and current methods are somewhat at a loss. This is the stage that pedigree analysis in statistical genetics was at some years ago, but the use of likelihood and MCMC methods have led to major progress since then (Thompson 1998). Social networks are more complex than pedigrees in one way, because pedigrees tend to have a tree structure, while social networks often have cycles, but progress does seem possible.

Most social data are spatial, but this fact has been largely ignored in sociological research. A major exception is Massey and Denton's (1993) study of residential segregation by race, reviving a much older sociological tradition of spatial analysis in American society (e.g., Duncan and Duncan 1957). More recently, the field of research on fertility and contraception in Asia (several major projects focused on China, Thailand, and Nepal) has been making fruitful use of satellite image and Geographic Information System (GIS) data (e.g., Entwisle et al. 1997).

More extensive use of spatial statistics in sociology seems likely. Spatial statistics has been making great progress in the past two decades. The two most fruitful approaches to modeling spatial dependence have turned out to be those based on geostatistics (Matheron 1971; Chilès and Delfiner 1999), and on Markov random fields (Besag 1974; Besag, York, and Mollié 1991). Geostatistics models spatial correlation taking account of distance explicitly. Markov random fields, on the other hand, are based on a notion of neighborhood: an observation is taken to depend directly on its neighbors, and to be conditionally independent of all other cases given its neighbors. Markov random fields seem promising for social data if they are fairly regularly spaced, but for unevenly spaced spatial units, geostatistics may find it easier to account for the spatial dependence. For social data, geographic distance may not be the most relevant; distances defined on the basis, for example, of flows of people or of information may be more germane for some applications. I do not know of any work on spatial statistical models based on distances of this type, however.

4.2. *Textual and Qualitative Data*

In its rawest form, a great deal of sociological data is textual—for example, interviews, answers to open-ended questions in surveys, and ethnographic accounts. How to analyze such data formally and draw inference from them remains a largely open question. Efforts at formal analysis have focused on standard content analysis, consisting mainly of counting words in the text in different ways. It seems likely that using the context in which words and clauses appear would yield better results. Promising recent efforts to do just this include Carley's (1993) map analysis, Franzosi's (1994) set theoretic approach, and Roberts's (1997) generic semantic grammar, but the surface has only been scratched. The human mind is very good at analyzing individual texts, but computers are not, at least as yet; in this way the analysis of textual data may be like other problems such as image analysis and speech recognition. A similar challenge is faced on a massive scale by information retrieval for the Web (Jones and Willett 1997), where most search engines are based on simple content analysis methods. The more contextual methods being developed in sociology might be useful in this area also.

Singer et al. (1998) have made an intriguing use of textual data analysis, blending quantitative and qualitative approaches. They took a standard unit-level data set with more than 250 variables per person, and converted them into written "biographies." They then examined the biographies for common features, and thinned them to more generic descriptions.

Another approach to the systematic analysis of some kinds of qualitative data has recently been pioneered by Raudenbush and Sampson (1999) under the name "ecometrics." Their work was motivated by the study of neighborhood characteristics that could be linked to crime, such as physical decay (e.g., abandoned buildings), physical disorder (e.g., graffiti), and social disorder (e.g., drug dealing on the street). A standard quantitative approach to this kind of problem has been to estimate neighborhood effects using aggregates of respondents from the neighborhood, but Raudenbush and Sampson argue persuasively that this does not provide independent or "objective" assessments of the environment based on direct observation. Their data consisted of videotapes and observer logs for about 23,000 street block segments (Sampson and Raudenbush 1999). They coded these data and developed a hierarchical model for assessing reliabilities and calculating physical and social disorder scales.

Raudenbush and Sampson place their work firmly in Reiss's (1971) framework of systematic social observation, defined to include explicit rules that permit replication, and means of observation that are independent of what is being observed. This seems important for formal analysis of and inference from qualitative, textual, and ethnographic data; the work of Carley (1993), Franzosi (1994) and Roberts (1997) is in this spirit.

Interestingly, Raudenbush and Sampson point out that the search for individual and ecological effects may overemphasize the individual component simply because the well-studied individual psychometric measures are likely to be better than the much less studied ecological ones. Indeed, I have noticed that in many sociological studies, the reported contextual and neighborhood effects are weak, and the point that this may be due to poor measures rather than to weak effects is interesting. Data of this kind cry out for spatial statistical analysis. Raudenbush and Sampson acknowledge this and list it as a topic for future research; their work to date has not accounted for spatial dependence.

4.3. *Narrative and Sequence Analysis*

Life histories are typically analyzed by reducing them to variables and doing regression and multivariate analysis, or by event-history analysis. Abbott and Hrycak (1990) argued that these standard approaches obscure vital aspects of a life history (such as a professional career) that emerge when it is considered as a whole. They proposed viewing life histories of this kind as analogous to DNA or protein sequences, using optimal alignment methods adapted from molecular biology (Sankoff and Kruskal 1983), followed up by cluster analysis, to detect patterns common to groups of careers. Stovel, Savage, and Bearman (1996) used these methods to describe changes in career systems at Lloyds Banks over the past century.

Subsequently, Dijkstra and Taris (1995) extended the ideas to include independent variables, and Abbott and Barman (1997) applied the Gibbs sampling sequence detection method of Lawrence et al. (1993), originally also developed for microbiology; this seems to work very well.

The approach is interesting, and there are many open statistical questions. These include questions about the alignment methodology—for example, how should the insertion, deletion, and replacement costs be determined? They also include questions about the clustering method: How many clusters are there? Which clustering method should be used? How should one deal with outliers? Perhaps a more explicitly model-based approach would help to answer these questions. Cluster analysis was long a somewhat ad hoc collection of methods, and reformulating it so that it is based on formal statistical models has helped provide principled answers to some of these questions in other contexts (e.g., Banfield and Raftery 1993; Fraley and Raftery 1998). An alternative approach to analyzing sequence data based on log-linear models has been developed by Yamaguchi and Kandel (1998).

4.4. *Simulation Models*

Another way to represent a social process in more detail is via a macro- or microsimulation model. Such models are often deterministic and quite complicated, representing systems by different compartments that interact, and each compartment by a set of differential or difference equations. They have been used, for example, to explore the implications of different theories about how domestic politics and war interact (Hanneman, Collins, and Mordt 1995), the social dynamics of collective action (Kim and Bearman 1997), and the role of sexual networks in the spread of HIV (Morris 1997 and references therein).

A difficulty with such models is that ways of estimating the many parameters involved, of assessing the fit of the model, and of comparing competing models are not well established; all this tends to be done by informal trial and error. Methods being developed to put inference for such models on a solid statistical footing in other disciplines may prove helpful in sociology as well (Guttorp and Walden 1987; Raftery, Givens, and Zeh 1995; Poole and Raftery 2000).

4.5. *Macrosociology*

Macrosociology deals with large entities, such as states and their interactions. As a result, the number of cases tends to be small, and the use of standard statistical methods such as regression is difficult. This was pointed out trenchantly by Ragin (1987) in an influential book. His own proposed alternative, qualitative comparative analysis, seems unsatisfactory because it does not allow for variability of any kind, and so is sensitive to small changes in the data and in the way the method is applied (Lieberson 1994).

One solution to the problem is to obtain an at least moderately large sample size, as Bollen and Appold (1993) were able to do, for example. Often, however, this is not possible, so this is not a general solution.

Another approach is to use standard regression-type models, but to do Bayesian estimation with strong prior information if available, which it often is from the practice, common in this area, of analyzing specific cases in great detail (Western and Jackman 1994). Bayes factors may also help, as they tend to be less stringent than standard significance tests in small samples and allow a calibrated assessment of evidence rather than forcing the rejection or acceptance of a hypothesis (Kass and Raftery 1995). They also provide a way of accounting for model uncertainty, which can be quite large in this context (Western 1996).

5. DISCUSSION

Statistical methodology has had a successful half-century in sociology, leading the way in providing models for cross-classifications, and developing well-adapted methods for unit-level data sets. This has contributed to the greatly improved level of scientific rigor in sociology today. New kinds of data and new challenges abound, and the area is ripe for statistical research.

What are the future directions? As is implicit in my categorization of generations, I feel that the questions posed by the types of data that have motivated the third generation of methods may well spark some of the most exciting developments in sociological methodology in the medium term. But there are others, particularly related to the kind of data that may emerge from current technological developments. For example, surveys carried out by giving computers to respondents and inviting them to respond online, perhaps sporadically or repeatedly over an extended period, may generate useful data with new methodological issues of repeated measures at unequal time intervals and missing data (or they may not work at all). More generally, the Web is generating vast amounts of social science data of new types, and developing methods for drawing valid conclusions from such data is bound to be a major future source of challenges.

One direction I would both predict and advocate is that future developments will be interdisciplinary, spanning the social sciences and beyond. This has not been the case for most of the twentieth century, during which one social science discipline after another made the leap to greater quantitative sophistication, but often in relative isolation from one another and from statistics as a whole. Psychology may have been the first to make this transition, with the work of Spearman and Thurstone early in the century, followed by economics, with the development of econometrics in the 1930s and 1940s by Haavelmo, Tinbergen, the Cowles Commission, and others. Then sociology made its move in the 1960s, with the work of Blalock, Duncan, Goodman, and others that we have been discussing here. In the 1990s, it has been the turn of political science, led by Gary King, Larry Bartels, and others, who have been adopting and adapting modern statistical methodology to their discipline and developing new methods in the process.

The pattern in each of these disciplines has been similar. The quantitative transition has tended to focus on, and in some cases create, the most advanced statistical methods available at the time, and to spawn a dynamic cadre of methodologists, which in the case of the disciplines that made the transition the longest time ago, psychology and economics, have coalesced into their own quasi-disciplines of psychometrics and econometrics. Subsequent quantitative methodological development has been slower in each discipline, however, and has tended to remain tied to the methods that were at the cutting edge at the time of the quantitative transition. Sociology has not escaped this pattern: there quantitative work remains dominated by the methods first developed in the 1960s and early 1970s (structural equation models with latent variables, generalized linear models, event-history analysis via the Cox model), and has focused on developments and refinements of these methods. As I have discussed, there are good reasons for this, and it has had a very positive effect on the field as a whole. However, the statistical methods of the 1990s, particularly Bayesian analysis via Markov chain Monte Carlo, have been eagerly adopted by the cohorts of young political scientists going through the excitement and turmoil of their own quantitative revolution, but have been slower to penetrate sociology.

Now, in an academic world more interdisciplinary than that of previous decades, the opportunity is there for all the social science disciplines to break out of the disciplinary straitjacket and to move their quantitative methodologies forward together. Several major institutions have launched interdisciplinary centers and initiatives focused on quantitative social science methodology in the past few years, providing resources for doing just this. The University of Washington has just established a new Center for Statistics and the Social Sciences. Harvard's new Center for Basic Research in the Social Sciences emphasizes social statistics. The new Center for Spatially Integrated Social Science at the University of California–Santa Barbara is another example, with a focus on spatial statistics. UCLA's young Statistics Department grew out of social statistics, and retains active interdisciplinary links to several social sciences. Columbia's new master's program in Quantitative Social Science is another interdisciplinary enterprise spanning the social sciences and statistics. At the University of Michigan, the new Quantitative Methodology Program is creating and reviving joint graduate programs between the Department of Statistics and several social science departments. These all join what is perhaps the most successful effort of this kind to date: the Social Statistics Department at the University of Southampton.

REFERENCES

Abbott, Andrew. 1998. "The Causal Devolution." *Sociological Methods and Research* 27:148–81.

Abbott, Andrew, and Emily Barman. 1997. "Sequence Comparison Via Alignment and Gibbs Sampling: A Formal Analysis of the Emergence of the Modern Sociological Article." *Sociological Methodology* 27:47–88.

Abbott, Andrew, and Alexandra Hrycak. 1990. "Measuring Sequence Resemblance," *American Journal of Sociology* 96:144–85.

Agresti, Alan. 1990. *Categorical Data Analysis.* New York: Wiley.

Aitchison, John. 1986. *The Analysis of Compositional Data.* London: Chapman and Hall.

Albert, James, and Siddartha Chib. 1993. "Bayesian Analysis of Binary and Polychotomous Response Data." *Journal of the American Statistical Association* 88:669–79.

Allison, Paul. 1982. "Discrete-Time Methods for the Analysis of Event Histories." *Sociological Methodology* 13:61–98.

———. 1984. *Event History Analysis.* Beverly Hills, CA: Sage.

Alwin, Duane F., and Robert M. Hauser. 1975. "The Decomposition of Effects in Path Analysis." *American Sociological Review* 40:37–47.

Amemiya, Takashi 1985. *Advanced Econometrics.* Cambridge, MA: Harvard University Press.

Arminger, Gerhard. 1998. "A Bayesian Approach to Nonlinear Latent Variable Models Using the Gibbs Sampler and the Metropolis-Hastings Algorithm." *Psychometrika* 63:271–300.

Baker, R. J., and John A. Nelder. 1977. *The GLIM System, Release 3, Generalized Linear Interactive Modeling.* Oxford, England: Numerical Algorithms Group.

Banfield, Jeffrey D., and Adrian E. Raftery. 1993. "Model-Based Gaussian and Non-Guassian Clustering." *Biometrics* 49:803–21.

Barnard, John, J. T. Du, Jennifer L. Hill, and Donald B. Rubin. 1998. "A Broader Template for Analyzing Broken Randomized Experiments." *Sociological Methods and Research* 27:285–317.

Bearman, Peter S. 1997. "Generalized Exchange." *American Journal of Sociology* 102:1383–415.

Beck, Nathaniel. 2000. "Political Methodology: A Welcoming Discipline." *Journal of the American Statistical Association* 95:651–54.

Becker, Mark P. 1989. "Using Association Models to Analyze Agreement Data: Two Examples." *Statistics in Medicine* 8:1199–207.

———. 1994. "Analysis of Cross-Classifications of Counts Using Models for Marginal Distributions: An Application to Trends in Attitudes on Legalized Abortion." *Sociological Methodology* 24:229–65.

Becker, Mark P., and I. Yang. 1998. "Latent Class Marginal Models for Cross-Classifications of Counts." *Sociological Methodology* 28:293–326.

Begg, Colin B., and R. Gray. 1984. "Calculation of Polytomous Logistic Regression Parameters Using Individualized Regressions." *Biometrika* 71:11–18.

Benzécri, J.-P. 1976. *L'Analyse des Données*. 2d ed. Paris: Dunod.

Bernhardt, Annette D., Martina Morris, and Mark S. Handcock. 1995. "Women's Gains or Men's Losses? A Closer Look at the Shrinking Gender Gap in Earnings." *American Journal of Sociology* 101:302–28.

Besag, Julian E. 1974. "Spatial Interaction and the Statistical Analysis of Lattice Systems" (with discussion). *Journal of the Royal Statistical Society*, Ser. B, 36:192–236.

Besag, Julian E., Jeremy York, and Annie Mollié. 1991. "Bayesian Image Restoration, with Two Applications in Spatial Statistics" (with discussion). *Annals of the Institute of Statistical Mathematics* 43:1–59.

Biblarz, Timothy J., and Adrian E. Raftery. 1993. "The Effects of Family Disruption on Social Mobility." *American Sociological Review* 58:97–109.

Biblarz, Timothy J., Adrian E. Raftery, and Alexander Bucur. 1997. "Family Structure and Social Mobility." *Social Forces* 75:1319–39.

Birch, M. W. 1963. "Maximum Likelihood in Three-Way Tables," *Journal of the Royal Statistical Society,* Ser. B, 25:220–33.

———. 1965. "The Detection of Partial Association, II: The General Case," *Journal of the Royal Statistical Society,* Ser. B, 27, 111–124.

Blalock, Hubert M. 1961. *Causal Inferences in Nonexperimental Research.* New York: W.W. Norton.

———. 1984. "Contextual-Effects Models: Theoretical and Methodological Issues." *Annual Review of Sociology* 10:353–72.

Blau, Peter M., and Otis Dudley Duncan. 1967. *American Occupational Structure.* New York: Free Press.

Boatwright, Peter, Robert McCullouch, and Peter Rossi. 1999. "Account-level Modeling for Trade Promotion: An Application of a Constrained Parameter Hierarchical Model." *Journal of the American Statistical Association* 94:1063–73.

Bock, R. D. 1989. *Multilevel Analysis of Educational Data.* San Diego, CA: Academic Press.

Bollen, Kenneth A. 1989. *Structural Equation Models with Latent Variables*. New York: Wiley.

Bollen, Kenneth A., and S. J. Appold. 1993. "National Industrial-Structure and the Global System." *American Sociological Review* 58:283–301.

Boyd, L. H., and G. R. Iversen. 1979. *Contextual Analysis: Concepts and Statistical Techniques.* Belmont, CA: Wadsworth.

Bradlow, Eric T., and Alan Zaslavsky. 1999. "A Hierarchical Latent Variable Model for Ordinal Data from a Customer Satisfaction Survey with 'No Answer' Responses." *Journal of the American Statistical Association* 94:43–52.

Browne, Michael W. 2000. "Psychometrics." *Journal of the American Statistical Association* 95:661–65.

Bryk, Anthony S., and Stephen W. Raudenbush. 1992. *Hierarchical Linear Models: Applications and Data Analysis Methods.* Newbury Park, CA: Sage.

Burt, Ronald S. 1987. "Social Contagion and Innovation: Cohesion Versus Structural Equivalence." *American Journal of Sociology* 92:1287–335.

Camic, Charles, and Yu Xie. 1994. "The Statistical Turn in American Social Science—Columbia University, 1890 to 1915." *American Sociological Review* 59:773–805.

Carley, Kathleen M. 1993. "Coding Choices for Textual Analysis: A Comparison of Content Analysis and Map Analysis." *Sociological Methodology* 23:75–126.

Celeux, Gilles, and Gérard Govaert. 1991. "Clustering Criteria for Discrete Data and Latent Class Models." *Journal of Classification* 8:157–76.

Charles, Maria, and David Grusky. 1995. "Models for Describing the Underlying Structure of Sex Segregation." *American Journal of Sociology* 100:931–71.

Chickering, D. Maxwell, and David Heckerman. 1997. "Efficient Approximations for the Marginal Likelihood of Bayesian Networks with Hidden Variables." *Machine Learning* 29:181–212.

Chilès, Jean-Paul, and Pierre Delfiner. 1999. *Geostatistics: Modeling Spatial Uncertainty.* New York: Wiley.

Clogg, Clifford C. 1992. "The Impact of Sociological Methodology on Statistical Methodology" (with discussion). *Statistical Science* 7:183–207.

———. 1995. "Latent Class Models." Pp. 311–59 in *Handbook of Statistical Modeling for the Social and Behavioral Sciences*, edited by G. Arminger, C. C. Clogg and M. E. Soble. New York: Plenum.

Clogg, Clifford C., Scott R. Eliason, and R. J. Wahl. 1990. "Labor Market Experiences and Labor Force Outcomes." *American Journal of Sociology* 95:1536–76.

Cornfield, Jerome 1951. "A Method of Estimating Comparative Rates from Clinical Data; Application to Cancer of the Lung, Breast and Cervix." *Journal of the National Cancer Institute* 11:1269–75.

———. 1962. "Joint Dependence of the Risk of Coronary Heart Disease on Serum Cholesterol and Systolic Blood Pressure: A Discriminant Function Analysis." *Federation Proceedings* 21:58–61.

Costner, Herbert L. 1969. "Theory, Deduction and Rules of Correspondence." *American Journal of Sociology* 75:245–63.

Cox, David R. 1970. *The Analysis of Binary Data.* London: Chapman and Hall.

———. 1972. "Regression Models and Life Tables" (with discussion). *Journal of the Royal Statistical Society*, Ser. B, 34, 187–220.

Daniels, Michael J., and Constantine Gatsonis. 1999. "Hierarchical Generalized Linear Models in the Analysis of Variations in Health Care Utilization." *Journal of the American Statistical Association* 94:29–42.

Datta, G. S., Partha Lahiri, T. Maiti, and K. L. Lu 1999. "Hierarchical Bayes Estimation of Unemployment Rates for the States of the U.S." *Journal of the American Statistical Association* 94:1074–82.

De Graaf, Nan. 1991. "Distinction by Consumption in Czechoslovakia, Hungary and the Netherlands." *European Sociological Review* 7:267–90.

Dempster, Arthur P., Nan M. Laird, and Donald B. Rubin. 1977. "Maximum Likelihood from Incomplete Data via the EM Algorithm" (with discussion). *Journal of the Royal Statistical Society*, Ser. B, 39:1–38.

Diekmann, Andreas. 1989. "Diffusion and Survival Models for the Process of Entry into Marriage." *American Journal of Mathematical Sociology* 14:31–44.

Dijkstra, W., and T. Taris. 1995. "Measuring the Agreement Between Sequences." *Sociological Methods and Research* 24:214–31.

DiPrete, Thomas A., and Jerry D. Forristal. 1994. "Multilevel Models: Methods and Substance." *Annual Review of Sociology* 20:331–57.

Duncan, Otis Dudley. 1961. "A Socioeconomic Index for All Occupations." Pp. 109–38 in *Occupations and Social Status*, edited by A. J. Reiss. New York: Free Press.

———. 1966. "Path Analysis." *American Journal of Sociology* 72:1–16.

———. 1975. *An Introduction to Structural Equation Models*. New York: Academic Press.

———. 1979. "How Destination Depends on Origin in the Occupational Mobility Table." *American Journal of Sociology* 84:793–803.

Duncan, Otis Dudley, and Beverly Duncan. 1957. *The Negro Population of Chicago*. Chicago: University of Chicago Press.

Durkheim, Emile. 1897. *Le Suicide*. Paris: Alcan. Translated by G. Simpson and J. A. Spaulding. 1951. New York: Free Press.

Eisenberg, Theodore. 2000. "Empirical Methods and the Law." *Journal of the American Statistical Association* 95:665–70.

Elliott, Michael R., and Roderick J. A. Little. 2000. "A Bayesian Approach to Combining Information from a Census, a Coverage Measurement Survey, and Demographic Analysis." *Journal of the American Statistical Association* 95:351–62.

Entwisle, Barbara, John B. Casterline, and H. A. A. Sayed. 1989. "Villages as Contexts for Contraceptive Behavior." *American Sociological Review* 54:1019–34.

Entwisle, Barbara, and William M. Mason. 1985. "Multilevel Effects of Socioeconomic Development and Family Planning Programs on Children Ever Born." *American Journal of Sociology* 91:616–49.

Entwisle, Barbara, William M. Mason, and A. I. Hermalin. 1986. "The Multilevel Dependence of Contraceptive Use on Socioeconomic Development and Family Planning Program Strength." *Demography* 23:199–215.

Entwisle, Barbara, Ronald R. Rindfuss, S. J. Walsh, T. P. Evans, and Sara R. Curran. 1987. "Geographic Information Systems, Spatial Network Analysis, and Contraceptive Choice." *Demography* 34:171–87.

Fahrmeir, Ludwig, and Leo Knorr-Held. 1997. "Dynamic Discrete-Time Duration Models: Estimation via Markov Chain Monte Carlo." *Sociological Methodology* 27:417–52.

Fay, Robert E. 1996. "Alternative Paradigms for the Analysis of Imputed Survey Data." *Journal of the American Statistical Association* 91:490–98.

Featherman, David L., and Robert M. Hauser. 1976. "Sexual Inequalities and Socioeconomic Achievement in the U.S., 1962–1973." *American Sociological Review* 41:462–83.

Featherman, David L., and Gillian Stevens. 1982. "A Revised Socioeconomic Index of Occupational Status: Applications in Analysis of Sex Differences in Attainment." Pp. 93–129 in *Measures of Socioeconomic Status*, edited by M. Powers. Boulder, CO: Westview.

Fienberg, Stephen E. 2000. "Contingency Tables and Log-Linear Models: Basic Results and New Developments." *Journal of the American Statistical Association* 95:643–47.

Fienberg, Stephen E., and William M. Mason. 1979. "Identification and Estimation of Age-Period-Cohort Effects in the Analysis of Discrete Archival Data." *Sociological Methodology* 10:1–67.

Fraley, Christina, and Adrian E. Raftery. 1998. "How Many Clusters? Which Clustering Method? Answers via Model-Based Cluster Analysis." *Computer Journal* 41:578–88.

Frank, Ove, and David Stauss. 1986. "Markov Graphs." *Journal of the American Statistical Association* 81:832–42.

Franzosi, Roberto. 1994. "From Words to Numbers: A Set Theory Framework for the Collection, Organization and Analysis of Narrative Data." *Sociological Methodology* 24:105–36.

Freeman, John, Glenn Carroll, and Michael T. Hannan. 1983. "The Liability of Newness: Age Dependence in Organizational Death Rates." *American Sociological Review* 48:692–710.

Freedman, David A. 1987. "As Others See Us" (with discussion). *Journal of Educational Statistics*, 12, 101–223.

Ganzeboom, Harry B. G., Ruud Luijkx, and Donald J. Treiman. 1989. "Intergenerational Class Mobility in Comparative Perspective." *Research in Social Stratification and Mobility* 9:3–79.

Gelman, Andrew, John B. Carlin, Hal S. Stern, and Donald B. Rubin. 1995. *Bayesian Data Analysis*. New York: Chapman and Hall.

Gilks, Walter R., Sylvia Richardson, and David J. Spiegelhalter, eds. 1996. *Markov Chain Monte Carlo in Practice*. London: Chapman and Hall.

Glass, David V. 1954. *Social Mobility in Britain*. Glencoe, IL: Free Press.

Goldstein, Harvey. 1995. *Multilevel Models in Educational and Social Research*, 2d ed. London: Griffin.

Goldstein, Harvey, M. Yang, R. Omar, R. Turner, and S. Thompson. 2000. "Meta-Analysis Using Multilevel Models with an Application to the Study of Class Size Effects." *Applied Statistics* 49:399–412.

Goodman, Leo A. 1971. "The Analysis of Multidimensional Contingency Tables: Stepwise Procedures and Direct Estimation Methods for Building Models for Multiple Classifications." *Technometrics* 13:33–61.

———. 1974a. "The Analysis of Systems of Qualitative Variables When Some of the Variables Are Unobservable." *American Journal of Sociology* 79:1179–259.

———. 1974b. "Exploratory Latent Structure Analysis Using Both Identifiable and Unidentifiable Models." *Biometrika* 61:215–31.

———. 1979. "Simple Models for the Analysis of Association in Cross-Classifications Having Ordered Categories." *Journal of the American Statistical Association* 74:537–52.

———. 1985. "The Analysis of Cross-Classified Data Having Ordered and/or Unordered Categories." *Annals of Statistics* 13:10–69.

Goodman, Leo A., and Michael Hout. 1998. "Statistical Methods and Graphical Displays for Analyzing How the Association Between Two Qualitative Variables Differs Among Countries, Among Groups, or Over Time: A Modified Regression-Type Approach" (with discussion). Pp. 175–262 in *Sociological Methodology 1998*, edited by Adrian E. Raftery. Cambridge, MA: Blackwell Publishers.

Grusky, David B., and Robert M. Hauser. 1984. "Comparative Social Mobility Revisited: Models of Convergence and Divergence in Sixteen Countries." *American Sociological Review* 49:19–38.

Guttorp, Peter, and Andrew T. Walden. 1987. "On the Evaluation of Geophysical Models." *Geophysical Journal of the Royal Astronomical Society* 91:201–10.

Haberman, Shelby J. 1979. *Analysis of Qualitative Data*, vol. 2. New York: Academic Press.

Hagenaars, Jacques A. 1988. "Latent Structure Models with Direct Effects Between Indicators: Local Dependence Models." *Sociological Methods and Research* 16: 379–406.

———. 1990. *Categorical Longitudinal Data: Log-Linear Panel, Trend and Cohort Analysis.* Newbury Park, CA: Sage.

Handcock, Mark S., and Martina Morris. 1998. "Relative Distribution Methods." *Sociological Methodology* 28, 53–98.

———. 1999. *Relative Distribution Methods in the Social Sciences.* New York: Springer-Verlag.

Hanneman, R. A., Randall Collins, and Gabriele Mordt. 1995. "Discovering Theory Dynamics by Computer Simulation: Experiments on State Legitimacy and Imperialist Capitalism." *Sociological Methodology* 25:1–46.

Hauser, Robert M., and John R. Warren. 1997. "Socioeconomic Indexes for Occupations: A Review, Update and Critique." *Sociological Methodology* 27:177–298.

Heckman, James J. 1979. "Sample Selection Bias as a Specification Error." *Econometrika* 47:153–61.

Heckman, James J., and V. Joseph Hotz. 1989. "Choosing Among Alternative Nonexperimental Methods for Estimating the Impact of Social Programs: The Case of Manpower Training" (with discussion). *Journal of the American Statistical Association* 84:862–80.

Hedges, Larry J., and Ingram Olkin. 1985. *Statistical Methods for Meta-Analysis.* New York: Academic Press.

Hill, D. H. 1997. "Adjusting for Attrition in Event-History Analysis." *Sociological Methodology* 27:393–416.

Hill, D. H., W. G. Axinn, and A. Thornton. 1993. "Competing Hazards with Shared Unmeasured Risk Factors." *Sociological Methodology* 23:245–77.

Holland, Paul. 1986. "Statistics and Causal Inference." *Journal of the American Statistical Association* 81:945–70.

Hosmer, David W., and Stanley Lemeshow. 1989. *Applied Logistic Regression.* New York: Wiley.

Hout, Michael. 1983. *Mobility Tables*. Beverly Hills, CA: Sage.

———. 1984. "Status, Autonomy and Training in Occupational Mobility." *American Journal of Sociology* 89:1379–409.

———. 1988. "Expanding Universalism, Less Structural Mobility: The American Occupational Structural in the 1980s." *American Journal of Sociology* 93:1358–400.

Jones, K. S., and Willett, P. 1997. *Readings in Information Retrieval*. San Francisco: Morgan Kaufman.

Jöreskog, Karl G. 1973. "A General Method for Estimating a Linear Structural Equation System." Pp. 85–112 in *Structural Equation Models in the Social Sciences*, edited by A. S. Goldberger and O. D. Duncan. New York: Seminar.

Kalmijn, M. 1991. "Status Homogamy in the United States." *American Journal of Sociology* 97:496–523.

Kass, Robert E., and Adrian E. Raftery. 1995. "Bayes Factors." *Journal of the American Statistical Association* 90:773–95.

Kass, Robert E., and Larry Wasserman. 1995. "A Reference Bayesian Test for Nested Hypotheses and Its Relationship to the Schwarz Criterion." *Journal of the American Statistical Association* 90:928–34.

Kim, Hyojoung, and Peter S. Bearman. 1997. "The Structure and Dynamics of Movement Participation." *American Sociological Review* 62:70–93.

Koster, Jan. 1996. "Markov Properties of Non-Recursive Causal Models." *Annals of Statistics* 24:2148–77.

Kuo, H. H. D., and Robert M. Hauser. 1996. "Gender, Family Configuration, and the Effect of Family Background on Educational Attainment." *Social Biology* 43:98–131.

Lang, Joseph B., and Alan Agresti. 1994. "Simultaneously Modeling Joint and Marginal Distributions of Multivariate Categorical Responses." *Journal of the American Statistical Association* 89:625–32.

Laumann, Edward O., J. Gagnon, R. Michael, and S. Michaels. 1994. *The Social Organization of Sexuality*. Chicago: University of Chicago Press.

Lawrence, C. E., S. F. Altschul, M. S. Boguski, J. S. Liu, A. F. Neuwald, and J. C. Wooton. 1993. "Detecting Subtle Sequence Signals." *Science* 262:208–14.

Lazarsfeld, Paul F. 1950. "The Logical and Mathematical Foundation of Latent Structure Analysis." Pp. 362–412 in *Studies in Social Psychology in World War II*. Vol. 4, *Measurement and Prediction*, edited by E. A. Schulman, P. F. Lazarsfeld, S. A. Starr, and J. A. Clausen. Princeton, NJ: Princeton University Press.

Lazarsfeld, Paul F., and Neil W. Henry. 1968. *Latent Structure Analysis*. Boston: Houghton Mifflin.

Lieberson, Stanley L. 1994. "More on the Uneasy Case for Using Mill-Type Methods in Small-N Comparative Studies." *Social Forces* 72:1225–37.

Lindley, Dennis V., and Adrian F. M. Smith. 1972. "Bayes Estimates for the Linear Model" (with discussion). *Journal of the Royal Statistical Society*, Ser. B, Methodological, 34:1–41.

Little, Roderick J. A. 1992. "Regression with Missing *X*'s: A Review." *Journal of the American Statistical Association* 87:1227–37.

Little, Roderick J. A., and Donald B. Rubin. 1987. *Statistical Analysis with Missing Data*. New York: Wiley.

———. 1989. "The Analysis of Social Science Data with Missing Values." *Sociological Methods and Research* 18:292–326.

Logan, John A. 1996. "Opportunity and Choice in Socially Structured Labor Markets." *American Journal of Sociology* 101:114–60.

———. 1997. "Estimating Two-Sided Logit Models." *Sociological Methodology* 28:139–73.

Long, J. Scott. 1984a. *Confirmatory Factor Analysis.* Newbury Park, CA: Sage.

———. 1984b. *Covariance Structure Models.* Newbury Park, CA: Sage.

———. 1997. *Regression Models for Categorical and Limited Dependent Variables.* Thousand Oaks, CA: Sage.

Longford, Nicholas. 1993. *Logistic Regression with Random Coefficients.* Princeton, NJ: Educational Testing Service.

Manski, Charles F. 1993. "Identification Problems in the Social Sciences." Pp. 1–56 in *Sociological Methodology 1993*, edited by Peter V. Marsden. Oxford, England: Blackwell Publishers.

———. 1995. *Identification Problems in the Social Sciences.* Cambridge, MA: Harvard University Press.

Manski, Charles C., and Daniel S. Nagin. 1998. "Bounding Disagreements About Treatment Effects: A Case Study of Sentencing and Recidivism." Pp. 99–137 in *Sociological Methodology 1998*, edited by Adrian E. Raftery. Cambridge, MA: Blackwell Publishers.

Marsden, Peter V., and Joel Podolny. 1990. "Dynamic Analysis of Network Diffusion Processes." Pp. 197–214 in *Social Networks Through Time*, edited by H. Flap and J. Weesie. Utrecht, Netherlands: ISOR.

Mason, William M., G.Y. Wong, and Barbara Entwisle. 1983. "Contextual Analysis Through the Multilevel Linear Model." Pp. 72–103 in *Sociological Methodology 1983–1984*, edited by S. Leinhardt. San Francisco: Jossey-Bass.

Massey, Douglas S., and Nancy A. Denton. 1993. *American Apartheid: Segregation and the Making of the Underclass.* Cambridge, MA: Harvard University Press.

Matheron, Georges. 1971. *The Theory of Regionalized Variables and Its Applications.* Paris: Ecole Nationale Supérieure des Mines.

Matsueda, Ross L., and Karen Heimer. 1987. "Race, Family Structure, and Delinquency: A Test of Differential Association and Social Control Theories." *American Sociological Review* 52:826–40.

Mayer, Karl Ulrich, and Nancy Brandon Tuma. 1990. *Event History Analysis in Life Course Research.* Madison: University of Wisconsin Press.

McCullagh, Peter, and John A. Nelder. 1989. *Generalized Linear Models.* London: Chapman and Hall.

Morris, Carl N. 1983. "Parametric Empirical Bayes Inference: Theory and Applications" (with discussion). *Journal of the American Statistical Association* 78:47–65.

Morris, Martina. 1997. "Sexual Networks and HIV." *AIDS* 11:S209-16.

Morris, Martina, Annette D. Bernhardt, and Mark S. Handcock. 1994. "Economic Inequality: New Methods for New Trends." *American Sociological Review* 59:205–19.

Muthén, Bengt. 1983. "Latent Variable Structure Equation Modeling with Categorical Data." *Journal of Econometrics* 22:43–65.

———. 1997. "Latent Variable Modeling of Longitudinal and Multilevel Data." *Sociological Methodology* 27:453–80.

Nakao, Keiko, and Judith Treas. 1994. "Updating Occupational Prestige and Socioeconomic Scores: How the New Measures Measure Up." Pp. 1–72 in *Sociological Methodology 1994*, edited by P. V. Marsden. Cambridge, MA: Blackwell Publishers.

Nelder, John A., and R. W. M. Wedderburn. 1972. "Generalised Linear Models." *Journal of the Royal Statistical Society*, Ser. A, 135:370–84.

Padgett, John F., and C. K. Ansell. 1993. "Robust Action and the Rise of the Medici." *American Journal of Sociology* 98:1259–319.

Pearl, Judea. 1998. "Graphs, Causality, and Structural Equation Models." *Sociological Methods and Research* 27:226–84.

Petersen, Trond. 1991. "The Statistical Analysis of Event Histories." *Sociological Methods and Research* 19:270–323.

———. 1995. "Models for Interdependent Event-History Data: Specification and Estimation." Pp. 317–76 in *Sociological Methodology 1995*, edited by Peter V. Marsden. Cambridge, MA: Blackwell Publishers.

Poole, David, and Adrian E. Raftery. 2000. "Inference from Deterministic Simulation Models: The Bayesian Melding Approach." *Journal of the American Statistical Association* 95:1244–55.

Raftery, Adrian E. 1986a. "Choosing Models for Cross-Classifications." *American Sociological Review* 51:145–46.

———. 1986b. "A Note on Bayes Factors for Log-Linear Contingency Table Models with Vague Prior Information." *Journal of the Royal Statistical Society*, Ser. B, 48:249–50.

———. 1991. "Bayesian Model Selection and Gibbs Sampling in Covariance Structure Models." Working Paper 92-4, Center for Studies in Demography and Ecology, University of Washington.

———. 1995. "Bayesian Model Selection in Social Research" (with discussion). *Sociological Methodology* 25:111–93.

———. 1996. "Approximate Bayes Factors and Accounting for Model Uncertainty in Generalized Linear Models." *Biometrika* 83:251–66.

———. 1999. "Bayes Factors and BIC: Comment on 'A Critique of the Bayesian Information Criterion for Model Selection.'" *Sociological Methods and Research* 27:411–27.

Raftery, Adrian E., Geof H. Givens, and Judith E. Zeh. 1995. "Inference from a Deterministic Population Dynamics Model for Bowhead Whales" (with discussion). *Journal of the American Statistical Association* 90, 402–30.

Raftery, Adrian E., and Michael Hout. 1985. "Does Irish Education Approach the Meritocratic Ideal? A Logistic Analysis." *Economic and Social Review* 16:115–40.

Raftery, Adrian E., Steven M. Lewis, and Akbar Aghajanian. 1995. "Demand or Ideation? Evidence from the Iranian Marital Fertility Decline." *Demography* 32:159–82.

Ragin, Charles. 1987. *The Comparative Method: Moving Beyond Qualitative and Quantitative Strategies*. Berkeley, CA: University of California Press.

Rao, J. N. K. 1996. "On Variance Estimation with Imputed Survey Data." *Journal of the American Statistical Association* 91:499–506.

Raudenbush, Stephen W., and Robert J. Sampson. 1999. "Ecometrics: Toward a Science of Assessing Ecological Settings, with Application to the Systematic Social Observation of Neighborhoods." *Sociological Methodology* 29:1–41.

Reiss, Albert J., Jr. 1971. "Systematic Observations of Natural Social Phenomena." *Sociological Methodology* 3:3–33.

Roberts, Carl W. 1997. "A Generic Semantic Grammar for Quantitative Text Analysis: Applications to East and West Berlin News Content from 1979." *Sociological Methodology*, 27, 89–130.

Roeder, Kathryn, G. S. Lynch, and Daniel S. Nagin. 1999. "Modeling Uncertainty in Latent Class Membership: A Case Study in Criminology." *Journal of the American Statistical Association* 94:766–76.

Rogoff, Nathalie. 1953. *Recent Trends in Occupational Mobility*. Glencoe, IL: Free Press.

Rubin, Donald, B. 1974. "Estimating Causal Effects of Treatments in Randomized and Nonrandomized Studies." *Journal of Educational Psychology* 66:688–701.

———. 1977. "Formalizing Subjective Notions About the Effect of Nonrespondents in Sample Surveys." *Journal of the American Statistical Association* 72:538–43.

———. 1987. *Multiple Imputation for Nonresponse in Surveys*. New York: Wiley.

———. 1996. "Multiple Imputation After 18+ Years." *Journal of the American Statistical Association* 91:473–89.

Sampson, Robert J., and Stephen W. Raudenbush. 1999. "Systematic Social Observations of Public Spaces: A New Look at Neighborhood Disorder." *American Journal of Sociology* 105:603–51.

Sankoff, D., and Kruskal, J. B. 1983. *Time Warps, String Edits, and Macromolecules*. Reading, MA: Addison-Wesley.

Schafer, Joseph L. 1997. *Analysis of Incomplete Multivariate Data*. London: Chapman and Hall.

Scheines, R., H. Hoijtink, and A. Boomsma. 1999. "Bayesian Estimation and Testing of Structural Equation Models." *Psychometrika* 64:37–52.

Schuessler, Karl F. 1980. "Quantitative Methodology in Sociology: The Last 25 Years." *American Behavioral Scientist* 23:835–60.

Schwarz, Gideon. 1978. "Estimating the Dimension of a Model." *Annals of Statistics* 6:461–64.

Singer, Burton, Carol D. Ryff, Deborah Carr, and W. J. Magee. 1998. "Linking Life Histories and Mental Health: A Person-Centered Strategy." *Sociological Methodology* 28:1–52.

Snijders, Tom A. B., and Roel J. Bosker. 1999. *Multilevel Analysis: An Introduction to Basic and Advanced Multilevel Modeling*. Beverly Hills, CA: Sage.

Sobel, Michael E. 1981. "Diagonal Mobility Models: A Substantively Motivated Class of Designs for the Analysis of Mobility Effects." *American Sociological Review* 46:893–906.

———. 1985. "Social Mobility and Fertility Revisited: Some New Methods for the Analysis of Mobility Effects Hypothesis." *American Sociological Review* 50:699–712.

———. 1990. "Effect Analysis and Causation in Linear Structural Equation Models." *Psychometrika* 55:495–515.

———. 1994. "Causal Inference in Latent Variable Models." Pp. 3–35 in *Latent Variables Analysis: Applications for Developmental Research*, edited by A. von Eye and C. C. Clogg. Thousand Oaks, CA: Sage.

———. 1995. "Causal Inference in the Social and Behavioral Sciences." Pp. 1–38 in *Handbook of Statistical Modeling for the Social and Behavioral Sciences*, edited by G. Arminger, C. C. Clogg, and M. E. Sobel. New York: Plenum.

———. 1997. "Measurement, Causation and Local Independence." Pp. 11–28 in *Latent Variable Modeling and Applications to Causality*, edited by M. Berkane. New York: Springer-Verlag.

———. 1998. "Causal Inference in Statistical Models of the Process of Socioeconomic Achievement: A Case Study." *Sociological Methods and Research* 27: 318–48.

———. 2000. "Causal Inference in the Social Sciences." *Journal of the American Statistical Association* 95:647–51.

Sobel, Michael E., Mark P. Becker, and Susan S. Minick. 1998. "Origin, Destination and Association in Occupational Mobility." *American Journal of Sociology* 104: 687–701.

Sorensen, Ann Marie. 1989. "Husbands' and Wives' Characteristics and Fertility Decisions: A Diagonal Mobility Model." *Demography* 26:125–35.

Spiegelhalter, David J., A. Philip Dawid, Steffan Lauritzen, and R. Cowell. 1993. "Bayesian Analysis in Expert Systems." *Statistical Science* 8:219–82.

Spirtes, Peter, Clark Glymour, and Richard Scheines. 1993. *Causation, Prediction and Search.* New York: Springer-Verlag.

Spirtes, Peter, Thomas S. Richardson, Christopher Meek, Richard Scheines, and Clark Glymour. 1998. "Using Path Diagrams as a Structural Equation Modeling Tool." *Sociological Methods and Research* 27:182–225.

Stern, R. D., and R. Coe. 1984. "A Model Fitting Analysis of Daily Rainfall Data" (with discussion). *Journal of the Royal Statistical Society*, Ser. A, 147:1–34.

Stovel, Katherine, M. Savage, and Peter S. Bearman. 1996. "Ascription into Achievement: Models of Career Systems at Lloyds Bank, 1890–1970." *American Journal of Sociology* 102:358–99.

Strang, David. 1991. "Adding Social Structure to Diffusion Models: An Event History Framework." *Sociological Methods and Research* 19:324–53.

Strang, David, and Nancy Brandon Tuma. 1993. "Spatial and Temporal Heterogeneity in Diffusion." *American Journal of Sociology* 99:614–39.

Thompson, Elizabeth A. 1998. "Inferring Gene Ancestry: Estimating Gene Descent." *International Statistical Review* 66:29–40.

Tobin, James. 1958. "Estimation of Relationships for Limited Dependent Variables." *Econometrika* 26:24–36.

Treiman, Donald J. 1977. *Occupational Prestige in Comparative Perspective*. New York: Academic Press.

Truett, J., Jerome Cornfield, and W. Kannel. 1967. "A Multivariate Analysis of the Risk of Coronary Heart Disease in Framingham." *Journal of Chronic Diseases* 20:511–24.

Tuma, Nancy Brandon. 1976. "Rewards, Resources, and Rates of Mobility: A Nonstationary Multivariate Stochastic Model." *American Sociological Review* 41:338–60.

Tuma, Nancy Brandon, and Michael T. Hannan. 1984. *Social Dynamics: Models and Methods*. Orlando, FL: Academic Press.

Udry, J. R., and Peter S. Bearman. 1998. "New Methods for New Research on Adolescent Sexual Behavior." Pp. 241–69 in *New Perspectives on Adolescent Risk Behavior*, edited by R. Jessor. Cambridge, England: Cambridge University Press.

Verma, T., and Judea Pearl. 1988. "Causal Networks: Semantics and Expressiveness." Pp. 352–59 in *Proceedings of the 4th Workshop on Uncertainty in Artificial Intelligence*. Mountain View, CA.

Warren, John R., Jennifer T. Sheridan, and Robert M. Hauser. 1998. "Choosing a Measure of Occupational Standing—How Useful Are Composite Measures in Analyses of Gender Inequality in Occupational Attainment?" *Sociological Methods and Research* 27:3–76.

Wasserman, Stanley, and K. Faust. 1994. *Social Network Analysis: Methods and Applications*, Cambridge, England: Cambridge University Press.

Wasserman, Stanley, and Philippa Pattison. 1996. "Logit Models and Logistic Regressions for Social Networks. 1. An Introduction to Markov Graphs and *p*," *Psychometrika* 61:401–25.

Weakliem, David L. 1992. "Does Social Mobility Affect Political Behavior?" *European Sociological Review* 8:153–65.

———. 1999. "A Critique of the Bayesian Information Criterion for Model Selection" (with discussion). *Sociological Methods and Research* 27:359–443.

Western, Bruce. 1996. "Vague Theory and Model Uncertainty in Macrosociology." *Sociological Methodology* 26:165–92.

Western, Bruce, and Simon Jackman. 1994. "Bayesian Inference for Comparative Research." *American Political Science Review* 88:412–23.

White, Harrison C. 1963. *An Anatomy of Kinship: Mathematical Models for Structures of Cumulated Roles.* Englewood Cliffs, NJ: Prentice-Hall.

Winship, Christopher, and Robert D. Mare. 1992. "Models for Sample Selection Bias." *Annual Review of Sociology* 18:327–50.

Wong, G. Y., and William M. Mason. 1985. "The Hierarchical Logistic Regression Model for Multilevel Analysis." *Journal of the American Statistical Association* 80:513–24.

Wright, Sewall. 1921. "Correlation and Causation." *Journal of Agricultural Research* 20:557–85.

Xie, Yu. 1992. "The Log-Multiplicative Layer Effect Model for Comparing Mobility Tables." *American Sociological Review* 57:380–95.

———. 1994. "Log-Multiplicative Models for Discrete-Time, Discrete-Covariate Event History Data," *Sociological Methodology*, 24, 301–40.

———. 2000. "Demography: Past, Present and Future." *Journal of the American Statistical Association* 95:670–73.

Xie, Yu, and Daniel Powers. 2000. *Statistical Methods for Categorical Data Models.* New York: Academic Press.

Yamaguchi, Kazuo. 1987. "Models for Comparing Mobility Tables: Towards Parsimony and Substance." *American Sociological Review* 52:482–94.

———. 1990. "Homophily and Social Distance in the Choice of Multiple Friends: An Analysis Based on Conditionally Symmetric Log-Bilinear Association Models." *Journal of the American Statistical Association* 85:356–66.

———. 1991. *Event History Analysis.* Newbury Park, CA: Sage.

———. 1992. "Accelerated Failure-Time Regression Models with a Regression Model of Surviving Fraction: An Application to the Analysis of 'Permanent Employment' in Japan," *Journal of the American Statistical Association* 87:284–92.

———. 1994. "Some Accelerated Failure-Time Models Derived from Diffusion Process Models: An Application to Diffusion Process Analysis." *Sociological Methodology* 24:267–301.

Yamaguchi, Kazuo, and Linda R. Ferguson. 1995. "The Stopping and Spacing of Childbirths and their Birth-History Predictors: Rational-Choice Theory and Event-History Analysis." *American Sociological Review* 60:272–98.

Yamaguchi, Kazuo, and Denise B. Kandel. 1998. "Parametric Event Sequence Analysis: Racial/Ethnic Differences in Patterns of Drug-Use Progression." *Journal of the American Statistical Association* 91:1388–99.

2

A FRAMEWORK FOR THE STUDY OF INDIVIDUAL BEHAVIOR AND SOCIAL INTERACTIONS

*Steven N. Durlauf**

Recent work in economics has begun to integrate sociological ideas into the modeling of individual behavior. In particular, this new approach emphasizes how social context and social interdependences influence the ways in which individuals make choices. This paper provides an overview of an approach to integrating theoretical and empirical analysis of such environments. The analysis is based on a framework due to Brock and Durlauf (2001, forthcoming). Empirical evidence on behalf of this perspective is assessed and some policy implications are explored.

1. INTRODUCTION

> Just as our political life is free and open, so is our day-to-day life in our relations with each other. We do not get into a state with our next-door neighbour if he enjoys himself in his own way, nor do we give him the type of black looks which, though they do no real harm, still do hurt people's feelings. We are free and tolerant in our private lives; but

I thank the John D. and Catherine T. MacArthur Foundation, National Science Foundation, Vilas Trust and Romnes Trust for financial support. Thanks go to Aimée Dechter for many helpful conversations. Special thanks go to William Brock; much of this paper describes our joint work and reflects our ongoing collaboration. Michael Sobel and two anonymous referees have provided exceptionally insightful suggestions on a previous draft. Artur Minkin, Eldar Nigmatullin and Chih Ming Tan have provided excellent research assistance.

*Department of Economics, University of Wisconsin–Madison

in public affairs we keep to the law. This is because it commands our deep respect. We give our obedience to those whom we put in positions of authority and we obey the laws themselves, especially those which are for the protection of the oppressed, and those unwritten laws which it is an acknowledged shame to break.
Pericles' *Funeral Oration to the Athenians*, c. 431–430 B.C.E.
Thucydides, *History of the Peloponnesian War* (2.37)

The Athenians owed to the plague the beginnings of a state of unprecedented lawlessness. Seeing how quick and abrupt were the changes of fortune which came to the rich who died and to those who had previously been penniless but now inherited their wealth, people now began openly to venture on acts of self-indulgence which before they used to keep dark. . . . As for what is called honour, no one showed himself willing to abide by its laws, so doubtful was it that one would survive to enjoy the name for it. It was generally agreed that what was both honourable and valuable was the pleasure of the moment.
Description of Effects of Plague in Athens, 430 B.C.E.
Thucydides, *History of the Peloponnesian War* (2.53)[1]

Among the many fascinating features of the Thucydides description of the Peloponnesian War, which may be the first recorded piece of social science in Western history, is his sensitivity to the panoply of sources of individual behavior. One cannot read his description of the interplay of powerful social norms, extreme forms of individualism, and the development of a sense of individual rights of citizenship among Athenians, and not reflect that the complexities required to understand the rise and fall of Athens are echoed in the most modern attempts to understand various social and political groupings. As illustrated by the influence of the plague on Athens, longstanding features of the Athenian "character" could precipitously vanish due to changes in individual incentives. And yet it is the Athenian character that determined both the world-historical achieve-

[1]Taken from the translation by R. Walters (New York: Penguin Books, 1978).

ment of the first democracy and the world-historical folly of the destruction of the Athenian empire through overambition and overcommitment.

This paper is designed to describe an approach for the formal modeling of social interactions. The framework is based upon standard economic models of individual choice, but it expands the determinants of these choices to include social factors that are frequently neglected in economic analyses. While social interactions, broadly defined to include phenomena ranging from societal norms to role models to networks, are a fundamental part of historical studies and other social sciences—especially sociology, of course—they have only recently begun to play a prominent role in economic thinking. This new research is explicitly designed to extend the domain of inquiry by economists into areas that have been the traditional domain of other social scientists. Economists are not making this attempt, however, out of the belief that the substantive ideas in other disciplines should be supplanted by economic models of decision making. Rather, the objective of this research program is to internalize within formal economic models a number of the substantive ideas and perspectives of these other disciplines. This new work therefore has a very ambitious objective: the melding of substantive ideas between economics and sociology in such a way as to produce more powerful models of individual behavior. The current paper describes one class of efforts at such a synthesis.[2]

At some level, virtually all economic models exhibit some form of interactions. However, in standard economic models, these interactions are usually mediated by markets. Once an agent knows the prices for different commodities in the economy, the fact that these prices reflect the supply and demand decisions of others is no longer relevant. The new interest in social interactions among economists stems from an increasing awareness that individual interdependences are far richer than those that are induced by markets. Of course, the preeminence of game theory in modern economic theory reflects a general movement away from market-mediated to direct models of interactions. The new interactions-based models in economics are at one level game-theoretic models. What distinguishes them is the use

[2]To be clear, sociology has generated many analyses that use formal methods to study the sorts of social dynamics I model in this article. Granovetter and Soong (1988) offer a particularly interesting example and one that is closely linked to a number of ideas I try to address.

of particular stochastic processes to uncover interesting properties of interacting populations.

Interactions-based thinking has assumed a particularly prominent role in recent studies of poverty and inequality. Durlauf (1999a) refers to this body of theories as a "memberships theory of inequality" in contrast to the family-based theories of inequality and mobility pioneered by Becker and Tomes (1979) and Loury (1981).[3] In one facet of this new approach, the impact of residential neighborhoods on the future prospects of children has been explored. Bénabou (1993, 1996a, 1996b) and Durlauf (1996a,b) construct models of persistent intergenerational inequality based on the presence of spillover effects from the educational and economic characteristics of a neighborhood on the human capital acquisition of children. In these types of models, children are assumed to be influenced by a range of community characteristics. One source of community influences is institutional—because of local public finance of education, the affluence of a community affects the level of per capita spending on schools.[4] Another source of community effects occurs via role models. If individual aspirations and assessment of educational effort depend on the observed education levels and associated occupations of adults in a community, then stratification of communities by income and education will induce cross-community differences in the educational efforts and attainment of chil-

[3] In fairness, Loury (1977) is a seminal contribution to group-based approaches to the study of inequality.

[4] There is considerable controversy concerning the effect of educational expenditure on educational outcomes. Hanushek (1986) has argued that this type of effect is negligible, when test scores are the outcome variable of interest. In contrast, Card and Krueger (1992) find that predictions of future wages are sensitive to educational quality. I do not take a strong stand on this question, except to say that the empirical literature has typically focused on linear models, whereas the effects may be nonlinear. Certainly Kozol (1991) is consistent with this view, in the sense that he documents how very poor schools are handicapped in the education they provide. One reason for this type of nonlinearity is that while schools may differ widely in the efficiency with which they use revenues, some minimum is needed for each educational quality level. Of course, nonlinearities may also imply that the Card and Krueger results are questionable. For example, Heckman, Layne-Farrar, and Todd (1996) find that the estimated effects of school resources on labor market outcomes vary widely according to what control variables are included and according to educational group. For example, it appears that school quality matters primarily for workers who end up going to college. My own view of this literature is that while some effects of school quality on student outcomes have been identified, little is known about the causal mechanisms or even functional forms.

dren. Empirical evidence which has argued to support the presence of these effects can be found in many studies.[5] A particularly important case is the use of quasi-experiments in which one can compare families that have been given incentives to move to lower poverty neighborhoods with those which have not. While issues of self-selection and interpretation represent serious caveats, analyses based on both the Gautreaux demonstration (Rubinowitz and Rosenbaum 2000) and the Moving to Opportunity demonstration (Katz, Kling, and Liebman 2001) strongly support the focus on group determinants of inequality.

The recent attention on interactions and inequality reflects the strong influence that sociological perspectives on poverty have had on economics. When William Julius Wilson (1987:8) claims

> . . . changes have taken place in ghetto neighborhoods, and the groups that have been left behind are collectively different than those that lived in these neighborhoods in earlier years. It is true that long-term welfare families and street criminals are distinct groups, but they live and interact in the same depressed community and they are part of the population that has, with the exodus of the more stable working- and middle-class segments, become increasingly isolated socially from mainstream patterns and norms of behavior.

or Elijah Anderson (1999:22–23) argues

> The inclination to violence springs from the circumstances of life among the ghetto poor—the lack of jobs that pay a living wage, limited basic public services (police response in emergencies, building maintenance, trash pickup, light-

[5]Important examples in the sociology literature include Brewster (1994a, b); Brooks-Gunn et al. (1993); Crane (1991); Sampson, Morenoff, and Earls (1999); Sampson, Raudenbush, and Earls (1997); South and Crowder (1999); and Sucoff and Upchurch (1998). A nice recent example in economics is Weinberg, Reagan, and Yankow (2000). In addition, much of the massive literature on social capital is in essence attempting to uncover group influences. That being said, as discussed in Brock and Durlauf (2000a, 2000b), Durlauf (2001), and Manski (1993, 2000), there are a host of statistical issues with this literature that call into question exactly what causal relations have been identified in the empirical literature.

> ing . . .), the stigma of race, the fallout from rampant drug use and drug trafficking, and the resulting alienation and absence of hope for the future. Simply living in such an environment places young people at special risk of falling victim to aggressive behavior. Although there are often forces in the community that can counteract the negative influences—by far the most important is a strong loving . . . family that is committed to middle class values—the despair is pervasive enough to have spawned an oppositional culture, that of "the street" as consciously opposed to those of mainstream society.

one finds exactly the sort of substantive ideas that the new theories of inequality are trying to embody. And in fact one sees frequent reference to the sociological literature in justifying memberships-based models of inequality and intergenerational mobility.

Another important source of evidence on social interaction effects is the experimental literature in social psychology; many interesting examples may be found in Aronson (1999). Perhaps the most impressive study in this regard is the celebrated Robbers Cave experiment, described in Brown (1986) as "the most successful experiment ever conducted on intergroup conflict." This experiment is described by Sherif et al. (1961), collaborators who studied the behavior of a group of teenage boys at an isolated retreat in Robbers Cave State Park in Oklahoma. A group of boys were initially placed in a common living quarters and associated social environment. Once friendships and other social relations developed, the experimenters announced that the boys were assigned to two groups, Rattlers and Eagles. The new assignments were essentially random, with the exception that strong friendship pairs were broken up. A set of competitive activities were initiated. Sherif et al. (1961) documents in great detail how the two groups developed strong internal senses of identity along with great animosity toward the other group, animosity that carried over beyond the competitive activities. Previous friendships disappeared, and attribution of negative stereotypes to the other group became commonplace. While the introduction of cooperative activities diminished the hostility, the experiment clearly demonstrated that group identification can strongly influence individual behavior.

Rich qualitative descriptions of the type found in Anderson (1999) or Mitchell Duneier (1992, 1999) and carefully constructed experiments such as the Robbers Cave study are an important reminder of the limits of the type of formal analysis that is used in this paper. Formal modeling of the type I describe, in many respects only crudely approximates the many subtleties that are associated with social interactions; phenomena related to personal identity that Anderson explores are a good example.[6] On the other hand, to the extent that the objective of a research program is the construction of predictive or evaluative distributions of the effects of alternative policies, then the sort of formalization I describe is essential. To take a classic example, the Coleman report on the determinants of educational outcomes was based upon and was ultimately in many ways discredited because of formal analysis. Alternatively, the most important work on the effects of Head Start and other social programs on individual outcomes has proceeded from the sort of quantitative social science I describe.[7]

This paper is organized as follows. Section 2 develops an abstract model of individual choice in the presence of social interactions. Section 3 shows how this model can be specialized to produce different behavioral rules. Section 4 develops some of the interesting properties of the binary choice model. Section 5 addresses a number of conceptual features of interactions-based models. Section 6 discusses statistical implementation. Section 7 describes some implications of these models for public policy. Section 8 provides conclusions.

2. A BASIC FRAMEWORK

In this section, I develop a baseline description of individual behavior with social interactions for a population of individuals indexed by $i = 1 \ldots I$. I will follow standard economic reasoning in assuming that these behaviors represent purposeful choices subject to some set of preferences, beliefs, and constraints facing each individual. In other words, the choice of each individual i, ω_i, is interpreted as maximizing some payoff (or utility) function V subject to a set Ω_i of possible choices that

[6] Akerlof and Kranton (2000) is an important recent effort at grappling with these issues.

[7] Heckman (2000) is a wonderful overview of the contribution of formal statistical analysis to furthering social science knowledge; Heckman's own research is the exemplar of the uses of quantitative methods in understanding both causal determinants of individual behavior as well as in the evaluation of effects of government policies.

are available to that individual. The goal of the analysis is to develop a probabilistic description of $\underset{\sim}{\omega}$, the vector of choices in the population.

The functional form of V embodies specific features about individual preferences. The primitive modeling assumption underlying the use of such a function is *not* that individuals literally possess these functions and explicitly calculate payoffs from alternative courses of action by using them. Rather, the primitive notion is that each individual possesses preference orderings over the space of possible choices he faces and chooses the one ranked highest. When these preference orderings fulfill certain axioms,[8] they may be mathematically represented by a payoff function; from this perspective an individual's observed choice is the one that maximizes the function among all available choices.

This maximization problem can be given a generic form:

$$\omega_i = argmax_{\omega \in \Omega_i} V(\omega, Z_i, \epsilon_i). \tag{1}$$

The payoff function V is expressed as possessing three distinct arguments. The first is of course the choice; the second is a vector of individual-indexed characteristics, Z_i, which allows for observable heterogeneity in how individuals evaluate choices; the third is a vector of individual-indexed characteristics ϵ_i, which is assumed to be unobservable to a modeler, but is known to individual i, thereby allowing for unobservable heterogeneity across individuals. Introducing unobservable as well as observable heterogeneity is important in developing the model in a direction that permits empirical implementation. This distinction is precisely the same as that between regressors and the disturbance in the specification of a linear regression. In fact, in empirical implementation, the ϵ_i terms will be interpreted in standard statistical fashion. For this reason, I will always assume they are independent across individuals and independent of all Z_i.

Should one start with a utility-based framework in order to develop decision rules? The answer to this question lies at the core of one of the deepest methodological differences between sociologists and economists, and can hardly be addressed, let alone resolved here. For the purposes of this paper, I use the utility language in order to illustrate how a researcher,

[8]These axioms typically impose certain forms of rationality on the individual, such as transitivity of preferences. See Mas-Colell, Whinston, and Green (1995, chap. 3, sec. C) for an introduction to the relationship between preferences and utility functions.

starting with standard economic reasoning, can arrive at a model that embodies substantive notions of social influences on behavior. My own judgment is that choice-based reasoning, at this level of abstraction, is tautological, in the sense that without an explicit description of the determinants of preferences, beliefs, and constraints, any behavior can be interpreted as utility-maximizing in the sense I have described. In turn, the social interactions approach attempts to enrich the choice-framework by introducing a substantive role for social determinants of behavior. Hence, the framework should be judged as to how these social determinants are embodied.

The incorporation of social interactions into the choice framework is, at one level, nothing more than a particular choice as to what variables to include in Z_i. Suppose that the individuals in this population define a group g in which social interactions occur. (It is straightforward to generalize the discussion to the case where individuals are members of distinct groups.) For example, interactions can then be incorporated into individual decisions by including variables that depend on i through variables that are determined at the level of g—i.e., interactions are modeled as the dependence of individual payoffs on variables that depend on characteristics of the group. The average education level among parents in a community or the average rate of cigarette smoking among teenagers in a given ethnic group are examples of such variables.

Of course, the substance of social explanations to behavior will depend on what variables are included and in how the individual payoffs depend on them. In developing this choice-based framework, it is important to distinguish between variables representing the influence that a group's characteristics have on its members and those variables representing the influence that a group's joint behaviors have on its members. Following Manski (1993), variables that measure the former represent *contextual* effects whereas variables that measure the latter are *endogenous* effects. In the context of youth behavior, role models constitute contextual effects whereas the contemporaneous behaviors of friends constitute endogenous effects. This language, of course, closely parallels usage from sociology (cf. Blalock 1984). This consideration means that it is convenient to separate Z_i into three distinct components: X_i, which represents a vector of variables that can vary across individuals within the group, Y_g, often called contextual effects, which represents a vector of variables that are common to all members of the same group and are predetermined with respect to group behavior, and $\mu_i(\underset{\sim}{\omega}|F_i)$, which captures endogenous effects, representing the beliefs of individual i concerning the choices of members of the group, given some information set F_i.

Contextual and endogenous effects represent group influences. The important difference between them is that contextual effects are usually treated as background variables for the analysis whereas endogenous effects refer to the social consequences of these choices. For example, consider the determination of the level of collegiality chosen by each member of an academic department. The overall level of collegiality in a department is an endogenous effect, if the choice of a level of collegiality by each department member is influenced by the collegiality of others. In contrast, suppose an individual's level of collegiality is influenced by his salary relative to the department average. The effect of his own salary on his behavior is an individual effect and so part of X_i, whereas the effect of others salaries on his behavior is a contextual effect and so is part of Y_g.[9]

The expression $\mu_i(\underset{\sim}{\omega}|F_i)$ refers to the subjective beliefs that individual i has about the choices of members of the population. These subjective beliefs are assumed to have the form of a conditional probability measure, but at this point, nothing is specified as to how these beliefs are formed, except that for individual i the beliefs do not reflect any information concerning ϵ_j for $j \neq i$. Later on, these beliefs will be made endogenous by specifying a relationship between them and the actual determinants of behaviors of the group. At first glance, the use of this expression in the payoff function might appear to be odd, in that each individual presumably knows his own choice and so should not be forming beliefs about it (ω_i is an element of $\underset{\sim}{\omega}$). The underlying idea is that each individual is affected by his beliefs about the choices of others, not himself; I use beliefs over all choices as an argument in the payoff function and implicitly assume that the payoff function for i is unaffected by i's beliefs about his own choice.

The decision to treat endogenous effects as occurring through beliefs concerning behavior rather than their actual behavior (i.e., the choice of $\mu_i(\underset{\sim}{\omega}|F_i)$ instead of the realized choices $\underset{\sim}{\omega}$ as an argument in the payoff function) makes the theoretical analysis of the model substantially simpler.[10] The appropriateness of this assumption, of course, will depend on the particular context in which the model is employed; one would think, for example, if an individual cares about the aggregate characteristics of a large group, then the expectations assumption makes particular sense.

[9] I thank Michael Sobel for suggesting this example.

[10] See Glaeser and Scheinkman (2000, 2001) for analyses that use realized behaviors in the payoff function.

The associated decision problem and choice of individual i can therefore be rewritten as:

$$\omega_i = argmax_{\omega \in \Omega_i} V(\underset{\sim}{\omega}, X_i, Y_g, \mu_i(\underset{\sim}{\omega}|F_i), \epsilon_i) \quad (2)$$

In order to close the model, it is necessary to specify how the subjective beliefs $\mu_i(\underset{\sim}{\omega}|F_i)$ are formed. Within economics, one standard assumption is that expectations are rational, which means that the subjective beliefs of individuals are consistent with the conditional probabilities that actually characterize the variables over which these beliefs are formed.

Operationally, rational expectations may be understood in two steps. First, consider the set of choices by members of the group. Suppose that each individual choice solves an optimization problem as described by equation (2). This means that the choice of each individual can be represented as determined by a choice function m,

$$\omega_i = m(X_i, Y_g, \mu_i(\underset{\sim}{\omega}|F_i), \epsilon_i) i = 1 \ldots I. \quad (3)$$

Stacking these I choice functions together, one has a vector function M (whose elements correspond to the m-functions for each individual) such that

$$\underset{\sim}{\omega} = M(X_1, \ldots, X_I, Y_g, \mu_1(\underset{\sim}{\omega}|F_1), \ldots, \mu_I(\underset{\sim}{\omega}|F_I), \epsilon_1 \ldots \epsilon_I). \quad (4)$$

What this formulation means is nothing more than that the individual characteristics of each member of the population (X_i's and ϵ_i's), the common group characteristics that affect them (Y_g), and the beliefs each has about the behavior of members of his group ($\mu_i(\underset{\sim}{\omega}|F_i)$'s), determine the set of choices made by members of the population. This is a restatement of the choice-based logic we have assumed for individual behavior. Notice as well that one could start with expressions such as (3) and (4) as the basis for analysis of the model. Empirical work on social interactions in both sociology and economics typically does this. What the choice-based derivation does is establish how such formulations emerge from a particular set of underlying behavioral assumptions.

This formulation is useful in that it allows us to describe the conditional probabilities of actual choices as a function of the individual characteristics, group characteristics, and beliefs of the group members. To see how this may be used to characterize rationality, suppose that each individual possesses an identical information set F from which he forms beliefs about the choices of others in the population. Further, assume that F consists of $X_1 \ldots X_I$ and Y_g. (This is a strong assumption on the amount of information individuals possess; reformulating the model with weaker information assumptions turns out not to add anything except cumbersome notation.) By construction, each individual uses this information to form identical beliefs $\mu^e(\underset{\sim}{\omega}|X_1,\ldots,X_I,Y_g)$. One can, using equation (4), compute the actual conditional probability of the vector of choices given the model and the information set F. From equation (4), it follows that

$$\mu(\underset{\sim}{\omega}|X_1,\ldots,X_I,Y_g) = \mu(\underset{\sim}{\omega}|X_1,\ldots,X_I,Y_g,\mu^e(\underset{\sim}{\omega}|X_1,\ldots,X_I,Y_g)). \qquad (5)$$

If there exists a probability measure $\mu(\underset{\sim}{\omega}|X_1,\ldots,X_I,Y_g)$ such that

$$\mu(\underset{\sim}{\omega}|X_1,\ldots,X_I,Y_g) = \mu(\underset{\sim}{\omega}|X_1,\ldots,X_I,Y_g,\mu(\underset{\sim}{\omega}|X_1,\ldots,X_I,Y_g)) \qquad (6)$$

then this measure $\mu(\underset{\sim}{\omega}|X_1,\ldots,X_I,Y_g)$ is a rational expectations solution to the model. In words, agents possess rational expectations conditional on the information set F when their beliefs given F, as represented by subjective conditional probabilities, are confirmed by the actual conditional probabilities which arise in the environment under study. For this reason, the concept of rational expectations is synonymous in these models with the ideas that beliefs are self-consistent.

Notice that all I have done is define the meaning of rational expectations Nothing has been established about the conditions under which a set of rational expectations exists, or if it exists, whether the set is unique. Properties such as these can only be assessed in the context of particular specifications of an environment.

The rational expectations assumption is controversial, and dissatisfaction with it has led over the last 15 years to a rich literature on bounded rationality (Rubinstein [1998] provides a profound overview of this work). However, the literature on interactions-based models has generally not incorporated this approach in an interesting fashion,[11] and I will assume

[11] In saying that bounded rationality or learning spillovers have not been dealt with in an "interesting" way, I mean that many if not most models that claim to be based on bounded rationality fail to generate insights that differ from models where agents interact through preferences. To be a bit more precise, one can model the effects of the behavior of peers on an individual as due to two distinct factors: (1) a psychological desire to conform to one's peers, which is a claim about interdependent preferences, and (2) an information effect whereby the behavior of others is used by an individual to determine which choice is better for him, which (when not formulated as an optimal extraction of information) is a form of bounded rationality. On the other hand, there is an important related literature on social learning in which the behavior of individuals alters the information sets of others in an environment in which each individual acts rationally conditional on a limited information set; see Bikhchandani, Hirshleifer, and Welch (1992) for a very nice analysis of this type.

rational expectations in what follows, for two reasons. First, the rationality assumption is in certain respects inessential for understanding the qualitative properties of these systems. For example, the rational expectations equilibria of a static model often prove to be the limit points of various learning schemes (see Brock and Durlauf [1998, 2001] and Glaeser and Scheinkman [2000] for specific examples of this). Second, the interesting qualitative properties of interactions-based models do not rely on rational expectations per se but rather are generated by the presence of feedbacks between group and individual behaviors.

Again, this abstract description of individual behaviors in a population under rational expectations incorporates very standard economic reasoning. Individual decisions are explicitly modeled as purposeful choices, and a consistency condition is imposed across the choices, in this case consistency of beliefs with the probabilistic structure of the population's behavior. This combination of individual maximization and self-consistency is no different from what occurs when one specifies a set of individual demand and supply functions for a group of commodities, where each individual takes prices as given, and then requires that prices clear markets.

3. BEHAVIORAL RULES

The choice-based framework described in Section 2 can be specialized in various ways. In this section, two different approaches are outlined.

3.1. *Linear Decision Rules*

Much of the empirical work on interaction effects has assumed that the behavior variable ω_i has continuous support and depends linearly on various individual and neighborhood effects. These assumptions permit a researcher to use standard regression methods for estimation, as will be seen in Section 5. While these regressions have typically not been developed via choice-based reasoning, it is straightforward to do so. Suppose that each individual makes a choice ω_i in order to minimize the squared distance from some ideal point ω_i^*

$$max_{\omega_i \in (-\infty,\infty)} - \tfrac{1}{2} E_i(\omega_i - \omega_i^*)^2 \tag{7}$$

and suppose that this ideal point ω_i^* is defined by

$$\omega_i^* = h_i + Jm_g + \epsilon_i,$$

where m_g is the expected value of the average choice in the population. It is immediate that actual behavior ω_i will follow

$$\omega_i = \omega_i^* = h_i + Jm_g + \epsilon_i. \tag{8}$$

This derivation is, of course, trivial and perhaps is a good example of how a choice-based perspective does not always add insight into an assumed behavioral rule. Nevertheless, one can develop a couple of implications of this type of model that are of interest. Suppose one takes the expected value of both sides of this equation, under the assumption that the values of all h_i are known to group members. Taking the expected value of both sides of (8),

$$m_g = h_g + Jm_g, \tag{9}$$

where $h_g = I^{-1} \sum_{i \in g} h_i$. It is immediately the case that self-consistency imposes the restriction

$$m_g = \frac{h_g}{1 - J}. \tag{10}$$

This solution has two relevant properties. First, the equilibrium expected choice level is unique as each value of h_g maps into a single m_g. Second, J cannot equal 1; in fact one can usually rule out $|J| > 1$ through analyzing dynamic analogs to this model.

3.2. *Binary Decision Rules*

Interesting theoretical models of social interactions have been developed in the context of binary decisions. Standard examples of these decisions include staying in school or dropping out, college attendance versus work, etc. I will assume that the two choices are coded 1 and -1. In this development, I will proceed in two steps, paralleling the derivations in Section 2. First, the model is formulated for an arbitrary set of subjective beliefs $\mu_i(\underset{\sim}{\omega}|F_i)$. Second, rational expectations will be imposed.

For the binary choice model, the individual decision process equation (2) can be expressed as

$$\omega_i = argmax_{\omega \in \{-1,1\}} V(\omega, X_i, Y_g, \mu_i(\underset{\sim}{\omega}|F_i), \epsilon_i) \tag{11}$$

At this point, of course, one still cannot say much about the structure of the group choices that are produced by such a general decision problem. One must place some assumptions on the structure of the $V(\cdot,\cdot,\cdot,\cdot,\cdot)$ function in order to see what insights interactions add to modeling an environment of this type as well as to making the model falsifiable. In this section, I will introduce some assumptions on the form of V that accomplish these goals, following the analysis in Brock and Durlauf (2001, forthcoming).

The first assumption is that the payoff function is additively separable into three distinct components, so that

$$V(\omega_i, X_i, Y_g, \mu_i(\underset{\sim}{\omega}|F_i), \epsilon_i) = u(\omega_i, X_i, Y_g) + S(\omega_i, X_i, Y_g, \mu_i(\underset{\sim}{\omega}|F_i)) + \epsilon_i(\omega_i) \qquad (12)$$

Here, $u(\omega_i, X_i, Y_g)$ denotes private deterministic utility, $S(\omega_i, X_i, Y_g, \mu_i(\underset{\sim}{\omega}|F_i))$ denotes social deterministic utility, and $\epsilon_i(\omega_i)$ denotes a private random utility. The distinction between deterministic and random utility is made from the perspective of the modeler—i.e., the model is analyzed under the assumption that only the distribution of the various $\epsilon_i(\omega_i)$'s are known. Notice that this error term is now made an explicit function of ω_i. What this means is that the two choices may have differential effects on the payoff function. So, for example, if one is choosing between a career as a musician ($\omega_i = 1$) or as a painter ($\omega_i = -1$), $\epsilon_i(1)$ represents unobservable musical talent and $\epsilon_i(-1)$ represents unobservable artistic talent.

The additive separability assumption is made for two reasons. First, separating out the random term $\epsilon_i(\omega_i)$ is essential in achieving analytic tractability for the model. Second, this formulation is attractive in terms of empirical implementation. It will turn out that when $S(\omega_i, X_i, Y_g, \mu_i(\underset{\sim}{\omega}|F_i))$ is omitted from the model, the individual behavioral rule reduces to that described by the standard binary choice model, hence one will be able to test for social interactions using relatively standard statistical methods.

The second assumption is that social utility possesses a particular functional form. Let $E_i(\omega_j|F_i)$ denote the subjective expected value that agent i assigns to the choice of agent j given his information set F_i. Social utility is assumed to take the form

$$S(\omega_i, X_i, Y_g, \mu_i(\underset{\sim}{\omega}|F_i)) = -\sum_{j \neq i} \frac{J_{i,j}}{2} (\omega_i - E_i(\omega_j|F_i))^2. \qquad (13)$$

The $J_{i,j}$ terms measure the magnitudes of the direct bilateral interactions between members of the population. If $J_{i,j} > 0$, then individual i derives higher utility (other things being equal) from making the same choice as he believes will be made by individual j; $J_{i,j} < 0$ in turn implies a utility benefit from acting differently.

By suitable choices of the $J_{i,j}$'s, one can, in principle, model a wide range of interactions. For example, suppose that there is a single individual k such that $J_{i,k}$ is relatively very large for all i. This person can be thought of as a leader in the group's behavior. Brock and Durlauf (1999) show how this type of formulation can be used to model the development of schools of thought in scientific communities. There is no requirement that the $J_{i,j}$ terms all have the same sign. When these signs differ, incentives to conform and deviate coexist. One example of this may be dialect use, where the choice of nonstandard forms of grammar and syntax appear to stem from a desire for membership in some groups and a rejection of identification with others. For example, as described in Chambers (1995), the dropping of the letter *g* in words ending in *-ing* is strongly associated with being poor and male in the United States, Britain, and Australia. This is generally explained by the need for poorer males to develop an identity that rejects conventional metrics of success. The framework described here would seem to be a natural way of exploring the use of African-American vernacular English versus standard dialects.

Finally, one completes the model by choosing a distribution for the random terms $\epsilon_i(\omega_i)$. This is done by assuming that the difference in the random utility terms is logistically distributed,

$$\mu(\epsilon_i(\omega_i) - \epsilon_i(-\omega_i) \leq z) = \frac{1}{1 + exp(-\beta_i z)}; \beta_i \geq 0. \tag{14}$$

As in the case of the other assumptions, this functional form provides benefits in terms of analytics as well as a way of linking the theoretical model to a statistical one. Notice that β_i indexes the support of the unobserved heterogeneity. Roughly speaking, the larger the value of β_i, the less likely are large draws of $|\epsilon_i(-\omega_i) - \epsilon_i(\omega_i)|$. The logistic error assumption is extremely useful in the development of theoretical models of social interactions as it allows for simple calculations of the equilibrium probability measure for choices, but the qualitative features of the these types of models do not depend on it.

Under these assumptions, it is possible to derive some parsimonious expressions to describe the set of population choices. Before doing so, there is a useful simplification that can be made. One can without loss of generality replace the general utility function $u(\omega_i, X_i, Y_g)$ with a linear function

$$u(\omega_i, X_i, Y_g) = h_i \omega_i + k_i, \tag{15}$$

where the slope term h_i and intercept term k_i are chosen so that

$$h_i + k_i = u(1, X_i, Y_g) \tag{16}$$

and

$$-h_i + k_i = u(-1, X_i, Y_g) \tag{17}$$

This simplification is allowable because choices are binary; so long as the new linear utility function matches the original u function when ω_i equals either -1 or 1—which is what equations (16) and (17) impose via the implied restrictions on h_i and k_i—it is irrelevant that it fails to match the original function for other values of ω_i.

The model now has enough detail to allow a parametric description of the conditional probabilities of the vector of choices $\underset{\sim}{\omega}$. One does this first by calculating

$$\mu(\omega_i | X_i, Y_g, \mu_i(\underset{\sim}{\omega} | F_i)), \tag{18}$$

the conditional probability of individual i's choice given his observable characteristics and beliefs. Since the choice ω_i is made only when the payoff from the choice exceeds that which would be generated by the choice $-\omega_i$, for any information set the conditional probability of ω_i is equal to the probability that the payoff at ω_i is greater than the payoff at $-\omega_i$—that is,

$$\begin{aligned} &\mu(\omega_i | X_i, Y_g, \mu_i(\underset{\sim}{\omega} | F_i)) \\ &\quad = \mu(V(\omega_i, X_i, Y_g, \mu_i(\underset{\sim}{\omega} | F_i), \epsilon_i(\omega_i)) \\ &\qquad > V(-\omega_i, X_i, Y_g, \mu_i(\underset{\sim}{\omega} | F_i), \epsilon_i(-\omega_i))). \end{aligned} \tag{19}$$

Substituting the social utility function (13) and the linearized deterministic private utility function (15) into equation (12), this inequality may be rewritten as

$$\mu\left(h_i\omega_i - \sum_{j\neq i}\frac{J_{i,j}}{2}(\omega_i - E_i(\omega_j|F_i)\right)^2 + \epsilon_i(\omega_i)$$

$$> -h_i\omega_i - \sum_{j\neq i}\frac{J_{i,j}}{2}(-\omega_i - E_i(\omega_j|F_i))^2 + \epsilon_i(-\omega_i))$$

$$= \mu(\epsilon_i(\omega_i) - \epsilon_i(-\omega_i) > -2h_i\omega_i - \sum_{j\neq i} 2J_{i,j}\omega_i E_i(\omega_j)). \quad (20)$$

Using equation (14), the logistic assumption for the errors, it is straightforward to manipulate this expression and conclude that

$$\mu(\omega_i|X_i Y_g, \mu_i(\underset{\sim}{\omega})) \propto exp(\beta_i h_i\omega_i + \sum_{j\neq i}\beta_i J_{i,j}\omega_i E_i(\omega_j)), \quad (21)$$

where "$\propto$" means "is proportional to."

Moving from individual to joint conditional probabilities is now trivial, since the random utility terms are independent across individuals. The joint probability measure for the population choices is

$$\mu(\underset{\sim}{\omega}|X_1,\ldots,X_I,Y_g,\mu_1(\underset{\sim}{\omega}|F_1),\ldots,\mu_I(\underset{\sim}{\omega}|F_I))$$

$$\propto \prod_i exp\left(\beta_i h_i\omega_i + \sum_{j\neq i}\beta_i J_{i,j}\omega_i E_i(\omega_j)\right). \quad (22)$$

Once one specifies the distributions across the population of private incentives, h_i—as derived through equations (16) and (17)—the probability distribution of unobserved heterogeneity, β_i, the interaction terms, $J_{i,j}$, and beliefs about the behaviors of others, $E_i(\omega_j)$, one has a complete characterization of the joint probability measure for observed behaviors $\underset{\sim}{\omega}$. This explicit mapping of the distributions of individual characteristics and interdependence terms $J_{i,j}$ into a distribution of individual behaviors is the hallmark of interactions-based models.

In the context of binary choice, rational expectation requires that the beliefs $E_i(\omega_j)$ coincide with the mathematical expectations $E(\omega_j)$ following the sort of self-consistency argument given by equation (18). Recalling the definition of the hyperbolic tangent function, $tanh(x) = (e^x - e^{-x})/(e^x + e^{-x})$, we can use equation (21) to verify that the expected value of each choice ω_i obeys

$$E(\omega_i|X_i,Y_g,\mu_i(\underset{\sim}{\omega}|F_i)) = tanh\left(\beta_i h_i + \sum_{j\neq i}\beta_i J_{i,j}E_i(\omega_j)\right). \quad (23)$$

A rational expectations equilibrium for this model requires that there exists a set of numbers $E(\omega_i)$ such that for all i and j

$$E(\omega_i) = tanh\Big(\beta_i h_i + \sum_{j \neq i} \beta_i J_{i,j} E(\omega_j)\Big), \; i = 1 \ldots I \tag{24}$$

The question of the existence of a rational expectations equilibrium is thus a fixed point problem for the set of I equations described by equation (24). Fortunately, this is an easy case to analyze. Since the $tanh(\cdot)$ function is continuous with range $[-1,1]$, Brouwer's fixed-point theorem may be immediately invoked (see Mas-Colell, Whinston, and Green [1995:952] for a statement of the theorem) to establish that at least one rational expectations solution exists.

4. PROPERTIES OF A BINARY CHOICE MODEL WITH SOCIAL INTERACTIONS

The binary choice model described in Section 3 can be specialized in many ways to incorporate different types of decisions, interactions environments, and the like. In order to elucidate the general properties of models of this type, it is useful to consider a baseline case that has been extensively analyzed in Brock and Durlauf (2001). This case assumes that for all i and j (1) $h_i = h$, (2) $\beta_i = \beta$, and (3) $J_{i,j} = J/I - 1 \geq 0$. Substantively, these assumptions do two things. First, the three assumptions eliminate all heterogeneity in individual behavior except that which is generated by the errors $\epsilon_i(\omega_i)$. Second, the social interactions have the property that each individual weighs the decisions of all others equally. This is obviously a strong restriction on the nature of conformity effects.

Under these assumptions, the system of equations described by (24) reduces to

$$E(\omega_i) = tanh\Big(\beta h + \frac{\beta J}{I-1} \sum_{j \neq i} E(\omega_j)\Big) \; \forall \; i, j. \tag{25}$$

Since each agent is associated with the same parameters β, h, and J, one can show that all expectations $E(\omega_i)$ are equal. This in turn implies that the group $m = I^{-1} \sum_j E(\omega_j)$ equals $E(\omega_i)$ and that the average choices of others relative to i, $m_{-i} = (I-1)^{-1} \sum_{j \neq i} E(\omega_j)$ must equal this same number. Therefore m will obey the functional relationship

$$m = tanh(\beta h + \beta J m). \tag{26}$$

Any m that is consistent with this equation is a possible equilibrium for expected average group-level behavior. At least one solution m solves this equation, as was discussed in the analysis of the binary choice model in Section 3.

4.1. *Multiple Equilibria*

Once the existence of an equilibrium expected choice level m has been established, a second question is to evaluate whether equation (26) possesses a unique solution. When multiple solutions exist, then the individual-level or micro-level structure of the model does not uniquely determine its macro-level characteristics. Why should one think that, in expectation, the average choice level is not uniquely determined? The answer lies in the assumption that $J \geq 0$. The magnitude of J influences the extent to which each individual makes a choice based on his or her beliefs concerning the choices of others. When this conformity effect is strong enough, it means that for many population members, the desire to conform to others dominates the other factors which influence choice. But when individual behavior is driven by a desire to be similar to others, this does not provide any information on what they actually do; rather it merely implies that whatever behaviors occur, there will be substantial within-group correlation due to conformity effects. Of course, the role of the conformity effect is determined by its strength relative to the private incentives agents face.

These considerations suggest that the number of equilibria should reflect an interplay of the various parameters of the model. Brock and Durlauf (2001) contains the following theorem that characterizes the number of equilibria in this model.

Theorem 1: Relationship between individual behavioral parameters and number of self-consistent equilibria in the binary choice model with social interactions

i. If $\beta J < 1$, then there exists a single solution to equation (26).
ii. If $\beta J > 1$ and $h = 0$, there exist three solutions to equation (26). One of these solutions is positive, one is zero and one is negative.
iii. If $\beta J > 1$ and $h \neq 0$, there exists a threshold H (which depends on βJ) such that
   a. for $|\beta h| < H$, there exist three solutions to equation (26) one of which has the same sign as h, and the others possessing opposite sign.

b. for $|\beta h| > H$, there exists a unique solution to equation (26) with the same sign as h.

This theorem provides a description of the ways in which private incentives, h, unobserved heterogeneity, β, and social incentives, J, combine to determine the number of self-consistent equilibria in this population. Notice that it is the interplay of private and social incentives that determines the multiplicity versus uniqueness of the equilibrium. Suppose that one fixes β and J so that $\beta J > 1$. In this case, different values of h will induce different numbers of equilibria. This is qualitatively illustrated in Figure 1.

A critical role is played by the βJ, in that large (in a sense specified in the theorem) values of this composite parameter are required for multiplicity. The role of J is easy to understand. Small values of J mean that the strength of endogenous interactions is weak, which mitigates against

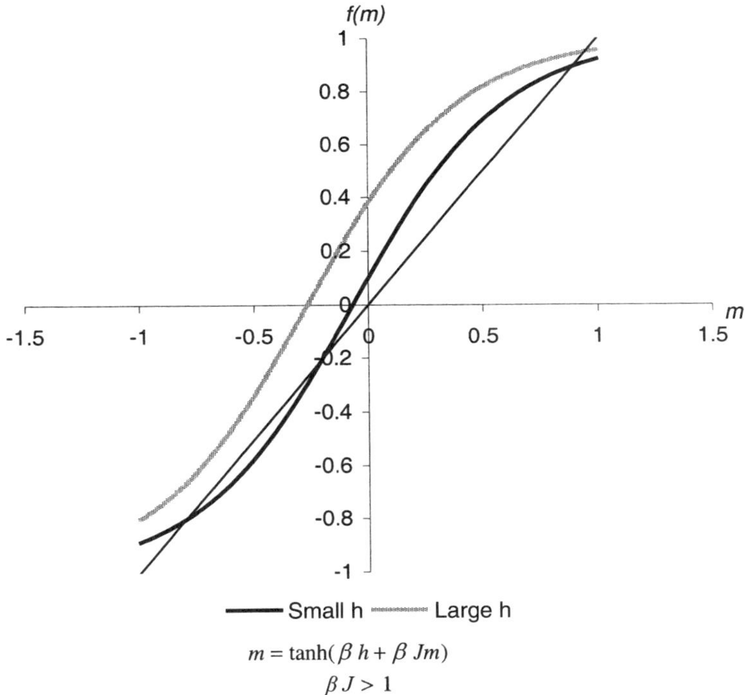

$$m = \tanh(\beta h + \beta Jm)$$
$$\beta J > 1$$

FIGURE 1. Equilibria for expected average choice.

self-consistent bunching of behavior. To understand the role of β, recall that small values of β imply that the likelihood of a large value of $|\epsilon_i(1) - \epsilon_i(-1)|$ is large. Hence for small β's, a relatively large percentage of the population will have draws of $\epsilon_i(1) - \epsilon_i(-1)$ which, roughly speaking, dominate the deterministic parts of their payoffs. Furthermore, the expected value of the percentage who are led to choose 1 due to the random utility draws will, in expectation, be the same as the expected value of the percentage of the population led to choose -1. In other words, small β's imply that a relatively small percentage of the population is susceptible to self-consistent bunching, in the sense that their decisions are likely to be dominated by the social utility component of their payoff functions. Now, consider what is needed for multiple self-consistent equilibria. Intuitively, what is needed is that enough of the population is susceptible to being influenced by the expected choices of others. But this requires, for fixed J, relatively large values of m. When the percentage of individuals whose behavior is dominated by the unobserved heterogeneity is high enough, then the range of possible values of m is restricted, which precludes the self-consistent bunching at multiple levels.

Under standard dynamic analogs to this static model, it turns out that the equilibria with the largest and smallest values of m are locally stable, whereas the equilibrium whose associated m lies between them is not.[12] One can ignore this "interior" equilibrium as it cannot be expected to arise in practice. Thus, when multiple equilibria are present, we can restrict attention to the possible equilibrium m^*_+, in which the average choice is expected to be positive, and m^*_-, in which the average choice is expected to be negative.

4.2. *Social Welfare*

The presence of multiple equilibria leads to the question of the relationship between a particular equilibrium and aggregate social welfare. In the baseline case of common h, β, and J values, it is natural to ask which equilibrium maximizes the expected average payoff in the population. Brock and Durlauf (2001) prove the following theorem

Theorem 2: Welfare rankings of equilibria

[12] These dynamic analogs typically assume that agents at t react to the expected average choice for $t - 1$.

i. If $h > 0$ (< 0) then the equilibrium associated with m^*_+ (m^*_-) provides a higher level of expected utility for each agent than the equilibrium associated with m^*_- (m^*_+).
ii. If $h = 0$, then the equilibrium associated with m^*_+ and the equilibrium associated with m^*_- provide equal levels of expected utility for each agent.

In words, when $h \neq 0$, individuals are better off when the average choice is of the same sign as h. Intuitively, when this holds, the social incentives to conform work in the same direction as the private incentives. On the other hand, when $h > 0$ and $m = m^*_-$, these incentives clash. In this case, the average member of the population would be better off if the other equilibrium prevailed. The existence of an inferior equilibrium in the sense described illustrates how individually rational decisions can be collectively undesirable.

5. CONCEPTUAL ISSUES OF INTERACTIONS-BASED MODELS

5.1. *Methodological Individualism*

Interactions-based models represent an effort to introduce richer sociological structure into economic theory. The absence of such structures has been the source of severe criticism of economic theory by social scientists who are not economists as well as among heterodox economists. Granovetter (1985) gives a typical critique:

> Classical and neoclassical economics operates, in contrast, with an atomized and *under*socialized conception of human action . . . The theoretical arguments disallow by hypothesis any impact of social structure and social relations on production, distribution, or consumption. (P. 55)

The interactions-based approach represents one way of answering this criticism without sacrificing any of the basic microeconomic behavioral assumptions of economics. I make this claim in two respects: one superficial and the other somewhat deeper.

First, the modeling exercise described in Sections 2, 3, and 4 illustrates how one can formally integrate group-level influences into individual decisions so long as these influences can be modeled as variables, as is done with Y_g and m_g. Self-consistency conditions of the type we have modeled impose whatever feedbacks exist between members of a group, in ways exactly analogous to the relationship between the modeling of individual demand schedules as functions of prices and the requirement that these prices clear markets.

This perspective on methodological individualism is quite similar to that taken by Elster (1989) in the context of studying social norms:

> I believe one can define, discuss, and defend a theory of social norms in a wholly individualistic framework. *A norm in this perspective is the propensity to feel shame and to anticipate sanctions by others at the thought of behaving in a certain forbidden way* . . . this propensity becomes a *social* norm when and to the extent that it is shared with other people . . . the social character of the norm is also manifest in the existence of higher-order norms that enjoin us to punish violators of the first-order norm. To repeat, this conception of a network of shared beliefs and common emotional reactions does not commit us to thinking of norms as supraindividual entities that somehow exist independently of their supports. (Pp. 105–106)

Second, the modeling framework I have described illustrates how social interactions lead to features of group behavior that are qualitatively different from those that arise in environments without such interactions. This is an example of the property of "emergence" that is a common feature of environments of this type. Emergence leads to the question of the relationship between these models and statistical mechanics models in physics, which is discussed next.

5.2. *Statistical Mechanics and Social Science*

The binary model of social interactions that I have described lies in a class of mathematical models originating in physics, specifically in the area of statistical mechanics.[13] These models were originally developed to explain how magnets arise in nature. A magnet occurs when, for a piece

[13] Yeomans (1992) is an accessible introduction to statistical mechanics.

of iron, a majority of the atoms spin up or spin down (spin being a binary property of atoms). In the early twentieth century, the existence of natural magnets was a major puzzle, as there are physical reasons why the ex ante probability that a given atom spins up or down (once external temperature considerations are removed) is $\frac{1}{2}$. The resolution of this puzzle, first instantiated in the celebrated Ising-Lenz model, is to assume that the probability that a given atom possesses a certain spin depends on the spins of the nearest neighbors to that atom. The subsequent statistical mechanics literature has extended analyses of this type to a wide range of alternative interaction structures that correspond to different choices of $J_{i,j}$.

For the purposes of social science, of course, the physical interpretation of these models is of no interest. What is of enormous interest are the mathematical properties of these systems, which have made the same mathematical models valuable in areas ranging from computer science (where neural networks have this mathematical structure) to biology (models of molecular evolution); Anderson and Stein (1984) is an accessible discussion of this. Among the many interesting properties of these systems are emergence, symmetry breaking, nonergodicity, phase transition, and universality. I provide a brief description of each property to clarify how it arises in the model that has been developed. Additional discussion may be found in Blume and Durlauf (2001) and Durlauf (1999b).

5.2.1. *Emergence*[14]

In a system of interacting agents, emergent properties are those that cannot be reduced to statements about the individual elements when studied in isolation. In physics, magnetism is an emergent phenomenon as it is a collective property of many iron atoms whose atomic spins are aligned; similarly, ice is a property of the way in which many water molecules are arrayed, not one molecule in isolation. The multiple equilibria described in Theorem 1 are examples of emergence in a socioeconomic context, as they constitute a property that arises only with respect to a group rather than for a single individual. Another example of emergence is Schelling's (1971) celebrated demonstration of how complete segregation is produced from mildly discriminatory preferences.

One important aspect of emergence is that it breaks any logical relationship between methodological individualism and reductionism. What I mean is that emergent properties cannot be understood through

[14] See Anderson (1972) for a physical perspective on emergence.

the individual elements of a system, as they are intrinsically collective. This is so even though the behaviors of these elements determine whether or not emergent properties are present.

5.2.2. *Symmetry Breaking*

Symmetry breaking occurs when, for a specification of symmetrically specified agents, asymmetric outcomes occur. In other words, suppose one starts with a set of identically specified agents. Do conditions exist under which their outcomes will differ? To see how this model exhibits symmetry-breaking, consider the case $h = 0$. Each agent is ex ante privately indifferent between the two choices—i.e., in the absence of any social interaction effect, the probability that agent chooses 1 (and of course -1) is $\frac{1}{2}$. However, when $J > 1$, the choices will bunch (in expected value) around one of the choices. Suppose that one has two groups of identically specified agents. It would be possible for one group to be associated with an equilibrium where most choices center on 1 whereas the other group centers on -1.

Symmetry breaking is important in modeling spatial agglomeration of agents (see Arthur [1987] and Krugman [1996] for a stochastic process/statistical mechanics perspective) into regions and cities. In such models, agents face identical incentives and possess identical characteristics, yet distinct bunching of the agents into subgroups will occur.

5.2.3. *Nonergodicity*

A probabilistic system is nonergodic if the conditional probabilities that describe the behavior of each element of the system conditional on the other elements fail to uniquely characterize the behavior of the system as a whole. The simplest example of a nonergodic system is a Markov chain whose transition probabilities are

$$\begin{bmatrix} 1 & 0 \\ 0 & 1 \end{bmatrix}$$

This conditional probability structure does not tell us which state of the system will be observed.

The cases where (26) exhibits multiple solutions are thus nonergodic. In these cases, one specifies the conditional probability choices of each member of the population and imposes self-consistency; however, this does not uniquely determine the aggregate behavior of the population. Multiple equilibria are a common feature of coordination games in economics, which are noncooperative environments in which individuals conform to one another; see Cooper (1997) for an overview. Such models typically embody conformity effects of the type that have been described.

5.2.4. *Phase Transition*

A model exhibits a phase transition when a small change in a model parameter induces a qualitative shift in the model's properties. The binary choice with social interactions model exhibits phase transitions along two dimensions. Recalling Theorem 1, holding h constant, there will be a threshold value H (which depends on h) such that if βJ moves from less than H to greater than H, the number of equilibria shifts from 1 to 3. On the other hand, for every $\beta J > 1$, there is a threshold K, depending on βJ, such that as h moves from less than K to greater than K, the number of equilibria shifts from 3 to 1.

5.2.5. *Universality*

A universal property of a system is one that does not depend on details of the system's micro-level specification. Such properties are found in many physical contexts; for example, magnetization of the type captured in the Ising-Lenz model does not depend on the nearest neighbor interaction structure and in fact occurs for a wide range of alternative interaction structures. Universality is extremely appealing from the perspective of social science modeling, since we often do not have any real justification for choosing interactions structures, forms of interaction effects, etc. outside of analytical convenience.

To see how this model exhibits some types of universality, suppose that each individual is associated with a neighborhood $g(i)$ that characterizes the set of individuals in the population with whom he wishes to conform; $\#(g(i))$ denotes the neighborhood's population size. Assume that all members of the neighborhood weight the expected choices of the others equally, so that $J_{i,j} = J/(\#(g(i)) - 1)$. A self-consistent equilibrium for this system is any set of solutions $E(\omega_1)\ldots E(\omega_I)$ to the set of I equations

$$E(\omega_i) = tanh\left(\beta h + \frac{\beta J}{\#(g(i)) - 1} \sum_{j \in g(i)} E(\omega_j)\right). \tag{27}$$

This mapping must possess at least one fixed point and hence at least one self-consistent equilibrium exists. Notice that any solution of the model with global interactions must also represent a solution to this model, so that

$$E(\omega_1) = E(\omega_2) = \ldots = E(\omega_I) = m = tanh(\beta h + \beta Jm). \tag{28}$$

Hence the properties we have found for the global interactions model occur for a wide variety of alternative interaction structures. This being said, universality has been relatively unexplored in social science applications of statistical mechanics. My judgment is that this is an important area for future work. One obvious possibility concerns Zipf's Law or the rank-size rule for city populations, which appears to occur for countries with very different socioeconomic structures. A number of interesting ideas along these lines appear in Krugman (1996).

6. STATISTICAL IMPLEMENTATION

In bringing social interactions models to data, a number of difficult statistical issues arise. In particular, under the assumption of rational expectations, there exist relationships between the various regressors that comprise the model. These relationships in turn influence identification. This possibility was first recognized by Wallis (1980) in the context of time series models. A seminal paper by Manski (1993) has developed this idea in the context of interactions-based models. Brock and Durlauf (forthcoming) provide both a survey of the relevant literature and many new results. See also Moffitt (2001) for a number of valuable insights into the relevant statistical issues.

6.1. *Linear-in-Means Models*

To see how an identification problem arises in interactions-based models, it is useful to start with a linear regression that is analogous to the theoretical model I have described in Section 3.1. For this empirical model, which is a generalization of the one studied by Manski (1993),[15] each agent is assumed to be a member of a group $g(i)$. An individual is assumed to be affected by contextual and endogenous characteristics that are specific to his group. In a typical data set one would expect that the observations represent individuals from different groups. Hence, each individual

[15] In Manski (1993), $Y_{g(i)}$ is assumed to equal $X_{g(i)}$, the average of X_i across all members of $g(i)$.

in the data set will be associated with an individually-indexed set of contextual effects $Y_{g(i)}$ and a distinct expected choice level among members of group $g(i)$, $m_{g(i)}$. As before, I assume that each individual possesses rational expectations and that the information set on which these expectations are formed includes all individual and contextual effects.

Relative to the linear model (8) the main modeling question is how to render (8) empirically operational while allowing for heterogeneity in the individual incentive terms h_i. Standard empirical practice assumes that these terms are linearly determined by the individual and contextual effects experienced by each individual

$$h_i = k + c'X_i + d'Y_{g(i)}. \tag{29}$$

Thus in the linear version of a social interactions model the behavior of a given individual is described by

$$\omega_i = k + c'X_i + d'Y_{g(i)} + Jm_{g(i)} + \epsilon_i \tag{30}$$

where ϵ_i is a regression error. The dependence of individual choices on averages of expected behaviors and contextual effects has led this structure to be called the linear-in-means model. The parameters of interest are k, c (an r-length vector), d (an s-length vector), and J. I assume that the available data include ω_i, X_i, $Y_{g(i)}$, and $X_{g(i)}$, where $X_{g(i)}$ equals the average of X's among members of neighborhood $g(i)$.[16]

To see how an identification problem arises, it is useful to work with the reduced form model for individual choices. Following the simple example in Section 3.2, one first computes the expected value of both

[16]This formulation differs from the hierarchical linear model (HLM) approach. well described in Bryk and Raudenbush (1992) that is popular in the sociology and education literatures. Relative to equation (29),

$$\omega_i = k + c'_{g(i)}X_i + \epsilon_i$$

$$c_{g(i)} = Jm_{g(i)} + DY_{g(i)} + \eta_i,$$

where J and D are $r \times 1$ and $r \times s$ matrices of coefficients and η_i is an r-length vector of errors. Relative to the linear-in-means model, there are two main differences. First, randomness in the coefficients is allowed. Second, when one substitutes the $c_{g(i)}$ equation into the ω_i equation described above, it is clear that one is in essence estimating a regression for ω_i where the regressors are the products of X_i with the various endogenous and contextual variables. Hence the two approaches estimate rather different behavioral models. I plan to explore the comparative merits of the approaches in future work.

sides of equation (30) for a given neighborhood $g(i)$. This leads to the expression

$$m_{g(i)} = k + c'X_{g(i)} + d'Y_{g(i)} + Jm_{g(i)}. \tag{31}$$

The expected average choice in the neighborhood can be solved for

$$m_{g(i)} = \frac{k + c'X_{g(i)} + d'Y_{g(i)}}{1 - J}. \tag{32}$$

Substituting this into (30), one can see that

$$\omega_i = \frac{k}{1-J} + c'X_i + \frac{1}{1-J}\, d'Y_{g(i)} + \frac{J}{1-J}\, c'X_{g(i)} + \epsilon_i. \tag{33}$$

This regression is in principle estimable by ordinary least squares. A potential identification problem occurs because of the possible linear dependence between $Y_{g(i)}$ and $X_{g(i)}$. For example, in the model studied by Manski (1993), it is assumed that $Y_{g(i)} = X_{g(i)}$—i.e., that the contextual effects that affect individuals are their expectations of the neighborhood averages of the same variables that affect them on an individual level. This is the source of the nonidentification or reflection problem that Manski (1993) examined.

On the other hand, this formulation makes clear that there are two paths by which identification may be achieved. First, in the presence of prior information on which individual and contextual variables influence individual behavior, it is possible that the spaces spanned by elements of $Y_{g(i)}$ and $X_{g(i)}$ are not identical, which may allow for identification. This follows from an analysis of the reduced form equation (33). This regression has $2r + s + 1$ regressors and $r + s + 2$ unknowns; it is easy to verify that if the regressors are linearly independent then the system is identified if $r > 0$ and overidentified if $r > 1$.

Furthermore, suppose we rewrite $X_{g(i)}$ as

$$X_{g(i)} = \Pi_0 + \Pi_1 X_i + \Pi_2 Y_{g(i)} + \eta_i \tag{34}$$

In this formulation, η_i is the part of $X_{g(i)}$ that cannot be predicted given a constant, X_i and $Y_{g(i)}$. Put differently, it is the part of $X_{g(i)}$ that cannot be predicted using those variables that are assumed in equation (30) to predict individual behavior. Notice that η_i can always be constructed by computing the regression (34). This allows us to rewrite the individual reduced form as

$$\omega_i = \frac{k}{1-J} + \frac{Jc'}{1-J}\Pi_0 + \left(c' + \frac{Jc'}{1-J}\Pi_1\right)X_i$$

$$+ \left(\frac{J}{1-J}d' + \frac{Jc'}{1-J}\Pi_2\right)Y_{g(i)} + \frac{J}{1-J}c'\eta_i + \epsilon_i. \quad (35)$$

Equation (34) identifies Π_0, Π_1, and Π_2. Since η_i is orthogonal to the other regressors in (35), the terms $k/(1-J) + Jc'/(1-J)\Pi_0$, $c' + Jc'/(1-J)\Pi_1$, and $J/(1-J)d' + Jc'/(1-J)\Pi_2$ respectively are identified from a regression of ω_i onto a constant, X_i, and $Y_{g(i)}$. Hence, this regression will have $r+s+1$ coefficients for $r+s+2$ unknowns. In order to identify the structural coefficients, it is necessary that the regressors η_i provide an additional estimate of some component of the vector $J/(1-J)c'$. This will give as many coefficients as there are unknowns. This in turn requires that η_i is not null—i.e., that there is some part of the neighborhood averages of the individual controls that do not lie in the space spanned by a constant, X_i, and $Y_{g(i)}$. In turn, a necessary condition for η_i to be non-null is that there is at least one regressor x_j such that its neighborhood average $x_{j,g(i)}$ is excluded from $Y_{g(i)}$ prior to the exercise. These arguments are the basis for the following theorem, which is taken from Brock and Durlauf (forthcoming).

Theorem 3: Necessary conditions for identification in the linear-in-means model with social interactions and rational expectations

In the linear-in-means model it is necessary for identification of the model's parameters that

i. The dimension of the linear space spanned by elements of 1, X_i and $Y_{g(i)}$ is $r+s+1$.[17]
ii. The dimension of the linear space spanned by the elements of 1, X_i, $Y_{g(i)}$ and $X_{g(i)}$ is at least $r+s+2$.

[17] The element 1 should be interpreted as a random variable whose value is 1 with probability 1.

6.2. *Nonlinear Models*

Notice that linearity plays a critical role in creating the potential for nonidentification. Suppose that instead of (30), the individual-level behavioral equation is

$$\omega_i = k + c'X_i + d'Y_{g(i)} + J\phi(m_{g(i)}) + \epsilon_i. \tag{36}$$

for some invertible function $\phi(\cdot)$. The rational expectations condition for this model is

$$m_{g(i)} = \psi(k + c'X_{g(i)} + d'Y_{g(i)}), \tag{37}$$

where $\psi(r) = (r - J\phi(r))^{-1}$. The associated reduced form equation equals

$$\omega_i = k + c'X_i + d'Y_{g(i)} + J\phi(\psi(k + c'X_{g(i)} + d'Y_{g(i)})) + \epsilon_i. \tag{38}$$

This is an example of a partially linear model (cf. Horowitz 1998). If $\phi(\cdot)$—and by implication $\psi(\cdot)$—is known, this equation is a standard nonlinear regression. Brock and Durlauf (forthcoming) verify that the parameters of this model are locally identified under weak assumptions on the variables in the system. Interestingly, the conditions for identification are weaker than the linear model when considered from the perspective of what relationship must exist between $X_{g(i)}$ and $Y_{g(i)}$. The reason for this is that the nonlinear function $\phi(\cdot)$ ensures that $m_{g(i)}$ and $Y_{g(i)}$ cannot be collinear, as is the potential source of nonidentification in the linear case.

6.3. *Binary Choice*

Using the linear model as background, I now consider identification in the binary choice model. This model will possess a likelihood function

$$\begin{aligned} &L(\underline{\omega}_I | X_i, Y_{g(i)}, m^e_{g(i)} \; \forall \; i) \\ &\quad = \prod_i \mu(\omega_i = 1 | X_i, Y_{g(i)}, m^e_{g(i)})^{(1+\omega_i)/2} \\ &\quad \cdot \mu(\omega_i = -1 | X_i, Y_{g(i)}, m^e_{g(i)})^{(1-\omega_i)/2} \\ &\quad \propto \prod_i (exp(\beta k + \beta c'X_i + \beta d'Y_{g(i)} + \beta J m^e_{g(i)})^{(1+\omega_i)/2} \\ &\quad \cdot exp(-\beta k - \beta c'X_i - \beta d'Y_{g(i)} - \beta J m^e_{g(i)})^{(1-\omega_i)/2}), \end{aligned} \tag{39}$$

where the assumption of rational expectations imposes the restriction

$$m^e_{g(i)} = m_{g(i)} = \int tanh(\beta k + \beta c'X + \beta d'Y_{g(i)} + \beta J m_{g(i)}) dF_{X|Y_{g(i)}} \quad (40)$$

under the assumption that agents only know $Y_{g(i)}$ within a neighborhood.[18] Notice the multiplicative structure of the parameters of the model; this makes it necessary to normalize the parameters in order to achieve identification, which can be done by setting $\beta = 1$.

The key question in terms of identification of the linear-in-means model is whether $m_{g(i)}$ is collinear with the other regressors in the individual behavioral equation due to self consistency. This same issue arises in the binary choice case. However, in the binary choice model, the expected value of a neighborhood choice is a nonlinear function of the other variables in the model. The technical appendix at the end of this paper gives a formal statement of the conditions under which the binary choice model with social interactions is identified, but the key intuition for identification follows from the nonlinearity built into (40). As the theorem indicates, there is no need for an exclusion restriction on the contextual variables in order to achieve identification, as was true in the linear-in-means model. This is an example of a more general phenomenon noted by McManus (1992)—namely, that lack of identification in parametric systems is typically associated with linearity.

This being said, the standard errors in estimating the binary choice model may be extremely large if the distributions of individual and contextual effects are such that (40) is "close" to linear. Exclusion restrictions of the type that generate identification in the linear model—i.e., the presence of elements of X_i in (39) whose group levels analogs do not appear in $Y_{g(i)}$—can facilitate accurate estimation for this case.

Finally, while identification has been established for the binary choice model, as well as for longitudinal analogs (Brock and Durlauf forthcoming), there has yet to be any investigation of issues that arise in the implementation of the models. The presence of latent expectations vari-

[18] It is technically convenient, in working with the binary choice model, to assume that the information sets for individuals take this form, rather than to assume each individual knows the distribution of X_i within his group, as was done in the linear case. This is so because, as seen in Manski (1988), identification arguments in the binary choice model are more subtle than for linear regressions; see Brock and Durlauf (forthcoming) for details.

ables (m_g's) that may not be uniquely determined by observables (due to multiple equilibria) suggests that computational issues, for example, will be far from trivial. Thus there is much additional research needed in order to fully understand how to apply interactions-based models to data.

7. IMPLICATIONS FOR PUBLIC POLICY

An interactions-based perspective on socioeconomic outcomes has important implications for the design and evaluation of public policy. How do interactions-based models affect the assessment of public policies? There are at least three respects in which one may explore this question.

From the perspective of policy assessment, interactions-based models make clear the importance of accounting for nonlinearities. To see this, suppose that a policymaker is assessing the effects of altering h, the private incentive of each individual within a population. Suppose as well that the equilibrium choice level for the population is described by equation (26). In the vicinity of a given equilibrium, the derivative of the equilibrium expected average choice m with respect to h is

$$\frac{dm}{dh} = \frac{\beta(1 - tanh^2(\beta h + \beta Jm))}{(1 - \beta J(1 - tanh^2(\beta h + \beta Jm)))}. \tag{41}$$

This is obviously highly nonlinear. However, the derivative is monotonically decreasing in h when $h > 0$, so one can at least infer that the marginal effect on a group will be higher the weaker the group's fundamentals, so long as the fundamentals have the same sign. However, because of the relationship between fundamentals and the number of equilibria, one must additionally ask whether nonmarginal changes in h will alter the number of equilibria. This creates the possibility that it is cost efficient to raise the private incentives for the relatively better off. For example, in Figure 1, when one moves from low to high h, the welfare inferior equilibria disappear.

A second implication for policy is implied by this equation. Suppose that a policymaker is considering whether to implement a system of subsidies to raise incentives for I individuals out of a population of I^2. Suppose each member of the population is described by equation (21) and these individuals do not form a single group but instead form I separate groups; as before, each group's equilibrium is described by (26). The policymaker is assumed to have two options: (1) raise incentives from h to

$h + dh$ for I individuals scattered across I different groups, or (2) raise incentives from h to $h + dh$ for all I members of a given group. Let m_1 denote the expected value of the average choice for I persons sampled across the I groups and m_2 denote the expected value of the average choice for the I members of a given group. Assuming that the groups are large, so that one can ignore the effect of the behavior of one individual on the group, then the total effect on behavior under the first policy option is

$$\frac{dm_1}{dh} = \beta(1 - tanh^2(\beta h + \beta Jm)). \tag{42}$$

Equation (41) gives the effect of the second policy. Therefore, the relative impact of the two policies is

$$\frac{dm_2}{dh}\bigg/\frac{dm_1}{dh} = \frac{1}{(1 - \beta J(1 - tanh^2(\beta h + \beta Jm)))} > 1. \tag{43}$$

These expressions differ because when the private incentives are affected for all members of a given group, the influences on individual behavior are magnified as the changes in the behavior of each person will simultaneously affect others in the population. The net effect of the change in private incentives on aggregate behavior will therefore be increased. This is known as a social multiplier in the literature. The presence of a social multiplier means that a cost benefit analysis would suggest concentrating expenditures in order to take advantage of the social multiplier that amplifies the effects of a higher h within a given group.

Third, interactions-based models suggest the importance of exploring alternatives to forms of redistribution that are designed to raise private incentives. One way to interpret welfare and other cash and/or in-kind aid programs is that they are forms of income redistribution. Such programs typically transfer (through taxes paid either contemporaneously or over time to retire government debt that funded the initial program) income from one group to another. An alternative form of equality-enhancing policies falls in the category of "associational redistribution" (Durlauf 1996c). These policies treat group memberships as potential objects of redistribution.

A number of past and current public policies are interpretable as promoting associational redistribution. For example, many education policies are attempts to engage in associational redistribution. Affirmative action in college admissions is nothing more than a choice of what criteria are used to construct student bodies. School busing for racial integration, while substantially less important now than 20 years ago, had exactly the same effect. Recent efforts to promote integration through magnet schools may be interpreted the same way.

Associational redistribution is a far more controversial class of policies than standard tax/transfer policies, as the visceral public hostility to affirmative action makes clear. Further, it seems clear that the development of a rigorous ethical defense of associational redistribution is more difficult than for income redistribution; even as egalitarian a thinker as Walzer (1983) finds various forms of quotas to be ethically problematic. While the presence of interactions in determining socioeconomic outcomes cannot, of course, resolve these complexities, their presence is nevertheless important in assessing whether particular forms of associational redistribution are just. For example, suppose one follows Roemer (1998) and concludes that society ought to indemnify individuals against adverse outcomes in life to the extent the outcomes are caused by factors outside their control. Clearly, ethnicity, residential neighborhood of youth, and the like are not variables that one chooses. Hence, the pursuit of equality of opportunity along the lines outlined by Roemer would require interventions to render these groupings irrelevant in predicting socioeconomic outcomes. One obvious and perhaps necessary way to achieve this is to alter those group memberships that are not immutable.

8. CONCLUSIONS

This paper has described a general model of social interactions that attempts to combine the rigorous choice-based modeling of economics with the richer social structures, interdependences, and contexts, which are the hallmark of sociology. The theoretical framework embodies methodological individualism, yet illustrates how social context means that it is impossible to reduce the analysis of aggregate behavior to individual level descriptions. In terms of conceptualizing behaviors, the approach allows one to integrate private incentives and social influences in a common structure. This framework is compatible with structural econometric analysis and so can be falsified using standard statistical methods.

In terms of future research, my own view is that the most important contributions can be made in the areas of statistical methodology and empirical work. As the survey of evidence suggests, the strongest evidence in favor of social interactions lies in those contexts most removed from the substantive phenomena that this new literature tries to address. Advances in this regard will probably require much more attention to data collection. For example, virtually no attention has been paid to the question of identifying which groups influence individuals as opposed to which groups are currently measured; as Manski (1993) argues, identification of relevant groups from data is probably impossible. Census tracts may have been chosen to approximate homogeneous neighborhoods, but this does not imply that they actually define reference groups. Detailed survey information may be needed to elicit information on what groups actually matter to individuals in a sample. An important effort in this respect is the Project on Human Development in Chicago Neighborhoods. Sampson, Morenoff, and Earls (1999), for example, show how the detailed survey data from this project help clarify some of the amorphous aspects of social capital discussions.

At a minimum, the framework helps to make clear, I believe, that the disciplinary barriers between sociology and economics are in many respects artificial. For phenomena such as inner city poverty, social pathologies, and the like, each field contains important and fundamental theoretical ideas that are not only compatible but in substantive ways complementary to one another. My own belief is that the continuing synthesis of choice-based reasoning with social interactions will prove to be one of the most promising areas of *socioeconomic* theory and empirical work.

TECHNICAL APPENDIX

Theorem 4: Identification in the binary choice model with social interactions and rational expectations

For the binary choice model with probability structure

$$\mu(\underline{\omega}|X_i, Y_{g(i)}, m^e_{g(i)}\ \forall\ i) \propto \prod_i exp(\beta k + \beta c' X_i \omega_i + \beta d' Y_{g(i)} \omega_i + \beta J m^e_{g(i)} \omega_i) \qquad \text{(A.1)}$$

and

$$m^e_{g(i)} = m_{g(i)} = \int tanh(\beta k + \beta c' X + \beta d' Y_{g(i)} + \beta J m_{g(i)}) dF_{X|Y_{g(i)}}, \qquad \text{(A.2)}$$

assuming β is normalized to 1, if

i. The support of the vector consisting of the elements of X_i and $Y_{g(i)}$ is not contained in a proper linear subspace of R^{r+s}.
ii. The support of the vector consisting of the elements of $Y_{g(i)}$ is not contained in a proper linear subspace of R^s.
iii. No element of X_i or $Y_{g(i)}$ is constant.
iv. There exists at least one group g_0 such that conditional on Y_{g_0}, X_i is not contained in a proper linear subspace of R_r.
v. None of the regressors in $Y_{g(i)}$ possesses bounded support.
vi. $m_{g(i)}$ is not constant across all groups g.

then, the parameters of the model (k, c, d, J) are identified relative to any distinct alternative $(\bar{k}, \bar{c}, \bar{d}, \bar{J})$.

Proof. See Brock and Durlauf (forthcoming).

REFERENCES

Akerlof, George. 1997. "Social Distance and Social Decisions." *Econometrica* 65: 1005–28.
Akerlof, George, and Rachel Kranton. 2000. "Identity and Economics." *Quarterly Journal of Economics* CVX, 719–53.
Anderson, Elijah. 1999. *Code of the Street*. New York: Norton.
Anderson, Philip. 1972. "More Is Different." *Science* 177, 393–96.
Anderson, Philip, and Daniel Stein. 1984. "Broken Symmetry, Emergent Properties, Dissipative Structures, Life: Are They All Related." In *Basic Notions of Condensed Matter Physics*, edited by P. Anderson. Menlo Park, CA: Addison Wesley.
Aronson, Elliot. 1999. *The Social Animal*, 8th ed., New York: W. H. Freeman.
Arthur, W. Brian. 1987. "Urban Systems and Historical Path Dependence." Pp. 85–97 in *Urban Systems and Infrastructure*, edited by R. Herman and J. Ausubel, Washington, D.C.: National Academy of Sciences/National Academy of Engineering.
Becker, Gary, and Nigel Tomes. 1979. "An Equilibrium Theory of the Distribution of Income and Intergenerational Mobility." *Journal of Political Economy* 87:1163–89.
Bénabou, Roland. 1993. "Workings of a City: Location, Education and Production." *Quarterly Journal of Economics*, 108:619–52.
———. 1996a. "Equity and Efficiency in Human Capital Investment: The Local Connection." *Review of Economic Studies* 62, 237–64.
———. 1996b. "Heterogeneity, Stratification, and Growth: Macroeconomic Effects of Community Structure." *American Economic Review* 86:584–609.

Bikhchandani, Sushil, David Hirshleifer, and Ivo Welch. 1992. "A Theory of Fads, Fashion, Custom, and Cultural Exchange as Information Cascades." *Journal of Political Economy* 100:992–1026.

Blalock, Herbert. 1984. "Contextual-Effects Models: Theoretical and Methodological Issues." *Annual Review of Sociology* 10: 353–72.

Blume, Lawrence, and Steven Durlauf. 2001. "The Interactions-Based Approach to Socioeconomic Behavior." Pp. 15–44 in *Social Dynamics*, edited by H. P Young and S. Durlauf. Cambridge, MA: MIT Press.

Brewster, Karen. 1994a. "Race Differences in Sexual Activity Among Adolescent Women: The Role of Neighborhood Characteristics." *American Sociological Review* 59: 408–24.

———. 1994b. "Neighborhood Context and the Transition to Sexual Activity Among Black Women." *Demography* 31: 603–14.

Brock, William, and Steven Durlauf, 1999. "A Formal Model of Theory Choice in Science." *Economic Theory* 14:113–30.

———. 2001. "Discrete Choice with Social Interactions." *Review of Economic Studies* 68, 2:235–60.

———. forthcoming. "Interactions-Based Models." *Handbook of Econometrics*, vol. 5, edited by J. Heckman and E. Leamer. Amsterdam: North-Holland.

Brooks-Gunn, Jeanne, Greg Duncan, P. Klebanov, and N. Sealand. 1993. "Do Neighborhoods Affect Child and Adolescent Development?" *American Journal of Sociology* 99:353–95.

Brown, Roger. 1986. *Social Psychology*. Cambridge, MA: Harvard University Press.

Bryk, Anthony, and Steven Raudenbush. 1992. *Hierarchical Linear Models: Applications and Data Analysis Methods*. New York: Sage.

Card, David, and Alan Krueger. 1992. "Does School Quality Matter? Returns to Education and the Characteristics of Public Schools in the United States." *Journal of Political Economy*: 1–40.

Chambers, Jack K. 1995. *Sociolinguistic Theory*. Oxford, England: Blackwell Publishers.

Coleman, James. 1990. *Foundations of Social Theory*. Cambridge, MA: Harvard University Press.

Cooper, Russell. 1997. *Coordination Games*, Cambridge, England: Cambridge University Press.

Crane, Jonathan. 1991. "The Epidemic Theory of Ghettos and Neighborhood Effects on Dropping Out and Teenage Childbearing." *American Journal of Sociology* 96: 1226–59.

Duneier, Mitchell. 1992. *Slim's Table*. Chicago: University of Chicago Press.

———. 1999. *Sidewalk*. New York: Farrar, Straus, and Giroux.

Durlauf, Steven. 1996a. "A Theory of Persistent Income Inequality." *Journal of Economic Growth* 1: 75–93

———. 1996b. "Neighborhood Feedbacks, Endogenous Stratification, and Income Inequality." Pp. 505–34 in *Dynamic Disequilibrium Modelling*, edited by W. Barnett, G. Gandolfo, and C. Hillinger. Cambridge, England: Cambridge University Press.

———. 1996c. "Associational Redistribution: A Defense." *Politics and Society* 24: 391–410.

———. 1997a. "Statistical Mechanics Approaches to Socioeconomic Behavior." Pp. 81–104 in *The Economy as a Complex Evolving System II*, edited by W. B. Arthur, S. Durlauf, and D. Lane. Redwood City: Addison-Wesley, forthcoming.

———. 1999a. "The Memberships Theory of Inequality: Ideas and Implications." Pp. 161–78 in *Elites, Minorities, and Economic Growth*, edited by E. Brezis and P. Temin. Amsterdam: North Holland.

———. 1999b. "How Can Statistical Mechanics Contribute to the Study of Science?" *Proceedings of the National Academy of Sciences* 96; 10582–84.

———. 2001. "On the Empirics of Social Capital." University of Wisconsin. Unpublished manuscript.

Elster, Jon. 1989. *The Cement of Society*. Cambridge, England: Cambridge University Press.

Glaeser, Edward, Bruce Sacerdote, and José Scheinkman. 1996. "Crime and Social Interactions." *Quarterly Journal of Economics*, 111, 507–48.

Glaeser, Edward, and José Scheinkman, 2000. "Nonmarket Interactions." Princeton University. Unpublished manuscript.

———. 2001. "Measuring Social Interactions." Pp. 83–132 in *Social Dynamics*, edited by S. Durlauf and H. P. Young. Cambridge, MA: MIT Press.

Granovetter, Mark. 1985. "Economic Action and Social Structure: The Problem of Embeddedness." *American Journal of Sociology* 91: 481–510.

Granovetter, Mark, and Roland Soong. 1988. "Threshold Models of Diversity: Chinese Restaurants, Residential Segregation, and the Spiral of Silence." Pp. 69–104 in *Sociological Methodology*, edited by C. Clogg. Cambridge, MA: Blackwell Publishers.

Hanushek, Eric. 1988. "The Economics of Schooling: Production and Efficiency in Public Schools." *Journal of Economic Literature* 24: 1141–77.

Hauser, Robert. 1970. "Context and Consex: A Cautionary Tale." *American Journal of Sociology* 75: 645–64.

Heckman, James. 2000. "Causal Parameters and Policy Analysis in Economics: A Twentieth Century Retrospective." *Quarterly Journal of Economics* 115: 45–97.

Heckman, James, Anne Layne-Farrar, and Petra Todd. 1996. "Does Measured School Quality Really Matter? An Examination of the Earnings-Quality Relationship." Pp. 192–289 in *Does Money Matter?* edited by G. Burtless. Washington, DC: Brookings Institution Press.

Horowitz, Joel. 1998. *Semiparametric Methods in Econometrics*. New York: Springer-Verlag.

Katz, Lawrence, Jeffrey Kling, and Jeffrey Liebman. 2001. "Moving to Opportunity in Boston: Early Impacts of a Randomized Mobility Experiment." *Quarterly Journal of Economics* 116: 607–54.

Krugman, Paul. 1996. *The Self-Organizing Economy*, Oxford, England: Blackwell Publishers.

Kozol, Jonathan. 1991. *Savage Inequalities*. New York: Crown.

Loury Glenn. 1977. "A Dynamic Theory of Racial Income Differences." Pp. 153–86 in *Women Minorities and Employment Discrimination*, edited by P. Wallace and A. LaMond. Lexington, MA: Lexington Books.

———. 1981. "Intergenerational Transfers and the Distribution of Earnings." *Econometrica* 49: 843–67.

Manski, Charles. 1988. "Identification of Binary Response Models." *Journal of the American Statistical Association* 83: 729–38.

———. 1993. "Identification of Endogenous Social Effects: The Reflection Problem." *Review of Economic Studies* 60: 531–42.

———. 2000. "Economic Analysis of Social Interactions", *Journal of Economic Perspectives* 14.3: 115–36.

Mas-Colell, Andrea, Michael Whinston, and Jerry Green. 1995. *Microeconomic Theory*. New York: Oxford University Press.

McManus, Douglas. 1992. "How Common Is Identification in Parametric Models?" *Journal of Econometrics* 53: 5–23.

Moffitt, Robert. 2001. "Policy Interventions, Low-Level Equilibria, and Social Interactions." Pp. 45–82 in *Social Dynamics*, edited by S. Durlauf and H. P. Young. Cambridge, MA: MIT Press.

Roemer, John. 1998. *Equality of Opportunity*. Cambridge, MA: Harvard University Press.

Rubinstein, Ariel. 1998. *Modeling Bounded Rationality*. Cambridge, MA: MIT Press.

Rubinowitz, Leonard, and James Rosenbaum. 2000. *Crossing the Class and Color Lines*, Chicago: University of Chicago Press.

Sampson, Robert, Jeffrey Morenoff, and Felton Earls. 1999. "Beyond Social Capital: Collective Efficacy for Children." *American Sociological Review* 64: 633–60.

Sampson, Robert, Steven Raudenbush, and Felton Earls. 1997. "Neighborhoods and Violent Crime: A Study of Collective Efficacy." *Science* 277: 918–24.

Schelling, Thomas. 1971. "Dynamic Models of Segregation." *Journal of Mathematical Sociology* 1: 143–86.

Sherif, Muzafer, O. Harvey, B. White, W. Hood, and C. Sherif. 1961. *Intergroup Conflict and Cooperation: The Robbers Cave Experiment*. Norman: Institute of Group Relations, University of Oklahoma; reprinted by Wesleyan University Press, 1988.

South, Scott, and Kyle Crowder. 1999. "Neighborhood Effects on Family Formation: Concentrated Poverty and Beyond." *American Sociological Review* 64: 113–32.

Sucoff, Clea, and Dawn Upchurch. 1998. "Neighborhood Context and the Risk of Childbearing Among Metropolitan-Area Black Adolescents." *American Sociological Review* 63: 571–85.

Wallis, Kenneth. 1980. "Econometric Implications of the Rational Expectations Hypothesis." *Econometrica* 48: 49–73.

Walzer, Michael. 1983. *Spheres of Justice*. New York: Basic Books.

Weinberg, Bruce, Patricia Reagan, and Jeffrey Yankow. 2000. "Do Neighborhoods Affect Work Behavior? Evidence from the NLSY79." Department of Economics, Ohio State University. Unpublished manuscript.

Wilson, William J. 1987. *The Truly Disadvantaged*. Chicago: University of Chicago Press.

Yeomans, Julia. 1992. *Statistical Mechanics of Phase Transitions*. Oxford, England: Oxford University Press.

COMMENT: INDIVIDUAL BEHAVIOR AND SOCIAL INTERACTIONS

*Samuel Bowles**

In recent years economists have discovered social exchange, reciprocity motives, poverty traps, cultural evolution, and contextual effects on behavior. Our excitement has been only slightly diminished by an occasional bemused observation that, like pre-Columbian North America, these were not exactly uninhabited territories awaiting our arrival. So the question is bound to come up: *What do economists know about social interactions that sociologists do not?* Steven Durlauf, who unlike many economists is no newcomer to sociological thinking, has written an arresting paper suggesting a possible answer: *Economists have a distinctive model of the way that individual action generates aggregate outcomes at the level of an entire population*, or what Durlauf calls the emergent properties of the system. When general equilibrium theory can be rescued from empirically vacuous "everything depends on everything" claims and from the particular assumptions of the dominant Walrasian (or neoclassical) paradigm, it has a lot to say about social interactions, as Durlauf's novel variant of this framework makes clear.

Of course, Durlauf makes no such claim: his model is a vehicle for importing sociological ideas into economics; he is not in the export business (which again distinguishes him from most economists with an interdisciplinary bent). But in this journal it is certainly worth asking what sociologists might take home from his efforts. The take-home here it is not the attention to system-level outcomes, for this is the bread and butter of social stratification research, historical sociology, and many other branches of sociology. Rather it is the economists' method of modeling emergent properties as the result of a strong version of intentional action in which the system-wide outcomes are represented as mutual best responses of reasonably well-informed individuals pursuing their autonomous projects. In this short note I want to say why what Durlauf has done

Thanks to the MacArthur Foundation for financial support and the Universita degli Studi di Siena for an ideal research environment.

*Santa Fe Institute and University of Massachusetts

is important, and suggest some possible extensions of his approach. To do this I need to recall some of the key features and disabilities of existing general equilibrium approaches.

Durlauf, like most economists, embraces methodological individualism because he wants to understand aggregate results: not why this particular person is without a job, but the rate of unemployment; not why this person is well off and that one poor, but the aggregate level of inequality and so on. But to explain aggregate outcomes we cannot simply sum the predicted individual behaviors, because the actions taken by each typically affect the constraints, beliefs, or preferences of the others. Taking account of these feedback effects can be done with population-level models that link individual actions to outcomes for the population as whole. There are just a few competing generic population-level models to choose from and Durlauf has provided an interesting hybrid, or perhaps even a new species.

Differing variants of population-level models may be distinguished by five key characteristics. The first is the way that each represents *content of social interactions*: Do individuals simply transact goods on competitive markets governed by complete contracts, or do they affect one another's well being in other ways also, as neighbors, voters, workmates, and family members? The second is the *technology of social interactions*: Does one's payoff to an action decrease with the number of others adopting the same action (selling goods to consumers with limited wants, traffic congestion, or other examples of overcrowding), or does one's payoff increase (industry-wide economies of scale, or participation in a strike)? The third is the process of individuals' *updating behaviors* in response to changes in the behaviors of others and chance events: Do they instantaneously optimize using complete knowledge of the population-level system or do they follow rules for appropriate behavior (rules of thumb, social norms), updating them only occasionally in response to local information? The fourth aspect of a population-level model is its *representation of outcomes*: Does the model identify a single state—perhaps a unique stable Nash equilibrium—as *the* outcome, or does the model study an explicit dynamical process whereby a population moves in a state space perhaps with many attractors and perhaps without ever settling exactly at any of them. The last aspect is the *normative properties of the relevant social outcomes*: Are the outcomes one would expect to obtain most (or much) of the time desirable according to some standard, or are suboptimal outcomes likely to persist over long periods?

The Walrasian general equilibrium model is one such population-level model: it aggregates the individual actions of producers and consumers to an economywide vector of prices, outputs, and resource allocation among competing uses. The only tractable versions of this model—and hence the only ones routinely taught—embody the five distinguishing characteristics listed as the first option in each of the above modeling choices: complete contracting is the only way people interact; constant or diminishing returns is assumed, individuals instantaneously adjust to new information, the aggregate outcome indicated by the model is a unique Nash equilibrium, and this equilibrium (under the assumptions of the Fundamental Theorem of Welfare Economics) is a Pareto-optimum.[1] These characteristics are summarized very schematically in the first column of Table 1.

A well-kept secret (even economics students are in the dark about this) is that markets in fact play no role in this model, and the allocation process is highly centralized. The equilibrium is implemented through the fiction that a single "auctioneer" announces a vector of prices, in response to which buyers and sellers announce their preferred transactions, the process continuing until the auctioneer hits on a price vector that if implemented would clear all markets. Buyers and sellers are then, but only then, permitted to do business (the auctioneer is also an enforcer) thus precluding out-of-equilibrium transactions. Buyers and sellers do not set prices (they are price takers); so the theory is silent on the question of how individuals adjust to disequilibria and how, as a result, markets may equilibrate. With these simplifying assumptions the model allows strong predictions about outcomes based solely on the knowledge of individual preferences, technologies, and the "initial" endowment of resources to each individual. For this reason and because of its tractability, the model has attracted wide application not only in economics, but in the social sciences generally, where analogies to competitive economic equilibrium are found in electoral competition, the marriage "market," and the like.

Other than the Walrasian general equilibrium model, the only fully developed class of population-level models are those depicting evolutionary dynamics of systems under the combined influences of chance, inheritance, and natural selection. The similarity between the two approaches

[1]Like the fundamental theorem, the uniqueness of equilibrium is not proved under any but highly stringent conditions; but in practice (that is, the undergraduate classroom and public policy rhetoric) uniqueness is routinely assumed (generally implicitly).

TABLE 1
Varieties of General Equilibrium Models

	Walrasian	Darwinian	Durlauf
Social interactions	Complete contracts: no nonmarket interactions	Fitness may be frequency-dependent	Nonmarket interactions
Technology of interactions	Nonincreasing returns (no positive feedbacks)	Unrestricted	Unrestricted (positive feedbacks possible)
Behavioral updating	Payoff maximizing with rational expectations	Payoff monotonic adaptive agents	Payoff max, rational expectations
System-level outcomes	Unique (stable) equilibrium	Multipeaked fitness landscapes	Multiple equilbria
Normative properties	Fundamental theorem of welfare economics	Fisher's Fundamental Theorem	Persistence of suboptimal outcomes

Note: Nothing in the Darwinian framework requires it but biological models commonly assume additive fitness (requiring no epistatic interactions) replicating the Walrasian complete-contracting framework in precluding interactions, which explains the similarity between the two fundamental theorems (Fisher 1930; Arrow 1951). Fisher's theorem does not hold where epistatic interactions or other nonadditive effects give rise to multiple equilibria (e.g., see, Wright 1931).

is hardly surprising: Charles Darwin got the idea of natural selection in 1838 while reading the classical economist Thomas Malthus. But there are important differences: While optimization is a behavioral postulate in the economic approach, it is necessarily an *as if* shortcut in biological modeling where the work of optimization is done through the process of competition and selection rather than through the conscious choice of strategies by individual members of a species. If the economic models make excessive demands on individual cognitive capacities, biological models applied to humans make far too few.

It is now easy to see the novelty and importance of Durlauf's contribution. He has embraced the standard economic (and biological) approach in generating theorems about emergent properties of a population of individuals who engage in payoff-monotonic updating of their behaviors. The key idea is that the outcomes of interest are asymptotically stable (self-correcting) equilibria of the implied dynamical system. But unlike the Walrasian approach, he models direct (meaning noncontractual) interactions between individuals (the Walrasian and additive fitness models are analogous to assuming his variable $J = 0$ and in this sense may be seen as degenerate cases of Durlauf's model). And because these direct interactions frequently produce positive feedbacks, his model accounts for generalized increasing returns (when $J_{ij} > 0$ individual i's payoff varies positively with j's choice of the same action. Durlauf refers to this as conformity; it generates the positive feedbacks characteristic of generalized increasing returns, which is how I refer to it). Theorem 1 then shows that these positive feedbacks (if strong enough relative to the stochastic elements in the system) may support three equilibria, one of which is not asymptotically stable.[2] The final property of his model—the possible persistence of suboptimal outcomes—follows immediately from the fact that only by unlikely accident will the two equilibria be normatively equivalent, and the population may spend significant amounts of time at the suboptimal one. (The Blume-Durlauf result that for very long time horizons the system will spend most of the time at or near the welfare-superior equilibrium is, as Durlauf notes, not of great practical impor-

[2] A quibble: Durlauf says we can "ignore" the unstable interior equilibrium, but this is not quite right, as it is analogous to the tipping point in a Schelling-type model, so its location may have an important bearing on the long-term dynamics of the system. If it is in the neighborhood of one of the stable equilibria, that equilibrium, though stable might not be persistent as small shocks would displace the system beyond the "tipping point" and into the basin of attraction of the other stable equilibrium.

tance because the persistence in the suboptimal equilibrium can endure far longer than is tolerable from a normative or policy standpoint).

Durlauf (singly, and with his frequent coauthors William Brock and Larry Blume) have produced a model that tractably formalizes essential aspects of social reality precluded in the Walrasian paradigm: included are noncontractual interactions, punctuated equilibria, poverty traps and other persistent but in principle avoidable blights on human well being, divergent development, and local uniformity combined with global heterogeneity. This is a major accomplishment and a welcome contribution to both economics and sociology.

I do have reservations about the model; they point to possible extensions, not to intrinsic shortcomings. Because Durlauf has deliberately crafted his model so as to be data friendly (another contrast with the Walrasian approach), let me illustrate my three concerns with an empirical problem.

Figure 1 presents a striking picture of divergent union densities in some of the advanced economies. Econometric estimates confirm a strong divergence from the mean, with a bifurcation at a density of about one-third (Bowles 2002). It is a strength of Durlauf's model that it would readily explain the observed phenomena: union membership is a binary choice for which $J > 0$, and the relevant underlying variables are such that the population will converge to some high level of density or to a low level depending on initial conditions.

But would this be an adequate explanation? My first concern is that among the most prominent direct social interactions not governed by complete contracts are those taking place between classes, and any treatment of divergent union densities would seemingly have to take class relationships into account. Durlauf's model is framed in terms of "horizontal" relationships among a multiplicity of people, not the "vertical" dyadic relationship of employer to worker, lender to borrower, and the like. I have in mind especially the employment relationship, in which the employer exchanges a wage for a contractually enforceable promise to show up at the appointed times, in the hope that what the employer needs but is not subject to contract—hard work of good quality—will result. The relationship between a bank and a borrower is no different, as the promise to repay the loan is unenforceable if the borrower is broke. In these situations the kinds of social exchange initially conceptualized by Peter Blau (1964), and formalized in principal agent models based on asymmetric information, appear to capture important aspects of the interaction that seem difficult to incorporate into Durlauf's model as it is currently specified.

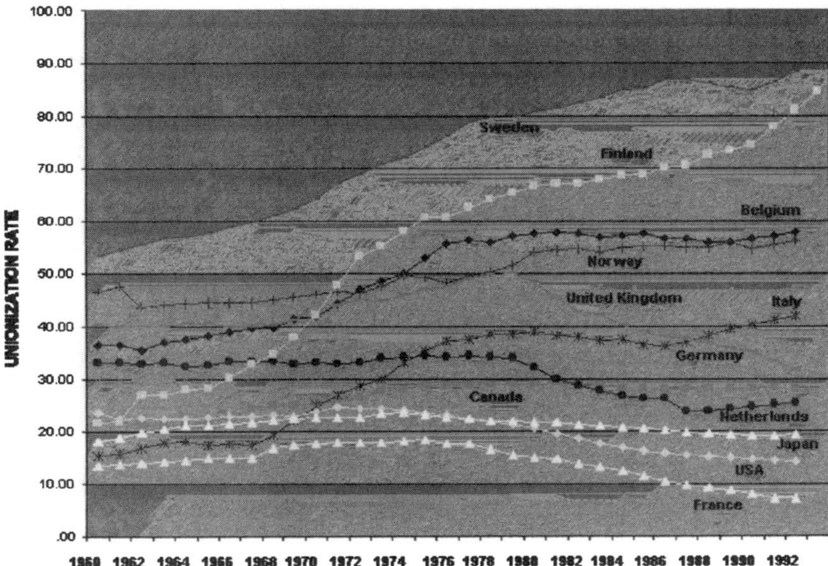

Note: Econometric analysis of these data demonstrate a significant divergence from the mean at the rate of 1.6 percent per annum, with densities exceeding a third tending to rise and less than a third declining.

Source: Luxemburg Income Study data set.

FIGURE 1. Union densities 1960–1992.

Second, and relatedly, understanding why union densities diverge would seem to require an analysis of not simply of what individuals do but of collective action including an account of why organizations like unions and employer organizations do what they do. This suggests that Durlauf's methodological individualism might be amended to incorporate multilevel interactions. I am not suggesting that organizations be simply posited as a *deus ex machina* but rather that the approach should be capable of producing organizations as outcomes, and then letting relationships among the organizations as well as among the individuals determine other outcomes. (I present a multilevel selection model of this type in Bowles [2001].)

My final concern is the one characteristic of the model that I pointedly did *not* yet mention: its rational expectations treatment of beliefs and the assumption of exogenous preferences. Nobody doubts that people learn from their environments, and most social scientists would agree that any concept of equilibrium must include an account of why the beliefs supporting the equilibrium are stationary in equilibrium. But this is a far cry from saying that the beliefs in equilibrium are true in the sense implied by the rational expectations account. I suspect that the relevant beliefs concerning union membership have been substantially influenced in all countries by pro and anti union rhetoric and that other beliefs relevant to the choice of union memberships would similarly be difficult to model in the rational expectations framework. The opposite concern applies to Durlauf's treatment of individual evaluations of outcomes: unlike beliefs, preferences are not subject to any updating at all. Given the extensive evidence that preferences are both situation-specific (or state dependent as this is called in economics, loss aversion is an example) and endogenous in the long run (responding to changes in institutions, residence patterns and the like) this seems a disability of the model (Nisbett and Ross 1991; Kahneman and Tversky 2000; Bowles 1998). I doubt that any convincing account of divergent union densities could ignore changing individual-specific evaluations of the status of being a union member.

Authors who produce a really good model share the fate of good chefs: the only decent form of appreciation is to ask for more. The above critical comments are just a way of telling the chef to keep on cooking.

REFERENCES

Arrow, Kenneth J. 1951. "An Extension of the Basic Theorems of Classical Welfare Economics." Pp. 507–32 in *Proceedings of the Second Berkeley Symposium on Mathematical Statistics and Probability*, edited by J. Neyman. Berkeley: University of California Press.

Blau, Peter. 1964. *Exchange and Power in Social Life*. New York: Wiley.

Bowles, Samuel. 1998. "Endogenous Preferences: The Cultural Consequences of Markets and Other Economic Institutions." *Journal of Economic Literature* 36: 75–111.

———. 2001. "Individual Interactions, Group Conflicts, and the Evolution of Preferences." Pp. 155–90 in *Social Dynamics*, edited by S. Durlauf and P. Young. Cambridge, MA, MIT Press.

———. 2002. *Economic Institutions and Behavior*. Princeton, NJ: Princeton University Press.

Fisher, R. A. 1930. *The Genetical Theory of Natural Selection*. Oxford, England: Clarendon Press.

Kahneman, Daniel, and Amos Tversky. 2000. *Choices, Values, and Frames*. Princeton, NJ: Princeton University Press.

Ross, L., and R. E. Nisbett. 1991. *The Person and the Situation: Perspectives of Social Psychology*. Philadelphia, PA: Temple University Press.

Wright, S. 1931. "Evolution in Mendelian Populations." *Genetics* 16:97–159.

COMMENT: MODELING SOCIAL INTERDEPENDENCE: IS IT IN THE STRUCTURE OR IN OUR HEARTS?

*Lin Tao**
*Christopher Winship**

1. INTRODUCTION

We want to congratulate Steven Durlauf on a most interesting and provocative paper. He reminds us that modeling the social interaction among and the social interdependence of individuals is a challenging task that is at the core of social science theory. As James Coleman (1990) has argued, understanding the link between the micro and the macro is one of the keys to the development of social science theory. The social interaction model proposed by Durlauf is certainly a welcomed effort in this direction.

In this comment we will focus on one specific question: Why are individuals' behaviors interdependent in Durlauf's model. We examine two possibilities: (1) the external structure of the choice problem people face induces externalities; or (2) individuals' "intrinsic" utilities are a function of choices made by other individuals. We also briefly discuss statistical estimation issues in Durlauf's model.

2. TYPES OF INTERDEPENDENCE

In the conventional economic and rational choice analysis, individuals are "egoists"—i.e., they do not care "intrinsically" about the actions or welfare of others and as such the behaviors or payoffs of others do not enter into their utility functions directly. Individuals become interdependent only when they interact under certain social conditions that result in each player's behaviors having consequences for others. People's buying and selling behavior in a market is one such example. The well-known

*Harvard University

Prisoner's Dilemma game is another. In both cases, the same action by an individual will bring different payoffs if others behave differently.

In the standard model, individuals' "intrinsic" utility functions are egoistic (e.g., people care only about their own monetary returns), but *after* the social context is taken into account, their payoff functions become potentially interdependent. We call this type of social interdependence "structurally induced." In this scenario, how people's choices interrelate depends on the specific social context (i.e., the social or game structure) in which the individuals interact. For example, the same egoistic players will cooperate in a coordination game (e.g., the Battle of the Sexes game) but be noncooperative in a Prisoner's Dilemma game. The structure of the game is critical in predicting how people interact.

The second type of interdependence is what we call "intrinsic interdependence." This refers to situations where individuals have some "intrinsic" interests in the actions and payoffs of others. Their concerns about others may include altruism (caring about the improvement of others' welfare), status competition (evaluating one's own payoff by comparing it with that of others), reciprocity (an inclination to reproduce the benevolent or malicious behaviors of others), or conformity (tendency to follow the majority). In these cases, the utility functions of the individuals include components of others' actions prior to the specification of the social structure in which they will interact.

A third logical possibility is where both "intrinsic" and "structurally induced" interdependence occur. An interesting example would be two individuals who are endowed with a "reciprocity" tendency playing the Prisoner's Dilemma (see Rabin 1993). Or imagine people who are ready to conform to the social roles of husband and wife playing the Battle of Sexes game.

The distinction between "structurally induced" and "intrinsic" interdependence is not trivial. In the case of structurally induced interdependence, it may be possible to change behavior by changing the structure in which individuals are embedded. For example, suppose we observe that people not only care about their own absolute income but also the relative rank order of their income. If such payoff interdependence is "structurally induced"—for instance, assuming people care about the rank order of their incomes because there are certain goods such as medical care that can only be obtained on a rank order basis—then changing the structure to make those goods available to everyone on a different basis may eliminate concerns over one's relative status. If, however, status concerns are inherently part of human nature—that is, psychological—then changes in the structural context may have no effect on the nature of the interdependence.

Durlauf's model is ambiguous as to why the social interdependence arises. At the heart of the paper is the following equation, which we will call the Durlauf equation:[1]

$$S_i = -\sum_j \frac{J_{i,j}}{2}(\omega_i - E_i(\omega_j | F_i))^2,$$

where ω_i and ω_j are choices of the individuals i and j, respectively. $J_{i,j}$ measures the tendency of i to "conform" to or to "deviate" from the expected action of j which is $E(\omega_j | F_i)$.

It is unclear whether the interdependence represented here is an inherent part of an individual's utility function that exists *prior* to any game structure, or a payoff function that is a product of given social context and structures. Note that under this specification an individual's payoff is not a function of other peoples' payoffs, but only their choices.

3. THE DURLAUF EQUATION AS A MODEL OF "STRUCTURALLY INDUCED" INTERDEPENDENCE

In reading the article we have the impression that the Durlauf equation is intended to be a generic "structurally induced" payoff function. The author moves from the equation directly to equilibrium analysis, which is legitimate only when the game structures within which the players interact are already captured by the equation. Game theory teaches us that the functional forms of payoff functions are highly dependent on the specific structure of a game—i.e., on the social context within which the interactions take place. The issue arises as to what extent the Durlauf equation can serve as a general payoff function characterizing social interdependence

[1]There are two reasons for us to focus on equation (13). First, other functional forms, such as equations (1) or (12) in his paper are not different from the generic payoff functions commonly seen in conventional game theory with perhaps the exception of the stochastic component in equation (12). The innovation in Durlauf's paper is equation (13). Second, the analytical results in the paper are all obtained with that specific functional form.

among social actors. If it is not general, then it is imperative to specify to what types of social situations it is applicable.

We show that the Durlauf equation is not a generally applicable payoff function by looking at some elementary games as examples. Consider the widely discussed Prisoner's Dilemma game.

		Player j	
		Cooperate	Defect
Player i	Cooperate	5, 5	−10, 10
	Defect	10, −10	0, 0

The first number in each cell is player i's payoff, the second is player j's.

Now consider a simplified version of the Durlauf equation (we leave out the stochastic component and the expected value function to simplify the presentation):

$$V_i = u_i(\omega_i) - \sum_j \frac{J_{i,j}}{2}(\omega_i - \omega_j)^2,$$

where ω_i and ω_j are choices of the individual i and j, respectively. $J_{i,j}$ measures the tendency of i to "conform" to or to "deviate" from the action of j which is ω_j. $u_i(\omega_i)$ is the constant utility one receives when playing ω_i. Let 1 represent the choice of "cooperate" and -1 represent "defect," the payoff function of player i should then satisfy:

$$\begin{cases} u(1) - (J/2)(1-1)^2 = 5 \\ u(1) - (J/2)(1+1)^2 = -10 \\ u(-1) - (J/2)(-1-1)^2 = 10 \\ u(-1) - (J/2)(-1+1)^2 = 0 \end{cases} \rightarrow \begin{cases} u(1) - u(-1) = 5 \\ u(1) - u(-1) = -20 \end{cases}$$

Obviously, there is no $u(1)$ and $u(-1)$ that can satisfy the above system of equations.

There are many other games whose structurally induced interdependence among the players cannot be represented by the Durlauf equation with suitable parameter values. Interested readers can verify that this is true of the Chicken game.

Of course, there are games that the Durlauf model describes well. For example, take a standard "Battle of the Sexes" game:

		Player j	
		Football	Opera
Player i	Football	5, 4	1, 1
	Opera	0, 0	4, 5

Let 1 represent the choice of going to "football" and -1 represent the choice of going to "opera." The payoff function of player i should satisfy

$$\begin{cases} u(1) - (J/2)(1-1)^2 = 5 \\ u(1) - (J/2)(1+1)^2 = 1 \\ u(-1) - (J/2)(-1-1)^2 = 0 \\ u(-1) - (J/2)(-1+1)^2 = 4 \end{cases}$$

If we let $u(1) = 5$, $u(-1) = 4$, and $J = 2$, they satisfy the above equations. That means the payoff function can indeed be represented by a Durlauf equation with suitable parameter values.

But note that the applicability of the Durlauf equation is highly sensitive to the payoff structure of a game. If we change the above payoff matrix slightly, even though the game still belongs to the Battle of the Sexes genre, no suitable parameter values for the Durlauf equation can be found. For instance, consider the following variant:

		Player j	
		Football	Opera
Player i	Football	5, 4	0, 0
	Opera	0, 0	4, 5

It can be verified that this payoff matrix can not be represented by the Durlauf equations, since it implies that $u(1) - u(-1) = 1$ and $u(1) - u(-1) = 0$ at the same time.

The above examples illustrate that social interdependence under structural constraints can take highly diverse forms and can be very sensitive to the specifics of the structure of a game. They show that the Durlauf equation is not a generally applicable functional form for describing the social interdependencies induced by various game structures. This raises the question of what types of situations can be modeled using the Durlauf equation and what types cannot, which should be answered by explicitly analyzing how the equation's form is derived from the underlying game structure.

Being explicit about the derivation of the model also provides insight into the relationship between the model's form and the structure it models. Two games can have similar payoff functions for different structural reasons. For example, people may "conform" both in a stock market and on a factory floor. In the former setting, it might be the presence of imperfect information that promotes individuals to imitate one another's behavior. In the latter, it could be the social sanctions attached to a norm that creates the incentive for workers to conform. Although the individuals' payoff function may in both situations be of the Durlauf functional form, the values of J (measuring people's tendency to conform) in those two situations may be determined by very different factors. The introduction of private information, for example, may weaken the incentive to conform (i.e., the J value) in the stock market but may have little effect among the norm-conforming factory workers. Conversely, a decrease in the opportunity for repeated interactions could have a large impact on the tendency to conform (the J value) among the workers since it weakens the foundation of the sanctioning mechanism, but may have little effect on behavior in the stock market.

4. THE DURLAUF EQUATION AS A MODEL OF "INTRINSIC" INTERDEPENDENCE

The Durlauf equation can also be viewed as a general representation of an individual utility function prior to any game structure. This would be an even more radical step from the conventional economic and rational choice models, though not unprecedented.

Traditional economic models seem to be incapable of explaining some robust experimental evidence. For example, individuals frequently cooperate in the one shot Prisoner's Dilemma game or the public goods provision game. During repeated plays, cooperative behavior declines over time but never vanishes as predicted by standard game theory. In the Ultimatum Game or the Dictator Game, people seem to be willing to share the wealth they can take as their own. In many games, some actors take actions to punish those who do not cooperate or have behaved "unfairly" at their own personal costs, contradicting the prediction of conventional models (Kagel and Roth 1995; Rabin 1998; Ostrom 2000).

One response to this evidence has been to rethink the traditional assumption that individuals are essentially "egoists."[2] Various researchers have proposed novel ways of modeling the individual's inherent utility functions and explored their consequences. Rabin (1993), for example, has developed utility functions where individuals value reciprocity—i.e., being kind to those who are kind to them and hurting those who hurt them. Rabin shows how his modified utility function can change the equilibria set of games. For instance, it allows the {cooperate, cooperate} strategy as well as the {defect, defect} strategy to be equilibria in the Prisoner's Dilemma game. More generally, it implies that under suitable parameter values, equilibria will only be either "mutual-min" (the players are mutually mean to each other) or "mutual-max" (the players are kind to each other).

Another example is Akerlof and Kranton's (2000) model of identity in which they adopt the assumption that individuals have inherent utilities attached to their identities. Behaviors of their own or of others that deviate from those prescribed by the identity cause utility loss and create the possibility of retaliation. They show that when it is costly for members of a subgroup to adopt the mainstream identity (e.g., for blacks as a result of the discrimination), equilibria can exist in which some or all members of the subgroup will choose an opposition identity and engage in activities economically detrimental to themselves (e.g., not aggressively seeking educational or work opportunities).

It would be most interesting to investigate whether the Durlauf equation can be adopted as a novel specification of an individual level utility function and to analyze the degree to which it can be used to represent different psychological and sociological models of individual choice. Altruism, for instance, as the inclination for improving others' welfare, cannot

[2]This is, of course, not the only response. Roth (1996), for example, proposes a model that only modifies the assumption of forward-looking rationality but keeps the assumption of self-interested actors.

be directly represented by the Durlauf equation since it is a function only of the actions, not the payoffs, of other players. For the same reason, status competition, defined as the tendency to evaluate one's own payoff by comparing it with those of others, cannot be directly represented by the model either. However reciprocity—i.e., the tendency to return the actions of others—can be represented by the Durlauf functional form. This is similarly true of conformity.

The consequences of adopting such a novel utility function also needs to be explored in both general terms and for specific games and social contexts. Some simple examples illustrate. Suppose we are applying the Durlauf utility function to any two-person symmetric game in the following way: We augment the payoff of each individual in a given cell of the payoff matrix by adding the Durlauf component $S = J(\omega_i - \omega_j)^2$ to his or her original payoff in that cell. We can generally conclude that any equilibrium that occurs on the diagonal of the payoff matrix before the augmenting will be preserved after the augmenting (under the assumption that $J > 0$, of course), since moving away from a diagonal cell will be further penalized after the augmenting. Therefore, {defect, defect} will still be an equilibrium in the Prisoner's Dilemma when individuals are endowed with this particular utility function. Also the equilibria set for the Battle of the Sexes game will be unchanged. Furthermore, any diagonal cell that was not an equilibrium can become one if J is sufficiently large as to offset the loss from moving away from an off diagonal equilibrium. This implies that a cooperative equilibrium can exist in a Prisoner's Dilemma under suitable values of J.

5. STATISTICAL IMPLEMENTATION

We applaud Durlauf's effort to provide a statistical implementation for his model. Too often theoretical models in economics remain just that—theoretical models that are never tested empirically. We are concerned, however, about the robustness of the parameter estimates to different assumptions about functional form. Durlauf points out that his model can be identified based on nonlinearities alone. The implication, however, is that assumptions about the nature of that nonlinearity are likely to lead to potentially quite different parameter estimates. This is something that should be explored through simulation studies. Alternatively, nonparametric estimators for the model should be developed. Obviously, the later course is quite ambitious.

6. CONCLUSION

Durlauf's paper should stimulate sociologists and economists alike to think seriously about the modeling of social interdependence of individual agents. Sociologists may find the notion of modeling the micro-process explicitly prior to carrying out empirical analyses productive. It allows for both better theoretical understanding of the relationship among the variables and of their potential effects on behavior. Economists may find the introduction of sociological perspectives and premises helpful in developing models that can both explain the mounting evidence that evades the conventional models and be applied to a much larger set of social interactions. Innovation along the boundary of sociology and economics is beneficial to both disciplines, and is critical to the development of a "social theory" envisioned by James Coleman (1990), or of a "socioeconomic" theory, as Durlauf calls it.

We have pointed out that Durlauf's model is not explicit about what produces its functional form (social structure or human psychology), and ambiguous about the level at which it positions itself (prior or post to the game structure). Although these ambiguities hinder attempts to justify, test, and apply the model, we see the issue as one of incompleteness rather than of inherent defects in the model. As always, there is more work to be done.

REFERENCES

Akerlof, George A., and Rachel E. Kranton. 2000. "Economics and Identity." *Quarterly Journal of Economics* 115:715–53.

Axelrod, Robert M. 1990. *The Evolution of Cooperation*. New York: Penguin Books.

Coleman, James. 1990. *Foundations of Social Theory*. Cambridge, MA: Harvard University Press.

Heckathorn, Douglas D. 1989. "Collective Action and the Second Order Free-Rider Problem." *Rationality and Society* 1(1): 78–100.

Kagel, John H., and Alvin E. Roth. 1995. *The Handbook of Experimental Economics*. Princeton, NJ: Princeton University Press.

Olson, Mancur. 1965. *The Logic of Collective Action; Public Goods and the Theory of Groups*. Cambridge, MA., Harvard University Press.

Ostrom, Elinor. 2000. "Collective Action and the Evolution of Social Norms." *Journal of Economic Perspectives* 14(3):137–58.

Rabin, Matthew. 1993. "Incorporating Fairness into Game Theory and Economics." *American Economic Review* 83:1281–302.

———. 1998. "Psychology and Economics." *Journal of Economic Literature* 36:11–46.

Roth, Alvin E. 1996. "Adaptive Behavior and Strategic Rationality: Evidence from the Laboratory and the Field." Pp. 255–73 in *The Rational Foundations of Economic Behavior: Proceedings of the IEA Conference Held in Turin, Italy*, edited by Kenneth J. Arrow et al. New York: St. Martin's Press.

Young, Peyton H. 1996. "The Economics of Convention." *Journal of Economic Perspectives* 10:105–22.

———. 1998. *Individual Strategy and Social Structure*. Princeton, NJ: Princeton University Press.

COMMENT: POTENTIAL APPLICATIONS AND EXTENSIONS FOR A BINARY CHOICE-BASED SOCIAL INTERACTION FRAMEWORK

*Aimée R. Dechter**

1. INTRODUCTION

Steven N. Durlauf describes a general binary-choice (response) based framework for studying social interactions that he developed with William A. Brock (Brock and Durlauf, 2001, forthcoming). Grounded in economic theory, this framework formalizes the influences of social structure in decision processes through individual preferences, which embody feelings about the choice in isolation and in relation to what is "known" (or believed) about the choices made by others. The statistical model is embedded in the theoretical framework and as such adds much needed analytic clarity. The framework has several useful features that allow for a description of the whole system, not just individual behavior. Its representation of what social influences are may be simplistic but that is a tradeoff for greater generality that makes the framework applicable to diverse areas and broad theories, and more importantly, permits it to encompass ostensibly dissimilar processes and structures. The framework provides the foundation from which others can elaborate and add specificity, and it provides the basis for theoretically informed empirical analyses that bear on longstanding debates in the social sciences and have practical significance for public policy. In this discussion I will (1) review selected features of the framework that may be particularly useful in sociology; (2) identify areas in sociology and demography where this framework may serve as the basis

I wish to acknowledge valuable discussions with Steven Durlauf, Michael Sobel, and Lawrence Wu. Preparation of this comment was partially supported with funding from the National Institute of Child Health and Human Development (HD 29550), and the Graduate School of the University of Wisconsin. Thanks go to John Carlson and Janet Clear for support from the library and administrative cores of the Center for Demography and Ecology, which receives core support from the National Institute of Child Health and Human Development (P30 HD05876).

*University of Wisconsin–Madison

for the development and testing of more powerful models and theories; and (3) discuss areas in which the framework can be extended.

2. SELECTED FEATURES OF THE FRAMEWORK

2.1. *Identification*

The framework resolves an important identification problem that arises in social interaction models. The ability to identify two distinct sources of social influence, so called "contextual effects," which operate through "fixed" characteristics of the reference group, and "endogenous effects," which generate feedback and social multipliers, is an important development.[1,2]

Further developments are needed to be able to identify the numerous sources of influence that can be classified into these two categories. The "contextual effects" include socialization (e.g., through role models or through the group's sanctions, stigmatization, and support of behaviors) to promote certain behaviors and diffusion of other information relevant to the behaviors. The "endogenous effects" include (1) diffusion of information about behavior (e.g., learning from others about the existence of the behaviors and how to conduct them); (2) learning from others (e.g., learning from the experiences of others and using this information to form expectations about the consequences of the behavior); and (3) social influences transmitted by internal desires (e.g., identity) to conform to or devi-

[1]Durlauf, like Manski (1995), Blalock (1984) and others, uses the term "endogenous effects" to describe the reinforcing relationship between group behaviors and individual behaviors. This usage can be traced back to Erbring and Young (1979). The term "contextual effects" has been used loosely in sociology, as Manski (1995, 2000) points out.

[2]Manski's 1995 results regarding the inability to identify the disparate effects of social interaction are for the linear-in-means framework. Durlauf demonstrates that there can be identification in this model if some combination of the contextual variables are known a priori to be linearly independent of the individual characteristics. Moreover, Brock and Durlauf (forthcoming) point out that correcting for the *individual level* self-selection mechanisms into the social contexts could facilitate identification by creating the type of nonlinearity/exclusion restrictions that allow for identification. Basically, the self-selection "correction" functions as an individual variable whose group average is not a contextual effect. Sociological perspectives can be useful to identify characteristics that are not expected to operate at both the individual and contextual level, and to identify measured variables that affect the selection into the social context but do not affect the behavioral outcome.

ate from the behavior of others and social norms.[3] Relatedly, the framework does not formalize how individuals and others communicate with each other to transmit these influences and as such there is no safeguard against interpreting the transmission of these social influences in implausible ways such as "social telepathy" (Erbring and Young, 1979).

2.2. *Payoff Function*

One important innovation of this framework is that social utility is introduced in the payoff function (i.e., the ordering of preferences), unlike earlier approaches which restrict the payoff function to private utility. The assumption in equation (12) that the components of the payoff function $V(\omega_i, X_i, Y_g, \mu_i(\underset{\sim}{\omega}|F_i), \epsilon_i)$ are additive does not imply that the three components—(1) private deterministic utility, $u(\omega_i, X_i, Y_g)$; (2) social deterministic utility, $S(\omega_i, X_i, Y_g, \mu_i(\underset{\sim}{\omega}|F_i))$; and (3) private random utility, $\epsilon_i(\omega_i)$—are in turn linear functions of their own respective components, ω_i (choice i); X_i (characteristics of individual i); Y_g, (characteristics of individual i's reference group); and $\mu_i(\underset{\sim}{\omega}|F_i)$ (beliefs about the choices of others conditional on information F_i).

Private deterministic utility is a function of individual and group characteristics that do not likely contribute to utility in a linear fashion. For example, in a neighborhood with high labor force participation, the influences of role models on a teenager whose parent is unemployed may differ from the influences on a teenager whose parent is employed. Similarly, living in a predominantly white (or African-American) neighborhood has different implications for an African-American child than a white child. More detailed specifications for private utility would be helpful to understand what parameters would allow the modeler to interpret the differences in the influences (i.e., when all permutations of $Y_g \times X_i$ vary freely).

Social utility is assumed to have the following functional form in equation (13):

$$S(\omega_i, X_i, Y_g, \mu_i(\underset{\sim}{\omega}|F_i)) = -\sum_{j \neq i} \frac{J_{i,j}}{2} (\omega_i - E_i(\omega_j|F_i))^2,$$

[3]Manski (2000) refers to the second and third forms as "expectations interactions" and "preference interactions," respectively. He provides a detailed discussion of the importance of identifying these two sources of influence individually for public policy.

where $E_i(\omega_j | F_i)$ denotes the subjective expected value that individual i assigns to the choice of individual j given i's information set F_i, for each individual member, i, of the reference group. The squared difference between individual i's choice and the expected choice for individual j (i.e., $\omega_i - E_i(\omega_j | F_i)$) is multiplied by parameter $J_{i,j}$, the bilateral interaction between members i and j of the reference group. This parameter represents how the individual feels about the behavior of others (i.e., a positive sign signifies that individual i prefers to make the same choice as he believes will be made by individual j in his reference group, and a negative sign signifies that i prefers to make a different choice). The social interaction models developed by Granovetter (1978) and Granovetter and Soong (1988) imply that social utility for an individual may be responsive only at some threshold (i.e., the number or proportion of the reference group that individual i believes have chosen the behavior). This suggests perhaps using a step function rather than a summation across individuals for the functional form, or incorporating the (subjective expected) prevalence of that choice into the bilateral interaction parameter. In general, the bilateral interaction parameter has the potential to build in flexibility into the framework. For example, social utility can vary with characteristics of the individual and the context by making the $J_{i,j}$'s a function of X_i and Y_g and differences between them. In theory the parameter could capture heterogeneity within the reference group with respect to the strength of ties (or identification with the group), hierarchies of positions (e.g., leaders) and sensitivity to reference group comparisons (e.g., some individuals may have cognitive constraints on behavior as a result of earlier indoctrination); however this information is rarely if ever measured.

It is critical to evaluate the empirical implications of choosing different sets of the bilateral interaction parameters. Generally, data collection efforts can help to reduce the number of parameters that need to be estimated parametrically. Further work is also needed to devise tests to evaluate the reasonableness and robustness of the assumptions made about these parameters. One strategy might be to evaluate the fit of the model under different sets of the parameters. These tests might also be useful for evaluating hypotheses that are characterized by these parameters.

2.3. *Formation of Subjective Beliefs*

Both Durlauf and Manski (1995) discuss the controversies surrounding the assumption of rational expectations, so I will comment only on the assumption that "each individual possesses an identical information set F from which he forms beliefs about the choices of others in the population." This assumption that beliefs are not formed conditionally on the characteristics of the individual forming the expectation may not be realistic because individual characteristics may determine how much information an individual knows about his reference group. For example, those with more education may be more informed than those with less education. In the presence of heterogeneity of social ties within a reference group, those loosely tied to the group may have less information about the group than those in the center of the group. Moreover, conditional on the information known, individuals may form beliefs differently depending on their characteristics or those of the group. A goal of data collection should be to assess these assumptions by eliciting as much information as possible from survey respondents about what they know about their reference group and how they use that information to make decisions (Manski 1995; Dominitz and Manski 1997).

2.4. *Multiple Equilibria*

The standard neoclassical model defines a single equilibrium, whereas this framework, by identifying multiple equilibria, allows for richer scenarios and insights. For example, the existence of multiple equilibria explains how inferior equilibria appear (e.g., persistent inter-generational inequality and poverty traps) and how individually rational decisions can be collectively undesirable. In terms of leverage for policy implications, poverty-related studies have found that changes at the margin often do not make a significant difference in outcomes; however, this may be because the values are close to equilibrium, whereas a large shock might be able to move the equilibrium to another one (e.g., from an inferior to an optimal one). One concern is how to recognize whether there really is an equilibrium or just shocks moving toward an equilibrium, especially for changing phenomena.

3. STATISTICAL MODELS

In contrast to Durlauf's statistical models which are grounded in (economic) theory, much of the empirical research on social context in sociology and demography have relied on conventional regression techniques and hazard models that are not linked to the theoretical model. Others have attempted to deal with some of the problems described by Blalock (1984), and DiPrete and Forristal (1994) by estimating what is often referred to as hierarchical or multilevel models, which are more appropriate than conventional regression models because they take into account the nested structure of the data, and acknowledge the covariance in the error terms of individuals in the same class (e.g., reference group or cluster). However, the reason that social ties influence behavior is left unspecified. Durlauf's models are conceptually different because of how the group characteristics and beliefs about the group's behaviors are incorporated into social utility. Moreover, if the multilevel models do not take into account social feedback mechanisms when they exist, the parameter estimates will not be consistent.

4. POTENTIAL APPLICATIONS IN SOCIOLOGY AND DEMOGRAPHY

Sociologists have long recognized that even when individual actors (people, firms, etc.) interact with markets and other institutions, these interactions can also be affected by social ties (Granovetter 1985; Coleman et al. 1957; Coleman 1988). However, few have taken the next step of formally modeling these processes. The exceptions, which include threshold models introduced by Granovetter (1978) and Granovetter and Soong (1988), endogenous feedback models advanced by Erbring and Young (1979), and diffusion models described by Strang (1991), have generated rich and complex hypotheses. They do not, however, derive from a general framework such as Durlauf's, and the statistical procedures for implementing these models are less well developed and not embedded in the theoretical model.[4]

Notwithstanding vigorous warnings by Hauser (1969, 1970, and 1974) more than 30 years ago about interpreting statistical associations between aggregate measures and individual outcomes as contextual effects, the empirical literature on social structure continues to suffer from underconceptualized analyses and loose interpretations, partially because of the gap between the theoretical frameworks and statistical models.[5] This gap is of particular concern in the poverty and education literatures, where empirical findings are often contradictory, resulting in

[4] Palloni (forthcoming) provides an in-depth review and critique of formal diffusion models.

[5] For example, inferences are drawn about neighborhood and school "effects" in models that do not incorporate feedback or allow for the identification of contextual and endogenous "effects." In some cases, coefficients for contextual characteristics are interpreted as "endogenous effects" (Manski 1995).

conflicting policy implications. Obviously there is great interest in understanding the relationship between social and school context and disadvantage, and the relationship between context and the behaviors that lead to further disadvantage. Unfortunately, as Jencks and Mayer (1990) point out, the debates often turn on unspecified assumptions and devolve into the ideological because of the difficulties in distinguishing empirically between hypotheses. As a result, empirical analyses have not made much headway in interpreting the behavioral outcomes of these social processes.

Further developments, such as those found in the framework presented by Durlauf, are needed to help narrow the gap between the theoretical discourse and the ability of empirical research to discern among competing hypotheses and explanations. Explanations for social change, secular trends, and other global phenomena are often construed as debates over two or more competing paradigms, one being cultural or social and the other structural or economic. The framework presented by Durlauf can help reconcile these debates because it is general and the statistical models are part of the theoretical framework. The framework allows for the effects of social relations to be fully consistent with a decision-making framework (by including social utility in the payoff function), thereby providing a common structure and methodology from which to evaluate each of these seemingly competing sets of hypotheses.

An example of a debate polarized in this way is the controversy surrounding the roles of diffusion, culture, and structural factors (e.g., economic development) in demographic transitions, and fertility differentials more generally.[6] To some extent the opposition between these two paradigms reflects incomplete frameworks (see Palloni forthcoming for a detailed review). Moreover, the empirical evidence regarding diffusion is often based not on direct measures but rather on the residual variation not explained by structural and economic factors. The potential for the framework to reconcile this debate is demonstrated by Durlauf and Walker (1998). They establish that the presence in the framework of social multipliers allows for modest economic development to lead to significant changes in fertility under conditions of strong social utility. As a result, diffusion and structural explanations can be mutually reinforcing, rather than competing explanations. The applications of this framework for behaviors related to contraception in particular are numerous, especially

[6] Diffusion theories are consistent with the empirical findings from the Princeton European fertility project that revealed historical geographic patterns of fertility decline that mirrored ethnic, language, and religious boundaries (two of these studies include Lesthaeghe 1977; Coale and Watkins 1986).

for explaining ethnic and geographic differences. Entwisle et al. (1996) find evidence that social interaction is important for contraceptive choice and may explain variation in the dominance of methods across villages in a rural district in Thailand. Bumpass et al. (2000) provide a persuasive social interaction hypothesis for the widely known but poorly understood dramatic ethnic differences in the prevalence of vasectomy in the United States, which they attribute to, among other explanations, ethnic differences in access to information about vasectomy resulting from differential contact with the medical system. These differences may account for the ethnic differences in the (mis)perceptions about the safety and consequences of vasectomy.[7] Even small ethnic differentials in social networks and contacts with the medical system could lead to large differentials because of the diffusion of information (or misinformation) across segregated social networks.

The framework can be applied to study the roles of networks and social ties for assorted other behaviors (e.g., migration, labor force outcomes, occupational and social closure, collective action). For example, it is consistent with the position taken by Marwell et al. (1988) that individuals know about and are influenced by the behavior of others in their reference group "and when interdependence is considered, individuals can find it "rational" to participate in collective action." The framework can also be useful for studying the spread of behavioral strategies across communities, college campuses, organizations, and firms, including the social interaction processes (e.g., recruitment through social networks, etc.) that have been used to describe participation in antiwar protests on college campuses in the United States, in the civil rights movement and in numerous other collective actions (e.g., McAdam 1988).

The theoretical framework may not be appropriate for contagion processes where other actors or nature have such great influence over outcomes that it would be awkward to assume that the effect of the outcome's prevalence in the population on an individual is mediated through a payoff function or that the contagion is transmitted through subjective beliefs. This does not imply that individuals are passive in these processes. On the contrary, decisions made regarding one's own behaviors and practices (e.g., unprotected sexual intercourse, installing alarms, and other health and safety related behaviors) that affect the outcome (e.g.,

[7] African Americans were much more likely to believe that vasectomy would impair a man's sexual ability (Bumpass et al., 2000:p. 34).

the transmission of disease, victimization) may be influenced by subjective beliefs about both the prevalence of the "contagion" in the population and the effects of those behaviors and practices on vulnerability to the contagion. Nevertheless, it may not be appropriate to characterize such outcomes as choices if the element of choice derives only from choices made regarding "right-hand side" variables, X_i.

5. REFERENCE GROUPS

5.1. *Identification and Formation of Reference Groups*

The framework is undertheorized with respect to the formation of reference groups and does not explicitly incorporate the process of reference group formation into the models. Other than social networks, perhaps, which may be observed, much of the literature relies on functional definitions of reference groups (e.g., it is a group from which individuals learn or are influenced through the behaviors and attitudes of the group's members); however, if a reference group can only be recognized when it influences, how does one test whether a particular behavior is influenced by social interaction?[8] The framework provides no means of verifying that the reference group (social world) is appropriate, other than perhaps estimating the models repeatedly with different reference groups and selecting the unit that seems to have the greatest effect. This imposes excessive data requirements and would appear to be tautological as well as burdensome.

It is well known that defining and identifying appropriate reference groups are looming conceptual and measurement problems. One reason is that social influences usually are not fixed in well-defined boundaries but often act on a continuum, whereas analyses require a discrete unit of analysis to measure characteristics and behaviors (Iversen 1991). No matter what the cutoff point is, there will be qualitative differences in the

[8] Portes and Sensenbrenner (1993) discuss the problem of instrumental-oriented definitions of social structure and specifically for the concept of social capital. A functional definition of reference groups is less troubling when the objective is to estimate a correctly specified model, and reference group characteristics are included only to serve as controls in order to measure individual-level associations between individual behaviors and individual-level characteristics. It may also be less problematic when the focus of the analysis is whether a specified collective is influencing behavior rather than on the question of whether a particular behavior is influenced by social interactions. The former may be of interest for policy research because spatial units or organizations may be regulated to some degree.

nature and closeness of the ties within the group. Another reason is that it is unclear what is meant by a community or network, especially because the boundaries are heterogeneous across individuals. Technology (e.g., the Internet) has complicated these issues even further by expanding the modes and nature of communication. Current characteristics and behaviors of reference groups may matter, as well as past characteristics and behaviors of earlier reference groups (i.e., lagged "effects"). A useful extension of the framework would be to handle lagged contexts and multiple levels of reference groups that may or may not be overlapping.

5.2. *Selection into Reference Groups*

People with whom one circulates are not randomly assigned and are systematically associated with individual characteristics and behaviors, both observed and unobserved. One of the major weaknesses of the empirical analyses of social context in the sociology literature is that they rarely acknowledge that individuals endogenously sort themselves into groups. The sorting may even be motivated by the individual's expectations about the effects of the group's characteristics and behaviors. Standard estimation techniques that ignore this selectivity may produce inconsistent estimates of contextual influences. Brock and Durlauf (forthcoming) demonstrate how the social interaction linear-in-means models can deal with self-selection into social groups and contexts. Experiments (e.g., the Moving to Opportunity demonstration, Gautreaux demonstration) have been implemented to try to address this problem. Natural experiments that might result in exogenous changes in reference groups include natural disasters (e.g., floods, earthquakes), and firm relocation. School redistricting may also provide the opportunity to study school effects; however, this may still be endogenous due to constituent pressure. Further developments in the framework should incorporate reference group selection, given some strong theoretical foundation.

6. IDENTITY

Durlauf's paper and many discussions of social interaction gloss over how identity and self-regulation allow for the influence of reference groups. Identity affects choices about behavior because of the desire for "self-realization"; however, identity permeates the social interaction process as well. Membership in a reference group not only reflects but may also reinforce or challenge an individual's sense of identity, and because of that reference groups' characteristics influence individual behavior by influencing one's sense of identity. Identity is not static since it is influenced by one's own beliefs and behaviors and those of others with whom one identifies. For this reason reference group formation should be treated as a dynamic process. Craig Calhoun (1991) provides an eloquent description of the impact that the 1989 Democracy movement in China had on him: "When *I* stood on Tiananmen Square in the evening of June 3, I felt a rush of adrenaline at early stages of the fighting, a macho impulse to be where the action was." Calhoun goes on to describe the actions of Chinese students in June who "were brave enough to risk death (but) who a month before had not been brave enough to be publicly identified with the boycott of classes." Prudent considerations won out, Calhoun argues, because his identity as a father and husband prevailed; however, he acknowledges that as the movement progressed, he identified more and more with the students. His experience demonstrates both the importance of social interaction for collective action, and how identities are responsive to both individual and collective behavior.

In Granovetter and Soong's (1988) threshold theory as well as in other theories in sociology, the composition of the reference group who have made the choice influences the susceptibility of the individual. The importance of identification with those who have chosen the behavior is supported by ethnographic research (e.g., Louie's 2001 study of immigrant workers demonstrates the importance of organizing union membership through ethnic associations because of identity). Identity may be incorporated into the theoretical framework in several ways. Specification of the bilateral interaction parameters, J_{ij}, can characterize differentials in influence across individuals in the reference group. The J_{ij}'s could in principle be specified as a function of differences between the characteristics of individuals i and j so that the interactions vary with the characteristics of the individual j with whom individual i is comparing himself. Of course this might be impossible due to data limitations on all individuals in the reference group and what may be most important is not a specific member of the reference group but rather some threshold number of members in the reference group with the same characteristics. Another extension of the framework could distinguish between the group characteristics of those who have (or who are believed to have) experienced the outcome, (e.g., $Y_{g|\omega=1}$) from those who have not (or who are believed to not have) experienced the outcome (e.g., $Y_{g|\omega=0}$). Another strategy is to stratify the reference group and "endogenous effect" by certain characteristics to reflect different degrees of influence (e.g., $Y_{g1}, Y_{g2}, \ldots, Y_{gn}$).

7. OTHER AREAS FOR FURTHER DEVELOPMENT

7.1. *Conceptualization of Influences*

There does not seem to be a strong theoretical motivation for using aggregate means, which could be masking huge amounts of variation, to represent social interaction influences. Extensions of the model might consider other group measures representing the distribution of characteristics (e.g., percentiles, variance, etc.).

7.2. *Dynamic Framework*

The binary choice-based framework is one approach chosen for convenience; however, a dynamic approach might be closer to actual behavior. A useful extension would be to develop a hazard-based framework (e.g., see Strang 1991) to specify individual and aggregate characteristics and behaviors as time-varying covariates and their relationships to the outcome as time dependent because characteristics of individuals change over time as do the characteristics and behaviors of the social context. Moreover, individuals move and are associated with different reference groups over time, and different contexts could influence behaviors at different times and have cumulative effects. A hazard-based framework would allow one to model the emergence of social phenomena at the beginning before some behavior or social context characteristic becomes prevalent in the reference group. This kind of framework would be particularly important for processes that change with the prevalence of the behavior or characteristics in the population. Of course the functional forms and assumptions in the static framework have resulted in appealing properties that may be lost with other specifications.

Characteristics of the individual and the reference group may change over time because of the social interaction process itself. For example, the process may have a direct impact on behavior and an indirect effect by altering individual characteristics and group characteristics making it difficult to identify "endogenous effects." In the presence of unmeasured heterogeneity, the composition of the reference group still at risk of the behavior may increasingly become composed of individuals with greater resistance. This may bias the parameters associated with the contextual and "endogenous effects" as well as the individual-level parameter estimates, clearly affecting aggregate patterns.

7.3. *Endogenous and Simultaneous Systems*

Many applications of this framework will involve explanatory variables that are jointly determined with the choice being modeled (e.g., teenage childbearing and dropping out of school) or suffer from omitted variable biases. It will be useful to add additional structure to the framework to deal with these problems; however, in the presence of feedback this will be complicated. If this poses too great a burden on the statistical estimation, it is unclear whether the priority should be to address these problems or deal with the social interaction feedback.

A variant on these problems is the presence of more than one endogenous macro-level variable. For example, a social interaction model of condom use would include beliefs about the prevalence of condom use in the reference group (actual prevalence would also be relevant if both partners are in the group), and also beliefs about the prevalence of sexually transmitted diseases (STDs). However, the prevalence of STDs is in turn a function of the prevalence of condom use. Other examples include the free-rider problem in vaccinations[9] and social interaction models of smoking and (beliefs about) the prevalence of smoking-related diseases.

8. CONCLUSION

The framework presented in this paper melds together theories about individual-level behavior with theories about social change and macro processes. Bringing macro-micro interdependencies into questions about individual behavior and about larger phenomena is important but daunting because it requires thinking about seemingly everything simultaneously. I think the theoretical framework provides a foundation to do this. It is not a remedy for all the difficulties inherent in modeling social context, many of which have been described by Hauser (1969, 1970, 1974), Blalock (1984), Iversen (1991), DiPrete and Forristal (1994), Manski (1995), and others, nor does it fully capture the complexity of social interactions and relations. Perhaps its greatest weaknesses are the under-theorization of both reference groups and the mechanisms through which so-called "contextual effects" and "endogenous effects" operate. Despite these and

[9]Prevalence of a disease may be low as a consequence of a high uptake of vaccinations in the population; however, free-riders will perceive their risks of contracting the disease to be low and will therefore be less likely to get vaccinated, which through feedback may both directly lower the likelihood of vaccinations for others on the one hand and increase the likelihood of contracting the disease, which in turn would raise the likelihood of vaccinations of others.

other drawbacks, this framework represents a significant advance in many dimensions. The development of a model that addresses endogenous feedback was one of the directions for future research called for in DiPrete and Forristal's 1994 review of multilevel models. The correspondence between the theoretical and statistical framework presented in this paper provides the rigor lacking in empirical research on social interactions. The innovations drawn from statistical mechanics provide powerful tools for interpreting observed patterns of behaviors and for understanding the implications of public policies and other external shocks, vis-à-vis social interactions. In short, Durlauf has presented an innovative and practical theoretical and statistical framework with many applications, and with great potential for further development.

REFERENCES

Blalock, Hubert. 1984. "Contextual-Effects Models: Theoretical and Methodological Issues." *Annual Review of Sociology* 10:353–72.

Brock, William A., and Steven N. Durlauf. 2001. "Discrete Choice with Social Interactions," *Review of Economic Studies* 68:235–60.

———. Forthcoming. "Interactions-Based Models." In *Handbook of Econometrics*. Vol. 5, edited by J. Heckman and E. Leamer. Amsterdam: North-Holland.

Bumpass, Larry, Elizabeth Thomson, and Amy L. Godecker. 2000. "Women, Men, and Contraceptive Sterilization." *Fertility and Sterility* 73:937–46.

Calhoun, Craig. 1991. "The Problem of Identity in Collective Action." Pp. 51–75. In *Macro-Micro Linkages in Sociology*, edited by J. Huber. Newbury Park, CA: Sage.

Coale, Ansley J., and Susan C. Watkins. 1986. *The Decline of Fertility in Europe*, Princeton, NJ: Princeton University Press.

Coleman, James, Elihu Katz, and Herbert Menzel. 1957. "The Diffusion of an Innovation Among Physicians." *Sociometry* 20:253–70.

Coleman, James S. 1988. "Social Capital in the Creation of Human Capital (in Sociological Analysis of Economic Institutions)." *American Journal of Sociology* 94: S95–120

DiPrete, Thomas A., and Jerry D. Forristal. 1994. "Multilevel Models: Methods and Substance." *Annual Review of Sociology* 20:331–57.

Dominitz, Jeff, and Charles F. Manski. 1997. "Using Expectations Data to Study Subjective Income Expectations." *Journal of the American Statistical Association Applications and Case Studies*, 92:855–67.

Durlauf, Steven N., and James R. Walker. 1998. "Social Interactions and Fertility Transitions." Presented at the workshop on "Social Processes Underlying Fertility Change in Developing Countries," January 29–30, 1998, organized by the Committee on Population, National Research Council, Washington, D.C.

Entwisle, Barbara, Ronald R. Rindfuss, David K. Guilkey, Aphichat Chamratrithirong, Sara R. Curran, and Yothin Sawangdee. 1996. "Community and Contraceptive Choice in Rural Thailand: A Case Study of Nan Rong." *Demography* 33:1–11.

Erbring, Lutz, and Alice A. Young. 1979. "Individuals and Social Structure: Contextual Effects as Endogenous Feedback." *Sociological Methods and Research* 7:396–430.

Granovetter, Mark S. 1978. "Threshold Models of Collective Behavior." *American Journal of Sociology* 83:1420–43.

———. 1985. "Economic Action, Social Structure, and Embeddedness." *American Journal of Sociology* 91:481–510.

Granovetter, Mark S., and Roland Soong. 1988. "Threshold Models of Diversity: Chinese Restaurants, Residential Segregation, and the Spiral of Silence." *Sociological Methodology* 18:69–104.

Hauser, Robert M. 1969. "Context and Consex: A Cautionary Tale." *American Journal of Sociology* 75:645–64.

———. 1970. "Hauser Replies." *American Journal of Sociology* 76:514–20.

———. 1974. "Contextual Analysis Revisited." *Sociological Methods and Research* 2:365–75.

Iversen, Gudmund R. 1991. *Contextual Analysis*. Newbury Park, CA: Sage.

Jencks, Christopher, and Susan E. Mayer. 1990. "The Social Consequences of Growing Up in a Poor Neighborhood." Pp.111–86 in *Inner-City Poverty in the United States*, edited by Laurence E. Lynn, Jr., and Michael G.H. McGeary. Washington, D.C.: National Academy Press.

Lesthaeghe, Ron J. 1977. *The Decline of Belgian Fertility, 1800–1970*. Princeton, NJ: Princeton University Press.

Louie, Miriam Ching Yoon. 2001. *Sweatshop Warriors: Immigrant Women Workers Take on the Global Factory*. Boston, MA: South End Press

Manski, Charles F. 1995. *Identification Problems in the Social Sciences*. Cambridge, MA: Harvard University Press.

———. 2000. "Economic Analysis of Social Interactions,"*Journal of Economic Perspectives*, 14:115–36.

Marwell Gerald, Pamela E. Oliver, and Ralph Prahl. 1988. "Social Networks and Collective Action: A Theory of the Critical Mass, III." *American Journal of Sociology* 94:502–34 .

McAdam Doug. 1988. *Freedom Summer*. New York: Oxford University Press.

Mouw, Ted, and Barbara Entwisle. 2001. "A Country of Strangers? The Effect of Social Class, Residential Proximity, and Mutual Activities on Multi-Racial Social Segregating in Schools." Presented at the Annual Meeting of the Population Association of America, Washington, DC.

Palloni, Alberto. Forthcoming. "Diffusion in Sociological Analysis: How Useful Is It for the Study of Fertility and Mortality?" In *Social Processes Underlying Fertility Changes in Developing Countries*, edited by J. Casterline and B. Cohen. National Research Council Press.

Portes, Alejandro, and Julia Sensenbrenner 1993. "Embeddedness and Immigration: Notes on the Social Determinations of Economic Action." *American Journal of Sociology* 98:1320–50.

Strang, David 1991. "Adding Social Structure to Diffusion Models: An Event History Framework." *Sociological Methods and Research* 19:324–53.

REJOINDER: DISCUSSIONS OF "A FRAMEWORK FOR THE STUDY OF INDIVIDUAL BEHAVIOR AND SOCIAL INTERACTIONS"

Steven N. Durlauf

I thank my discussants for a set of interesting comments that will certainly be valuable to me in pursuing future work on social interactions.

RESPONSE TO BOWLES

As is usual, Samuel Bowles has made some very insightful comments and given me much to think about. His discussion brings up a nice example where the sort of framework I describe may not be all that useful. Specifically, he argues that if one wants to understand the evolution of unionization, an individual-level explanation of the type I developed in "A Framework . . ." would seem to be inadequate. The reason for this is that unionization seems to be intrinsically linked to class as well as to individual relationships. So, while one might argue that the attractiveness of union membership depends on whether coworkers are also union members (for reasons such as bargaining power), this is clearly only one part of the story since unions are agents of collective action.

I fully agree with this criticism and think the union example nicely illustrates where models of the type I examine need better development. Put more generally, once one argues that individual decisions are interdependent, it is natural to ask what sorts of institutions, norms, etc., arise in response to these interdependences. Unions arise as ways to coordinate bargaining and deal with the interdependencies induced when workers can act as substitutes. For the contexts I discuss, neighborhood effects help explain how neighborhood compositions evolve, as families face incentives to choose communities on the basis of their neighbors. A complete theory of social interactions needs to account for the evolution of higher order structures in addition to the ones on which I focus.

Bowles also points out that the rationality assumption I impose on individuals is problematic. This point is well taken; it is no exaggeration to say that much of the interesting recent work on microeconomics has involved efforts to move beyond rational expectations assumptions of the type I employ. As Aimée Dechter points out in her discussion, ongoing work by Charles Manski suggests ways in which subjective expectations can be captured from survey data; this seems a very important research program. I am personally less sympathetic to Bowles's other concern that the model does not embody any mechanism for preferences to evolve. For the time scales for which I envision a model like this to operate, I believe that changes in preferences can be reduced to allowing the values of the X_i's and $Y_{n(i)}$'s to vary across time. At a minimum, Bowles' criticism needs to be put in a specific context to assess its force.

RESPONSE TO TAO AND WINSHIP

Lin Tao and Christopher Winship provide the most critical of the three discussions and question both some aspects of the theory as well as the statistical implementation of the model. I will review their concerns and indicate where I agree and where their remarks are unpersuasive or incorrect.

The first issue raised by Tao and Winship concerns the interpretation of the social utility term. They correctly point out that social interdependences can be intrinsic in that my utility depends, presumably for psychological reasons, on the choices others make. Alternatively, interdependences can arise for "structurally induced" reasons. One example of this would be the dependence of one person's choices on the choices of others because of the information content in the choices. So, for example, if others repeatedly make a particular choice, I may infer the choice is relatively better for me as well, assuming similar preferences, constraints, etc. Tao and Winship assert that the paper is ambiguous on how to interpret the social utility term. This claim is a fair one, in the sense that in our work William Brock and I have treated conformity effects as a primitive in the payoff functions and not as something that occurs as an equilibrium consequence of an agent's relationships to others. In our development of these models, Brock and I have favored the psychological or intrinsic interpretation. Specifically, we have argued that evidence ranging from ethnography to social psychology to linguistics is consistent with a role for intrinsic conformity effects in influencing individual behavior. So, to the extent that the nature of the social interactions we model needs to be explicated, it is most appropriate to regard the conformity effects we model as a psychological primitive.

However, the subsequent discussion of intrinsic versus structural interpretations of social utility is rather misguided and in some respects incorrect. One problem is the failure of Tao and Winship to provide any substantive reasons to worry about the lack of attention to the distinction between intrinsic and structural explanations for the applications I envision for the model. (For this reason, Aimée Dechter's discussion is much more persuasive on the related points.) When I propose conformity effects as a way to explain community differences in out-of-wedlock births, it seems of little consequence whether the functional form used to describe this can or cannot also capture Prisoner's Dilemma–type payoffs.

Further, Tao and Winship make some conceptual mistakes in their efforts to contrast my model with various 2×2 games that they assert are "structural" forms of interactions. The reason for these mistakes is that Tao and Winship assume that the specification of the payoff matrix for a given game is equivalent to specifying the game. In fact, the payoff matrices in Prisoner's Dilemma games and the like are themselves black boxes in the sense that they do not emerge from some deeper micro-level description of how individuals interact. Put differently, the payoff functions in these games are assumed in exactly the same way that the generalized conformity effect is assumed in my model. To treat the payoff matrices of games as structural rather than intrinsic is to misunderstand the nature of such games. What game theory teaches us, contrary to Tao and Winship's misstatement on this issue, is that the observed play for a given payoff structure depends on the structure of the game—that is, how agents form beliefs, whether they will interact repeatedly, etc.

In contrast to the ill-posed games that Tao and Winship present, the model in "A Framework . . ." is very standard from the perspective of game theory. The model I present uses an expectational form of the one-shot Nash equilibrium concept: Agents make choices on the basis of their beliefs about others'choices, agents only interact once, and these beliefs are required to be self-consistent in the sense that these beliefs are rational. These seem like reasonable assumptions given the noncooperative environments I wish to study.

Independent of their misinterpretations, Tao and Winship raise an interesting issue by exploring the question of what sort of payoff matrices for 2×2 games can be captured by the generalized conformity effect and identify some standard payoff matrices that cannot be placed in the framework I develop. There is a simple reason why this happens in Tao and Winship's examples: the generalized conformity effect embodies certain types of symmetry that are inconsistent with the logic of games such as the Prisoner's Dilemma. In my framework, agent i's dependence on j depends only on whether the two of them make similar or different choices, not on which particular choices make them so. In other words, $J_{i,j}$ weights $(\omega_i - \omega_j)^2$ regardless of what values these take on. In the Prisoner's Dilemma, in contrast, agent i receives a very different payoff if he confesses and j does not, as opposed to the case where j confesses and i does not.

In fact, there is a simple way to extend the social utility functions I work with to account for such asymmetries—namely, by replacing J with J_+ and J_-, which depend on agent i's choice. This allows social utility to differ according to whether agent i chooses $+1$ or -1. To see how this allows my general framework to incorporate the Prisoner's Dilemma, notice that the calculations by Tao and Winship are now

$$u(1) - \frac{J_+}{2}(1-1)^2 = 5$$

$$u(1) - \frac{J_+}{2}(1+1)^2 = -10$$

$$u(-1) - \frac{J_-}{2}(-1-1)^2 = 10$$

$$u(-1) - \frac{J_-}{2}(-1+1)^2 = 0.$$

It is easy to verify that these constraints imply $J_+ = -7.5$ and $J_- = 5$. (Notice that arbitrary 2×2 games can now be mapped into my payoff function since, as the Prisoner's Dilemma example illustrates, introducing separate parameters J_+ and J_- in essence changes the number of unknowns in the four equations that map my payoff function into the 2×2 game's payoff matrix from 3 to 4.) Brock and Durlauf (2001) explore this type of asymmetry in the social utility function. Perhaps not surprisingly, this generalization is somewhat difficult to study analytically although some results are obtained there.

Finally, Tao and Winship also express concern over the analysis of statistical identification in the paper. They point out that for the binary choice model of social interactions, the identification theorem is parametric, in the sense that the analysis is developed under the assumption that the difference in the model's random utility terms is logistically distributed. This point is well taken (although to be fair, the identification conditions are relevant to most of the extant papers that model binary choice with neighborhood effects) and I am currently exploring identification in semiparametric environments.

At the same time, Tao and Winship's concern needs to be placed in context. As Brock and Durlauf (forthcoming) show, there is nothing special about the logistic assumption per se; parametric duration data models are also identified for the same reasons as the binary choice model. So, at best, their criticism really is equivalent to saying that when one works with a nonlinear model, if one mispecifies the nature of the nonlinearity, then there are problems of parameter interpretation, consistency, etc. Finally, I would note that Brock and Durlauf (forthcoming) provides some results on nonparametric identification of neighborhood effects, using bounds-type arguments of the type pioneered by Manski.

RESPONSE TO DECHTER

Aimée Dechter provides a wide-ranging discussion of the strengths and weaknesses of my framework from the perspective of sociology. She identifies a number of weaknesses of the framework as it is currently developed. Dechter also provides a number of interesting suggestions on how the social interactions model can be employed in sociological contexts.

In terms of criticisms, there are two that I think deserve to be highlighted. The first concerns the identification of reference groups. The identification results Brock and I have developed all presuppose that these groups are known. Dechter is quite correct that this assumption is problematic. One of the reasons that survey data is important, I think, is in adding plausibility to assumptions concerning what reference groups matter for individuals. Similarly, this is one of the reasons why ethnographic studies are very relevant to formal analyses. That being said, I do not wish to sound too much like a Pollyanna: identification of references groups is a serious issue in this literature and has received far too little attention.

Second, Dechter points out that the model is psychologically underdeveloped. In particular, she argues that the determinants of self-identity and self-regulation are far more complex than the simple functional forms

I employ. Dechter notes how these notions are fluid in ways that the model does not address. I think these criticisms are valid and important. Notice that relative to Bowles, Dechter is not arguing that one needs an evolutionary mechanism for preferences but rather that self-identity and self-regulation require a more sophisticated view of what one means by preferences than I have allowed.

Dechter's description of the model's shortcoming reflects ideas that, while of longstanding importance in sociology, have only recently begun to permeate into economics (cf. Akerlof and Kranton's [2000] work on identity). What I hope my paper has accomplished is a demonstration that economic modeling and sociological insights can be integrated, so I regard Dechter's many interesting suggestions as a useful outline for future research in this area.

3

ANALYSIS OF CATEGORICAL RESPONSE PROFILES BY INFORMATIVE SUMMARIES

Zvi Gilula†
*Shelby J. Haberman**

A categorical profile is a vector of observed values of several categorical variables that share a common context. Statistical analysis of categorical profiles may involve study of the joint distribution of the profiles or study of the relationship of the profiles to explanatory variables. Such analysis entails special difficulties due to the very large number of possible categorical profiles and due to the very strong relationships among the responses. Given the complex nature of the relationships among the variables, large samples are required for analysis. These large samples generally render useless traditional methods of model fitting based on tests of goodness of fit. Alternatively, model quality may be assessed in terms of descriptive power, as measured by information-theoretic criteria.

A useful method of data description involves summary statistics derived from the data. A new approach combining log-linear models and summary statistics results in insightful and parsimonious description of categorical profiles. The analysis of summary statistics results in the use of log-linear models that differ substantially from those commonly employed in the analysis of profile data. Special measures are introduced for comparison of

Research for this article was partially supported by National Science Foundation grants DMS9303713 and DMS9505799 and by United States–Israel Binational Fund grant 92-00064. The authors gratefully acknowledge comments by Yu Xie and thank two referees for comments and suggestions that led to a substantial improvement in the article.

†Hebrew University, Jerusalem, Israel
*Northwestern University

the descriptive power associated with different choices of summary statistics and for comparison of the number of parameters required for each model. Estimates for these special measures are proposed, and large-sample properties are considered in order to find asymptotic confidence intervals, providing an added inferential value to the proposed methods of analysis.

Through use of an empirical example of responses to questions concerning legal abortions, it is shown that models based on very succinct summaries of responses involve remarkably little information loss, thus describing the data relatively accurately and parsimoniously.

1. INTRODUCTION

A categorical profile is a vector of observed values of a set of categorical variables, where the variables do not necessarily have the same range but share a common context. Such profiles commonly arise in sociological research. For example, the General Social Survey of the National Opinion Research Center has typically employed six questions concerning grounds for legalized abortion. These questions, listed in Table 1, describe six conditions under which the respondent may or may not approve of a legalized abortion. The responses to these questions thus share a common context. Categorical profiles are also frequently encountered in the psychological, educational, and biological sciences and in marketing research.

Statistical analysis of categorical profiles usually involves study of the following two properties of the data:

TABLE 1
Questions on Abortion Used in the General Social Survey

Question	Text
The questions are introduced by the statement, "Please tell me whether or not you think it should be possible for a pregnant woman to obtain a legal abortion if . . ."	
A	there is a strong chance of serious defect in the baby.
B	she is married and does not want any more children.
C	the woman's own health is seriously endangered by the pregnancy.
D	the family has a very low income and cannot afford any more children.
E	she became pregnant as a result of rape.
F	she is not married and does not want to marry the man.

A. The joint distribution of the profiles.
B. The relationship of the profiles to explanatory variables.

For analysis of properties A and B, a model-based approach is quite common. However, categorical profiles have the following two special characteristics that require suitable methodological solutions.

1. In typical cases, there is a very large number of possible categorical profiles.
2. There is a frequently encountered tendency of a large fraction of subjects to use only a very limited number of the possible profiles.

The categorical profiles defined by Table 1 illustrate both characteristics 1 and aspect 2.

- Characteristic 1: If the responses to each question are coded as "yes," "no," or other (no answer or "don't know"), then there are $3^6 = 729$ possible categorical profiles. To avoid analyses of very sparse contingency tables requires sample sizes of many thousands.
- Characteristic 2: As can be seen in Table 2, 25,400 subjects in the General Social Survey from 1972 to 1993 were asked to respond to the six abortion questions. Of these, 21,479 (84.6 percent) used only 14 of 729 possible response profiles! The fact that profiles are usually not uniformly distributed gives certain profiles an exceptional importance in description of the data. For instance, the first profile in Table 2 describes 34 percent of the data. The eighth profile in that table accounts for almost an additional 18 percent, so that a majority of all subjects use one of two profiles.

Given characteristics 1 and 2 of the categorical profiles defined in Table 1, any analysis of the data involves study of a very sparse contingency table, even in the study of the joint distribution of the profile variables (property A). This situation exists even though there are 25,400 observations. Indeed, of the 729 possible profiles, only 118 are used by more than five respondents. The issue of sparseness is much more serious in the study of the relationship of the profile variables to explanatory variables such as year of survey, age of respondent, sex of respondent, race of respondent, geographical division of respondent, education of respondent, and religion of respondent (property B). As noted by Haberman

TABLE 2
Common Response Profiles for Questions on Abortion Question Response

A	B	C	D	E	F	Frequency	Fraction
Yes	Yes	Yes	Yes	Yes	Yes	8,624	.340
Yes	Yes	Yes	Yes	Yes	No	631	.025
Yes	Yes	Yes	No	Yes	Yes	345	.014
Yes	Yes	Yes	No	Yes	No	385	.015
Yes	No	Yes	Yes	Yes	Yes	677	.027
Yes	No	Yes	Yes	Yes	No	930	.037
Yes	No	Yes	No	Yes	Yes	559	.022
Yes	No	Yes	No	Yes	No	4,536	.179
Yes	No	Yes	No	No	No	978	.039
Other	Other	Other	Other	Other	Other	236	.009
No	No	Yes	No	Yes	No	874	.034
No	No	Yes	No	No	No	852	.034
No	No	No	No	Yes	No	226	.009
No	No	No	No	No	No	1,626	.064

(1977a; 1977b; 1979, sec. 6.3), customary large-sample approximations for the distributions of maximum-likelihood estimates and likelihood-ratio chi-square tests for a log-linear model may still apply when the sample size is large but the contingency table under study is sparse, provided that the number of independent parameters in the model studied is relatively small and provided that the likelihood-ratio chi-square compares the proposed log-linear model to a more general log-linear model in which the number of independent parameters is also relatively small. The results of Haberman apply to a study of both properties A and B.

In practice, very large sample sizes such as those encountered in the analysis of the 25,400 responses in the General Social Survey make customary model-fitting techniques virtually useless even when the basic requirements of Haberman (1977a, 1977b) are met. A slight discrepancy between a true probability of a categorical profile and a probability assigned to that profile by a proposed model often results in a huge value of the likelihood-ratio chi-square statistic. As a consequence, the conclusion is typically reached that the underlying model is inappropriate.

This paper offers a new methodology for the analysis of categorical profiles. This methodology is appropriate for data with characteristics 1 and 2 even when the sample size is very large. Summarization of data is combined with log-linear models to approximate either the joint unconditional distribution of the observed categorical profiles or the joint conditional distribution of the observed categorical profiles given the observed explanatory variables.

The approach to summarization involves the means of summary variables that depend on the responses or on both the responses and the explanatory variables. For example, in the data under study, one might consider the average number of times a subject responds "yes." As shown in Section 2.7, this approach is very flexible and results in novel log-linear models.

The approach to use of log-linear models adopted here is somewhat different than that commonly employed. Here goodness of fit is replaced by the descriptive or *predictive* power of a model. As suggested in Gilula and Haberman (1994, 1995, 2000), predictive power is defined and measured by information-theoretic techniques. Section 2 provides the necessary background concerning information theory for readers unfamiliar with the relevant material. These measures are based on the logarithmic penalty function developed by Savage (1971), among others. It should be emphasized that the theory developed in this paper *does not* prescribe abandonment of tests of goodness of fit but rather advocates that models not passing the goodness-of-fit test may still be methodologically valuable and that their value in such cases is in their predictive or descriptive power. The assumption here is that relatively few nontrivial log-linear models are valid in typical cases of categorical profiles. This issue is discussed in Section 2.8 from a technical standpoint and illustrated in the analysis of Section 4 of the abortion responses of the General Social Survey. This issue is also examined in Sections 2.8 and 4. As evident from results of Section 4, very concise summaries of the data can be obtained that appear to provide nearly all information that can be obtained concerning the data.

The techniques developed in Sections 2, 2.6, and 2.8 have an important added value. They can be extended to other areas that may appear very far removed from the subject of log-linear models. This point is considered in the models examined in Section 2.7. For example, a number of scaling techniques have been used to analyze categorical profiles. These scaling techniques correspond to summary statistics of the type employed in Section 2. Consequently, *for the first time*, the quantitative information provided by Guttman scaling (1950) or by correspondence analysis or canonical analysis (Schriever 1983; Greenacre 1984; Van de Geer 1993) may be formally evaluated. In this fashion, very different scaling methods can now be compared.

Latent-class models (Lazarsfeld and Henry 1968; Goodman 1974a, 1974b; Haberman 1979, ch. 10; Heinen 1996) are natural candidates for use with categorical profiles. Indeed, Haberman (1979, ch. 10) illustrates use of latent-class analysis by use of the General Social Survey responses to three of the abortion questions for the years 1972 to 1974. In special cases, latent-class models are log-linear models. This situation applies in the case of the Goodman (1975) generalization of Guttman (1950) scaling and in the case of the Rasch (1960) model. Many of the techniques developed in this article remain relevant in the case of latent-class analysis, although latent-class models do not necessarily correspond to summary statistics derived from the data.

2. MODELS AND DATA SUMMARIES

To describe formally the relationships between models and data summaries, let Y_k, $1 \leq k \leq K$, $K \geq 1$, be categorical random response variables and X_j, $1 \leq j \leq J$, $J \geq 1$, be discrete or continuous real random explanatory variables defined on a population S. For $1 \leq k \leq K$, the categorical random variable Y_k assumes integer values from 1 to $C_k \geq 2$. The categorical response profile variable $\mathbf{Y}$ is the K-dimensional vector of responses Y_k, $1 \leq k \leq K$. For a population member s in S, $\mathbf{Y}$ has value $\mathbf{Y}(s)$, and Y_k has value $Y_k(s)$ for $1 \leq k \leq K$. The J-dimensional profile $\mathbf{X}$ of explanatory variables is the vector of explanatory variables X_j, $1 \leq j \leq J$. For a population member s of the population S, $\mathbf{X}$ has value $\mathbf{X}(s)$, and X_j has value $X_j(s)$ for $1 \leq j \leq J$. Let Q be the set of $C = \prod_{k=1}^{K} C_k$ possible categorical profiles. Let T be the range of the explanatory profile $\mathbf{X}$, so that T contains all J-dimensional vectors $\mathbf{x}$ such that $\mathbf{X}(s) = \mathbf{x}$ for some member s of the population S. Inferences concerning the data are based on a simple random sample s_i, $1 \leq i \leq n$, of size $n \geq 1$ from the population S. The observed data are the responses $Y_{ik} = Y_k(s_i)$, $1 \leq k \leq K$, $1 \leq i \leq n$, and the observed explanatory variables $X_{ij} = X_j(s_i)$, $1 \leq j \leq J$, $1 \leq i \leq n$. The observed response profiles are the vectors $\mathbf{Y}_i$ of responses Y_{ik}, $1 \leq k \leq K$, and the vectors $\mathbf{X}_i$ of explanatory variables X_{ij}, $1 \leq j \leq J$.

For example, in the case of the General Social Survey, the data available are from 1972 to 1993, with no surveys in 1979, 1981, and 1992 and with no use of the abortion questions in 1986. The abortion questions are used with about two out of every three respondents from 1988 to 1993. Given these results, one might let S be the population of pairs $s = (s_1, s_2)$ such that s_2 is a year in which the abortion question was asked and s_1 is an adult in the noninstitutional English-speaking adult population of the United States at the time of the survey in year s_1. For a pair $s = (s_1, s_2)$, let the weight $w(s)$ be the probability that a member s_1 of the adult noninstitutional population of the United States in year s_2 is asked the abortion questions. Let the expectation E on S be defined for every real function Z on S to be the weighted average

$$E(Z) = \frac{\sum_{s \in S} w(s)Z(s)}{\sum_{s \in S} w(s)}.$$

The corresponding probability P is defined for each subset A of the population S so that

$$P(A) = \frac{\sum_{s \in A} w(s)}{\sum_{s \in S} w(s)}.$$

The actual sampling procedure used in the General Social Survey has not been constant over time and full details are not readily obtained from publicly available data. For the purposes of this discussion, the simplifying assumption is made that the observations s_i, $1 \leq i \leq n = 25{,}400$, can be regarded as a simple random sample from S.

In the case of the $K = 6$ abortion questions in the General Social Survey, each response to an abortion question is coded from 1 to 3, with code 1 for "yes," code 3 for "no," and code 2 for any other response ("don't know" or "no answer"). For integers k from 1 to K, there are $C_k = 3$ responses to question k, and Y_k is the variable on S such that, for $s = (s_1, s_2)$ in S, $Y_k(s)$ is the response of subject s_1 to question k for year s_2. Here question 1 corresponds to reason A, question 2 corresponds to reason B, etc. The set Q of possible response profiles contains $C = 729$ members. The profile (1,1,1,1,1,1) corresponds to a response of "yes" to all questions, while (1,3,1,3,1,3) corresponds to a response of "yes" for reasons A, C, and E and a response of "no" for reasons B, D, and F. The $J = 13$ explanatory variables are defined as in Table 3. The set T consists of all values $\mathbf{X}$ assumed in the population S.

The unconditional joint probability distribution of the response profile $\mathbf{Y}$ may be described fully by means of the probabilities

$$p_{\mathbf{Y}}(\mathbf{y}) = P(\{s \in S : \mathbf{Y}(s) = \mathbf{y}\})$$

assigned to each possible categorical profile $\mathbf{y}$ in Q. One may then define the probability function $\mathbf{p_Y}$ of the response profile variable $\mathbf{Y}$ to be the

TABLE 3
Explanatory Variables for Questions on Abortion Attitudes

Variable	Variable Description
X_1	Year of interview minus 1982
X_2	Indicator for male
X_3	Indicator for black
X_4	Indicator for nonblack and nonwhite respondent
X_5	Indicator for current residence in North Central states
X_6	Indicator for current residence in South
X_7	Indicator for current residence in West
X_8	Minimum of 89 and reported age in years (50 if no response)
X_9	Indicator for no report of age in years
X_{10}	Minimum of 20 and years of education (12 if no response)
X_{11}	Indicator for no report of years of education
X_{12}	Indicator for religion reported to be Catholic
X_{13}	Indicator for religion not reported or neither Protestant nor Catholic

function on Q such that $\mathbf{p_Y}$ has value $p_\mathbf{Y}(\mathbf{y})$ at $\mathbf{y}$ in Q. Obviously, each $p_\mathbf{Y}(\mathbf{y})$ is nonnegative and

$$\sum_{\mathbf{y}\in Q} p_\mathbf{Y}(\mathbf{y}) = 1.$$

2.1. *Entropy and the Logarithmic Penalty Function*

A basic measure of dispersion for the categorical profile $\mathbf{Y}$ is the Shannon (1948) entropy

$$\mathrm{Ent}(\mathbf{Y}) = -\sum_{\mathbf{y}\in Q} p_\mathbf{Y}(\mathbf{y})\log p_\mathbf{Y}(\mathbf{y}),$$

where the convention is adopted that $0\log 0 = 0$. This measure of dispersion has the fundamental properties that $\mathrm{Ent}(\mathbf{Y})$ is nonnegative, with $\mathrm{Ent}(\mathbf{Y}) = 0$ if and only if, for some $\mathbf{y}$ in Q, the probability is 1 that $\mathbf{Y} = \mathbf{y}$, so that the profile variable $\mathbf{Y}$ is constant with probability 1. The entropy measure achieves its maximum value of $\log C$ if $\mathbf{Y}$ satisfies the equiprobability condition that each probability $p_\mathbf{Y}(\mathbf{y})$ is $1/C$. Shannon (1948) uses entropy in information theory to measure the information provided by $\mathbf{Y}$.

A rationale for use of the entropy measure of dispersion is provided by Savage (1971), whose argument is a generalization of earlier arguments by Good (1952) and Mosteller and Wallace (1964, pp. 191–92). Because the response profile $\mathbf{Y}$ is a vector of categorical variables, prediction of the specific value of $\mathbf{Y}$ is not appropriate. It is more desirable to use probabilistic prediction of the profile $\mathbf{Y}$, so that probabilities are assigned to each possible value of $\mathbf{Y}$. For instance, the same issue arises in weather forecasts in which precipitation probabilities are provided rather than a simple statement that rain will (or will not) occur.

In probabilistic prediction of $\mathbf{Y}$, each profile $\mathbf{y}$ in the set Q of categorical profiles is assigned probability $f(\mathbf{y}) \geq 0$. Probabilities are required to be consistent, so that $\sum_{\mathbf{y}\in Q} f(\mathbf{y}) = 1$. Let prediction accuracy be assessed by use of a nonnegative penalty which depends only on the value of categorical profile variable $\mathbf{Y}$ and on the probability assigned to the value assumed by $\mathbf{Y}$. Thus, for some nonnegative extended real function $g_{\mathbf{y}}$ on the interval $[0,1]$ of real numbers from 0 to 1, a penalty of $g_{\mathbf{y}}(f(\mathbf{y}))$ is assessed if $\mathbf{Y} = \mathbf{y}$. The expected penalty is then

$$E(g_{\mathbf{Y}}(f(\mathbf{Y}))) = \sum_{\mathbf{y}\in Q} p_{\mathbf{Y}}(\mathbf{y}) g_{\mathbf{y}}(f(\mathbf{y})).$$

Let the only optimal value of f be the probability function $p_{\mathbf{Y}}$, no matter what distribution $\mathbf{Y}$ may have, and let the minimum possible expected penalty be 0. Savage (1971) demonstrates that for $C \geq 3$ these conditions imply that, for some real number $b > 0$, $g_{\mathbf{y}}(x) = -b\log(x)$ for $0 \leq x \leq 1$ and $\mathbf{y}$ in Q. Note that $-\log 0 = \infty$. Thus the expected penalty must be

$$-bE(\log f(\mathbf{Y})) = -b \sum_{\mathbf{y}\in Q} p_{\mathbf{Y}}(\mathbf{y}) \log f(\mathbf{y}).$$

The minimum possible expected penalty is then $b\,\mathrm{Ent}(\mathbf{Y})$.

The choice of the scale factor b has no effect on comparisons of expected penalties for different values of f. It is convenient to let $b = 1$, so that the penalty from use of the probability function f as a predictor is the logarithmic penalty $-\log f(\mathbf{y})$ for $\mathbf{Y} = \mathbf{y}$. If $\mathbf{Y}'$ is a categorical profile variable with values in Q with probability function g and if f is a probability function as defined above, then the expected penalty from prediction of $\mathbf{Y}'$ by f is

$$B(g,f) = -\sum_{\mathbf{y}\in Q} g(\mathbf{y}) \log f(\mathbf{y}).$$

One has

$$B(g,f) \geq B(g,g), \tag{1}$$

with $B(g, f) = B(g, g)$ only if $g = f$. In the case of $\mathbf{Y}$, the expected penalty

$$B(p_{\mathbf{Y}}, f) = E(-\log f(\mathbf{Y})) = -\sum_{\mathbf{y}\in Q} p_{\mathbf{Y}}(\mathbf{y})\log f(\mathbf{y})$$

is at least as large as the entropy

$$\mathrm{Ent}(\mathbf{Y}) = B(p_{\mathbf{Y}}, p_{\mathbf{Y}}),$$

with $B(p_{\mathbf{Y}}, f) = \mathrm{Ent}(\mathbf{Y})$ only if $f = p_{\mathbf{Y}}$.

2.2. *Probability Prediction Functions*

As in Gilula and Haberman (1994, 1995), an extension of the Savage (1971) argument may be considered in which the profile $\mathbf{Y}$ is predicted by a probability prediction function q. Here q is a function on the population S. For each population member s of S, $q(s)$ is a probability function on Q with value $q(\mathbf{y}, s) \geq 0$ at $\mathbf{y}$ in Q, and, for each response $\mathbf{y}$ in Q, the variable $q^*(\mathbf{y})$ on S which assigns probability $q(\mathbf{y}, s)$ to $\mathbf{y}$ for population member s in S is a real random variable. Note that the assumption that $q(s)$ is a probability function implies that $\sum_{\mathbf{y}\in Q} q(\mathbf{y}, s) = 1$. Let $q(\mathbf{Y})$ be the random variable on S such that, for each member s of the population S, $q(\mathbf{Y})$ has valued $q(\mathbf{Y}(s), s)$ equal to the probability assigned to the observed profile $\mathbf{Y}(s)$. The quality of q as a predictor of $\mathbf{Y}$ is assessed by use of the expectation

$$H(q) = E(-\log q(\mathbf{Y})).$$

One has $H(q) = B(p_{\mathbf{Y}}, f)$ if q is a constant probability prediction function with $q(s) = f$ for each member s of the population S. Thus the entropy $\mathrm{Ent}(\mathbf{Y})$ is the smallest expected penalty $H(q)$ obtained by use of a constant prediction function.

As noted in Gilula and Haberman (1994), a reduced expected penalty (an increased quality of prediction) may be achievable by use of explanatory variables. The conditional entropy $\mathrm{Ent}(\mathbf{Y}|\mathbf{X})$ of $\mathbf{Y}$ given $\mathbf{X}$ may be defined to be the smallest expected penalty $H(q)$ obtained by use of a prediction function q such that, for some function b defined on the range T of $\mathbf{X}$, $q = b(\mathbf{X})$. Because q can be chosen so that $q(s) = p_{\mathbf{Y}}$ for each s in S, it follows that

$$0 \leq \mathrm{Ent}(\mathbf{Y}|\mathbf{X}) \leq \mathrm{Ent}(\mathbf{Y}).$$

To find the conditional entropy $\mathrm{Ent}(\mathbf{Y}|\mathbf{X})$, conditional probabilities may be used. Consider any definition of the conditional probability distribution of $\mathbf{Y}$ given $\mathbf{X}$. Under this definition, for $\mathbf{x}$ in T and $\mathbf{y}$ in Q, let $p_{\mathbf{Y}|\mathbf{X}}(\mathbf{y}|\mathbf{x})$ denote the conditional probability that $\mathbf{Y} = \mathbf{y}$ given that $\mathbf{X} = \mathbf{x}$. Let p be the conditional probability prediction function of $\mathbf{Y}$ given $\mathbf{X}$, so that p is the function on S such that $p(s)$, s in S, is the function on Q with value $p(\mathbf{y}, s)$ equal to $p_{\mathbf{Y}|\mathbf{X}}(\mathbf{y}|\mathbf{X}(s))$ for the possible categorical profile $\mathbf{y}$ in Q. Let a be the function on T such that $p = a(\mathbf{X})$. For $q = b(\mathbf{X})$, (1) and standard results concerning conditional expectations may be applied to show that

$$\begin{aligned}\mathrm{Ent}(\mathbf{Y}|\mathbf{X}) &= H(p)\\ &= E(B(a(\mathbf{X}), a(\mathbf{X})))\\ &\leq H(q)\\ &= E(B(a(\mathbf{X}), b(\mathbf{X}))),\end{aligned}$$

with $H(q) = H(p)$ if and only if q and p are equal with probability 1. Because the set of s in S with $p(s) = p_{\mathbf{Y}}$ has probability 1 if and only if $\mathbf{X}$ and $\mathbf{Y}$ are independent, it follows that the entropy $\mathrm{Ent}(\mathbf{Y})$ of the categorical profile $\mathbf{Y}$ equals the conditional entropy $\mathrm{Ent}(\mathbf{Y}|\mathbf{X})$ of $\mathbf{Y}$ given the explanatory profile $\mathbf{X}$ if and only if $\mathbf{X}$ and $\mathbf{Y}$ are independent.

If the conditional entropy $\mathrm{Ent}(\mathbf{Y}|\mathbf{X}) = 0$, then $\mathbf{X}$ is essentially a perfect predictor of the categorical profile $\mathbf{Y}$, for some function g on T exists such that $\mathbf{Y} = g(\mathbf{X})$ with probability 1. Given these properties of entropy, Theil (1970) and Haberman (1982) use the ratio

$$\frac{\mathrm{Ent}(\mathbf{Y}) - \mathrm{Ent}(\mathbf{Y}|\mathbf{X})}{\mathrm{Ent}(\mathbf{Y})}$$

to measure the value of $\mathbf{X}$ as a predictor of $\mathbf{Y}$. The ratio varies from 0 to 1 for $\mathrm{Ent}(\mathbf{Y}) > 0$, with 1 corresponding to essentially perfect prediction of $\mathbf{Y}$ by $\mathbf{X}$ and 0 corresponding to independence of $\mathbf{X}$ and $\mathbf{Y}$.

2.3. *Log-Linear Models*

As emphasized in Gilula and Haberman (1994, 1995), even though the conditional probability prediction function p is an optimal probability prediction function for prediction of the response profile $\mathbf{Y}$ by use of a function of the explanatory profile $\mathbf{X}$, other choices of prediction functions dependent on $\mathbf{X}$ may be more appropriate. Considerations may include inability to estimate p accurately from sample data or a desire for a simple form for the prediction function. In practice, *there is a tradeoff between simplicity and accuracy*. If q is a simple probability prediction function dependent on $\mathbf{X}$ and if $H(q)$ is only slightly larger than $\text{Ent}(\mathbf{Y}|\mathbf{X})$, then q may be a better probability prediction function than p.

Log-linear models provide an attractive approach for determination of suitable probability prediction functions. As in Haberman (1979, chap. 6), multinomial response models will be considered. To define the class of models under study, let D be a nonnegative integer that will represent the number of independent parameters in the model, and let M, the prediction set, be the set of probability prediction functions that satisfy the model. For $D = 0$, let M be the set $M(0)$ containing the single prediction function q such that $q(\mathbf{y}, s) = 1/C$ for all $\mathbf{y}$ in Q and s in S. For $D > 0$, let $Z_d(\mathbf{y})$, $\mathbf{y}$ in Q, $1 \leq d \leq D$, be random variables on S with finite expectations. Let $Z_d(\mathbf{y})$ have value $Z_d(\mathbf{y}, s)$ at s in S. For a given integer d, $1 \leq d \leq D$, $Z_d(\mathbf{y}, s)$, $\mathbf{y}$ in Q, s in S, may be a dummy variable associated with a particular profile $\mathbf{z}$ in Q, a dummy variable associated with a possible value y_k of the response variable Y_k, a dummy variable associated with a pair y_k and $y'_{k'}$ of values of the response variables Y_k and $Y_{k'}$, $1 \leq k < k' \leq K$, or a product of score variables $u(\mathbf{y})v(\mathbf{X}(s))$ for a real variable u defined on the set Q of possible categorical profiles and a real variable v defined on the set T of possible values of the explanatory vector. Because prediction of $\mathbf{Y}$ by $\mathbf{X}$ is of interest, assume that any dependence of $Z_d(\mathbf{y}, s)$ on the population member s involves the explanatory vector $\mathbf{X}(s)$, so that $Z_d(\mathbf{y}, s) = Z_d(\mathbf{y}, s')$ whenever s and s' are in S and $\mathbf{X}(s) = \mathbf{X}(s')$. Let the prediction set M be the set of prediction functions q such that, for some real β_d, $1 \leq d \leq D$, q satisfies the log-linear model equations

$$\mu(\mathbf{y}, s) = \sum_{d=1}^{D} \beta_d Z_d(\mathbf{y}, s) \tag{2}$$

and

$$q(\mathbf{y}, s) = \frac{\exp \mu(\mathbf{y}, s)}{\sum_{\mathbf{z} \in Q} \exp \mu(\mathbf{z}, s)} \tag{3}$$

for all $\mathbf{y}$ in Q and s in S. As in Haberman (1979, chap. 6), q may be said to satisfy a multinomial response model. The functions $Z_d(\mathbf{y})$, $\mathbf{y}$ in Q, $1 \leq d \leq D$, may be termed *generators* of the prediction set M. To permit D to be properly defined as the number of independent parameters associated with the prediction set M, assume the parameters β_d are identified, so that each q in M satisfies (2) and (3) for a unique β_d, $1 \leq d \leq D$. This identifiability requirement is also supplemented by the requirement that $q = q'$ whenever q and q' are in M and q and q' are equal with probability 1.

A series of examples of log-linear models for categorical profiles are given in Section 2.7. The following two simple examples illustrate the basic notation used.

Example 1: The saturated model without explanatory variables. Let the prediction set $M(S)$ consist of all prediction functions q such that $q(s) = f$, s in S, for some probability function f such that $f(\mathbf{y}) > 0$ for each $\mathbf{y}$ in Q. Thus the conditional probability prediction function p is in $M(S)$ if $\mathbf{X}$ and $\mathbf{Y}$ are independent and $p_{\mathbf{Y}}(\mathbf{y})$ is positive for each possible categorical profile $\mathbf{y}$ in Q. To construct the corresponding log-linear model, let $D = D(S) = C - 1$ and let $\mathbf{z}_c$, $0 \leq c \leq C - 1$ be the C distinct members of the set Q of possible profiles. To find generators for $M(S)$, let $Z_d(\mathbf{y}, s)$ be 1 for $\mathbf{y} = \mathbf{z}_d$ and 0 for $\mathbf{y} = \mathbf{z}_d$ for $1 \leq d \leq D$, $\mathbf{y} \in Q$, and s in S. Because no $Z_d(\mathbf{y})$ depends on the population member s, if (2) and (3) hold, then $q(s) = f$, s in S, for the probability function f on Q such that

$$f(\mathbf{z}_d) = \begin{cases} \dfrac{\exp \beta_d}{1 + \sum\limits_{d'=1}^{D} \exp \beta_{d'}}, & 1 \leq d \leq C - 1, \\[2ex] \dfrac{1}{1 + \sum\limits_{d'=1}^{D} \exp \beta_{d'}}, & d = 0. \end{cases}$$

Clearly $f(\mathbf{y}) > 0$ for each possible profile $\mathbf{y}$ in Q, and $\sum_{\mathbf{y} \in Q} f(\mathbf{y}) = 1$. On the other hand, if $q(s) = f$, s in S, for a probability function f such that $f(\mathbf{y}) > 0$ for each $\mathbf{y}$ in Q, then (2) and (3) hold for

$$\beta_d = \log[f(\mathbf{z}_d)/f(\mathbf{z}_0)], \quad 1 \leq d \leq D.$$

If f is the probability function $p_{\mathbf{Y}}$ of $\mathbf{Y}$ and if $p_{\mathbf{Y}}(\mathbf{y}) > 0$ for all categorical profiles $\mathbf{y}$ in Q, then β_d, $1 \leq d \leq D$, are the relative odds that $\mathbf{Y}$ is $\mathbf{z}_d$ rather than $\mathbf{z}_0$. Because different orderings of the members of the set Q of possible profiles are available, it follows that the generators of $M(S)$ are not uniquely determined. The prediction set $M(S)$ corresponds to the saturated model for the responses $\mathbf{Y}$ in which no substantial assumptions are made concerning the joint distribution of $\mathbf{Y}$ and the relationship of $\mathbf{Y}$ to $\mathbf{X}$ is not considered.

Example 2: The saturated model for a categorical explanatory variable. Let F be a function defined for any $\mathbf{x}$ in the range T of $\mathbf{X}$. Assume that $F(\mathbf{X})$ is a categorical random variable with values from 1 to $b \geq 1$, and let $p_F(a)$ be positive, where $p_F(a)$ is the marginal probability that $F(\mathbf{X}) = a$, $1 \leq a \leq b$. For example, in the abortion example, $F(\mathbf{X})$ might be the sex X_2 of the respondent, so that $F(\mathbf{x}) = x_2$ for $\mathbf{x}$ in T and $b = 2$. Let $M(C, F)$ consist of all probability prediction functions q on S such that q is a function $q = c(F)$ of F for some function c on the integers 1 to b such that $c(a)$ has values $c(\mathbf{y}, a) > 0$ for all $\mathbf{y}$ in Q and integers a from 1 to b. In this fashion, the conditional probability prediction function p is in $M(C, F)$ if, for $\mathbf{x}$ in the range T of $\mathbf{X}$ and $a = F(\mathbf{x})$, the conditional probability $p_{\mathbf{Y}|\mathbf{X}}(\mathbf{y}|\mathbf{x})$ that $\mathbf{Y} = \mathbf{y}$ in Q given that $\mathbf{X} = \mathbf{x}$ is the same as the conditional probability $p_{\mathbf{Y}|F}(\mathbf{y}|a) > 0$ that $\mathbf{Y} = \mathbf{y}$ given that $F(\mathbf{X}) = a$.

In the corresponding log-linear model, there are $D = D(C, F) = (C-1)b$ independent parameters. Define $\mathbf{z}_c$, $0 \leq c \leq C-1$, as in Example 1, so that the $\mathbf{z}_c$ are the distinct possible categorical profiles in Q. Let $Z_d(\mathbf{y})$ be defined for $1 \leq d \leq D(C, F)$ and $\mathbf{y}$ in Q so that $Z_d(\mathbf{y}, s) = 1$ if $\mathbf{y} = \mathbf{z}_c$ and $Z_d(\mathbf{y}, s) = 0$ if $\mathbf{y} = \mathbf{z}_c$, $F(\mathbf{X}(s)) = a$, $1 \leq c \leq C-1$, $1 \leq a \leq b$, and $d = c + (a-1)(C-1)$. In this fashion, if $q = e(F)$, $e(\mathbf{y}, a) > 0$ for $\mathbf{y}$ in Q and $1 \leq a \leq b$, and $\sum_{\mathbf{y} \in Q} e(\mathbf{y}, a) = 1$ for $1 \leq a \leq b$, then (2) and (3) hold with

$$\beta_d = \log[e(\mathbf{z}_c, a)/e(\mathbf{z}_0, a)]$$

for $1 \leq a \leq b$, $1 \leq c \leq C-1$, and $d = c + (a-1)(C-1)$. If $e(\mathbf{y}, a)$ is the conditional probability $p_{\mathbf{Y}|F}(\mathbf{y}|a) > 0$ that $\mathbf{Y} = \mathbf{y}$ in Q given that $F(\mathbf{X}) = a$, $1 \leq a \leq b$, then β_d, $1 \leq c \leq C-1$, $d = c + (a-1)(C-1)$, is the conditional log odds, given that $F(\mathbf{X}) = a$, that $\mathbf{Y} = \mathbf{z}_c$ rather than $\mathbf{z}_0$.

Conversely, if (2) and (3) hold for some β_d, $1 \leq d \leq D(C, F)$, then $q = e(F)$, where for $0 \leq c \leq C-1$, $1 \leq a \leq b$, $d = c + (a-1)(C-1)$, $g = 1 + (a-1)(C-1)$, and $h = a(C-1)$,

$$e(\mathbf{z}_c, a) = \begin{cases} \dfrac{\exp \beta_d}{1 + \sum_{d'=g}^{h} \exp \beta_{d'}}, & 1 \leq c \leq C-1, \\[2ex] \dfrac{1}{1 + \sum_{d'=g}^{h} \exp \beta_{d'}}, & c = 0. \end{cases}$$

For $\mathbf{y}$ in Q, $e(\mathbf{y}, a) > 0$ for $1 \leq a \leq b$. For $1 \leq a \leq b$, $\sum_{\mathbf{y} \in Q} e(\mathbf{y}, a) = 1$.

2.4. *Optimal Prediction*

To study optimal prediction, let $Z_d(\mathbf{Y})$, $1 \leq d \leq D$, denote the random variable with value $Z_d(\mathbf{Y}(s), s)$ at member s of the population S. The variable $Z_d(\mathbf{Y})$ should be distinguished from $Z_d(\mathbf{y})$. For $\mathbf{y}$ in Q, let $\delta_{\mathbf{y}}$ be the function on Q such that $\delta_{\mathbf{y}}(\mathbf{z})$, $\mathbf{z}$ in Q, is 1 for $\mathbf{y} = \mathbf{z}$ and 0 for $\mathbf{y} = \mathbf{z}$. Then

$$Z_d(\mathbf{Y}) = \sum_{\mathbf{y} \in Q} \delta_{\mathbf{y}}(\mathbf{Y}) Z_d(\mathbf{y}).$$

In a similar manner, let $\mu(\mathbf{y})$, $\mathbf{y}$ in Q, be the random variable with value $\mu(\mathbf{y}, s)$ at s in S, and let $\mu(\mathbf{Y})$ be the random variable with value $\mu(\mathbf{Y}(s), s)$ at s in S. The expectations $E(Z_d(\mathbf{Y}))$, $1 \leq d \leq D$, and the joint distribution of the generators $Z_d(\mathbf{y})$, $\mathbf{y}$ in Q, $1 \leq d \leq D$, determine the expected penalty $H(q)$ for prediction of the response profile $\mathbf{Y}$ by a probability prediction function q that satisfies (2) and (3). To verify this claim, observe that the linearity properties of expectations and the equation

$$\mu(\mathbf{y}) = \sum_{d=1}^{D} \beta_d Z_d(\mathbf{y})$$

lead to

$$\begin{aligned} H(q) &= E\left(\mu(\mathbf{Y}) - \log \sum_{d=1}^{D} \exp \mu(\mathbf{y})\right) \\ &= \sum_{d=1}^{D} \beta_d E(Z_d(\mathbf{Y})) - E\left(\log \sum_{\mathbf{z} \in Q} \exp \mu(\mathbf{y})\right). \end{aligned} \tag{4}$$

Given (4), the expectations $E(Z_d(\mathbf{Y}))$, $1 \leq d \leq D$, may be termed *sufficient expectations* under the constraint that the probability prediction function q is in M. The usage is analogous to terminology for sufficient statistics; however, in the present case, the sufficient expectations are population characteristics of the profile variables $\mathbf{X}$ and $\mathbf{Y}$ rather than sample characteristics associated with the observations $\mathbf{X}_i$ and $\mathbf{Y}_i$, $1 \leq i \leq n$. Analogous results for estimation are provided in Section 2.8.

As a simple illustration of sufficient expectations, in Example 1, the sufficient expectations $E(Z_d(\mathbf{Y})) = p_{\mathbf{Y}}(\mathbf{z}_d)$ for $1 \leq d \leq D$. Because

$$p_{\mathbf{Y}}(\mathbf{z}_0) = 1 - \sum_{d=1}^{D} p_{\mathbf{Y}}(\mathbf{z}_d),$$

knowledge of the sufficient expectations is equivalent to knowledge of the unconditional probability distribution of $\mathbf{Y}$. Similarly, in Example 2, the sufficient expectations $E(Z_d(\mathbf{Y}))$, $1 \le d \le D$, are the joint probabilities $p_{F\mathbf{Y}}(a, \mathbf{z}_c)$ that $\mathbf{Y} = \mathbf{z}_c$ and $F(\mathbf{X}) = a$ for $1 \le c \le C - 1$ and $1 \le a \le b$. Given that the marginal probabilities $p_F(a)$ are known for $1 \le a \le b$, knowledge of the sufficient expectations is equivalent to knowledge of the conditional distribution of $\mathbf{Y}$ given $F(\mathbf{X})$.

The standard for optimal prediction of $\mathbf{Y}$ by a member of the prediction set M is the minimum $I(M) \ge \mathrm{Ent}(\mathbf{Y}|\mathbf{X})$ of the expected penalties $H(q)$ for probability prediction functions q in the prediction set M. Thus the minimum loss of expected penalty from use of q in M rather than p as a probability prediction function is

$$\kappa(M) = I(M) - \mathrm{Ent}(\mathbf{Y}|\mathbf{X}) \ge 0.$$

If p is in M, then $\kappa(M) = 0$. In this fashion, the optimal probability prediction function q in M may be regarded as an approximation to the conditional probability prediction function p. The measure $\kappa(M)$ assesses the extent to which p may be approximated by a member of the prediction set M.

The optimal probability prediction function q in M is the unique probability prediction function in M that satisfies $H(q) = I(M)$. If the conditional probability prediction function p is in M, then $q = p$ and $I(M) = \mathrm{Ent}(\mathbf{Y}|\mathbf{X})$. If $D = 0$, then $I(M) = \log C$. Optimal prediction for $D > 0$ is discussed in Appendix A.

To illustrate optimal probability prediction, consider Example 1. In this case, for $p_{\mathbf{Y}}(\mathbf{y}) > 0$ for all $\mathbf{y}$ in Q, results in Appendix A imply that the optimal probability prediction function q satisfies the conditions $q(s) = f$ for s in S, $f(\mathbf{y}) > 0$ for $\mathbf{y}$ in Q, and

$$f(\mathbf{z}_d) = p_{\mathbf{Y}}(\mathbf{z}_d)$$

for $1 \le d \le D$. It follows that $f = p_{\mathbf{Y}}$, so that

$$I(M(S)) = \mathrm{Ent}(\mathbf{Y})$$

and

$$\kappa(M(S)) = \mathrm{Ent}(\mathbf{Y}) - \mathrm{Ent}(\mathbf{Y}|\mathbf{X}).$$

In Example 2, for $p_{\mathbf{Y}|F}(\mathbf{y}|a) > 0$ for $\mathbf{y}$ in Q and $1 \leq a \leq b$, a similar argument shows that the optimal probability prediction function q satisfies the condition

$$q(\mathbf{y}, s) = p_{\mathbf{Y}|F}(\mathbf{y}|F(\mathbf{X}(s)))$$

for $\mathbf{y}$ in Q and s in S. Thus

$$I(M(C,F)) = \mathrm{Ent}(\mathbf{Y}|F(\mathbf{X}))$$

and

$$\kappa(M(C,F)) = \mathrm{Ent}(\mathbf{Y}|F(\mathbf{X})) - \mathrm{Ent}(\mathbf{Y}|\mathbf{X}),$$

where

$$\mathrm{Ent}(\mathbf{Y}|F(\mathbf{X})) = -\sum_{a=1}^{b} \sum_{\mathbf{y} \in Q} p_{F\mathbf{Y}}(a, \mathbf{y}) \log p_{\mathbf{Y}|F}(\mathbf{y}|a)$$

is the conditional entropy of $\mathbf{Y}$ given $F(\mathbf{X})$.

2.5. *Information from Summaries*

The concept of sufficient expectations may be used to evaluate the information that can be obtained from summary expectations. Note that, for any categorical profile variable $\mathbf{Y}'$ with values in Q, if $\mathbf{Y}'$ and $\mathbf{Y}$ have the same sufficient expectations, so that

$$E(Z_d(\mathbf{Y}')) = E(Z_d(\mathbf{Y})), \quad 1 \leq d \leq D, \tag{5}$$

and if q in M satisfies $H(q) = I(M)$, then the expected penalty from use of q to predict $\mathbf{Y}'$ is

$$H'(q) = E(-\log q(\mathbf{Y}')) = H(q) = I(M).$$

Thus knowledge of the sufficient expectations implies a guaranteed minimum expected penalty of $I(M)$.

In general, no way exists to guarantee a smaller minimum expected penalty than $I(M)$. Gilula and Haberman (2000) provide the following argument. Let q be the optimal probability prediction function in the prediction set M. Because q is dependent on $\mathbf{X}$, $q = b(\mathbf{X})$ for some function b on T, and (4) and (11) imply that

$$I(M) = E(B(b(\mathbf{X}), b(\mathbf{X}))).$$

Let q' be any probability prediction function that is a function of the explanatory profile $\mathbf{X}$, so that $q' = b'(\mathbf{X})$ for a function b' on T. Let $\mathbf{Y}'$ be a categorical profile variable on S with values in Q such that $p' = q$ is the conditional probability prediction function of $\mathbf{Y}'$ given $\mathbf{X}$. Then the categorical profile variables $\mathbf{Y}'$ and $\mathbf{Y}$ have the same sufficient expectations, so that (5) holds. The expected penalty for probability prediction of $\mathbf{Y}'$ by q' is

$$\begin{aligned} H'(q') &= E(-\log q'(\mathbf{Y}')) \\ &= E(B(b(\mathbf{X}), b'(\mathbf{X}))) \\ &\geq E(B(b(\mathbf{X}), b(\mathbf{X}))) \\ &= I(M), \end{aligned}$$

with $H'(q') > I(M)$ if q' and q differ with positive probability. Thus the optimal probability prediction function q in M is essentially the only q' in M such that $H'(q') \leq I(M)$ for all categorical profile variables $\mathbf{Y}'$ on S such that (5) holds. Given this result, the minimum expected penalty $I(M)$ can be regarded as the information available from the sufficient expectations $E(Z_d(\mathbf{Y}))$, $1 \leq d \leq D$.

Thus in Example 1, the entropy $\text{Ent}(\mathbf{Y})$ is the information available concerning $\mathbf{Y}$ based on the unconditional probability distribution of $\mathbf{Y}$. In Example 2, the conditional entropy $\text{Ent}(\mathbf{Y}|F(\mathbf{X}))$ is the information available concerning $\mathbf{Y}$ based on the conditional probability distribution of $\mathbf{Y}$ given $F(\mathbf{X})$ and based on the marginal probability distribution of $F(\mathbf{X})$.

2.6. *Comparison of Prediction Sets*

In typical analyses of categorical profiles, it is natural to expect that more than one prediction set (model) is appropriate for data description. Therefore, it is desirable to develop a methodology for comparing competing prediction sets. Such methodology is developed in Gilula and Haberman (1994) for a specific class of conditional log-linear models but can be applied to categorical profiles. Let M and M' be two competing prediction sets defined as in Section 2.3. Let M have D independent parameters, and let M' have D' independent parameters. No necessary relationship between M and M' exists in general; however, in what may be termed the hierarchical case, M' is a subset of M, so that the log-linear model associated with M is at least as general as the log-linear model associated with M' and $D' \leq D$. Define the difference in predictive value of models M and M' as

$$\Delta(M', M) = I(M') - I(M) = \kappa(M') - \kappa(M).$$

The difference $\Delta(M', M)$ is positive if the prediction set M permits better prediction of $\mathbf{Y}$ than does M', while $\Delta(M', M)$ is negative if prediction set M' permits better prediction of $\mathbf{Y}$ than does M. In the hierarchical case, $\Delta(M', M)$ is nonnegative.

For instance, in Examples 1 and 2, $M(S)$ is included in $M(C, F)$, so that

$$\Delta(M(S), M(C, F)) = \text{Ent}(\mathbf{Y}) - \text{Ent}(\mathbf{Y}|F(\mathbf{X}))$$

is nonnegative, with $\Delta(M(S), M(C, F)) = 0$ only if $F(\mathbf{X})$ and $\mathbf{Y}$ are independent. To better understand typical values of $\Delta(M(S), M(C, F))$, consider the following elementary example adapted from Gilula and Haberman (1994). Let $K = 1$, $C_1 = 2$, and $b = 2$. Let the marginal probabilities $p_1(1)$ and $p_1(2)$ of Y_1 both be 0.5, and let the marginal probabilities $p_F(1)$ and $p_F(2)$ also be 0.5. Let c be the conditional probability that $Y_1 = 1$ given that $F(\mathbf{X}) = 1$. In this case, the marginal constraints imply that c is also the conditional probability that $Y_1 = 2$ given that $F(\mathbf{X}) = 2$. At the same time, $1 - c$ is the conditional probability that $Y_1 = 2$ given $F(\mathbf{X}) = 1$ and the conditional probability that $Y_1 = 1$ given that $F(\mathbf{X}) = 2$. If $c = 0.8$, as might be the case were Y_1 and $F(\mathbf{X})$ rather strongly related, then $\Delta(M(S), M(C, F))$ is 0.1927. If $c = 0.6$, as might be the case were Y_1 are $F(\mathbf{X})$ associated to a modest extent, then $\Delta(M(S), M(C, F)) = 0.0201$.

For D and D' positive, the measure $\Delta(M', M)$ can also be interpreted as a measure of the value of sufficient expectations. Let $Z_d(\mathbf{y})$, $\mathbf{y}$ in Q, $1 \leq d \leq D$, generate M, and let $Z'_d(\mathbf{y})$, $\mathbf{y}$ in Q, $1 \leq d \leq D'$, generate M'. Let the joint distribution of $Z_d(\mathbf{y})$, $\mathbf{y}$ in Q, $1 \leq d \leq D$, be known, and let the joint distribution of $Z'_d(\mathbf{y})$, $\mathbf{y}$ in Q, $1 \leq d \leq D'$, be known. Then $\Delta(M', M)$ can also be regarded as a comparison of the information provided by $E(Z_d(\mathbf{y}))$, $\mathbf{y}$ in Q, $1 \leq d \leq D$, to the information provided by $E(Z'_d(\mathbf{y}))$, $\mathbf{y}$ in Q, $1 \leq d \leq D'$.

An alternative criterion for model comparison is analogous to the R^2 criterion of regression analysis. Let $I(M')$ be positive. Then

$$\Lambda(M', M) = \Delta(M', M)/I(M')$$

measures the relative improvement achieved by use of M rather than M'. The larger the value of $\Lambda(M', M)$, the more the prediction set M is preferable to the prediction set M'. In the hierarchical case, $\Lambda(M', M)$ is between 0 and 1. In Examples 1 and 2, if $p_{\mathbf{Y}}(\mathbf{y}) > 0$ for at least two categorical profiles $\mathbf{y}$ in Q, then $\Lambda(M(S), M(C, F))$ is the Theil (1970) uncertainty coefficient for prediction of $\mathbf{Y}$ by $F(\mathbf{X})$. For the case of $K = 1$, $C_1 = b = 2$, $p_1(1) = p_2(1) = p_F(1) = p_F(2) = 0.5$ and c equal to the conditional probability that $Y_1 = 1$ given $F(\mathbf{X}) = 1$, for the strong relationship case of $c = 0.8$, $\Lambda(M(S), M(C, F)) = 0.2781$, for the moderate relationship case of $c = 0.6$, $\Lambda(M(S), M(C, F)) = 0.0290$.

Another important aspect of model comparison is parsimony. If $I(M) < I(M')$ and if $D < D'$, then the prediction set M clearly is preferable to the prediction set M', for fewer parameters have led to a better prediction. On the other hand, if $I(M) < I(M')$ but $D > D'$, then it is necessary to consider the value of the improved accuracy of prediction relative to the cost of additional model complexity. No universal criteria are available for measurement of costs of complexity, so that the tradeoff between prediction accuracy and the number of parameters is context-dependent. However, to aid in examination of the tradeoff, for $D' = D$, the measure

$$\nu(M', M) = \Delta(M', M)/(D - D')$$

is used for the accuracy gained per independent parameter from use of a prediction function that satisfies model M rather than model M'. Larger values of $\nu(M', M)$ provide increasing indication that M is preferable to M', with M' clearly preferable to M if $\nu(M', M)$ is negative and $D' < D$. In this paper, $\nu(M', M)$ will provide the basis for analyses designed to indicate the relative importance of different model components. In Examples 1 and 2,

$$\nu(M(S), M(C, F)) = \frac{\text{Ent}(\mathbf{Y}) - \text{Ent}(\mathbf{Y}|F(\mathbf{X}))}{(C-1)(b-1)}$$

for $b > 1$. In the example with $K = 1$ and $C_1 = b = 2$, $\nu(M(S), M(C, F))$ and $\Delta(M(S), M(C, F))$ are equal.

The criteria for model comparison in this section are criteria for populations. Thus, in the case of the General Social Survey, they apply if the entire adult noninstitutionalized population of the United States is observed for all years under study. Use of random samples to estimate the parameters of this section is considered in Section 2.8. In that section, appropriate model comparsions based on sampling are considered. Analysis considers chi-square tests, the Akaike (1974) information criterion (AIC), and the Schwarz (1978) Bayesian information criterion (BIC).

2.7. *Examples of Models and Sufficient Expectations*

The following eight examples illustrate some of the possible approaches for construction of log-linear models for categorical profiles and for summarization of results. The examples shown are only a few of the vast variety of possible models (prediction sets) appropriate for analysis of categorical profile data.

Example 3: Mutual independence of response variables. Let the marginal probabilities $p_k(y_k) > 0$, $1 \leq y_k < C_k$, of the responses Y_k be given for $1 \leq k \leq K$. Because

$$p_k(C_k) = 1 - \sum_{y_k=1}^{C_k-1} p^k_{y_k}$$

for $1 \leq k \leq K$, this information specifies the marginal distributions of the variables Y_k for $1 \leq k \leq K$. The corresponding prediction set $M(I)$ consists of functions q on S such that, for s in S, (3) holds and

$$\mu(\mathbf{y}, s) = \sum_{k=1}^{K} \lambda^k_{y_k}$$

for some $\lambda^k_{y_k}$, $1 \leq y_k \leq C_k$, $1 \leq k \leq K$, such that

$$\sum_{y_k=1}^{C_k} \lambda^k_{y_k} = 0, \quad 1 \leq k \leq K.$$

In this case, there are $D(I) = \sum_{k=1}^{K}(C_k - 1)$ independent parameters, and $p_k(y_k)$, $1 \leq y_k < C_k$, $1 \leq k \leq K$, provide sufficient expectations. The optimal prediction function q satisfies

$$q(\mathbf{y}, s) = \prod_{k=1}^{K} p_k(y_k)$$

for $\mathbf{y}$ in Q and s in S. The conditional probability prediction function p can be defined to be in $M(I)$ if and only if $\mathbf{Y}$ and $\mathbf{X}$ are independent and the responses Y_k, $1 \le k \le K$, are mutually independent.

The entropy of each individual response Y_k is

$$\mathrm{Ent}(Y_k) = -\sum_{y_k=1}^{C_k} p_k(y_k) \log p_k(y_k),$$

so that the minimum expected penalty is

$$I(M(I)) = \sum_{k=1}^{K} \mathrm{Ent}(Y_k).$$

If $M(S)$ is defined as in Example 1, then $M(I)$ is a subset of $M(S)$. The information loss from use of $M(I)$ rather than $M(S)$ as a prediction set is

$$\Delta(M(I), M(S)) = \sum_{k=1}^{K} \mathrm{Ent}(Y_k) - \mathrm{Ent}(\mathbf{Y}),$$

so that $\Delta(M(I), M(S))$ may be regarded as a measure of the mutual dependence of the responses Y_k, $1 \le k \le K$. An alternative measure is $\Lambda(M(I), M(S))$.

On the other hand, the information gain from use of $M(I)$ rather than the trivial prediction set $M(0)$ is

$$\Delta(M(0), M(I)) = \sum_{k=1}^{K} [\log C_k - \mathrm{Ent}(Y_k)],$$

where $\log C_k - \mathrm{Ent}(Y_k)$ measures the reduction in dispersion of the response Y_k relative to the dispersion of a categorical random variable which assumes C_k values with equal probability.

Example 4: Conditional independence of response variables given an explanatory variable. Define F as in Example 2. Let the joint probabilities $p_{kF}(y_k, a) > 0$ that $Y_k = y_k$ and $F(\mathbf{X}) = a$ be known for $1 \le y_k < C_k$ and $1 \le a \le b$. A similar argument to that used in Example 3 shows that the given information specifies the bivariate distribution of $F(\mathbf{X})$ and Y_k for $1 \le k \le K$. The corresponding prediction set $M(CI, F)$ consists of probability prediction functions q such that, for s in S, (3) holds and

$$\mu(\mathbf{y}, s) = \sum_{k=1}^{K} \lambda_{y_k}^{k} + \sum_{k=1}^{K} \lambda_{y_k F(s)}^{kF}$$

for some $\lambda^k_{y_k}$, $1 \le y_k \le C_k$, $1 \le k \le K$, and $\lambda^{kF}_{y_k a}$, $1 \le y_k \le C_k$, $1 \le a \le b$, such that

$$\sum_{y_k=1}^{C_k} \lambda^k_{y_k} = 0, \quad 1 \le k \le K,$$

$$\sum_{y_k=1}^{C_k} \lambda^{kF}_{y_k a} = 0, \quad 1 \le k \le K, 1 \le a \le b,$$

and

$$\sum_{a=1}^{b} \lambda^{kF}_{y_k a} = 0, \quad 1 \le y_k \le C_k, 1 \le k \le K.$$

There are $D(CI, F) = bD(I)$ independent parameters associated with the prediction set $M(CI, F)$. Sufficient expectations are $p_{kF}(y_k, a)$, $1 \le y_k < C_k$, $1 \le k \le K$, $1 \le a \le b$. If the conditional probability prediction function p is in $M(C, F)$, then the Y_k, $1 \le k \le K$, are conditionally independent given $F(\mathbf{X})$ and the conditional probability that $\mathbf{Y} = \mathbf{y}$ in Q given $\mathbf{X} = \mathbf{x}$ depends only on $F(\mathbf{x})$.

The optimal probability prediction function for q in $M(C, F)$ satisfies

$$q(\mathbf{y}, s) = \prod_{k=1}^{K} \frac{p_{kF}(y_k, F(\mathbf{s}))}{p_F(F(\mathbf{X}(s)))}$$

for s in S and $\mathbf{y}$ in Q. Let

$$\text{Ent}(Y_k, F(\mathbf{X})) = -\sum_{y_k=1}^{C_k} \sum_{a=1}^{b} p_{kF}(y_k, a) \log p_{kF}(y_k, a)$$

denote the entropy of the pair $(Y_k, F(\mathbf{X}))$ for $1 \le k \le K$, and let

$$\text{Ent}(F(\mathbf{X})) = -\sum_{a=1}^{b} p_F(a) \log p_F(a)$$

be the entropy of $F(\mathbf{X})$. For $1 \le y_k \le C_k$, $1 \le k \le K$, and $1 \le a \le b$, let $p_{k|F}(y_k|a)$ be the conditional probability $p_{kF}(y_k, a)/p_F(a)$ that $Y_k = y_k$ given that $F = a$. Let

$$\begin{aligned}\mathrm{Ent}(Y_k|F(\mathbf{X})) &= -\sum_{a=1}^{b}\sum_{y_k=1}^{C_k} p_{kF}(y_k,a)\log p_{k|F}(y_k|a)\\ &= \mathrm{Ent}(Y_k,F(\mathbf{X})) - \mathrm{Ent}(F(\mathbf{X}))\end{aligned}$$

be the conditional entropy of Y_k given $F(\mathbf{X})$. Then the minimum expected penalty is

$$\begin{aligned}I(M(CI,F)) &= \sum_{k=1}^{K}\sum_{a=1}^{b} \mathrm{Ent}(Y_k,F(\mathbf{X})) - b\,\mathrm{Ent}(F(\mathbf{X}))\\ &= \sum_{k=1}^{K} \mathrm{Ent}(Y_k|F(\mathbf{X})).\end{aligned}$$

The prediction set $M(I)$ of Example 2 is included in the prediction set $M(CI,F)$, and the difference in minimum expected penalty for the two prediction sets is

$$\Delta(M(I),M(C,F)) = \sum_{k=1}^{K}[\mathrm{Ent}(Y_k) - \mathrm{Ent}(Y_k|F(\mathbf{X}))] \geq 0,$$

with $\Delta(M(I),M(C,F)) = 0$ if and only if Y_k and $F(\mathbf{X})$ are independent for $1 \leq k \leq K$. The difference per parameter is

$$\nu(M(I),M(C,F)) = \frac{\Delta(M(I),M(C,F))}{(b-1)D(I)}.$$

On the other hand, the prediction set $M(C,F)$ of Example 2 is included in $M(CI,F)$, so that the difference in minimum expected penalties is

$$\Delta(M(CI,F),M(C,F)) = \sum_{k=1}^{K}\mathrm{Ent}(Y_k|F(\mathbf{X})) - \mathrm{Ent}(\mathbf{Y}|F(\mathbf{X})).$$

The difference per parameter is

$$\nu(M(CI,F),M(C,F)) = \frac{\Delta(M(CI,F),M(C,F))}{b[C-1-D(I)]}.$$

Example 5: Two-way interactions of response variables. Let the number K of response variables be at least 2. For $1 \leq k < k' \leq K$, let $p_{kk'}(y_k,y_{k'})$ denote the joint probability that $Y_k = y_k$ and $Y_{k'} = y_{k'}$, $1 \leq y_k \leq C_k$, $1 \leq y_{k'} \leq C_{k'}$. Define $p_k(y_k)$ as in Example 3. Consider probability prediction given $p_k(y_k)$, $1 \leq y_k < C_k$, $1 \leq k \leq K$, and $p_{kk'}(y_k,y'_{k'})$, $1 \leq$

$y_k < C_k$, $1 \le y'_{k'} < C_{k'}$, $1 \le k < k' \le K$. Note that the given probabilities specify the bivariate distributions of Y_k and $Y_{k'}$ for $1 \le k < k' \le K$. The corresponding log-linear model is a model with all main effects and two-way interactions. The prediction set $M(T)$ consists of probability prediction functions q that satisfy (3) and

$$\mu(\mathbf{y}, s) = \sum_{k=1}^{K} \lambda^k_{y_k} + \sum_{k'=2}^{K} \sum_{k=1}^{k'-1} \lambda^{kk'}_{y_k y_{k'}} \tag{6}$$

for

$$\sum_{y_k=1}^{C_k} \lambda^k_{y_k} = 0, \quad 1 \le k \le K,$$

$$\sum_{y_k=1}^{C_k} \lambda^{kk'}_{y_k y'_{k'}} = 0, \quad 1 \le y'_{k'} \le C_{k'}, 1 \le k \le K,$$

and

$$\sum_{y'_{k'}=1}^{C_{k'}} \lambda^{kk'}_{y_k y'_{k'}} = 0, \quad 1 \le y_k \le C_k, 1 \le k \le K.$$

There are

$$D(T) = D(I) + \sum_{k'=2}^{K} \sum_{k=1}^{k'-1} (C_k - 1)(C_{k'} - 1)$$

independent parameters. No closed-form expression for $I(M(T))$ is available.

The prediction set $M(T)$ may be employed to measure the information provided by a correspondence analysis or principal components analysis of the categorical profile $\mathbf{Y}$ based on the variables $\delta_{y_k}(Y_k)$, $1 \le y_k < C_k$, $1 \le k \le K$, where, for a real number c, δ_c is the Kronecker function on the real line with value $\delta_c(b)$ at b in R equal to 1 for $b = c$ and equal to 0 for $b = c$. Knowledge of these quantities is equivalent to knowledge of $p_k(y_k)$, $1 \le y_k < C_k$, and $p_{kk'}(y_k, y'_{k'})$, $1 \le y_k < C_k$, $1 \le y'_{k'} < C_{k'}$. Thus the prediction set of this example measures the information $I(M(T))$ available from the specified correspondence analysis. Obviously, the prediction set $M(I)$ of Example 3 is included in $M(T)$, so that an indication of the potential added value of bivariate distributions is provided by $\Delta(M(I), M(T))$, $\nu(M(I), M(T))$, or $\Lambda(M(I), M(T))$.

Example 6: Guttman scaling. In the Goodman (1975) generalization of Guttman (1950) scaling, all response variables are dichotomous ($C_k = 2$ for $1 \le k \le K$), at least two response variables are present ($K \ge 2$), and the variables have been ordered so that typically $Y_k \le Y_{k'}$ for $1 \le k < k' \le K$. The summary information used is the marginal probabilities $p_k(y_k)$, $1 \le y_k < C_k$, and the individual probabilities $p_{\mathbf{Y}}(\mathbf{v}_k)$, $0 \le k \le K$, where $\mathbf{v}_k$, the kth scale type, has coordinates v_{ik}, $1 \le i \le K$, equal to 1 for $i + k \le K$ and 2 for $i + k > K$. Thus the given information specifies the marginal distributions of the responses Y_k for $1 \le k \le K$ and the probability of the kth scale type for $0 \le k \le K$. The prediction set $M(G)$ consists of probability prediction functions q that satisfy a multivariate quasi-independence model in which (3) holds and

$$\mu(\mathbf{y}, s) = \begin{cases} \sum_{k=1}^{K} \lambda_{y_k}^{k} + \gamma_i, & \mathbf{y} = \mathbf{v}_i, 0 \le i \le k, \\ \sum_{k=1}^{K} \lambda_{y_k}^{k}, & \text{otherwise.} \end{cases}$$

Here $\lambda_{y_k}^{k}$ is defined as in Example 3. There are $D(G) = D(I) + K + 1 = 2K + 1$ independent parameters. As in Example 5, no closed-form expression for $I(M(G))$ is available. Clearly, $M(I)$ is included in $M(G)$. One may employ $\Delta(M(I), M(G))$, $\nu(M(I), M(G))$, or $\Lambda(M(I), M(G))$ to measure the effectiveness of the Guttman scale relative to simple use of marginal probabilities.

Example 7: Two-way interactions of responses and a categorical explanatory variable. A generalization of Examples 4 and 5 has a prediction set $M(T, F)$ which consists of probability prediction functions q such that (3) holds and

$$\mu(\mathbf{y}, s) = \sum_{k=1}^{K} \lambda_{y_k}^{k} + \sum_{k'=2}^{K} \sum_{k=1}^{k'-1} \lambda_{y_k y_{k'}}^{kk'} + \sum_{k=1}^{K} \lambda_{y_k F(s)}^{kF}.$$

The parameter constraints are the same as in Examples 4 and 5. There are $D(T, F) = D(T) + (b - 1)D(I)$ independent parameters. The log-linear model is the one conditional on $F(\mathbf{X})$ with all main effects for the variables Y_k, $1 \le k \le K$, and all two-way interactions for the variables Y_k, $1 \le k \le K$, and $F(\mathbf{X})$.

Sufficient expectations are the marginal probabilities $p_{kF}(y_k, a)$, $1 \le y_k < C_k$, $1 \le a \le b$, and $p_{kk'}(y_k, y'_{k'})$, $1 \le y_k < C_k$, $1 \le y'_{k'} < C_{k'}$. The given expectations specify the bivariate distributions of Y_k and $Y_{k'}$ for $1 \le k < k' \le K$ and of $F(\mathbf{X})$ and Y for $1 \le k \le K$. This information is the basis for a conventional correspondence or canonical correlation analysis based on the predicted variables $\delta_{y_k}(Y_k)$, $1 \le y_k < C_k$, $1 \le k \le K$, and the explanatory variables $\delta_a(F(\mathbf{X}))$, $1 \le a < b$. Thus $I(M(T, F))$ measures the information concerning $\mathbf{Y}$ provided by the correspondence analysis.

Example 8: Symmetric interactions associated with category counts. Let C_k be the same for all k from 1 to $K \ge 2$. Assume that categories for different response variables are comparable in meaning, as is the case in the example concerning abortion attitudes. Define U_y to be the number of responses Y_k, $1 \le k \le K$, with value y, $1 \le y \le C_1$. Let the given information be the marginal probabilities $p_k(y_k)$, $1 \le y_k < C_k$, $1 \le k \le K$, and the covariances $\text{cov}(U_y, U_z)$ of U_y and U_z for $1 \le y \le z < C_1$. The given marginal probabilities determine the expectations of the counts U_y for $1 \le y < C_k$, so that the known information includes the expectations of $U_y U_z$ for $1 \le y \le z < C_1$. The equation

$$U_{C_1} = K - \sum_{y=1}^{C_1 - 1} U_y \tag{7}$$

shows that the given information specifies the expectations of the counts U_y for $1 \le y \le C_1$ and the covariances of U_y and U_z for $1 \le y \le z \le C_1$. The corresponding prediction set $M(ST)$ is the set of all prediction functions q in $M(T)$ with the symmetry property that (6) holds and, for fixed y and z from 1 to C_1, $\lambda_{yz}^{kk'}$ is the same for $1 \le k < k' \le K$ and

$$\lambda_{yz}^{kk'} = \lambda_{zy}^{kk'}.$$

Thus there are

$$D(ST) = D(I) + \frac{1}{2} C_1(C_1 - 1)$$

independent parameters. The model is a type of multivariate quasi-symmetry model.

Example 9: Symmetric interactions and scored responses. In Example 8, assign category y_k of variable Y_k the numerical score

$$t(y_k) = y_k - \frac{1}{2}(C_1 + 1)$$

for $1 \leq y_k \leq C_k = C_1$, and let

$$V = \sum_{k=1}^{K} t(Y_k) = \sum_{y=1}^{C_1} t(y)U_y \tag{8}$$

be the sum of the response scores. Let Υ be the possible values of V, so that v is in Υ if $v + K(C_1 - 1)/2$ is a nonnegative integer not greater than $K(C_1 - 1)$. Let $v' = K(C_1 - 1)/2$ denote the largest value in Υ, so that $-v'$ is the smallest value in Υ. In the case of the data on abortion attitudes, $V = U_3 - U_1$ is the difference between the number of negative responses ("no") and the number of positive responses ("yes"), so that V provides an indication of overall position on legalized abortion. In this case, Υ consists of the integers from -6 to 6, and $v' = 6$. Let the information available be the expectations $E(t(Y_k))$ of the response scores for $1 \leq k \leq K$, the probability $p_V(v)$ that $V = v$ for v in Υ and $-v' < v < v'$, the expectations $E(U_y)$ for any integer y such that $y \geq 2$ and $y \leq C_1 - 1$, and the covariances $\text{cov}(U_y, U_z)$ for any integers y and z such that $2 \leq y \leq z \leq C_1 - 1$. In the case of abortion attitudes, the sufficient expectations are the difference

$$E(t(Y_k)) = p_k(3) - p_k(1)$$

between the probability of a response "no" to question k and the probability of a response "yes" to question k for $1 \leq k \leq K = 6$, the expectation $E(U_2)$ of the number U_2 of responses "don't know" or "no answer" provided by a subject, the variance $\text{var}(U_2) = \text{cov}(U_2, U_2)$ of U_2, and the probability $p_V(v)$ that the difference $V = U_3 - U_1$ between the number of responses "no" and the number of responses "yes" is v for integers v such that $-5 \leq v \leq 5$.

As in Example 8, the summary information provides more than may at first be apparent. Knowledge of the mean response scores $E(t(Y_k))$ for $1 \leq k \leq K$ specifies the expected sum of response scores

$$E(V) = \sum_{k=1}^{K} E(t(Y_k)).$$

The expectation

$$E(V) = \sum_{v \in \Upsilon} v p_V(v),$$

and

$$1 = \sum_{v \in \Upsilon} p_V(v),$$

so that $p_V(v')$ and $p_V(-v')$ may be determined from the given information. Thus the distribution of V is determined. Given (7) and (8), it follows that U_1 and U_{C_1} are affine functions of V and of any counts U_y such that $2 \leq y \leq C_1 - 1$. Thus the given information determines the expectations $E(U_y)$ of the counts U_y for all integers y from 1 to C_1 and determines the covariance of U_y and U_z for all integers y and z from 1 to C_1.

The corresponding prediction set $M(V)$ consists of all prediction functions q such that (3) holds and such that

$$\mu(\mathbf{y}, s) = \sum_{k=1}^{K} \lambda_{y_k}^{k} + \sum_{k=2}^{K} \sum_{k'=1}^{k-1} \lambda_{y_k y_{k'}}^{kk'} + \gamma_v \tag{9}$$

for $\mathbf{y}$ in Q, $v = \sum_{k=1}^{K} t(y_k)$, and s in S for some unknown parameters $\lambda_{y_k}^{k}$, $\lambda_{y_k y_{k'}}^{kk'}$, and γ_v. The $\lambda_{y_k y_{k'}}^{kk'}$ satisfy the constraints in Examples 5 and 8 and satisfy the constraint that

$$\sum_{y_1=1}^{C_1} t(y_1)\lambda_{y_1 y_2}^{12} = 0$$

for $1 \leq y_2 \leq C_2 = C_1$, the γ_v are defined for v in Υ so that $\gamma_{v'}$ and $\gamma_{-v'}$ are 0, and

$$\lambda_{y_k}^{k} = \tau_k t(y_k) + \rho_{y_k}, \quad 1 \leq y_k \leq C_k, 1 \leq k \leq K,$$

for some real τ_k, $1 \leq k \leq K$, and some real ρ_y, $1 \leq y \leq C_1$, such that

$$\sum_{k=1}^{K} \tau_k = \sum_{y=1}^{C_1} \rho_y = \sum_{y=1}^{C_1} t(y)\rho_y = 0.$$

If $C_1 = 2$, then the $\lambda_{y_k y'_{k'}}^{kk'}$ are all 0 and, as in Tjur (1982) and Agresti (1993), $M(V)$ corresponds to the log-linear model that corresponds to the conditional Rasch (1960) model. If $C_1 > 2$ and $K = 2$, then $M(V)$ corresponds to the log-linear model in Agresti (1993) derived from a multinomial Rasch (1960) model with scored responses. (See also Goodman [1972].) If $C_1 > 2$ and $K > 2$, then one has a restricted version of the Agresti (1993) log-linear model based on the multinomial Rasch (1960) model with scored responses.

To examine these claims, consider nonnegative integers u_z, $1 \leq z \leq C_1$, with sum $\sum_{z=1}^{C_1} u_z = K$. Let $\mathbf{u}$ be the vector with coordinates u_z for $1 \leq z \leq C_1$. Let $\psi(\mathbf{u})$ be the set of possible response profiles $\mathbf{y}$ with coordinates y_k for $1 \leq k \leq K$ such that u_z of the y_k equal z for $1 \leq z \leq C_1$. As in Agresti (1993), under (9), the probabilities $q(\mathbf{y}, s)$ assigned to the events $\mathbf{Y} = \mathbf{y}$ for possible response profiles $\mathbf{y}$ in Q correspond to a conditional probability

$$\frac{\exp\left[\sum_{k=1}^{K} \tau_k t(y_k)\right]}{\sum_{\mathbf{y}' \in \psi(\mathbf{u})} \exp\left[\sum_{k=1}^{K} \tau_k t(y'_k)\right]} \tag{10}$$

that $\mathbf{Y} = \mathbf{y}$ given that $U_z = u_z$ for z from 1 to C_1. This conditional probability depends only on the scores $t(y_k)$ and on the coefficients τ_k for $1 \leq k \leq K$.

For $K > 2$ and $C_1 > 2$, the proposed model differs from the Agresti (1993) model in that stronger restrictions are placed on interactions. Let $k(1)$ and $k(2)$ be integers such that $1 \leq k(1) < k(2) \leq K$, and let $\mathbf{z}$ be a response profile in Q with coordinates z_k for k from 1 to K such that $z_{k(1)}$ and $z_{k(2)}$ are both less than C_1. Let $c(1)$ and $c(2)$ be positive integers such that $z_{k(1)} + c(1)$ and $z_{k(2)} + c(2)$ are no greater than C_1. Let $\mathbf{y}_{ab}$, $0 \leq a \leq 1$, $0 \leq b \leq 1$, be response profiles defined so that the response for item k is

$$y_{kab} = \begin{cases} z_k + ac(1), & k = k(1), \\ z_k + bc(2), & k = k(2), \\ z_k, & k = k(1), k = k(2), \end{cases}$$

Then the cross-product ratio

$$\left[\frac{q(\mathbf{y}_{00}, s)q(\mathbf{y}_{11}, s)}{q(\mathbf{y}_{10}, s)q(\mathbf{y}_{01}, s)}\right]$$

is determined by $c(1)$, $c(2)$, $z_{k(1)}$, $z_{k(2)}$, and $\sum_{k=1}^{K} t(z_k)$.

In the case of the data on abortion attitudes, the λ_2^k parameter, which corresponds to the responses "don't know" or "no answer," is a constant ρ_2 for each response Y_k. The constraints on ρ_y for $1 \leq y \leq 3$ imply that $\rho_1 = \rho_3$ and $\rho_2 = -2\rho_3$, so that

$$\lambda_1^k = -\tau_k + \rho_3,$$
$$\lambda_2^k = -2\rho_3,$$
$$\lambda_3^k = \tau_k + \rho_3,$$

and

$$\tau_k = \frac{1}{2}(\lambda_3^k - \lambda_1^k).$$

Constraints on interactions imply that λ_{11}^{11}, λ_{13}^{11},λ_{31}^{11}, and λ_{33}^{11} are the same, λ_{12}^{11}, λ_{21}^{11}, λ_{23}^{11}, and λ_{32}^{11} are all $-2\lambda_{11}^{11}$, and λ_{22}^{11} is $4\lambda_{11}^{11}$. Thus the only parameter directly associated with the responses "don't know" or "no answer" is ρ_2.

For $K > 2$, the prediction set $M(V)$ does not include $M(ST)$, and $M(ST)$ does not include $M(V)$. There are

$$D(V) = KC_1 - 1 + \frac{1}{2}(C_1 + 1)(C_1 - 2)$$

independent parameters.

Example 10: Two-way interactions associated with average responses and explanatory variables. In Example 9, consider the addition of covariates. Let the covariates be real functions F_g, $1 \le g \le h$, defined on the range T of the explanatory profile $\mathbf{X}$ in such a fashion that $F_g(\mathbf{X})$ is a real random variable with finite variance. Let $\mathbf{F}$ denote the h-dimensional function with coordinates F_g for $1 \le g \le h$.

In addition to the information available in Example 9, let the covariances of V and $F_g(\mathbf{X})$ be known for $1 \le g \le h$, and let the joint distribution of $\mathbf{F}$ be known. Given that the joint distribution of the $\mathbf{F}$ is known, given that F_g has positive variance, given that the distribution of V is known, and given that V has positive variance, knowledge of the correlation of V and $F_g(\mathbf{X})$ is the same as knowledge of the covariance of V and $F_g(\mathbf{X})$. If F_g is a dummy variable that only assumes the values 0 and 1 and $F_g = 1$ with positive probability, then knowledge of the conditional expectation of V given $F_g = 1$ is equivalent to knowledge of the covariance of F_g and V.

The corresponding prediction set $M(V, \mathbf{F})$ is the set of probability prediction functions q that satisfy (3) and satisfy the equation

$$\mu(\mathbf{y}, s) = \sum_{k=1}^{K} \lambda_{y_k}^k + \sum_{k'=2}^{K} \sum_{k=1}^{k'-1} \lambda_{y_k y_{k'}}^{kk'} + \gamma_v + \sum_{g=1}^{h} \zeta_g V(s) F_g(\mathbf{X})(s)$$

where $\lambda^k_{y_k}$ and $\lambda^{kk'}_{y_k y'_{k'}}$ satisfy the constraints of Examples 4, 5, 8, and 9, γ_v satisfies the conditions of Example 9, and $v = \sum_{k=1}^{K} t(y_k)$.

For any possible value **f** of $\mathbf{F}(\mathbf{X})$, the $q(\mathbf{y}, s)$ for **y** in Q correspond to a conditional probability of $\mathbf{Y} = \mathbf{y}$ given $V = v$ and $\mathbf{F}(\mathbf{X}) = \mathbf{f}$ that is the same as the conditional probability of $\mathbf{Y} = \mathbf{y}$ given $V = v$. Thus for a conditional probability prediction function p in $M(V, \mathbf{F})$, the conditional distribution of **Y** given $V = v$ and $\mathbf{F}(\mathbf{X}) = \mathbf{f}$ is the same as the conditional distribution of **Y** given $V = v$. Thus the relationship between **Y** and $\mathbf{F}(\mathbf{X})$ is determined by the relationship between V and $\mathbf{F}(\mathbf{X})$. In addition, given that $\mathbf{F}(\mathbf{X})$ is f, the conditional log odds that $V = v$ rather than v', v in Υ, is

$$(v - v') \sum_{g=1}^{k} \zeta_g f_g.$$

Comparison of $M(V)$ and $M(V, \mathbf{F})$ provides an indication of the value of the $F_g(\mathbf{X})$, $1 \leq g \leq h$, in prediction of **Y**.

In the abortion example, $\mathbf{F}(\mathbf{X})$ will be taken to be **X**.

2.8. *Estimation*

In typical cases, the measures and parameters developed in Sections 2 to 2.7 must be estimated from the sample observations $\mathbf{X}_i$ and $\mathbf{Y}_i$ for $1 \leq i \leq n$. The methods developed by Gilula and Haberman (1994, 1995) for conditional log-linear models and Haberman (1989) for exponential response models may be applied without difficulty. Given a probability prediction function q, the expected penalty function $H(q)$ has the estimate

$$H_n(q) = -n^{-1} \sum_{i=1}^{n} \log[q(\mathbf{Y}_i), s_i].$$

The estimated minimum expected penalty $I_n(M)$ is the minimum of $H_n(q)$ for q in M, with q_n in M an estimated optimal probability prediction function if $H_n(q_n) = I_n(M)$. An estimated optimal probability prediction function q_n is, conditional on the $\mathbf{X}_i$, $1 \leq i \leq n$, a maximum-likelihood estimate of the conditional probability prediction function p under the model that p is in M.

In the trivial case of a prediction set M with $D = 0$ independent parameters, the only element of M is the constant probability prediction function e such that $e(s)$ assigns value $1/C$ to each member of Q. In this case,

$$H_n(e) = H(e) = \log C,$$

so that the minimum expected penalty $I(M) = \log C$ has the trivial estimate $I_n(M) = \log C$. The unique estimated optimal probability prediction function q_n is e.

If the prediction set M has $D > 0$ independent parameters and M is generated by $Z_d(\mathbf{y})$ for $\mathbf{y}$ in Q and $1 \leq d \leq D$, then, for q in M, the estimated expected penalty $H_n(q)$ is determined by the joint sample distribution of the $Z_d(\mathbf{y}, s_i)$, $\mathbf{y}$ in Q, $1 \leq d \leq D$, for $1 \leq i \leq n$, and by the sample means

$$\bar{Z}_d = n^{-1} \sum_{i=1}^{n} Z_d(\mathbf{Y}_i, s_i)$$

for $\mathbf{y}$ in Q and $1 \leq d \leq D$. As in Section 2.4, if (2) and (3) hold, then

$$H_n(q) = \sum_{d=1}^{D} \beta_d \bar{Z}_d - n^{-1} \sum_{i=1}^{n} \log \sum_{\mathbf{y} \in Q} \exp \sum_{d=1}^{D} \beta_d Z_d(\mathbf{y}, s_i).$$

Thus the sample means $\bar{Z}_d$, $1 \leq d \leq D$, provide a sample data summary which provides all information concerning the response variable $\mathbf{Y}$, which is used in the sample to assess the quality of the probability prediction of $\mathbf{Y}$ by a q in M. For further details concerning estimation of the optimal prediction function q_n, see Appendix B.

If M' is a prediction set with D' independent parameters, then $\Delta(M', M)$ is estimated by

$$\Delta_n(M', M) = I_n(M') - I_n(M),$$

$\Lambda(M', M)$ is estimated by

$$\Lambda_n(M', M) = \Delta_n(M', M)/I_n(M')$$

if $I_n(M') > 0$, and $\nu(M', M)$ is estimated by

$$\nu_n(M', M) = \Delta_n(M', M)/(D - D')$$

if $D = D'$.

2.9. *Normal Approximations*

In typical cases, $I_n(M)$, $\Delta_n(M',M)$, $\Lambda_n(M',M)$, and $\nu_n(M',M)$ have normal approximations that may be employed to obtain approximate confidence intervals. The conditions required are minimal. In the case of M and in the case of $D > 0$ independent parameters, let $Z_d(\mathbf{y})$, $\mathbf{y}$ in Q, $1 \leq d \leq D$, generate M, assume that the $Z_d(\mathbf{y})$ have finite variances, and assume that the optimal probability prediction function q in M is defined. Similarly, in the case of M' and in the case of $D' > 0$ independent parameters, let $Z'_d(\mathbf{y})$, $\mathbf{y}$ in Q, $1 \leq d \leq D'$, generate M', assume that the $Z'_d(\mathbf{y})$ have finite variances, and assume that the optimal probability prediction function q' in M' is defined. Under these circumstances, the probability approaches 1 that there is a unique estimated optimal probability prediction function q_n in M and a unique estimated optimal probability prediction function q'_n in M'. Normal approximations are always available for the distributions of $I_n(M)$ and $\Delta_n(M',M)$. If $D = D'$, then a normal approximation for $\nu_n(M',M)$ is available. If $I_n(M') > 0$, then a normal approximation for $\Lambda_n(M',M)$ is available. Appropriate formulas are provided in Appendix C for normal approximations and for approximate confidence intervals.

Application of normal approximations requires caution. As noted in Gilula and Haberman (1994, 1995), the expectation $E(I_n(M))$ cannot exceed $E(H_n(q)) = I(M)$. In general, $n[I(M) - E(I_n(M))]$ converges to a constant $g(M)$ described in Appendix C. If the conditional probability prediction function p is in the prediction set M, then $g(M)$ is $D/2$. In some cases, $g(M)$ remains $D/2$ even if p is not in M. It is reasonable to expect problems with the normal approximation if D^2/n is not small, a result not surprising given Haberman (1977a, 1977b). For comparison of models, it is reasonable to expect that normal approximations will be problematic if either the number D of independent parameters of prediction set M or the number D' of independent parameters of prediction set M' is large relative to the square root $n^{1/2}$ of the sample size n.

3. COMPARISON OF PREDICTION SETS UNDER SAMPLING

In this section, three common approaches are considered for comparison of prediction sets under sampling: (1) hypothesis tests; (2) the Akaike (1974) information criteria, which is compared to a modification of Gilula and Haberman (1994, 1995); and (3) the Schwarz (1978) Bayesian information criterion.

3.1. *Hypothesis Tests*

If the prediction set M' is included in the prediction set M, then

$$L^2(M',M) = 2n\Delta_n(M',M)$$

is the likelihood-ratio chi-square statistic for the null hypothesis that the conditional probability prediction function p is in M' and the alternative hypothesis that p is in M. If p is in M', then $\Delta(M',M) = 0$ and $L^2(M',M)$ has an approximate chi-square distribution on $D - D'$ degrees of freedom. If $\Delta(M',M) > 0$, then $L^2(M',M)$ approaches ∞ as the sample size increases, so that, for any positive significance level α, the probability approaches 1 that $L^2(M',M)$ is significant at level α. It is possible that $\Delta(M',M) = 0$ but p is not in M'. This case is considered in Appendix C. As will be evident in Section 4, observed significance levels encountered in model comparisons will be very small.

The statistic $L^2(M',M)$ may still be defined if M' is not included in M. This statistic is twice the logarithm of the likelihood ratio for the null hypothesis that p is in M' and the alternative hypothesis that p is in M. As noted in Appendix C, if $\Delta(M',M) = 0$ and the optimal probability prediction function in M' is also the optimal probability prediction function in M, then the distribution of $L^2(M',M)$ is approximately the difference of two nonnegative random variables Γ and Γ' described in Appendix C. If $\Delta(M',M) = 0$ but the optimal probability prediction function in M' is not the optimal probability prediction function in M, then it follows from Appendix C that $n^{-1/2}L^2(M',M)$ has an approximate normal distribution with asymptotic mean 0 and asymptotic standard deviation $2\tau(\Delta, M', M)$, where $\tau(\Delta, M', M)$ is defined in Appendix C. If $\Delta(M',M) > 0$, then $L^2(M',M)$ approaches ∞ as the sample size increases. If $\Delta(M',M) < 0$, then $L^2(M',M)$ approaches $-\infty$ as the sample size increases.

3.2. *The Akaike Information Criterion*

Akaike (1974) proposes that two prediction sets M and M' be compared by use of the statistics $nI_n(M) + D$ and $nI_n(M') + D'$. Thus the prediction set M is preferred if

$$A_n(M',M) = \Delta_n(M',M) + (D' - D)/n$$

is positive, while M' is preferred if $A_m(M', M)$ is negative. In large samples, for any real $\epsilon > 0$, the probability approaches 1 that

$$|n^{1/2}[A_n(M', M) - \Delta_n(M', M)]| < \epsilon.$$

Thus $A_n(M', M)$ has the same normal approximation as $\Delta_n(M', M)$. If $\Delta(M', M) > 0$, the probability approaches 1 that M is preferred. If $\Delta(M', M) < 0$, then the probability approaches 1 that M' is preferred. If $\Delta(M', M)$ is 0, then the limiting probability that M is preferred is positive but less than 1.

The Akaike criterion is based on probability prediction of a new categorical profile variable $\mathbf{Y}'$ with a conditional distribution given $\mathbf{X}$ equal to the conditional distribution of $\mathbf{Y}$ given $\mathbf{X}$. Let q_n be the estimated optimal prediction function in M. Then q_n may be used for probability prediction of $\mathbf{Y}'$, and $H(q_n)$ measures the expected penalty for probability prediction of $\mathbf{Y}'$ by use of q_n. As in Gilula and Haberman (1994), the difference $n[H(q_n) - H_n(q)]$ is increasingly well approximated by the difference $n[H_n(q) - I_n(M)]$ as the sample size becomes large. As evident from Section 2.9, $n[H_n(q) - I_n(M)]$ is a random variable with mean approximated by $g(M)$. It follows that $H(q_n)$ may be approximated by $I_n(M) + 2g(M)/n$. If the conditional probability prediction function p is in M, then $H(q_n)$ is approximated by

$$I_{na}(M) = I_n(M) + \frac{1}{n}D.$$

Similarly, let q_n' be the estimated optimal prediction function in M'. Then $H_n(q_n')$ may be approximated by $I_{na}(M')$ if p is in M'. Thus the Akaike criterion

$$A_n(M', M) = I_{na}(M') - I_{na}(M)$$

approximates the difference $H(q_n') - H(q_n)$ under the condition that p is in the prediction sets M and M'. This restriction is a weakness of the Akaike criterion in our case in which no presumption exists that the conditional probability function p is in either M or M'.

A more general comparison criterion is obtained by estimation of $g(M)$ and $g(M')$. Let $\hat{g}(M)$ denote the sample estimate of $g(M)$. Then $H(q_n)$ can be approximated by

$$I_{ng}(M) = I_n(M) + \frac{1}{n}\hat{g}(M)$$

without any assumptions concerning the conditional probability prediction function p, and $A_n(M',M)$ can be replaced by

$$A'_n(M',M) = I_{ng}(M') - I_{ng}(M) = \Delta_n(M',M) + \frac{1}{n}[\hat{g}(M') - \hat{g}(M)].$$

This change does not have fundamental effects on large-sample properties. For real $\epsilon > 0$, the probability approaches 1 that

$$n^{1/2}|A'_n(M',M) - \Delta_n(M',M)| < \epsilon.$$

Thus the normal approximations for $A'_n(M',M)$ and $A_n(M',M)$ are the same. In addition, in Example 1, $\hat{g}(M(S)) = C - 1$, and in Example 2, $\hat{g}(M(C,F)) = b(C-1)$, so that

$$A'_n(M(S),M(C,F)) = A_n(M(S),M(C,F)).$$

3.3. *The Bayesian Information Criterion*

In the Schwarz (1978) approach to model comparison, the model that p is in M is compared to the model that p is in M' by comparison of $nI_n(M) + (1/2)D \log n$ and $nI_n(M') + (1/2)D' \log n$. Let

$$I_{ns}(M) = I_n(M) + \frac{D \log n}{2n}$$

and

$$B_n(M',M) = I_{ns}(M') - I_{ns}(M) = \Delta_n(M',M) + \frac{1}{2n}(D' - D)\log n.$$

The prediction set M is preferred if $B_n(M',M)$ is positive, and prediction set M' is preferred if $B_n(M',M)$ is negative. The criterion $B_n(M',M)$ has the same basic large-sample properties as $\Delta_n(M',M)$. For any real $\epsilon > 0$, the probability approaches 1 that

$$n^{1/2}|B_n(M',M) - \Delta_n(M',M)| < \epsilon.$$

Thus $B_n(M,M)$ and $\Delta_n(M',M)$ have the same normal approximation. If $\Delta(M',M) > 0$, then the probability approaches 1 that M is preferred. If $\Delta(M',M) < 0$, then the probability approaches 1 that M' is preferred. The preference situation is a bit different than in the Akaike (1974) case if $\Delta(M',M) = 0$. In this case, if $D' < D$ and M' is included in M, then the probability approaches 1 that M' is preferred. If $D' > D$ and M' includes M, then the probability approaches 1 that M is preferred.

The rationale for the Schwarz criterion is based on a Bayesian model which assumes that a positive prior probability exists that the conditional probability prediction function p is in M and a positive prior probability exists that p is in M'. Given that p is in M and $D > 0$, it is assumed that the parameters β_d, $1 \leq d \leq D$, in (2) have a joint continuous prior probability distribution with positive density. A similar assumption is made concerning the condition that p is in M'. Schwarz (1978) shows that, given that p is in M or M', the posterior log odds that p is in M rather than M' differs from $nB_n(M', M)$ by no more than a finite function of the $\bar{Z}_d$ for d from 1 to D and the corresponding variables $\bar{Z}'_d$ for d from 1 to D', where $\bar{Z}'_d$ is defined in a manner analogous to that used to define $\bar{Z}_d$ in Section 2.8.

Two issues arise in interpretation of the Schwarz criterion in terms of Bayesian inference. The first involves the accuracy of the approximation. On the one hand, it is possible to find prior parameter distributions under which the difference between $nB_n(M', M)$ and the posterior log odds approaches 0 as the sample size becomes large (Kass and Wasserman 1995). On the other hand, variations in the choice of prior distribution can have very large effects on posterior odds, so that the Schwarz criterion can be very far from the appropriate posterior odds (Kass and Raftery 1995). A more fundamental issue is that the assumption that a restricted probability model has a positive probability of being true is a very strong assumption, especially in the context of sociology. Even in the case of well-established laws of physics, the difficulty of successfully measuring the same quantity in a consistent fashion is impressive, as evident in Jeffreys (1961, p. 307) in a discussion of comparisons of use of gold, platinum, and glass to measure the gravitational constant. It appears far more honest to admit that models are rarely true and to assess their value as approximations than to claim that they may be true and try to find statistical procedures that can be used to hide their falsity.

Nonetheless, the main reported large-sample properties of $B_n(M', M)$ remain without use of the Bayesian framework.

4. APPLICATION TO DATA ON ABORTION ATTITUDES

In the analysis of the data on abortion attitudes, prediction sets (models) with a limited number of independent parameters have been emphasized in order to ensure that large-sample approximations are reliable. In some instances, other prediction sets are employed to provide bounds for possible results or to indicate alternatives that might be investigated. As described in Section 2.8, for a sample of size n, $I_n(M)$ measures the quality of probability prediction associated with prediction set M. Small values of $I_n(M)$ reflect successful probability prediction. As in Appendix C, the symbol $\hat{\sigma}$ is used to designate an estimated asymptotic standard deviation used in computation of approximate confidence intervals. Thus $\hat{\sigma}(I_n(M))$ is the estimated asymptotic standard deviation of the estimated minimum expected penalty $I_n(M)$ associated with the prediction set M.

When interpreting the results, it is important to determine upper and lower bounds for quality of prediction. The saturated model with prediction set $M(S)$ (Example 1) provides a lower bound $I_n(M(S)) = 2.800$ for the minimum estimated expected penalty $I_n(M)$ for a prediction set M that does not use explanatory variables. The prediction set $M(S)$ has $D(S) =$ 728 independent parameters, so that this prediction set is not attractive in terms of parsimony. Indeed, $M(S)$ has the maximum number of independent parameters of any prediction set that does not involve explanatory variables. At the other extreme, for the trivial equiprobability model $M(0)$ with $D = 0$ independent parameters (Section 2.3), the minimum estimated expected penalty is $I_n(M(0)) = I(M(0)) = 6.592$. Hence, for any prediction set M, $I_n(M) \leq 6.592$ and $I(M) \leq 6.592$. Thus the estimated difference $\Delta_n(M(0), M)$ between the minimum estimated expected penalty for M and the minimum estimated expected penalty for $M(0)$ cannot exceed

$$I_n(M(0)) - I_n(M(S)) = 3.792$$

if the prediction set M is included in $M(S)$.

The prediction sets considered in the analysis of the abortion data are $M(0)$, $M(I)$ (Example 3, mutual independence of response variables), $M(ST)$ (Example 8, symmetric interactions associated with category counts), $M(V)$ (Example 9, two-way interactions associated with average responses), and $M(V, \mathbf{X})$ (Example 10, two-way interactions associated with average responses and explanatory variables). Tables 5 to 9 provide the basic summary data used in the analyses. Tables 10 and 11 summarize the basic results required for analysis of the data on abortion attitudes by use of prediction sets just described. In Table 10, recall that $I_{na}(M)$ is the Akaike criterion, Section 3.2, $I_{ng}(M)$ is the modification of the Akaike (1974) criterion of Gilula and Haberman (1994, 1995) (Section 3.2), $I_{ns}(M)$ is the Schwarz (1978) criterion (Section 3.3). It should be noted that the differences between $I_n(M)$, $I_{na}(M)$, $I_{ng}(M)$, and $I_{ns}(M)$ are negligible, as

TABLE 4
Marginal Sample Distributions of Response Variables

Question	Response	Frequency	Fraction
A	Yes	19,973	.786
	Other	936	.037
	No	4,491	.177
B	Yes	10,663	.420
	Other	1,062	.042
	No	13,675	.538
C	Yes	22,162	.873
	Other	808	.032
	No	2,430	.096
D	Yes	11,874	.467
	Other	1,129	.044
	No	12,397	.488
E	Yes	20,086	.791
	Other	1,153	.045
	No	4,161	.164
F	Yes	10,948	.431
	Other	1,179	.046
	No	13,273	.523

can be expected given the large sample size. As a consequence, the discussion in this section will emphasize $I_n(M)$.

To aid in understanding results reported in Table 11, consider as an example the comparison of prediction sets $M(V)$ and $M(ST)$. The prediction set $M(V)$ involves four more independent parameters than does $M(ST)$. The change in minimum estimated expected penalty $\Delta_n(M(ST),$

TABLE 5
Average Responses Scores

Question	Average
A	−0.609
B	0.118
C	−0.777
D	0.021
E	−0.627
F	0.092

TABLE 6
Response Counts: Sample Means and Variances

Response	Mean Count	Variance
Yes	3.768	4.077
Other	0.247	0.676
No	1.983	3.729

$M(V))$ is only 0.030. This small change is quite accurately estimated, as is evident from the estimated asymptotic standard deviation $\hat{\sigma}(\Delta_n(M(ST), M(V)))$ of 0.002. The Akaike (1974) comparative measure $A_n(M(ST), M(V))$ of Section 3.2, the Gilula and Haberman (1994, 1995) comparative measure $A'_n(M(ST), M(V))$ of Section 3.2, and the Schwarz (1978) criterion $B_n(M(ST), M(V))$ of Section 3.3 are all 0.030. Examination of these comparative information measures for the entire table reveals negligible differences between them, again an expected result given the large sample sizes. Discussion in this section will emphasize $\Delta_n(M', M)$.

The proportional reduction in minimum estimated expected penalty $\Lambda_n(M(ST), M(V)) = 0.010$ is quite small. As evident from the estimated asymptotic standard deviation $\hat{\sigma}(\Lambda_n(M(ST), M(V))) = 0.001$, the

TABLE 7
Sample Distribution of Response Score Sums

Sum	Relative Frequency
−6	0.340
−5	0.013
−4	0.075
−3	0.017
−2	0.089
−1	0.018
0	0.206
1	0.018
2	0.087
3	0.013
4	0.052
5	0.009
6	0.064

TABLE 8
Sample Correlations of Response Score Sums and Explanatory Variables

Variable	Correlation
X_1	0.029
X_2	0.034
X_3	0.100
X_4	0.018
X_5	0.030
X_6	0.106
X_7	−0.083
X_8	0.139
X_9	0.039
X_{10}	−0.246
X_{11}	0.066
X_{12}	0.072
X_{13}	−0.162

TABLE 9
Sample Means of Response Scores for Selected Subgroups

Group	Count	Sample Mean
All subjects	25,400	−3.521
Male	11,183	−3.612
Female	14,217	−3.450
White	21,401	−3.626
Black	3,513	−2.923
Other race	486	−3.210
Northeast	5,183	−3.879
North Central	7,004	−3.403
South	8,337	−3.157
West	4,353	−3.962
No reported age	108	−2.012
Reported age	25,292	−3.523
No reported education	83	−0.771
Reported education	25,317	−3.530

TABLE 10
Estimated Expected Penalties for Prediction Sets

M	D	$I_n(M)$	$I_{na}(M)$	$I_{ng}(M)$	$I_{ns}(M)$	$\hat{\sigma}(I_n(M))$
$M(0)$	0	6.592	6.592	6.592	6.592	0.000
$M(I)$	12	4.211	4.212	4.212	4.214	0.016
$M(ST)$	15	2.880	2.881	2.881	2.883	0.013
$M(V)$	19	2.850	2.851	2.854	2.854	0.013
$M(V,\mathbf{X})$	32	2.790	2.791	2.791	2.796	0.013

Note: The number of independent parameters associated with M is denoted by D.

coefficient $\Lambda_n(M(ST), M(V))$ is quite well determined. The reduction per parameter in minimum estimated expected penalty is only $\nu_n(M(ST), M(V)) = 0.008$. This small reduction is nonetheless far larger than its estimated asymptotic standard deviation $\hat{\sigma}(\nu_n(M(ST), M(V)))$ of 0.000 (that is, the estimate is less than 0.0005). The likelihood-ratio chi-square statistic $L^2(M(ST), M(V))$ of 1,539 is very large. Although $M(V)$ does not include $M(ST)$ and $M(ST)$ does not include $M(V)$, it is obvious from the large-sample approximations described in Appendix C that such a large likelihood-ratio chi-square is extremely unlikely if the conditional probability prediction function is in both $M(ST)$ and $M(V)$. More strikingly, in Table 11, the likelihood-ratio chi-square statistics for all other pairs of prediction sets are much larger. As noted in the introduction, use of likelihood-ratio chi-squares for assessment of prediction quality is practically useless for the sample size under study.

As evident from examination of prediction set $M(V)$, a prediction set contained in $M(S)$ with a quite modest number of independent parameters is very effective for probability prediction. The set $M(V)$ has only $D(V) = 19$ independent parameters, yet $I_n(M(V))$ is 2.850. Thus the difference $\Delta_n(M(0), M(V)) = 3.742$ is *98.7 percent of the maximum potential value of $\Delta_n(M(0), M)$ for a prediction set M in $M(S)$ and 96.5 percent of the maximum potential value of $\Delta_n(M(I), M)$ for a prediction set M in $M(S)$*. The ratio $\Lambda_n(M(0), M(V))$ is 0.568, and the reduction in estimated expected penalty per parameter is estimated to be $\nu_n(M(0), M(V)) = 0.197$.

The information required for estimation for the prediction set $M(V)$ is the table of sample means of response scores for the six abortion questions (Table 5), the fraction of observed subjects for whom the difference V between the number of responses "no" and the number of responses

TABLE 11

Estimated Statistics for Comparison of Prediction Sets

M	M'	$D-D'$	$\Delta_n(M',M)$	$\hat{\sigma}(\Delta_n(M',M))$	$L^2(M',M)$	$A_n(M',M)$	$A'_n(M',M)$	$B_n(M',M)$	$\Lambda_n(M',M)$	$\hat{\sigma}(\Lambda_n(M',M))$	$\nu_n(M',M)$	$\hat{\sigma}(\nu_n(M',M))$
$M(I)$	$M(0)$	12	2.380	0.016	12,092	2.380	2.380	2.378	0.361	0.002	0.198	0.001
$M(ST)$	$M(0)$	15	3.712	0.013	18,854	3.711	3.711	3.708	0.563	0.002	0.247	0.001
$M(ST)$	$M(I)$	3	1.331	0.014	6,762	1.331	1.331	1.331	0.316	0.006	0.444	0.004
$M(V)$	$M(0)$	19	3.742	0.013	19,008	3.741	3.741	3.738	0.568	0.002	0.197	0.001
$M(V)$	$M(I)$	7	1.362	0.013	6,916	1.361	1.361	1.360	0.323	0.003	0.194	0.002
$M(V)$	$M(ST)$	4	0.030	0.002	1,539	0.030	0.030	0.030	0.010	0.001	0.008	0.000
$M(V,\mathbf{X})$	$M(0)$	32	3.802	0.013	19,313	3.800	3.800	3.795	0.577	0.002	0.119	0.000
$M(V,\mathbf{X})$	$M(I)$	20	1.421	0.014	7,221	1.421	1.421	1.417	0.338	0.003	0.071	0.001
$M(V,\mathbf{X})$	$M(ST)$	17	0.090	0.003	4,582	0.090	0.090	0.087	0.031	0.001	0.005	0.000
$M(V,\mathbf{X})$	$M(V)$	13	0.060	0.002	3,043	0.059	0.059	0.057	0.021	0.001	0.005	0.000

Note: There are D independent parameters associated with M and D' independent parameters associated with M'.

"yes" is v for $-5 \leq v \leq 5$ (Table 7), and the sample mean and sample variance of the number U_2 of responses "don't know" and "no answer" provided by individual subjects (Table 6). Note that in Table 5, the sample mean for item k is the difference between the fraction $f_k(3)$ of subjects who answer "no" and the fraction $f_k(1)$ of subjects who answer "yes" to this item. As is evident, the sample means vary considerably. The means for questions A, C, and E are quite low, for the minimum possible mean is -1 and the maximum possible mean is 1. These results correspond in Table 4 to the high fraction of respondents who favor legality of abortions in cases involving the mother's health, birth defects, or rape. The means for questions B, D, and F are relatively close to 0. They reflect the fact that for other reasons for legal abortion, the fraction of subjects in favor is roughly comparable to the fraction of subjects opposed. In Table 7, the use of other responses is modest, for the average number U_2 of such responses per subject is 0.247. The maximum possible value is 6. Alternatively, the average fraction of subjects who give a response of "don't know" or "no answer" to a question is

$$6^{-1} \sum_{k=1}^{6} f_k(2) = 0.247/6 = 0.041,$$

or about 4.1 percent per question. The sample variance for the number U_2 of other responses is 0.676, a quite large value given the relatively small sample mean. Note that the estimated variance of U_2 would be

$$\sum_{k=1}^{6} f_k(2)[1 - f_k(2)] = 0.237$$

were responses independent (Example 3, prediction set $M(I)$). Table 2 provides further insight into this matter. The 236 subjects who only use the other responses account for 1,416 (22.6 percent) of the 6,267 uses of other responses by all 25,400 subjects. Table 2 also provides insight into the observed distribution in Table 7 of the summary variable V. The value -6 is observed only if "yes" is the response to each question. Thus the relative frequency 0.340 of $V = -6$ is the same as the relative frequency of each response "yes." In like fashion, $V = 6$ corresponds to responses of "no" for all questions. The response $V = 0$ can be obtained for a number of distinct categorical profiles. It is notable that the relative frequency of $V = 0$ is 0.206, while 0.179 is the relative frequency of responses "yes" for reasons A, C, and E and responses "no" for reasons B, D, and F. The relative frequency is 0.009 for the categorical profile for each response "don't know" or "no answer."

As evident from Table 4, the marginal probabilities $p_k(y_k)$ are quite far from the value of $1/3$ associated with equiprobability. It is not surprising that the nonuniform marginal distributions of the responses Y_k can be used with prediction set $M(I)$ to greatly reduce the estimated expected penalty from the value obtained with $M(0)$. One has $I_n(M(I)) = 4.211$, so that the reduction in estimated expected log penalty is

$$\Delta_n(M(0), M(I)) = 2.380,$$

the estimated reduction per independent parameter is $\nu_n(M(0), M(I)) = 0.198$, and the proportional reduction in estimated expected penalty is

$$\Lambda_n(M(0), M(I)) = 0.361.$$

The average entropy

$$K^{-1} \sum_{k=1}^{K} \mathrm{Ent}(Y_k) = K^{-1} I(M(I))$$

of an individual response is estimated to be

$$4.211/6 = 0.702.$$

This average is slightly larger than $\log 2 = 0.693$, the maximum possible average entropy achievable if only responses "yes" and "no" had positive probability.

It is clear from the information measures that the mutual dependence of the response variables is quite strong. Observe that the change in expected penalty from use of $M(V)$ rather than $M(I)$ is

$$\Delta_n(M(I), M(V)) = 1.362,$$

the proportional reduction in estimated expected penalty is

$$\Lambda_n(M(I), M(V)) = 0.323,$$

and the estimated reduction in expected penalty per parameter is

$$\nu_n(M(I), M(V)) = 0.194.$$

Because $M(V)$ is included in $M(S)$,

$$\Delta(M(I), M(S)) \geq \Delta(M(I), M(V))$$

and

$$\Lambda(M(I), M(S)) \geq \Lambda(M(I), M(V)).$$

Given the small value of $\hat{\sigma}(\Lambda_n(M(I), M(V)))$, there appears to be very strong evidence that the measure $\Lambda(M(I), M(S))$ of mutual dependence of the responses Y_k, $1 \leq k \leq K = 6$, is at least 0.30. Because, $I_n(M(S))$ is 2.800, $I_n(M(V))$ is only 0.050 larger than the smallest possible value of $I_n(M)$ for M included in $M(S)$, and no estimated value $\Lambda_n(M(I), M)$ can be greater than 0.335 for M included in $M(S)$. As a comparison, $\Lambda(M(I), M(S))$ would have a similar value, 0.333, if each response had the same entropy $\text{Ent}(Y_k)$, if the first four responses Y_1 to Y_4 were mutually independent, and if Y_4, Y_5, and Y_6 were always identical, so that only four distinct responses were present. As already noted in Table 6, the sample variance of U_2 is very large relative to the sample mean of U_2.

It should also be noted from Table 6 that the variances of the counts U_1 and U_3 are also quite large relative to their means. In the case of U_1, the sample variance of 4.077 is much larger than the estimated variance of

$$\sum_{k=1}^{6} f_k(1)[1 - f_k(1)] = 1.182$$

appropriate for independent responses. Similar comments apply to U_3. These results are consistent with the large estimated change in penalty of

$$\Delta_n(M(I), M(ST)) = 1.331$$

and of the very large reduction per independent parameter of

$$\nu_n(M(I), M(ST)) = 0.444.$$

The added information required for $M(ST)$ rather than $M(I)$ is only three statistics, the variances of U_1 and U_2 and the covariance of U_1 and U_2. Given the variances of U_1, U_2, and U_3, the covariance of U_1 and U_2 may be determined, for

$$U_3 = 6 - U_1 - U_2$$

and

$$\text{cov}(U_1, U_2) = \frac{1}{2}\,[\text{var}(U_3) - \text{var}(U_1) - \text{var}(U_2)].$$

Despite a difference of 57 in the number of independent parameters, the prediction set $M(ST)$ for symmetric two-factor interaction performs rather well compared with the prediction set $M(T)$ for two-factor interaction. One has $I_n(M(T)) = 2.821$, so that the estimated difference in minimum expected penalty is $\Delta_n(M(ST), M(T)) = 0.059$ and loss per parameter is $\nu_n(M(ST), M(T)) = 0.001$. It should be noted that large sample approximations associated with $M(T)$ may not be fully satisfactory. In addition to any question raised by the value of

$$[D(T)]^2/n = 72^2/25400 = 0.204,$$

there is the added problem that several pairs of responses are quite rare. For example, only eight subjects answered "no" to question B and "yes" to question C. One might still ask whether in the case of the abortion data, there is a prediction set $M(ST1)$ that includes $M(S)$, is included in $M(T)$, can be used to account for most of the difference between $I_n(M(ST))$ and $I_n(M(T))$, and has relatively few independent parameters. In this example, a reasonable candidate does exist. One may divide the reasons for abortions into two groups. Questions A, C, and E involve grounds for abortion that are typically regarded as more compelling than are the grounds in questions B, D, and F. One may define $M(ST1)$ to consist of prediction functions q such that (3) holds, (6) holds, and the $\lambda^{kk'}_{y_k y'_{k'}}$ are constrained so that

$$\lambda^{kk'}_{y_k y'_{k'}} = \lambda^{13}_{y_k y'_{k'}} = \lambda^{13}_{y'_{k'} y_k}$$

for k and k' odd,

$$\lambda^{kk'}_{y_k y'_{k'}} = \lambda^{24}_{y_k y'_{k'}} = \lambda^{42}_{y'_{k'} y_k}$$

for k and k' even,

$$\lambda^{kk'}_{y_k y'_{k'}} = \lambda^{12}_{y_k y'_{k'}}$$

for k odd and k' even, and

$$\lambda^{kk'}_{y_k y'_{k'}} = \lambda^{12}_{y'_{k'} y_k}$$

for k even and k' odd. In this case, $I_n(M(ST1)) = 2.832$ and $M(ST1)$ has $D(ST1) = 22$ independent parameters. The improvement over $M(ST)$ per parameter is modest, for

$$\nu_n(M(ST), M(ST1)) = 0.007,$$

but the corresponding value $\nu_n(M(ST1), M(T))$ is only 0.0002 and $\Delta_n(M(ST1), M(T))$ is only 0.011, so that progress beyond $M(ST1)$ is very difficult for a prediction set M included in the prediction set $M(T)$ for two-factor interactions.

Table 8 provides the added information required for use of explanatory variables. Because several explanatory variables are dummy variables, Table 9 has been used to provide sample means for selected subgroups relevant to computation of $I_n(M(V, \mathbf{X}))$. In examination of Table 9, it may be helpful to note that the sample standard deviation of V is 2.403. The information in Tables 8 and 9 suggests a modest relationship between the explanatory variables and the score variable V. Sample correlation coefficients are of modest size, and differences between groups in sample means of V are relatively small. This impression of a modest relationship is supported by the observed value of $I_n(M(V, \mathbf{X}))$ of 2.790. The gain in estimated expected penalty relative to use of $M(V)$ is

$$\Delta_n(M(V), M(V, \mathbf{X})) = 0.060,$$

the proportional reduction in estimated expected penalty is

$$\Lambda_n(M(V), M(V, \mathbf{X})) = 0.021,$$

and the reduction per parameter in estimated expected penalty is

$$\nu_n(M(V), M(V, \mathbf{X})) = 0.005.$$

As evident from Table 11, estimated asymptotic standard deviations of measures comparing $M(V)$ and $M(V, \mathbf{X})$ are quite small. It is not the case that the explanatory variables are unrelated to the response variables. The correlations observed in Table 8 are of modest size, but they clearly indicate that the population correlations are not 0. For example, in the case of the education variable X_{10}, a standard test of independence of the sum V of the responses based on the sample correlation coefficient yields a normal deviate of -39.27! Even in the case of the indicator X_4 for a nonblack and nonwhite respondent, the normal deviate for a test of independence of V and X_4 is 2.885, even though the sample correlation of 0.0181 is quite small in magnitude. As evident from the example in Section 2.6, the observed changes in minimum estimated expected penalty are consistent with a moderate relationship between the explanatory variables and the responses. It is also evident that the relationship among responses is far stronger than the relationship between the response variables and the explanatory variables. A substantial fraction of the relationship between response and explanatory variables is accounted for by the education variable X_{10}, for $I_n(M(V, X_{10})) = 2.820$ and

$$\Delta_n(M(V, X_{10}), M(V, \mathbf{X})) = 0.030$$

is about half of $\Delta_n(M(V), M(V, \mathbf{X}))$. It is also worth noting that $I_n(M(V, \mathbf{X}))$ is smaller than $I_n(M(S))$ despite a very large difference between the 32 independent parameters associated with $M(V, \mathbf{X})$ and the 728 independent parameters associated with $M(S)$.

One important issue in the relationship of education to the sum V of scored responses is that large differences in educational level do appear to matter. The observed relationship is somewhat reduced in size due to the relatively small observed variation in education. The sample standard deviation of X_{10} is 3.214, a value much smaller than the range of X_{10}, which is 20. Among 332 subjects with 20 or more completed years of education, the average value of V is -4.608, a value only 1.392 above -6, the minimum possible value of V. Among 89 subjects with zero completed years of education, the average value of V is -1.056. One might be concerned that subjects not reporting their education appear in Table 9 to differ considerably from subjects who do report education; however, few subjects do not report education. As a consequence, $I_n(M(V, (X_{10}, X_{11})))$ is 2.818, a value only slightly smaller than $I_n(M(V, X_{10}))$.

The analysis in this section does not lead to a unique best description of the data under study. Nonetheless, some basic conclusions can be reached. The estimated measures $I_n(M(V))$ and $I_n(M(ST))$ are much smaller than $I_n(M(I))$, so that responses are very strongly dependent. The relative success of $M(ST)$ indicates that the strong dependence among responses can be summarized with considerable effectiveness by use of just the marginal distributions of the responses together with the variances of the counts U_y for y from 1 to 3. The alternative summarization approach that has considerable success uses the mean and variance of U_2, the differences $p_k(3) - p_k(1)$, $1 \leq k \leq 6$, and the distribution of the sum V of the response scores. The variable V provides a convenient tool for the summarization of relationships of explanatory variables to the six response variables. Use of correlations of V with explanatory variables provides a modest but noticeable improvement in the prediction of response profiles. It appears that the basic demographic variables used in this example as explanatory variables have only a modest relationship with attitudes toward legal abortions. Much of the relationship of explanatory variables with attitudes toward legal abortions appears to involve education of respondent.

5. CONCLUSIONS

The methodology developed in this paper is novel in the sense that it deviates from traditional model fitting. The approach advocated associates summary statistics and log-linear models in a unique matter that yields analytic tools especially suited for analysis of categorical profiles.

Parsimonious summarization of data is one of the basic tasks of statistical work. The information criteria and log-linear models developed in Section 2 provide a basis for judging the effectiveness of a particular data summary in terms of the predictive power of the log-linear model associated with the data summary and in terms of the number of real-valued statistics required for the summary. Thus both parsimony of description and effectiveness of description are considered. As shown in Section 4, quite succinct summaries of data can be remarkably effective with categorical profile data.

Implementation of the methodology developed in this paper is, for the most part, feasible with SPSS. Detailed information can be obtained from the authors. The authors also have Fortran 90 computer programs available that are more specifically oriented toward the approach used in the paper.

The approaches adopted in this paper have application outside of pure sociology. For example, special treatment of frequent profiles appears to be important in longitudinal marketing surveys in which brand loyalty is of great interest. Due to the sequential nature of the data and due to interest in prediction of future purchases, the exact type of model appropriate in the marketing contrasts appears somewhat different than the type of models considered in this paper (see Nordmoe [1993]).

APPENDIX A: CHARACTERISTICS OF OPTIMAL PREDICTION FUNCTIONS

To describe the optimal probability prediction function for $D > 0$ independent parameters, Theorems 1 to 3 in Gilula and Haberman (1995) may be applied. For $1 \leq d \leq D$ and for a probability prediction function q in M, let $e_d(q)$ be the random variable on the population S with value

$$e_d(q, s) = \sum_{\mathbf{y} \in Q} q(\mathbf{y}, s) Z_d(\mathbf{y}, s)$$

at population member s in S. Thus $e_d(p, s)$ is the conditional expected value of $Z_d(\mathbf{Y})$ given that $\mathbf{X}$ is $\mathbf{X}(s)$, and $E(e_d(p))$ is equal to the sufficient expectation $E(Z_d(\mathbf{Y}))$. To the extent that a probability prediction function q in M approximates the conditional probability prediction function p, $e_d(q)$ approximates $e_d(p)$ and $E(e_d(q))$ approximates $E(e_d(p)) = E(Z_d(\mathbf{Y}))$. Gilula and Haberman (1995) show that q is the unique optimal probability prediction function in M if and only if

$$E(e_d(q)) = E(Z_d(\mathbf{Y})), \quad 1 \leq d \leq D, \tag{11}$$

so that, for $1 \leq d \leq D$, $E(e_d(q))$ is equal to the sufficient expectations $E(Z_d(\mathbf{Y}))$. For an alternative interpretation, observe that if $\mathbf{Y}'$ is a response profile on S such that q is the conditional probability prediction function of $\mathbf{Y}'$, then $e_d(q, s)$, s in S, is the conditional expectation of $Z_d(\mathbf{Y})$ given that $\mathbf{X}$ has value $\mathbf{X}(s)$ and

$$E(e_d(q)) = E(Z_d(\mathbf{Y}')),$$

so that $\mathbf{Y}'$ and $\mathbf{Y}$ have the same sufficient expectations.

APPENDIX B: ESTIMATION OF THE OPTIMAL PREDICTION FUNCTION

To estimate the optimal prediction function when $D > 0$, consider the sample means

$$\bar{e}_d(q) = n^{-1} \sum_{i=1}^{n} e_d(q, s_i)$$

of the $e_d(q, s_i)$, $1 \leq i \leq n$, for a probability prediction function q.

An estimated optimal prediction function q_n in M, if it exists, satisfies the equation

$$\bar{e}_d(q_n) = \bar{Z}_d, \quad 1 \le d \le D.$$

Computations can be performed, at least in principle, by use of standard computer programs for computation of maximum-likelihood estimates for log-linear models.

For a simple case, in Example 1, let the frequency $n_{\mathbf{Y}}(\mathbf{y})$ be the number of observations $\mathbf{Y}_i$, $1 \le i \le n$, equal to $\mathbf{y}$ in Q, and let the relative frequency

$$f_{\mathbf{Y}}(\mathbf{y}) = \frac{n_{\mathbf{Y}}(\mathbf{y})}{n}.$$

If $n_{\mathbf{Y}}(\mathbf{y}) > 0$ for each possible categorical profile $\mathbf{y}$ in Q, then the estimated optimal prediction function q_n in $M(S)$ satisfies

$$q_n(\mathbf{y}, s) = f_{\mathbf{Y}}(\mathbf{y})$$

for $\mathbf{y}$ in Q and population member s in the population S. Otherwise, no estimated optimal prediction function in $M(S)$ exists. Nonetheless, it is always the case that

$$I_n(M(S)) = -\sum_{\mathbf{y} \in Q} f_{\mathbf{Y}}(\mathbf{y}) \log f_{\mathbf{Y}}(\mathbf{y}).$$

The sample data summary corresponding to $M(S)$ is based on the relative frequencies $f_{\mathbf{Y}}(\mathbf{z}_c)$ for $1 \le c \le C - 1$. The estimate $I_n(M(S))$ is an estimate of the entropy $\mathrm{Ent}(\mathbf{Y})$.

In Example 2, let the frequency $n_{F\mathbf{Y}}(a, \mathbf{y})$ be the number of observations with $F(\mathbf{X}_i) = a$, $1 \le a \le b$, and $\mathbf{Y}_i = \mathbf{y}$ in Q, and let the relative frequency

$$f_{F\mathbf{Y}}(a, \mathbf{y}) = \frac{n_{F\mathbf{Y}}(a, \mathbf{y})}{n}.$$

Let $n_F(a)$ be the number of observations with $F(\mathbf{X}_i) = a$, and let

$$f_{\mathbf{Y}|F}(\mathbf{y}|a) = \frac{n_{F\mathbf{Y}}(a, \mathbf{y})}{n_F(a)}$$

if $n_F(a) > 0$. If $n_F(a) = 0$, let

$$f_{\mathbf{Y}|F}(\mathbf{y}|a) = f_{\mathbf{Y}}(\mathbf{y}).$$

If $n_{F\mathbf{Y}}(a, \mathbf{y}) > 0$ for each possible categorical profile $\mathbf{y}$ in Q and each possible value a of F, then the estimated optimal prediction function q_n in $M(C, F)$ satisfies

$$q_n(\mathbf{y}, s) = f_{\mathbf{Y}|F}(\mathbf{y}|F(\mathbf{X}(s)))$$

for $\mathbf{y}$ in Q and population member s in the population S. Otherwise, no estimated optimal prediction function in $M(S)$ exists. Nonetheless, it is always the case that

$$I_n(M(S)) = -\sum_{a=1}^{b} \sum_{\mathbf{y} \in Q} f_{F\mathbf{Y}}(a, \mathbf{y}) \log f_{\mathbf{Y}|F}(\mathbf{y}|a).$$

The sample data summary corresponding to $M(S)$ is based on the relative frequencies $f_{F\mathbf{Y}}(a, \mathbf{z}_c)$ for $1 \leq a \leq b$ and $1 \leq c \leq C - 1$.

APPENDIX C: NORMAL APPROXIMATIONS

Gilula and Haberman (1994, 1995) may be applied to obtain the normal approximations of Section 2.9. Let $\tau(I, M)$ be the standard deviation of $\log q(\mathbf{Y})$. Then $n^{1/2}[I_n(M) - I(M)]$ has an approximate normal distribution with mean 0 and standard deviation $\tau(I, M)$. Thus

$$\sigma(I_n(M)) = \tau(I, M)/n^{1/2}$$

may be termed the asymptotic standard deviation (ASD) of $I_n(M)$. For construction of confidence intervals, estimate $\sigma(I_n(M))$ by the estimated asymptotic standard deviation (EASD)

$$\hat{\sigma}_n(I_n(M)) = \left\{ \frac{1}{n^2} \sum_{i=1}^{n} [-\log q_{in} - I_n(M)]^2 \right\}^{1/2},$$

where $q_{in} = q_n(\mathbf{Y}_i, s_i)$ for $1 \leq i \leq n$. Let $0 < \alpha < 1$ and let $z_{\alpha/2}$ be the value such that a standard normal deviate is greater than $z_{\alpha/2}$ with probability $\alpha/2$. If $\tau(I, M) > 0$, then an approximate confidence interval for $I(M)$ of level $1 - \alpha$ has lower bound

$$I_n(M) - z_{\alpha/2}\hat{\sigma}_n(I_n(M))$$

and upper bound

$$I_n(M) + z_{\alpha/2}\hat{\sigma}_n(I_n(M)).$$

Let $\tau(\Delta, M', M)$ be the standard deviation of $u = \log q(\mathbf{Y}) - \log q'(\mathbf{Y})$. Then $n^{1/2}[\Delta_n(M', M) - \Delta(M', M)]$ has an approximate normal distribution with mean 0 and standard deviation $\tau(\Delta, M', M)$. Thus the ASD of $\Delta_n(M', M)$ is

$$\sigma(\Delta_n(M', M)) = \tau(\Delta, M', M)/n^{1/2}.$$

Let $q'_{in} = q'_n(\mathbf{Y}_i, s_i)$ and $u_{in} = \log q_{in} - \log q'_{in}$ for $1 \le i \le n$. The EASD of $\Delta_n(M', M)$ is

$$\hat{\sigma}(\Delta_n(M', M)) = \left\{ \frac{1}{n^2} \sum_{i=1}^{n} [u_{in} - \Delta_n(M', M)]^2 \right\}^{1/2}.$$

For $\tau(\Delta, M', M) > 0$, the approximate confidence interval for $\Delta(M', M)$ of level $1 - \alpha$ has lower bound

$$\Delta_n(M', M) - z_{\alpha/2}\hat{\sigma}(\Delta_n(M', M))$$

and upper bound

$$\Delta_n(M', M) + z_{\alpha/2}\hat{\sigma}(\Delta_n(M', M)).$$

For $D = D'$, let $\tau(\nu, M', M)$ be $\tau(\Delta, M', M)/|D - D'|$. Then $n^{1/2}[\nu_n(M', M) - \nu(M', M)]$ has an approximate normal distribution with mean 0 and standard deviation $\tau(\nu, M', M)$. The ASD of $\nu_n(M', M)$ is then

$$\sigma(\nu_n(M', M)) = \tau(\nu, M', M)/n^{1/2},$$

and the EASD of $\nu_n(M', M)$ is

$$\hat{\sigma}(\nu_n(M', M)) = \hat{\sigma}(\Delta_n(M', M))/|D - D'|.$$

For $\tau(\nu, M', M) > 0$, the approximate confidence interval for $\nu(M', M)$ of level $1 - \alpha$ has lower bound

$$\nu_n(M', M) - z_{\alpha/2}\hat{\sigma}(\nu_n(M', M))$$

and upper bound

$$\nu_n(M', M) + z_{\alpha/2}\hat{\sigma}(\nu_n(M', M)).$$

For $I(M') > 0$, let

$$v = \frac{u + \Lambda(M',M)\log q'}{I(M')}$$

and let $\tau(\Lambda, M', M)$ be the standard deviation of v. Then $n^{1/2}[\Lambda_n(M',M) - \Lambda(M',M)]$ has an approximate normal distribution with mean 0 and standard deviation $\tau(\Lambda, M', M)$. The ASD of $\Lambda_n(M',M)$ is

$$\sigma(\Lambda_n(M',M)) = \tau(\Lambda, M', M)/n^{1/2},$$

and the EASD of $\Lambda_n(M',M)$ is

$$\hat{\sigma}(\Lambda_n(M',M)) = \frac{1}{[nI_n(M')]^2}\sum_{i=1}^{n} v_{in}^2,$$

where

$$v_{in} = u_{in} + \Lambda_n(M',M)\log q'_{in}, \quad 1 \le i \le n.$$

For $\tau(\Lambda, M', M) > 0$, the approximate confidence interval for $\Lambda(M',M)$ of level $1 - \alpha$ has lower bound

$$\Lambda_n(M',M) - z_{\alpha/2}\hat{\sigma}(\Lambda_n(M',M))$$

and upper bound

$$\Lambda_n(M',M) + z_{\alpha/2}\hat{\sigma}(\Lambda_n(M',M)).$$

To study bias in estimation, apply Gilula and Haberman (1994, 1995) to show that $n[I(M) - E(I_n(M))]$ converges to $g(M)$. If $D = 0$, $g(M) = 0$. For $D > 0$ independent parameters, let the trace $\mathrm{tr}(\mathbf{A})$ of a D by D matrix $\mathbf{A}$ be the sum of the diagonal elements of $\mathbf{A}$. Let $\boldsymbol{\Psi}$ be the D by D covariance matrix of the $Z_d(\mathbf{Y})$, $1 \le d \le D$. Let $\boldsymbol{\Phi}$ be the D by D approximation to $\boldsymbol{\Psi}$ with row d and column d' equal to

$$\Phi_{dd'} = E(\phi_{dd'}),$$

where $\phi_{dd'}$ is the random variable with value at s in S of

$$\phi_{dd'}(s) = \left[\sum_{\mathbf{y}\in Q} Z_d(\mathbf{y},)Z_{d'}(\mathbf{y},s)q(\mathbf{y},s)\right] - e_d(q,s)e_{d'}(q,s).$$

Let

$$\boldsymbol{\Xi} = \boldsymbol{\Phi}^{-1}\boldsymbol{\Psi}.$$

Then $g(M)$ is $(1/2)\mathrm{tr}(\boldsymbol{\Xi})$. If the conditional probability prediction function p is in M, then $g(M) = D/2$. The coefficient $g(M')$ is defined in an analogous fashion.

In the study of chi-square statistics, it is helpful to note that $2n[I_n(M) - H_n(q)]$ converges in distribution to a nonnegative random variable Γ with expectation $2g(M)$ and variance $v(M)$. For $D = 0$, $v(M) = 0$. For $D > 0$,

$$v(M) = 2\,\mathrm{tr}(\boldsymbol{\Xi}\boldsymbol{\Xi}).$$

If the conditional probability prediction function p is in M, then Γ has a chi-square distribution with D degrees of freedom. The coefficient $v(M')$ is defined in a similar manner. Thus $2n[I_n(M') - H_n(q')]$ converges in distribution to a nonnegative random variable Γ' with expectation $g(M')$ and variance $v(M')$. If p is in M', then Γ' has a chi-square distribution with D' degrees of freedom. In the case of the $L^2(M', M)$ statistic, if $\Delta(M', M) = 0$ and if $q' = q$, then $L^2(M', M)$ has an asymptotic distribution $\Gamma - \Gamma'$. In the case of M' included in M, $\Gamma \geq \Gamma'$. If p is in M and M' and M' is included in M, then $\Gamma - \Gamma'$ has a chi-square distribution on $D - D'$ degrees of freedom.

REFERENCES

Agresti, Alan. 1993. "Computing Conditional Likelihood Maximum Likelihood Estimates for Conditional Rasch Models Using Simple Loglinear Models with Diagonal Parameters." *Scandinavian Journal of Statistics* 20:63–71.

Akaike, Hirotugu. 1974. "A New Look at the Statistical Identification Model." *IEEE Transactions on Automatic Control* 19:716–23.

Gilula, Zvi, and Shelby Joel Haberman. 1994. "Conditional Log-linear Models for Analyzing Categorical Panel Data." *Journal of the American Statistical Association* 89:645–56.

———. 1995. "Prediction Functions for Analysis of Categorical Panel Data." *The Annals of Statistics* 23:1130–42.

———. 2000. "Probability Prediction by Summary Statistics: An Information-Theoretic Approach." *Scandinavian Journal of Statistics* 27:521–34.

Good, Irving J. 1952. "Rational Decisions." *Journal of the Royal Statistical Society*, Ser. B, 14:107–14.

———. 1963. "Maximum Entropy for Hypothesis Formulation, Especially for Multidimensional Contingency Tables." *Annals of Mathematical Statistics* 34:911–34.

Goodman, Leo A. 1972. "Some Multiplicative Models for the Analysis of Cross-classified Data." *Proceedings of the Sixth Berkeley Symposium on Mathematical Statistics and Probability* 1:649–96.

———. 1974a. "The Analysis of Systems of Qualitative Variables When Some of the Variables Are Unobservable. Part I—a Modified Latent Structure Approach." *American Journal of Sociology* 79:1179–259.

———. 1974b. "Exploratory Latent Structure Analysis Using Both Identifiable and Unidentifiable Models." *Biometrika* 61:215–31.

———. 1975. "A New Model for Scaling Response Patterns: An Application of the Quasi-Independence Concept." *Journal of the American Statistical Association* 70:755–68.

Greenacre, Michael J. 1984. *Theory and Application of Correspondence Analysis*. New York: Academic Press.

Guttman, Louis. 1950. "The Basis for Scalogram Analysis." Pp. 413–72 in *Measurement and Prediction, Studies in Social Psychology in World War II*, vol. 4, edited by Samuel A. Stouffer et al. Princeton, NJ: Princeton University Press.

Haberman, Shelby J. 1977a. "Maximum Likelihood Estimates in Exponential Response Models." *Annals of Statistics* 5:815–41.

———. 1977b. "Log-linear Models and Frequency Tables with Small Expected Cell Counts." *Annals of Statistics* 5:1148–69.

———. 1979. *Analysis of Qualitative Data*. Vol. 2, *New Developments*. New York: Academic Press.

———. 1982. "Analysis of Dispersion of Multinomial Responses." *Journal of the American Statistical Association* 77:568–80.

———. 1989. "Concavity and Estimation." *Annals of Statistics* 17:1631–61.

———. 1996. *Advanced Statistics*. Vol. 1, *Description of Populations*. New York: Springer Verlag.

Heinen, T. 1996. *Latent Class and Discrete Latent Trait Models: Similarities and Differences*. Thousand Oaks, CA: Sage.

Jeffreys, Harold. 1961. *Theory of Probability*, 3d ed. London: Oxford University Press.

Kass, Robert E., and Adrian E. Raftery. 1995. "Bayes Factors." *Journal of the American Statistical Association* 90:773–95.

Kass, Robert E., and Larry Wasserman. 1995. "A Reference Bayesian Test for Nested Hypotheses and Its Relationship to the Schwarz Criterion." *Journal of the American Statistical Association* 90:928–34.

Lazarsfeld, Paul F., and Neil W. Henry. 1968. *Latent Structure Analysis*. Boston: Houghton-Mifflin.

Mosteller, Frederich, and David L. Wallace. 1964. *Inference and Disputed Authorship: The Federalist*. Reading, MA: Addison-Wesley.

Nordmoe, Erie D. 1993. "Entropy-Based Prediction of Categorical Response Variables in Scanner Panel Data." Ph.D. dissertation, Department of Statistics, Northwestern University, Evanston, IL.

Rasch, George. 1960. *Probabilistic Models for Some Intelligence and Attainment Tests*. Copenhagen: Nielsen and Lydiche.

Savage, Leonard J. 1971. "Elicitation of Personal Probabilities and Expectations." *Journal of the American Statistical Association* 66:783–801.

Schriever, B. F. 1983. "Scaling of Order Dependent Categorical Variables with Correspondence Analysis." *International Statistical Review* 51:225–38.
Schwarz, Gideon. 1978. "Estimating the Dimension of a Model." *Annals of Statistics* 6:461–64.
Shannon, Claude E. 1948. "A Mathematical Theory of Communication." *Bell System Technical Journal* 27:379–423, 623–56.
Theil, Henri. 1970. "On the Estimation of Relationships Involving Qualitative Variables." *American Journal of Sociology* 76:103–54.
Tjur, Tye. 1982. "A Connection Between Rasch's Item Analysis Model and Multiplicative Poisson Model." *Scandinavian Journal of Statistics* 9:23–30.
Van de Geer, John P. 1993. *Multivariate Analysis of Categorical Data: Applications and Theory*. Newbury Park, CA: Sage.

4

STATISTICAL METHODS AND GRAPHICAL DISPLAYS FOR ANALYZING HOW THE ASSOCIATION BETWEEN TWO QUALITATIVE VARIABLES DIFFERS AMONG COUNTRIES, AMONG GROUPS, OR OVER TIME

PART II: SOME EXPLORATORY TECHNIQUES, SIMPLE MODELS, AND SIMPLE EXAMPLES

*Leo A. Goodman**
*Michael Hout**

We introduce some simple models that can be viewed as special cases of the general model and general approach to analyzing the association in multiway tables that we first presented in 1998. We use two empirical examples to demonstrate the flexibility and utility of the simple models introduced here and of our general approach.

A preliminary version of this paper was presented at the annual meeting of the American Sociological Association, San Francisco, August 1998. We acknowledge the financial support of the Survey Research Center at the University of California, Berkeley. Louis Andre Vallet and Yu Xie provided us with useful comments.
*University of California, Berkeley

In previous work we introduced a modified regression-type approach for analyzing how the association between two qualitative variables might vary from category-to-category of a third qualitative variable (Goodman and Hout 1998a, 1998b). The two empirical examples we investigated—cross-national differences in the association between occupational origins and destinations in an intergenerational mobility table and changes over time in the relationship between religion and voting behavior in U.S. presidential elections—demonstrated the flexibility of our approach. However, those two examples did not provide an opportunity to illustrate some of the other special merits of the modified regression-type approach. In the present paper, we illustrate some of these other special merits. We shall show here how the general model used with this approach can incorporate various simplifications—for example, simplifications of the kind that were introduced earlier in the context of the analysis of cross-classified data having ordered categories (e.g., see Goodman 1979a, 1984) and other simplifications as well. In doing so we also uncover some unanticipated features of the model.

1. A REGRESSION-TYPE APPROACH

Consider a cross-classification of three qualitative variables (say, row, column, and layer variables) in which the association between the row variable and the column variable is of special interest, and the question of how the row-column association varies among the levels of the layer variable is also of interest. Let F_{ijk} denote the expected frequency in row i (for $i = 1, \ldots, I$), column j (for $j = 1, \ldots, J$), and layer k (for $k = 1, \ldots, K$) of the three-way cross-classification. Let $\theta_{ij|k}$ denote the corresponding odds-ratio in the two-way subtable formed from rows i and $i + 1$ and columns j and $j + 1$ in the k-th layer (for $i = 1, \ldots, I - 1$, $j = 1, \ldots, J - 1$, and $k = 1, \ldots, K$). Thus we have

$$\begin{aligned}\theta_{ij|k} &= (F_{ijk}F_{i+1,j+1,k})/(F_{i,j+1,k}F_{i+1,j,k}) \\ &= (F_{ijk}/F_{i+1,j,k})/(F_{i,j+1,k}/F_{i+1,j+1,k}) \\ &= (F_{ijk}/F_{i,j+1,k})/(F_{i+1,j,k}/F_{i+1,j+1,k}). \qquad (1)\end{aligned}$$

For the $I \times J \times K$ table, the model presented in the Goodman and Hout (1998a) article can be described by the simple formula,

$$\ln \theta_{ij|k} = a_{ij} + b_{ij}\phi_k, \tag{2}$$

where ln denotes the natural logarithm, a_{ij} and b_{ij} denote the intercept and slope, respectively, in the straight-line (linear) relationship between $\ln \theta_{ij|k}$ and ϕ_k (for $k = 1, \ldots, K$), and ϕ_k denotes the score pertaining to the k-th layer of the three-way cross-classification. For expository purposes, the intercepts and slopes in the straight-line formulas in (2) are designated by using the letters a and b, respectively, as is done in the usual formula for a straight line—namely, $Y = a + bX$ (where Y and X are quantitative variables). In the Goodman and Hout (1998a) article, the Greek letters μ and μ' were used (instead of a and b) since that notation was more consistent with the other related notation used in that article.

The log-odds-ratios, $\ln \theta_{ij|k}$, describe the association between the row variable and the column variable at the k-th layer of the layer variable, based on the 2×2 subtable formed from rows i and $i + 1$ and columns j and $j + 1$ in the k-th layer. The layer scores, ϕ_k, can be assigned *a priori*, or they can be estimated from the observed data (as was done in the Goodman and Hout (1998a) article). Formula (2) states that the $\ln \theta_{ij|k}$ lie on the straight line with intercept a_{ij} and slope b_{ij} ($for\ k = 1, \ldots, K$). The intercepts, a_{ij}, are the values that the $\ln \theta_{ij|k}$ take when (and if) ϕ_k equals zero; the slopes, b_{ij}, capture the cross-layer variation in the $\ln \theta_{ij|k}$. The graphical displays introduced in the Goodman and Hout (1998a) article are simple two-dimensional displays of these straight-line relationships that use estimates of the intercepts, a_{ij}, and the slopes, b_{ij}, obtained from the data under the specified model in order to draw the straight lines. In most displays we array the layer scores, ϕ_k, on the x-axis and the log-odds-ratios, $\ln \theta_{ij|k}$, on the y-axis; we make a separate panel for each combination of i and j.

When the simple straight-line formulas in (2) are congruent with the observed data, we can then consider various special cases. Are the slopes, b_{ij}, equal to each other, for all combinations of i and j or for some combinations of i and j? Are the intercepts, a_{ij}, equal to each other, for all combinations of i and j or for some combinations of i and j? Are some or all of the slopes equal to zero? Are some or all of the intercepts equal to zero? Each of these questions can be investigated using the methods presented in the Goodman and Hout (1998a) article. (The question pertaining to equal slopes (for all combinations of i and j) and the question pertaining to zero intercepts (for all combinations of i and j) can also be considered using the models in Yamaguchi (1987) and in Xie (1992), respectively.)

1.1. *Special Cases of the General Model*

Various models that pertain to the association between two qualitative variables can be used in order to obtain more parsimonious models that might fit a set of observed data. For example, if the uniform association model (UA) is used for the two-factor association parameters that pertain to the intercepts (the a_{ij}), and the full association (FA) model is used for the two-factor association parameters that pertain to the slopes (the b_{ij}), model (2) can be replaced by the more parsimonious formula,

$$\ln \theta_{ij|k} = a + b_{ij}\phi_k, \tag{3}$$

for $i = 1, \ldots, I - 1$, $j = 1, \ldots, J - 1$, and $k = 1, \ldots, K$. The Goodman-Hout modified regression-type approach can be applied with model (3) in order to answer one of the simple questions that arise naturally in an investigation of the straight-line relationships described in (2)—namely, are the intercepts, a_{ij}, in (2) equal to each other? If this question is answered in the affirmative, then the uniform association model can be used to describe the association between the row variable and column variable when $\phi_k = 0$; and the intercept, a, in model (3) describes the magnitude of this association. (Considering the score, ϕ_k, pertaining to the k-th layer of the layer variable, it should be noted that there may or may not be a particular layer—for example, the k^*-th layer—for which $\phi_{k^*} = 0$.) The $b_{ij}\phi_k$ term in model (3) can then be used to describe how much the magnitude and pattern of this association is modified when the score ϕ_k for the k-th layer is not equal to zero. We use graphical displays in this paper to interpret the straight-line relationships implied by the general model in equation (2) and by various special cases of this general model, including the simple model described by equation (3).

1.2. *Identification of Layer Scores*

The layer scores, ϕ_k, can be estimated from the data or assigned *a priori*, as we noted here earlier (see also Goodman and Hout 1998a). Let us now consider briefly the situation in which the layer scores are to be estimated from the data. We start with the model in equation (2). In this case, in order for the layer scores to be identifiable, two of the scores, ϕ_k, need to be specified in advance or otherwise restricted (as we shall spell out in more detail below). And in order to compare the results obtained using the model in equation (3) with the corresponding results obtained using the model in equation (2), we would also, for comparative purposes, impose the same two restrictions on the layer scores of the former model. However, when we consider the conditions necessary for the layer scores to be identifiable for the model in equation (3), we obtain this surprising result: Only one layer score needs to be specified in order for the layer scores to be identifiable for the model in equation (3). Thus, in order to apply the model in equation (3) as fully as possible (without introducing unnecessary constraints), only one layer score would be specified. We say this model is of type I. And when comparing results obtained using the model in equation (3) with the corresponding results obtained using the model in equation (2), we would specify the same two identifying restrictions on both the model in equation (2) and the one in equation (3). We say that the model in equation (3) with two identifying restrictions on the layer scores is of type II.

To see how the identification of layer scores works, consider what happens if the layer scores in equations (2) and (3) are transformed from ϕ_k to ϕ'_k, where,

$$\phi'_k = d\phi_k, \quad \text{with} \quad d \neq 0. \tag{4}$$

This transformation will not change the basic form of equation (2), nor will it change the basic form of equation (3). These equations can remain completely unchanged by the transformation (4) simply by replacing the b_{ij} in equations (2) and (3) by $b'_{ij} = b_{ij}/d$. On the other hand, if the layer scores in equations (2) and (3) are transformed from ϕ_k to ϕ''_k, where

$$\phi''_k = c + d\phi_k, \quad \text{with} \quad c \neq 0 \quad \text{and} \quad d \neq 0, \tag{5}$$

this transformation will not change the basic form of equation (2), but it will change the basic form of equation (3). Simply by replacing the b_{ij} in equation (2) by $b'_{ij} = b_{ij}/d$ and by replacing the a_{ij} in this equation by $a'_{ij} = a_{ij} - b_{ij}c/d$, equation (2) remains completely unchanged; but the basic form of equation (3) will be changed if the intercept, a, in this equation is replaced by $a'_{ij} = a - b_{ij}c/d$. In particular, the restriction $a'_{ij} = a'$ will not hold for all i and j.

Because of the differences between equations (2) and (3) noted in the preceding paragraph, we find that the parameters in the full association (FA) model with regression-type layer effect will be identifiable if two of the layer scores (say, ϕ_1, and ϕ_K) are specified; whereas, the parameters in the uniform association (UA) model with regression-type layer effect will be identifiable if only one of the layer scores (say, ϕ_1) is specified. Any convenient values can be specified in order to identify the others. Since the two scores that are specified (say, ϕ_1 and ϕ_K) in the FA model with regression-type layer effect can be transformed into any other two scores (say, ϕ_1'' and ϕ_K'') using transformation (5), the basic form of this model will remain unchanged regardless of what are the specified values of the two scores. Similarly, since the one score that is specified (say, ϕ_1) in the UA model with regression-type layer effect can be transformed into any other score (say, ϕ_1') using transformation (4), the basic form of this model will remain unchanged regardless of what is the specified value of the score.

When one layer score (say, ϕ_1) is specified in the UA model with regression-type layer effect, and the other layer scores (and the other parameters in the model) are estimated using the observed data (i.e., the observed frequencies) in the three-way cross-classification table of interest, the expected frequencies estimated under the model will usually differ from the corresponding expected frequencies estimated under this same model in the case where two layer scores (say, ϕ_1 and ϕ_K) are specified. In the case when one layer score (say, ϕ_1) is specified in the UA model with regression-type layer effect, we call this a UA model of type I; and in the case when two layer scores (say, ϕ_1 and ϕ_K) are specified in this model, we call this a UA model of type II. The expected frequencies estimated under a UA model of type I will be equal to the corresponding expected frequencies estimated under a UA model of type II only when the two specified layer scores (say, ϕ_1 and ϕ_K) in the UA model of type II are proportional to the corresponding layer scores obtained under the UA model of type I (where the corresponding layer score ϕ_1 is specified in this model of type I, and the corresponding layer score ϕ_K is estimated under the model). The UA model of type II is more parsimonious than the corresponding UA model of type I.

When more than one layer score is specified in the UA model with regression-type layer effect, or when more than two layer scores are specified in the FA model with regression-type layer effect, the corresponding models that are obtained are more parsimonious. More generally, we could consider here UA models and FA models with regression-type layer effect in which a given subset of the K layer scores are specified and the remaining layer scores (i.e., the layer scores that are not included in the given subset) are estimated (together with the other parameters in the model) using the observed data in the three-way cross-classification table.

The only limit on the number of layer scores that can, in principle, be specified in advance is the number of layers itself. When all of the layer scores (ϕ_k, for $k = 1, \ldots, K$) are specified, the models obtained from equations (2) and (3) correspond to log-linear models for the expected frequencies; we refer to these special cases as regression-type models with layer scores specified (LSS). When some of the layer scores are not specified (and the scores that are not specified are estimated using the observed data), the models obtained from equations (2) and (3) correspond to log-bilinear models for the expected frequencies (e.g., see Goodman 1986).

Table 1 presents the formulas for the degrees of freedom for testing various association models that will be considered in this paper, including the two types of models (namely, type I and type II) obtained with equation (3), the uniform association (UA) models with regression-type layer effect. The relationship between these models and the models in Yamaguchi (1987) and Xie (1992) will also be discussed in Section 2.2 of the present paper.

TABLE 1

Degrees of Freedom for Testing Selected Association Models Pertaining to Two-way Association for a Table with I Categories (Rows) for the Row Variable and J Categories (Columns) for the Column Variable as the Table Varies Across K Categories (Layers) of a Layer Variable

Model	DF
Conditional independence (null association at each layer)	$(I-1)(J-1)K$
Uniform association (UA) with null layer effect on association	$(I-1)(J-1)K-1$
Layer-specific UA	$(IJ-I-J)K$
UA with additive layer effect	$(IJ-I-J)K$
UA with multiplicative layer effect	$(IJ-I-J)K$
UA with regression-type layer effect (type I)	$(IJ-I-J)(K-1)-1$
UA with regression-type layer effect (type II)	$(IJ-I-J)(K-1)$
Null three-factor interaction (full two-way association [FA] with null layer effect on association)	$(I-1)(J-1)(K-1)$
FA with additive layer effect	$(IJ-I-J)(K-1)$
FA with multiplicative layer effect	$(IJ-I-J)(K-1)$
FA with regression-type layer effect	$(IJ-I-J)(K-2)$

2. EXAMPLE 1. JOB SATISFACTION AND SELF-EMPLOYMENT STATUS

In our first example we examine how the association between job satisfaction and self-employment status varies among occupational groups. The data are shown in Table 2.[1] The counts in Table 2 pertain to the 2,070 persons who were active in the labor force and who had no missing data on job satisfaction, self-employment status, or occupation. There are five categories of job-satisfaction based on answers to the question: "On a scale from one to five, how much do you like your job? One is 'I hate my job' and five is 'I love my job'" (Of the 2,098 persons with jobs, 23 gave no answer to the question). Self-employment status is coded "self" or "other" based on answers to the question: "Are/were you employed by someone else, are/were you in business for yourself, or do/did you work without pay in a family business or farm?" The respondents who said they were in business for themselves are coded "self-employed;" the others are coded "other" (two persons gave no answer to this question). Our classification of self-employment status is consistent with that used by the U.S. Bureau of Labor Statistics (www.bls.gov/bconcepts.htm; see also Bogue 1985). Detailed occupations are grouped into four broad categories: "Professional or Managerial," "Routine white collar," "Skilled blue collar" and "Semi-skilled or unskilled blue collar." Farm owners and managers are classed as "Skilled blue collar"; farm laborers are classed as "Semiskilled or unskilled blue collar." Three persons with valid data on self-employment and job satisfaction gave a response to the occupation question that was too vague to code.

Self-employed people like their jobs better than workers who are employed by others. As the "all occupations (%)" row shows, a higher percentage of self-employed people chose category five—"I love my job"—and higher percentages of employees chose the other four categories. The two-way association is statistically significant at conventional levels; the likelihood-ratio chi-square value (L^2) is 54.29 and the Pearson

[1]The source of the data is a survey of American adults in 1991 described in Hout, Wright, and Sanchez Jankowski (1992). Random digit dialing (rdd) methods were used to draw a sample that is representative of households with at least one telephone and at least one adult who speaks English. We use weights to adjust for the higher probability that households with more than one telephone will be sampled and the higher probability that an individual who is the only adult in a sampled household will be interviewed. Repeated call-backs mitigated some of the factors that might make the sample unrepresentative and produced a response rate of 69 percent.

TABLE 2
Cross-Classification of Job Satisfaction by Self-Employment Status by Occupation: United States, 1991

	Job Satisfaction					
Self-Employment Status	"Hate it" 1	2	3	4	"Love it" 5	Total
Professional/Managerial						
Other	7	21	82	203	191	504
Self-employed	0	2	11	44	88	145
Routine White Collar						
Other	16	20	109	187	195	527
Self-employed	0	1	8	16	11	36
Skilled Blue Collar						
Other	6	17	88	98	100	309
Self-employed	1	2	12	18	62	95
Unskilled Blue Collar						
Other	24	29	95	96	150	394
Self-employed	2	4	9	15	30	60
All Occupations						
Other	53	87	374	584	636	1,734
Self-employed	3	9	40	93	191	336
All Occupations (%)						
Other	3	5	22	34	37	100
Self-employed	1	3	12	28	57	100

Source: "Class Structure and Consciousness Survey." Survey Research Center, University of California, Berkeley, 1991.

chi-square value (X^2) is 53.08 with 4 degrees of freedom. The UA model for the two-way table fits the data very well ($L^2 = 2.82$; $X^2 = 2.98$; DF = 3); and the log-odds-ratio for contrasting employees with the self-employed and each of the first four job-satisfaction categories ($j = 1, \ldots, 4$) with the next higher job-satisfaction category expected under UA is .478. (Its asymptotic standard error is .072.)

From Table 2, we see that only three self-employed people classify themselves in job-satisfaction category 1 (they "hate it") and just nine more put themselves in job-satisfaction category 2. Combining job satisfaction categories 1 and 2 will facilitate the graphical display of the observed data. We cannot justify combining them if there is evidence of three-way interaction among job-satisfaction, self-employment status, and occupation, in the corresponding $2 \times 2 \times 4$ table obtained by restricting attention to the first two job-satisfaction categories in Table 2. Nor can we justify combining them if the conditional distribution of self-employment status, given occupation, is different in job-satisfaction category 1 from the corresponding conditional distribution in job-satisfaction category 2. Chi-square tests indicate that neither assumption is violated.[2] Thus we replace the $2 \times 5 \times 4$ table (Table 2) by the corresponding $2 \times 4 \times 4$ table in which job-satisfaction category 1 is combined with job-satisfaction category 2 for the remainder of our analysis. Table 3 presents the goodness-of-fit chi-square values obtained when various models of the association between job satisfaction and self-employment status by occupation are applied to the data in the resulting $2 \times 4 \times 4$ table.

2.1. *Models Based on Uniform Association*

We first focus our attention on the models in Table 3 obtained using equation (3), and then we shall consider the corresponding models obtained using the more general equation (2). When equation (3) is applied (to the $2 \times 4 \times 4$ table) with $a_j = 0$ and $b_j = 0$ (for all j),[3] we obtain the usual model of conditional independence between job satisfaction and self-employment status, given occupation (with $(2 - 1)(4 - 1)4 = 12$DF for the $2 \times 4 \times 4$ table); and when equation (3) is applied with $b_j = 0$ (for all j), we obtain the UA model for the association between job satisfaction and self-employment status, with null effect of occupation on this association (with $12 - 1 = 11$ DF for the $2 \times 4 \times 4$ table). These are models M0 and M1 in Table 3. From the corresponding goodness-of-fit chi-square values in Table 3, we see that each of the models M0 and M1 would be rejected when the usual statistical criteria are used ($L^2 = 67.49$ and $X^2 = 65.88$, with 12 DF for model M0; and $L^2 = 20.65$ and $X^2 = 21.13$,with 11 DF for model M1), although model M1 clearly is preferable to model M0. The estimated UA parameter is $a_j = .485$ for all j. (Its asymptotic standard error is .075.)

[2]With respect to the three-factor interaction in the $2 \times 4 \times 4$ table, the chi-square values are $L^2 = 1.86$ and $X^2 = 1.36$, each with 3 DF. With respect to the conditional association between job-satisfaction and self-employment status, given occupation, in the $2 \times 4 \times 4$ table, the corresponding chi-square values are $L^2 = 2.65$ and $X^2 = 1.82$ with 4 DF.

[3]With $I = 2$, the i subscript is always 1, so we dispense with showing it in the remainder of this example.

TABLE 3

Goodness-of-Fit Statistics for Selected Models of the Association Between Job Satisfaction and Self-Employment Status by Occupation, United States, 1991 ($N = 2,070$)

No.	Model	L^2	X^2	DF	p	BIC
M0	Conditional independence	67.49	65.88	12	<.01	−24
M1	Uniform association (UA) with null layer effect on association	20.65	21.13	11	.04	−63
M2	Layer-specific UA	7.27	7.30	8	.51	−54
$M3^+$	UA with additive layer effect	7.27	7.30	8	.51	−54
$M3^\times$	UA with multiplicative layer effect	7.27	7.30	8	.51	−54
M3*	UA with regression-type layer effect (model I)	1.79	1.76	5	.88	−36
M3**	UA with regression-type layer effect (model II)	1.81	1.81	6	.94	−44
M4*	UA with regression-type layer effect (model I), $b_1 = b_2 = 0$	2.00	2.00	7	.96	−51
M4**	UA with regression-type layer effect (model II), $b_1 = b_2 = 0$	2.02	2.04	8	.98	−59
M5	UA with regression-type layer effect, layer score specified (LSS), $b_1 = b_2 = 0$	2.20	2.22	10	.99	−74
M6	UA with regression-type layer effect, layer score specified (LSS), $b_1 = b_2 = 0$	3.08	3.22	10	.98	−73
M7	Full association (FA) with null layer effect on association	18.63	18.76	9	.03	−50
$M8^+$	FA with additive layer effect	6.48	6.28	6	.37	−39
$M8^\times$	FA with multiplicative layer effect	3.74	3.41	6	.71	−42
M8*	FA with regression-type layer effect	1.74	1.69	4	.78	−29
M9*	FA with regression-type layer effect, $b_1 = b_2 = 0$	1.96	1.91	6	.92	−44

Figure 1 presents a graphical display of the association between job satisfaction and self-employment status for the four occupational categories, comparing the observed association (circles) with the corresponding expected association (horizontal lines) under model M1. To describe the association in the 2×4 table pertaining to the relationship between job satisfaction and self-employment status, for the occupational categories, we use $(2 - 1)(4 - 1) = 3$ panels in Figure 1. There are four job-satisfaction categories (namely, job-satisfaction category 1+2 in which the first two job-satisfaction categories in Table 2 were combined, and job-satisfaction categories 3, 4, and 5 from Table 2); and there are two categories describing self-employment status. The first panel in Figure 1 presents the log-odds-ratio obtained from the 2×2 subtable that compares job-satisfaction category 1+2 with job-satisfaction category 3 for the two self-employment status categories; the second panel presents the log-odds-ratio obtained from the 2×2 subtable that compares job-satisfaction category 3 with job-satisfaction category 4 for the two self-employment status categories; the third panel presents the log-odds-ratio obtained from the 2×2 subtable that compares job-satisfaction category 4 with job-satisfaction category 5 for the two self-employment status categories. In each of the three panels in Figure 1, we include the relevant observed log-odds-ratios for the four occupational categories;[4] we also include there the 95 percent confidence intervals (the vertical lines or line-segments) for the observed log-odds-ratios, which are obtained directly from the corresponding observed frequencies. Figure 1 presents us with a picture that indicates in which ways model M1 fits the observed data and in which ways it does not fit the observed data. The 95 percent confidence intervals for 10 of the 12 observed log-odds-ratios overlap the estimated value of a (.485), but the chi-square test statistics from model M1 in Table 3 are as large as they turn out to be, in part because only two of the observed log-odds-ratios lie within the 95 percent confidence interval of a (the lower and upper bounds of which are .339 and .632, respectively).

The other UA models considered in Table 3 (namely, model M2 and the M3 and M4 models, M5, and M6) are all congruent with the

[4]The observed log-odds-ratio (or the observed association) is obtained using formula (1) with the observed frequencies in the $2 \times 4 \times 4$ table, replacing the corresponding expected frequencies in this formula. The expected log-odds-ratio (or the expected association) is obtained using formula (1) with the expected frequencies estimated under a model. The expected log-odds-ratios estimated under model M1 are displayed in Figure 1 by the horizontal line in each panel of the graphical display.

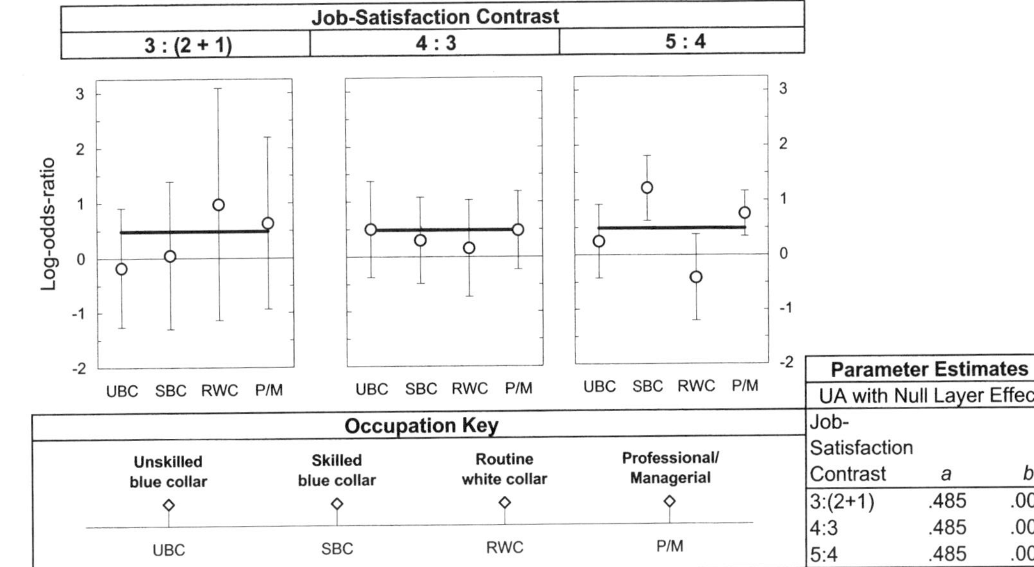

FIGURE 1. Log-odds-ratios for association between job satisfaction and self-employment status by occupation, United States, 1991: Observed (circles) and expected (horizontal lines) under uniform association model with null layer effect on association; i.e., Model M1 in Table 3 ($L^2 = 20.65$; DF = 11).

Note: Vertical lines indicate the 95 percent confidence intervals based on the observed log-odds-ratios.

observed data in the $2 \times 4 \times 4$ table, when the usual statistical criteria are used. M2 can be obtained by fitting UA to the 2×4 table at each layer ($k = 1,\ldots,4$); we label this model layer-specific UA. M2 can also be obtained by fitting the additive layer effects model (Yamaguchi 1987) with UA constraints on both the intercepts and slopes—i.e.,

$$\ln \theta_{ij|k} = a + b\phi_k, \tag{6}$$

for $i = 1, j = 1, 2, 3$; and $k = 1,\ldots,4$. It could also be obtained by fitting the multiplicative layer effects model (Xie 1992) with uniform slopes:

$$\ln \theta_{ij|k} = b'\phi_k, \tag{7}$$

for $i = 1$; $j = 1, 2, 3$; and $k = 1,\ldots,4$ where $a_j = 0$ for all j. We call the models in equations (6) and (7) models $M3^+$ and $M3^\times$, respectively.

The straight-line relationship in equation (6) can be obtained from Figure 2 simply by adjusting the layer scores, ϕ_k, so that (1) a straight line is then obtained in each panel, and (2) when $\phi_k = 0$, then $\ln \theta_{ij|k} = a$. The straight-line relationship in equation (7) can be obtained from Figure 2 in the same way that the straight line in equation (6) can be obtained, with the location of the layer scores, ϕ_k, adjusted so that when $\phi_k = 0$, then $\ln \theta_{ij|k} = 0$.[5]

Figure 2 presents the expected log-odds-ratios under model M2 (lines) with the corresponding observed log-odds-ratios (circles). The expected log-odds-ratios vary among occupations within panels but the corresponding expected log-odds-ratios do not vary from panel to panel. The occupational categories are ordered so that the expected log-odds-ratios increase from left to right. We have drawn Figure 2 with equal intervals between the occupations; using the layer scores from either $M3^+$ or $M3^\times$ would vary those intervals and make the lines straight as with equation (6) or (7). All 12 of the expected log-odds-ratios are within the 95 percent confidence intervals of the corresponding observed log-odds-ratios, but only 6 of the 12 observed log-odds-ratios fall within the 95 percent confidence interval of the corresponding expected log-odds-ratio.[6]

[5] With respect to both equations (6) and (7), it is not necessary that $\phi_k = 0$ for any of the particular layers—i.e., for any of the particular values of $k = 1,\ldots,4$.

[6] The confidence intervals for the expected log-odds-ratios are not shown in the figure, but they can be calculated from the asymptotic standard errors shown in the lower-right portion of the figure.

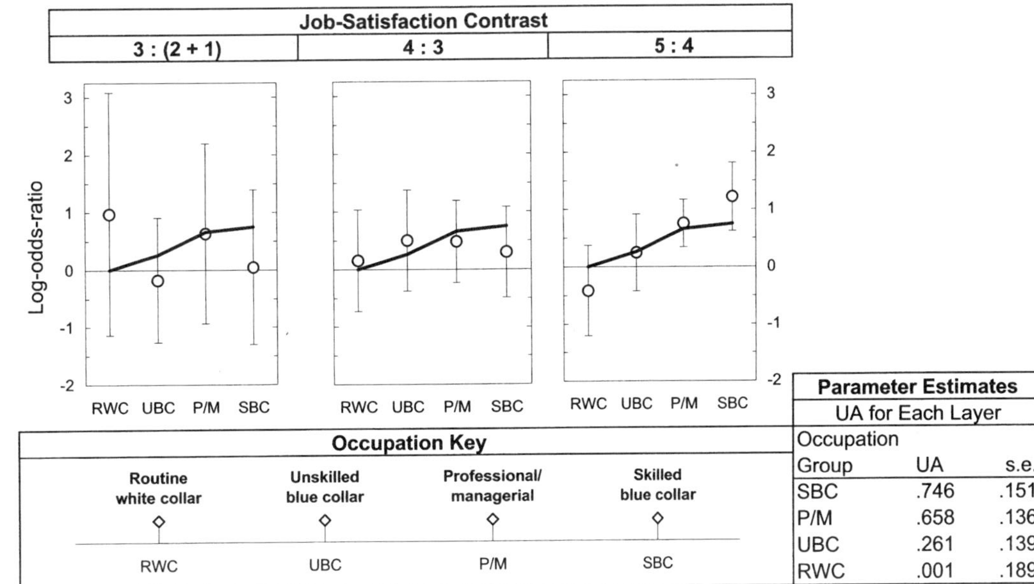

Parameter Estimates		
UA for Each Layer		
Occupation Group	UA	s.e.
SBC	.746	.151
P/M	.658	.136
UBC	.261	.139
RWC	.001	.189

FIGURE 2. Log-odds-ratios for association between job satisfaction and self-employment status by occupation, United States, 1991: Observed (circles) and expected (lines) under layer-specific uniform association model; i.e., Model M2 in Table 3 ($L^2 = 7.27$; DF = 8).

Note: Vertical lines indicate the 95 percent confidence intervals based on the observed log-odds-ratios.

Next we consider the models obtained when equation (3) is applied with no constraints imposed on the slopes (b_j). These are the UA models for the association between job satisfaction and self-employment status with a regression-type effect of occupation on this association. With one layer score specified in advance, we obtain model M3*; with two layer scores specified in advance, we obtain model M3**. We chose to specify $\phi_k = 1$ for skilled blue collar/farmer category for both M3* and M3**, and $\phi_{k'} = -1$ for routine white collar category for M3**; other choices would produce exactly the same expected frequencies (and therefore the same goodness-of-fit results). We present in Figure 3 a graphical display of the association between job satisfaction and self-employment status for the four occupational categories, comparing the observed association (circles) with the corresponding expected association (lines) under model M3**. We do not include a graphical display for model M3* here, since its graphical display is very similar to the graphical display for model M3** presented in Figure 3.

Note that the lines describing the expected association in Figure 3 are more congruent with the corresponding circles describing the observed association than are the lines tracing the expected frequencies of models M1 and M2 in Figures 1 and 2, respectively. The regression-type model improves upon models M1 and M2 by letting the slopes vary across panels. The maximum-likelihood estimates of b_1 and b_2 turn out to be close to zero (as in M1) while the maximum-likelihood estimate of b_3 turns out to be far from zero (as in M2). Better fit comes at a cost; model M3** is less parsimonious than models M1 and M2.

We next consider a modification of model M3** that Figure 3 suggests. The new model (M4**) specifies that $b_1 = b_2 = 0$. This model is as parsimonious as model M2 and more parsimonious than model M3**. We present in Figure 4 the graphical display of the association between job satisfaction and self-employment status for the four occupational categories, comparing observed association (circles) with the expected association (lines) under model M4**. This graphical display provides a simple, parsimonious picture that describes in what way the association between job satisfaction and self-employment status is affected by occupational category and in what way this association is not affected by occupational category.

Let us compare Figure 4 for model M4** with Figure 1 for model M1. This comparison helps us to see why model M1 would be rejected when the usual statistical criteria are used, while model M4** would be

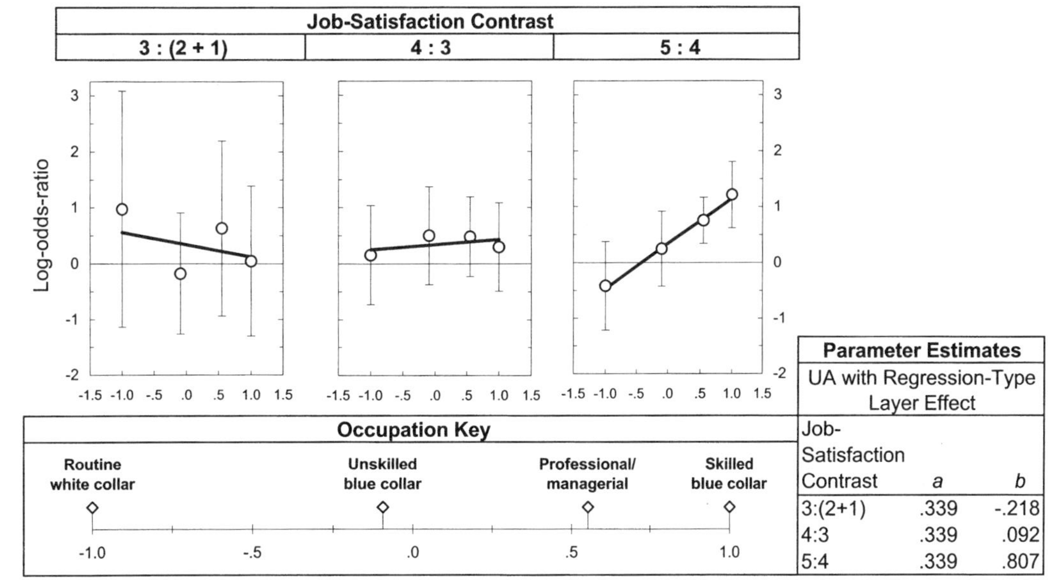

FIGURE 3. Log-odds-ratios for association between job satisfaction and self-employment status by occupation, United States, 1991: Observed (circles) and expected (lines) under uniform association model with regression-type layer effect (II); i.e., Model M3** in Table 3 ($L^2 = 1.81$; DF = 6).

Note: Vertical lines indicate the 95 percent confidence intervals based on the observed log-odds-ratios.

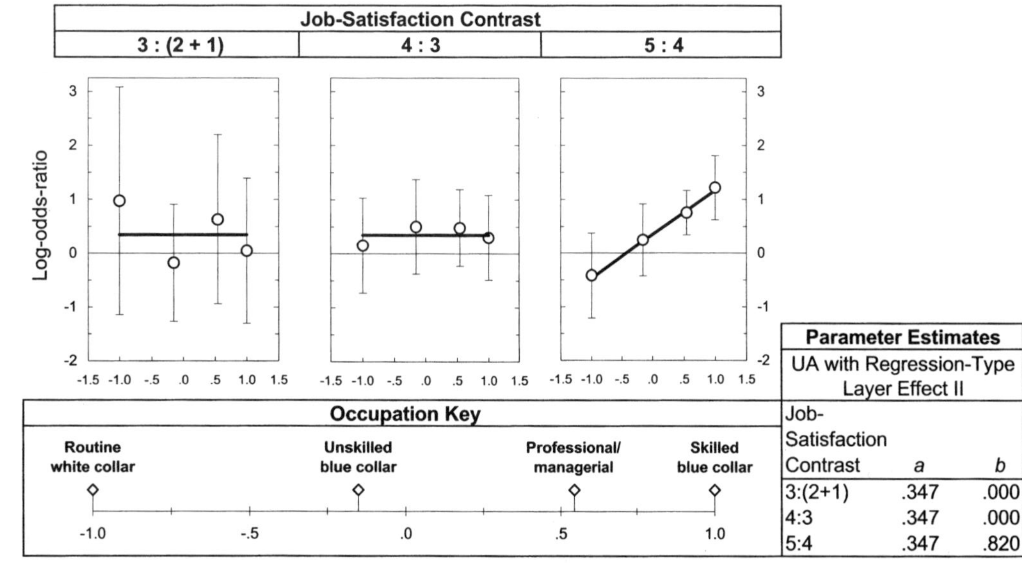

Parameter Estimates		
UA with Regression-Type Layer Effect II		
Job-Satisfaction Contrast	*a*	*b*
3:(2+1)	.347	.000
4:3	.347	.000
5:4	.347	.820

FIGURE 4. Log-odds-ratios for association between job satisfaction and self-employment status by occupation, United States, 1991: Observed (circles) and expected (lines) under uniform association model with regression-type layer effect(II) and with the first two slopes constrained to equal zero; i.e., Model M4** in Table 3 ($L^2 = 2.02$; DF = 8).

Note: Vertical lines indicate the 95 percent confidence intervals based on the observed log-odds-ratios.

accepted. We see from Figure 4 that model M4** fits the observed data very well indeed; while from Figure 1 we see that model M1 fails to take note of the effect of occupation on the association between job satisfaction and self-employment status in the third panel in Figure 1. For example, from the third panel in Figure 1, we see that the 95 percent confidence interval for the observed log-odds-ratio does not include the estimated expected association under model M1 for the routine white-collar worker and skilled blue-collar worker/farmer categories—i.e., for the occupational category with the lowest layer score and the one with the highest layer score. In addition, with respect to the first two panels in Figures 1 and 4, from the comparison of the observed association in these panels with the corresponding expected association estimated under models M1 and M4**, we see that the expected association between job satisfaction and self-employment status under model M1 is 40 percent too large (the estimate is .485 under model M1, while it is .347 under model M4**).

From Figure 4 we see that occupation can be described as having a simple linear effect on the association between job satisfaction and self-employment status in the third panel (comparing job-satisfaction category 5 with job-satisfaction category 4, for the two self-employment status categories), and the effect of occupation on this association is null in the other two panels of this figure.[7] In the third panel of Figure 4, the association was more positive for each of the two blue-collar categories (namely, the skilled worker/farmer and unskilled blue-collar categories) than for the corresponding two white-collar categories (namely, the professional/managerial category and the routine white-collar category), and more positive for the upper-status category within each of the white-collar and blue-collar categories (namely, the professional/managerial category and the skilled blue-collar/farmer category) than for the corresponding lower-status category within each of the white-collar and blue-collar categories (namely, the routine white-collar category and the unskilled blue-collar category). The association in this panel increased from being negative for lower-status white-collar workers to being positive for lower-status blue-collar workers, to being more positive for upper-status white-collar workers, to being still more positive for upper-status blue-collar workers. Also, from the three panels of Figure 4, we see that the uniform association in

[7]Note that the association between self-employment status and job satisfaction is not null; the vertical line representing this two-way association is horizontal at $a = .347$. Only the layer effect is null in this model.

the first two panels for each of the occupational categories is slightly larger than the association in the third panel for the unskilled blue-collar workers (since the occupational score for the unskilled blue-collar workers is slightly less than zero).

We next consider the BIC scores presented in Table 3 for each of the UA models considered up to this point in the paper. From Table 3 we see that, if the BIC criterion were used to select a preferred model, the first choice would be model M1, and the second choice would be model M4**. On the other hand, as we noted earlier herein, if the usual statistical criteria are used, model M1 would be rejected, and model M4** would be viewed as being congruent with the observed data; and the discussion earlier herein of the comparison of Figure 1 for model M1 with Figure 4 for model M4** would illustrate why we prefer model M4** to model M1 in this application.

We observe that the estimated layer score (ϕ_k) for the unskilled blue-collar category is very close to zero, and the estimated ϕ_k for the professional/managerial category is very close to .5. We use a layer-score specified version of model 3** in which we fix $\phi_2 = 0$ and $\phi_3 = .5$ to create model M5. Specifying the layer scores in this way saves two degrees of freedom but has a trivial effect on fit (see Table 3). At this point, if the BIC criterion were used to select a preferred model, M5 would be it. Considering our earlier comments about model M4** and observing the close resemblance between models M4** and M5 (comparing Figures 4 and 5), we are indifferent between these two models.

The pattern of layer scores we specified for model M5 allows more distance (twice as much to be precise) between the first two occupation categories as between the second and third or between the third and fourth. We next consider a model (M6) that is similar to model M5 in specifying that $a_j = a$ for all j and $b_1 = b_2 = 0$, but M6 also specifies equally spaced layer scores for all occupations (-1 for the routine white-collar category, $-1/3$ for the unskilled blue-collar category, 1/3 for the professional/managerial category, and 1 for the skilled blue-collar/farmer category). Model M6 has the same number of degrees of freedom (10) as model M5, and it fits the observed data nearly as well ($L^2 = 3.08$; $X^2 = 3.22$). A difference of .88 between the L^2 for models M5 and M6 is small relative to the baseline of 67.49 for model M0, and the BIC values are nearly equal to each other (-74 and -73, respectively). Thus for some purposes the equidistant scores may be sufficient.

FIGURE 5. Log-odds-ratios for the association between job satisfaction and self-employment status by occupation, United States, 1991: Observed (circles) and expected (lines) under Model M5 in Table 3 ($L^2 = 2.20$; DF = 10).

Note: Vertical lines indicate the 95 percent confidence intervals based on the observed log-odds-ratios.

2.2. *Models with Unconstrained Intercepts*

In our discussion of the results presented in Table 3, we have been considering so far those models that can be obtained using equation (3) (namely, models M1 and M2, the M3 and M4 models, and models M5 and M6). Next we consider the other models included in Table 3 (namely, model M7, the M8 models, and model M9*). Each of these models can be viewed as models obtained using the more general equation (2).

When equation (2) is applied to the $2 \times 4 \times 4$ table with $b_j = 0$ (for all j), we obtain the usual model of null three-factor interaction in the three-way table. With this model, the full two-way association (FA) model is used to describe the association between job satisfaction and self-employment status, with null effect of occupation on this association. This is model M7 in Table 3. From the corresponding goodness-of-fit chi-square values in Table 3, we see that model M7 would be rejected when the usual statistical criteria are used ($L^2 = 18.63$; $X^2 = 18.76$; DF $= 9$).

The other FA models in Table 3 (namely, the M8 models and model M9*) are all congruent with the observed data in the $2 \times 4 \times 4$ table, when the usual statistical criteria are used. When equation (2) is applied with $b_j = b$ (for all j), we obtain the FA model with additive layer effect, and when equation (2) is applied with $a_j = 0$ (for all j), we obtain the FA model with multiplicative layer effect. These are models $M8^+$ and $M8^\times$ in Table 3.[8] Then when equation (2) is applied with no constraints imposed on the intercepts, a_j, and on the slopes, b_j, we obtain the FA model with regression-type layer effect (model M8*). Model M9* is a simplification of model M8* with the constraint $b_1 = b_2 = 0$; it is as parsimonious as models $M8^+$ and $M8^\times$, and it is more parsimonious than M8*. Table 1 shows the formulas for the degrees of freedom for model M7 and the M8 models. Model M9* has two more degrees of freedom than M8* has.

[8] Model $M8^+$, which is the FA model with additive layer effect, was introduced in Yamaguchi (1987); model $M8^\times$, which is the FA model with multiplicative layer effect, was introduced in Xie (1992). As we noted earlier, if these two FA models are replaced by the corresponding two UA models (namely, the UA model with additive layer effect and the UA model with multiplicative layer effect), then the two UA models thus obtained will be equivalent to each other (e.g., see models $M3^+$ and $M3^\times$ in Table 3). In addition to the FA model with additive layer effect, Yamaguchi (1987) also considered various special cases of that model (including the UA model with additive layer effect); in addition to the FA model with multiplicative layer effect, Xie (1992) also considered various special cases of that model. Also see Xie (1998) and Goodman and Hout (1998b).

The results presented in Table 3 for model M7, the M8 models, and model M9* are somewhat similar to the corresponding results presented in this table for model M1 and the M3 and M4 models. Of course, each of the models based on the UA model, which were obtained using equation (3), will be more parsimonious than the corresponding model based on the FA model, which were obtained using equation (2). Since the graphical display pertaining to each of the models based on the FA model turn out to be similar to the graphical display pertaining to the corresponding model based on the UA model (namely, Figures 1 to 5), we do not include here the graphical displays pertaining to the FA models.

At various points in this paper we have considered three types of constraints on the parameters of the full association model with regression-type layer effects:

1. Constraints on the intercepts, a_j, that transform the FA model into the UA model (compare model M3* with M8*, and M4* with M9*)
2. Constraints on the slopes, b_{ij} (compare model M3* with M4*, M3** with M4**, and M8* with M9*)
3. Constraints on the layer scores (compare model M3* with M3**, M4* with M4**, and M4** with M5 and M6)

In this application we arrive at two attractive specifications by applying all three kinds of constraints (i.e., models M5 and M6). Model M5 fits nearly as well as less parsimonious models and better than related models with the same number of degrees of freedom. The BIC values suggest that models M5 and M6 are the preferred models for these data.

Substantively, we learn that self-employed people tend to like their jobs more than employees do. When people with labor force experience were asked to rate their job satisfaction on a scale from 1 to 5 (where 1 = "I hate it," and 5 = "I love it"), the odds on rating their job satisfaction 3 instead of 1 or 2, and 4 instead of 3, were 40 percent higher among the self-employed than among employees in each of four occupational categories. The contrast between the fifth and fourth categories differs according to occupation. Among routine nonmanual workers, the self-employed are actually somewhat less likely than employees to "love" their jobs—i.e., they are less likely than employees to score their jobs 5, and more likely to score them 4. Among unskilled blue collar workers, the general pattern holds exactly—i.e., the odds on a 5 rating instead of a 4 are 40 percent higher among the self-employed than among employees. Among the professionals and managers, the odds on a 5 rating instead of a 4 are 114 percent higher for the self-employed than for the employees. The disparity between the self-employed and employees is greatest among skilled blue-collar workers and farmers; the odds on a 5 rating instead of a 4 are 227 percent higher for the self-employed than for the employees.[9]

The ϕ_k scores do not result in a unidimensional ranking of the occupational categories according to prestige, socioeconomic status, percent female, or any other well-known property of occupations. They do result in a two-dimensional ranking as we already noted in Section 2.1 (p. 207). The occupation scores are higher for each of the two blue-collar categories (namely, the skilled worker/farmer and unskilled blue-collar categories) than for the corresponding two white-collar categories (namely, the professional/managerial category and the routine white-collar category), and more positive for the upper-status category within each of the white-collar and blue-collar categories (namely, the professional/managerial category and the skilled blue-collar/farmer category) than for the corresponding lower status category within each of the white-collar and blue-collar categories (namely, the routine white-collar category and the unskilled blue-collar category).

2.3. *Partitioning Association*

The pattern and strength of association are the focus of most data analysis, but a partitioning of the total conditional nonindependence between the row and column variables can also be of interest. The likelihood ratio chi-square value obtained for testing model M0 was $L^2 = 67.49$ (DF = 12). We can view this value of L^2 as, in some sense, an indication of the magnitude of the total conditional nonindependence between job satisfaction and self-employment status, given occupation. We shall proceed to partition this total conditional nonindependence into components as suggested by some of the results presented in Figures 4 and 5 pertaining to models M4** and M5. In particular, the specification that $b_1 = b_2 = 0$ reveals no three-way interaction among self-employment status, job satisfaction, and occupation for the contrasts involving the first two job-

[9]The percentage differences in this paragraph were computed from the parameter estimates from model M5 in Table 3. First, $100(\exp(.334) - 1) = 40$ percent. Second, using the equation $100(\exp(a + b_3\phi_3) - 1) = 100(\exp(.334 + .850(.5)) - 1) = 114$ percent. Third, using the equation $100(\exp(a + b_3\phi_4) - 1) = 100(\exp(.334 + .850) - 1) = 227$ percent.

satisfaction contrasts (namely, 1+2:3 and 3:4). This result suggests a partitioning that distinguishes job-satisfaction categories 1+2, 3, and 4 from 5. The three-way $2 \times 4 \times 4$ cross-classification in Table 2 can be partitioned into, say, a $2 \times 3 \times 4$ subtable and a $2 \times 2 \times 4$ table (e.g., see Goodman 1968). We shall let **T**, **T**′, and **T**″ denote the full $2 \times 4 \times 4$ cross-classification table, the corresponding $2 \times 3 \times 4$ subtable, and the corresponding $2 \times 2 \times 4$ table, respectively. In particular, we form the $2 \times 3 \times 4$ subtable **T**′ by dropping job-satisfaction category 5 from the $2 \times 4 \times 4$ table **T**; we form the corresponding $2 \times 2 \times 4$ table **T**″ with two self-employment statuses (as before), two job-satisfaction categories (the first category is obtained combining job-satisfaction categories 1+2, 3, and 4, and the second category is just category 5), and four occupational categories (as before).

Model M0 is the model of conditional independence between self-employment status and job satisfaction, given occupation, applied to the cross-classification table **T**; we shall let M0′ and M0″ denote the corresponding models of conditional independence applied to cross-classification tables **T**′ and **T**″, respectively. We noted earlier that there were 12 DF for testing model M0; there are 8 DF for testing model M0′ and 4 DF for testing model M0″. Note that 8 DF plus 4 DF equal 12 DF. The preliminary partitioning of the conditional nonindependence between self-employment status and job satisfaction in table **T** is to note that 7.79 of the total of 67.49 is due to the conditional nonindependence in table **T**′ and 59.70 is due to the conditional nonindependence in table **T**″ (see Table 4).

The conditional nonindependence in each of table **T**′ and table **T**″ can, in turn, be partitioned (e.g., see Goodman 1970). Recall that model M1 was the model of UA with null layer effect applied to what we are now referring to as table **T**. By parallel construction, model M1′ denotes the model of UA with null layer effect applied to cross-classification table **T**′. The L^2 from applying model M1′ to table **T**′ is 2.00 with 7 DF; by subtraction, it explains $7.79 - 2.00 = 5.79$ or 74 percent of the conditional nonindependence in table **T**′ while using just 1 DF.[10] Applying the model of no three-way interaction to table **T**″, we obtain $L^2 = 16.45$ (with 3 DF); by subtraction, then, the two-way partial association between self-employment status and job satisfaction explains $59.70 - 16.45 = 43.25$ or

[10]The uniform association effect in table **T**′ is statistically significant, with $L^2 = 5.79$ on 1 DF.

TABLE 4
The Components of the Total Conditional Nonindependence Between Job Satisfaction and Self-Employment Status, Given Occupation, in Cross-Classification Table T

Component	L^2	DF	Percentage Explained
Preliminary Partitioning of M0 in Cross-Classification Table **T**			
0. Total conditional nonindependence (M0, in **T**)	67.49	12	100
1. Conditional nonindependence in **T**′ (M0′, in **T**′)	7.79	8	12
2. Conditional nonindependence in **T**″ (M0″, in **T**″)	59.70	4	88
Partitioning of M0′ in Cross-Classification Table **T**′			
0. Conditional nonindependence in **T**′ (M0′, in **T**′)	7.79	8	100
1. Uniform association effect in **T**′ (M0′ − M1′, in **T**′)	5.79	1	74
2. Unexplained residual in **T**′ (M1′, in **T**′)	2.00	7	26
Partitioning of M0″ in Cross-Classification Table **T**″			
0. Conditional nonindependence in **T**″ (M0″, in **T**″)	59.70	4	100
1. Two-factor partial association effect in **T**″	43.25	1	72
2. Three-factor interaction effect in **T**″	16.45	3	28
A Composite Partitioning of M0 in Cross-Classification Table **T**			
0. Total conditional nonindependence in **T**	67.49	12	100
1. Uniform association effect in **T**′	5.79	1	9
2. Two-factor partial association effect in **T**″	43.25	1	64
3. Three-factor interaction effect in **T**″	16.45	3	24
4. Unexplained residual in **T**′	2.00	7	3

Note: See text for definition of cross-classification tables **T**, **T**′, and **T**″.

72 percent of the nonindependence in table **T**″. A composite breakdown of nonindependence in table **T** brings together each of these elements. We find that 9 percent of the total is attributable to the uniform association effect in table **T**′, 64 percent is attributable to two-way partial association in table **T**″, 24 percent is attributable to three-way interaction in table **T**″, and the remaining 3 percent is an unexplained residual in table **T**′.

3. EXAMPLE 2. SOCIAL MOBILITY IN THREE COUNTRIES REVISITED: NONFARM MOBILITY

In our previous work we used our methods to reanalyze the cross-national differences in social mobility that Yamaguchi (1987) and Xie (1992) had previously analyzed. That reanalysis revealed a different pattern of association with respect to immobility in farming than elsewhere in the table. We will now explore the efficacy of some of our simpler models when applied to nonfarm mobility. With four rows for occupational origin, four columns for occupational destination, and three layers for country, we show the counts and category names in Table 5.

Strong association between origins and destinations remains after the farm categories are removed, as indicated by the corresponding large chi-square values for the $4 \times 4 \times 3$ table (e.g., $L^2 = 2{,}683.75$; DF = 27). The three-way interaction is a relatively small part of that overall association ($L^2 = 50.66$; DF = 18), but it is nonetheless statistically significant at conventional levels.[11] Our question is whether any of the models we have been considering—the additive, multiplicative, or regression-type models (or some simplification of them)—are useful for understanding the three-way interaction. With the goodness-of-fit chi-square values presented in Table 6,

[11] The cross-national differences in mobility that involves farm origins, farm destinations, or both are more substantial (see Goodman and Hout 1998a).

TABLE 5
Cross-Classification of Origin by Destination by Country

	Destination			
Origin	Upper Nonmanual	Lower Nonmanual	Upper Manual	Lower Manual
United States, 1973				
Upper nonmanual	1,275	364	274	272
Lower nonmanual	1,055	597	394	443
Upper manual	1,043	587	1,045	951
Lower manual	1,159	791	1,323	2,046
Britain, 1974				
Upper nonmanual	474	129	87	124
Lower nonmanual	300	218	171	220
Upper manual	438	254	669	703
Lower manual	601	388	932	1,789
Japan, 1975				
Upper nonmanual	127	101	24	30
Lower nonmanual	86	207	64	61
Upper manual	43	73	122	60
Lower manual	35	51	62	66

TABLE 6
Goodness-of-Fit Statistics for Selected Models of the Association Between Origins and Destinations in Mobility Tables from Britain, Japan, and the United States

No.	Model	L^2	X^2	DF	p	BIC
H0	Null association	2,683.75	2,776.24	27	<.001	2,413
H1	Full association (FA) with null layer effect on association	50.66	49.89	18	<.001	−130
H2$^+$	FA with additive layer effect	42.38	42.03	16	<.001	−118
H2$^\times$	FA with multiplicative layer effect	30.36	30.79	16	.016	−130
H2*	FA with regression-type layer effect	5.43	5.50	8	.711	−75
H3*	FA with regression-type layer effect LSS	5.52	5.59	9	.787	−85
H4*	DA with regression-type layer effect LSS	6.53	6.60	14	.951	−134

Note: LSS = layer score specified; DA = diagonals association; see text for design matrix.

we see that our question is answered in the affirmative. Compare model H1 in Table 6 with, for example, models H2*, H3*, and H4*.

Figure 6 is a graphical display that highlights the difference between the model of no three-way interaction and the full association (FA) model with regression-type layer effect. Each panel shows the observed log-odds-ratio for a combination of origins and destinations plotted against the country scores obtained from model H2*, and the corresponding log-odds-ratios expected under the model of no three-way interaction (model H1) and the FA model with regression-type layer effect (model H2*). The lines representing the expected log-odds-ratios under model H1 are all horizontal ($b_{ij} = 0$ for $i = 1,\ldots,4, j = 1,\ldots,4$); model H1 is characterized by no difference among countries in the association between origins and destinations. All of the gray lines representing expected log-odds-ratios under model H2* have slopes that differ from the horizontal. The largest slopes are the ones that involve the diagonal contrasts for nonmanual occupations—namely, $b_{22} = .570$ and $b_{11} = .472$. Three other slopes are also substantial—namely, $b_{12} = .441$, $b_{13} = -.372$, and $b_{21} = -.385$; the fourth-largest slope (in absolute value) is $b_{23} = -.232$. The expected log-odds-ratios under both model H1 and model H2* are very close for the United States; the observed and expected log-odds-ratios for the two models differ much more for Japan. That is because the U.S. sample is 11 times larger than the Japanese sample (13,619 compared with 1,212).

The graphical displays in Figure 6 suggest two kinds of simplifications for model H2*. First, the country scores are nearly evenly spaced, $\phi_2 - \phi_1 = .54$, and $\phi_3 - \phi_2 = .46$, suggesting that we might consider a

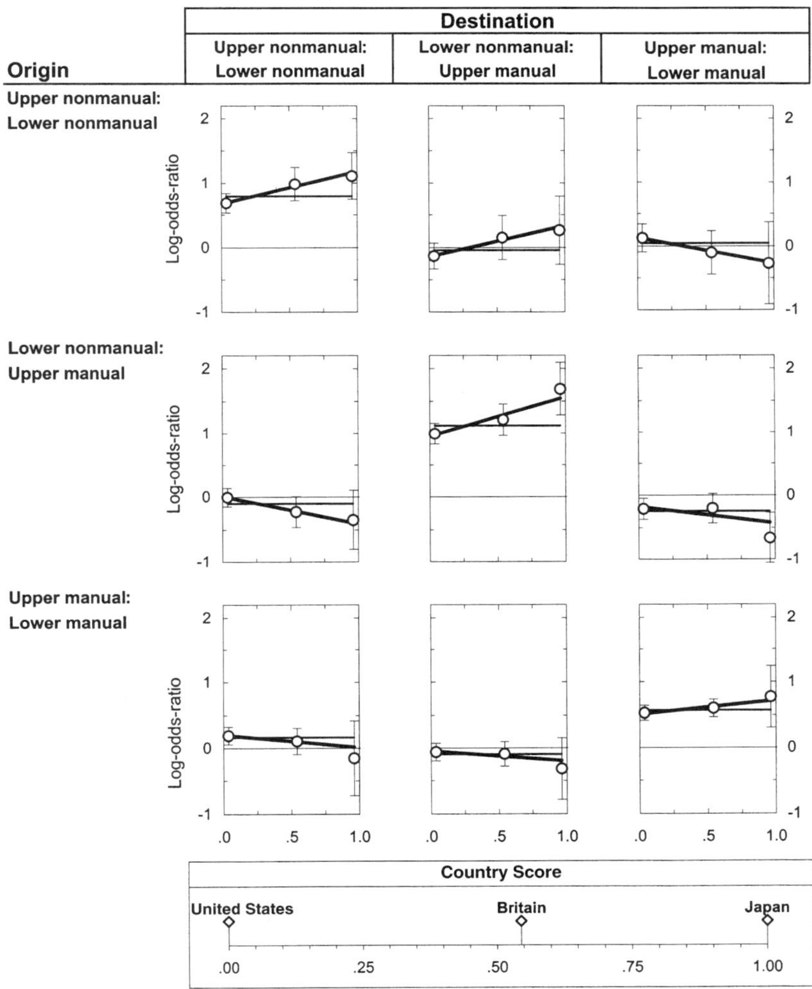

FIGURE 6. Log-odds-ratios observed and expected under the full association (FA) model with null layer effect on association and the FA Model with regression-type layer effect for the country score; i.e., Model H2* in Table 6 ($L^2 = 5.43$; DF = 8).

Note: In each panel, the horizontal line shows the expected log-odds-ratios under the FA model with null layer effect and the slanted line shows expected log-odds-ratios under the FA model with regression-type layer effect; the circles show the observed log-odds-ratios; the vertical lines show the 95 percent confidence intervals for the observed log-odds-ratios.

layer-score-specified (LSS) model in which $\phi_1 = 0$, $\phi_2 = .5$, and $\phi_3 = 1$. Second, several of the observed and expected log-odds-ratios for the United States are close to zero. With the United States as the referent country—i.e., $\phi_1 = 0$—we could construct a model in which some of the expected log-odds-ratios for the United States are zero by constraining the intercepts, a_{ij}, to be zero for the appropriate combinations of i and j.

We begin modifying model H2* with the first type of constraint and specify a model (call it model H3*) in which $\phi_k = \{0, .5, 1\}$ for $k = 1, 2, 3$. Model H3* saves one degree of freedom, and constraining the country scores in this way only adds .09 to the corresponding goodness-of-fit chi-square values. We use the graphical display in Figure 6 and a similar one based on model H3* as a guide to determine which intercepts, a_{ij}, to constrain. We also make use of Featherman and Hauser's (1978, pp. 166–73) extensive analysis of the U.S. table. In particular, the design matrix for their topological model of the U.S. table (dropping the farm row and column) is

$$\begin{matrix} 2 & 4 & 6 & 6 \\ 3 & 4 & 7 & 6 \\ 6 & 6 & 6 & 6 \\ 6 & 6 & 6 & 4 \end{matrix}$$

which implies that $a_{12} = a_{23} = -a_{13}$ and that $a_{31} = a_{32} = 0$. Comparing those expectations with Figure 6, we see that the observed and expected log-odds-ratios corresponding to a_{12} and a_{23} are indeed about as far below the origin as the observed and expected log-odds-ratios corresponding to a_{13} are above it. Furthermore, the observed and expected log-odds-ratios corresponding to a_{32} are close to the origin, and the 95 percent confidence interval based on that observed log-odds-ratio overlaps the origin. The only feature of the Featherman and Hauser model not realized in the data is the implication that the expected log-odds-ratio corresponding to a_{31} is equal to 0; the observed value is far enough from zero that the 95 percent confidence interval based on the observed log-odds-ratio does not overlap the origin, and the value expected under model H3* (.19) also differs from zero. It is, however, very close to a_{13}, and it has nearly the same magnitude but the opposite sign from a_{12} and a_{23}. We also note from Figure 6 that the observed and expected log-odds-ratios corresponding to a_{21} are very close to zero.

With all of these considerations in mind, we develop model H4* with the following properties:

$$\phi_1 = 0, \phi_2 = .5, \phi_3 = 1,$$

$$a_{12} = a_{23} = -a_{13} = -a_{31} \quad \text{and}$$

$$a_{21} = a_{32} = 0.$$

We call this the diagonals association (DA) model because $a_{12} = a_{23}$ and $a_{21} = a_{32}$. It is related to the diagonals parameter models introduced by Goodman (1972; see also Goodman 1979b, 1979c). In particular, diagonals parameter models imply a DA pattern in the log-odds-ratios.

The DA model (model H4*) fits the data very well. The goodness-of-fit chi-square values are only 1.10 larger than the corresponding values for the FA model with regression-type layer effect, and it has five more degrees of freedom; its goodness-of-fit chi-square values are also only 1.01 larger than the corresponding values for model H3* and it has four more degrees of freedom than H3*. At this point, if the BIC criterion were used to select a preferred model, model H4* would be it. (With BIC, note that model H1 would be preferred over models $H2^{+}$, H2*, and H3*, and models H1 and $H2^{\times}$ would be equally preferred. On the other hand, see how much better model H2* fits the observed data in Figure 6 than does model H1). In Figure 7, we show the observed log-odds-ratios and those expected under model H4*. The fit is very tight. Perhaps some further simplification could come to light by constraining some of the slopes to be equal to one another, but the usefulness of parsimonious models is amply demonstrated by model H4*.

4. CONCLUSION

In this paper we have considered a number of simplifications to the regression-type approach presented in Goodman and Hout (1998a, 1998b). We have shown the usefulness of our approach for discerning patterns of three-way interaction in tables of job satisfaction and social mobility that other approaches would have missed. We have also uncovered an unanticipated property of the uniform association model when coupled with the regression-type layer effects. In particular we have identified two versions of the uniform association model that differ according to whether one or two of the layer scores are fixed. Finally, we have introduced a

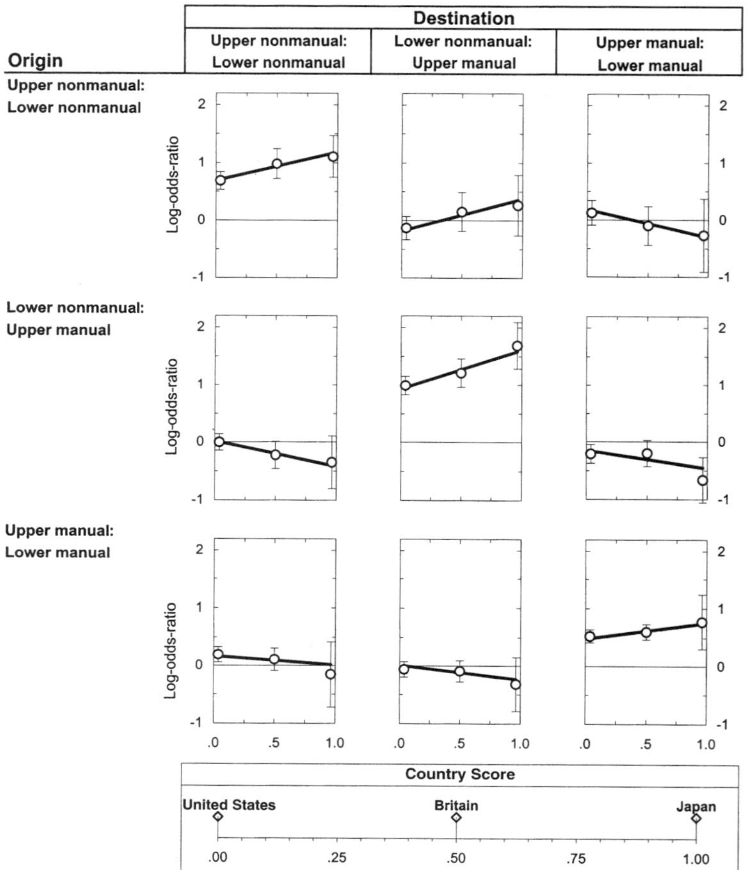

FIGURE 7. Log-odds-ratios observed and expected under diagonals association (DA) model with regression-type layer effect and layer score specified (LSS) for the country score; i.e., Model H4* in Table 6 ($L^2 = 6.53$; DF = 14). *Note*: In each panel, the gray line shows expected log-odds-ratio under the DA model with layer score specified; the circles show the observed log-odds-ratios; the vertical lines show the 95 percent confidence intervals based on the observed log-odds-ratios.

diagonals association (DA) model that bears a resemblance to the diagonals-parameter models of Goodman (1972, 1979b, 1979c). The DA model is an additional useful tool for building parsimonious models.

REFERENCES

Bogue, Donald J. 1985. *The Population of the United States*. New York: Free Press.

Duncan, Otis Dudley. 1979. "How Destination Depends on Origin in the Occupational Mobility Table." *American Journal of Sociology* 84:793–803.

Featherman, David L., and Robert M. Hauser. 1978. *Opportunity and Change*. New York: Academic Press.

Goodman, Leo A. 1968. "The Analysis of Cross-Classified Data: Independence, Quasi-Independence, and Interactions in Contingency Tables With or Without Missing Entries." *Journal of the American Statistical Association* 63:1091–131.

———. 1970. "The Multivariate Analysis of Qualitative Data: Interactions Among Multiple Classifications." *Journal of the American Statistical Association* 65:226–56.

———. 1972. "Some Multiplicative Models for the Analysis of Cross-Classified Data." Pp. 649–96 in *Proceedings of the Sixth Berkeley Symposium on Mathematical Statistics and Probability*, edited by Lucien LeCam et al. Berkeley: University of California Press.

———. 1979a. "Simple Models for the Analysis of Association in Cross-Classifications Having Ordered Categories." *Journal of the American Statistical Association* 74: 537–52.

———. 1979b. "Multiplicative Models for the Analysis of Occupational Mobility Tables and Other Kinds of Cross-Classification Tables." *American Journal of Sociology* 84:804–19.

———. 1979c. "Multiplicative Models for Square Contingency Tables with Ordered Categories." *Biometrika* 66: 413–18.

———. 1984. *The Analysis of Cross-Classified Data Having Ordered Categories*. Cambridge, MA: Harvard University Press.

———. 1986. "Some Useful Extensions of the Usual Correspondence Analysis Approach and the Usual Log-Linear Models Approach in the Analysis of Contingency Tables" (with discussion). *International Statistical Review* 54:243–70.

Goodman, Leo A., and Michael Hout. 1998a. "Statistical Methods and Graphical Displays for Analyzing How the Association Between Two Qualitative Variables Differs Among Countries, Among Groups, or Over Time: A Modified Regression-type Approach." *Sociological Methodology* 28: 175–230.

———. 1998b. "Understanding the Goodman-Hout Approach to the Analysis of Differences in Association and Some Related Comments." *Sociological Methodology* 28:249–62.

Hout, Michael, Erik Olin Wright, and Martín Sanchez Jankowski. 1992. "Class Structure and Consciousness Survey." Survey Research Center, University of California, Berkeley.

Xie, Yu. 1992. "The Log-Multiplicative Layer Effect Model for Comparing Mobility Tables." *American Sociological Review* 57:380–95.

———. 1998. "The Essential Tension Between Parsimony and Accuracy." *Sociological Methodology* 28: 237–48.

Yamaguchi, Kazuo. 1987. "Models for Comparing Mobility Tables: Toward Parsimony and Substance." *American Sociological Review* 52:482–94.

5

LATENT CLASS FACTOR AND CLUSTER MODELS, BI-PLOTS, AND RELATED GRAPHICAL DISPLAYS

*Jay Magidson**
Jeroen K. Vermunt†

We propose an alternative method of conducting exploratory latent class analysis that utilizes latent class factor models, and compare it to the more traditional approach based on latent class cluster models. We show that when formulated in terms of R mutually independent, dichotomous latent factors, the LC factor model has the same number of distinct parameters as an LC cluster model with R+1 clusters. Analyses over several data sets suggest that LC factor models typically fit data better and provide results that are easier to interpret than the corresponding LC cluster models. We also introduce a new graphical "bi-plot" display for LC factor models and compare it to similar plots used in correspondence analysis and to a barycentric coordinate display for LC cluster models. New results on identification of LC models are also presented. We conclude by describing various model extensions and an approach for eliminating boundary solutions in identified and unidentified LC models, which we have implemented in a new computer program.

1. INTRODUCTION

Latent class (LC) analysis is becoming one of the standard data analysis tools in social, biomedical, and marketing research. While the traditional

The authors wish to thank Jeremy F. Magland, Leo A. Goodman, and Peter G. M. van der Heijden for their helpful comments.
*Statistical Innovations
†Tilburg University

LC model was introduced by Lazarsfeld and Henry (1968) for dichotomous variables and formalized and extended to nominal variables by Goodman (1974a, 1974b), variants have been proposed for ordinal (Clogg 1988; Uebersax 1993; Heinen 1996) and continuous indicators (Wolfe 1970; McLachlan and Basford 1988; Fraley and Raftery 1998), as well as for combinations of variables of different scale types (Lawrence and Krzanowski 1996; Moustaki 1996; Hunt and Jorgensen 1999; Vermunt and Magidson 2001). This paper concentrates on exploratory LC analysis with nominal and ordinal indicators.

In an exploratory LC analysis, the usual approach is to begin by fitting a 1-class (independence) model to the data, followed by a two-class model, a three-class model, etc., and continuing until a model is found that provides an adequate fit (Goodman 1974a, 1974b; McCutcheon 1987). We refer to such models as LC cluster models since the T nominal categories of the latent variable serve the same function as the T clusters desired in cluster analysis (McLachlan and Basford 1988; Hunt and Jorgensen 1999; Vermunt and Magidson 2001).

Van der Ark and Van der Heijden (1998) and Van der Heijden, Gilula, and Van der Ark (1999) showed that exploratory LC analysis can be used to determine the number of dimensions underlying the responses on a set of nominal items. A LC model with three classes, for example, can be seen as a two-dimensional model similar to a two-dimensional joint correspondence analysis (JCA). However, within the context of LC analysis, a more natural manner of specifying the existence of two underlying dimensions for a set of items is to specify a model containing two latent variables.

Goodman (1974b), Haberman (1979), and Hagenaars (1990, 1993) proposed restricted 4-class LC models yielding confirmatory LC models with two latent variables. Their approach is confirmatory since, as in confirmatory factor analysis, it requires *a priori* knowledge on which items are related to which latent variables. In *exploratory* data analysis settings, we do not know beforehand which items load on the same latent variable. Hence, in exploratory analyses with several latent variables, this approach has limited practical applicability.

In this paper, we propose combining the exploratory model fitting strategy of the traditional LC model with the possibility of increasing the number of latent variables to study the dimensionality of a set of items. Our alternative model-fitting sequence involves increasing the number of latent variables (factors) rather than the number of classes (clusters). We call the latter sequence the LC factor approach because of the natural analogy to standard factor analysis. The basic LC factor model contains R mutually independent, dichotomous latent variables. To exclude higher-order interactions, logit models are specified on the response probabilities. An interesting feature of the basic R-factor model is that it has exactly the same number of parameters as an LC cluster model with T = R+1 clusters. In Section 2, we describe the two types of exploratory LC models using the log-linear formulation introduced by Haberman (1979).

Section 3 compares the use of LC cluster and factor models in several examples and describes various graphical displays that facilitate the interpretation of the results obtained from these models. In particular, we consider some variations of the ternary diagram originally proposed by Van der Ark and Van der Heijden (1998) for LC cluster models, and introduce a new display (called a "bi-plot") for LC factor models to represent various kinds of information in a two-dimensional factor space. These two graphs are compared to each other and to similar displays used in correspondence analysis.

Section 4 describes some important extensions of the basic LC factor model, such as various model modifications needed for a more confirmatory analysis and for the inclusion of covariates. In Section 5, we discuss identification issues. The paper ends with some final remarks regarding the applicability of these models.

2. TWO APPROACHES FOR EXPLORATORY LC ANALYSIS

In this section we describe and compare two competing alternative approaches for exploratory LC analysis. The traditional approach utilizes LC cluster models, while the alternative is based on LC factor models. For the sake of simplicity of exposition, below we use the log-linear formulation of LC models introduced by Haberman (1979). In Appendix A, we give the alternative probability formulation of the two types of LC models as well as the relationship between the two formulations.

2.1. *The LC Cluster Model*

For concreteness, consider four nominal variables denoted A, B, C, and D. Let X represent a nominal latent variable with T categories. The log-linear representation of the LC cluster model with T classes is

$$\ln(F_{ijklt}) = \lambda + \lambda_t^X + \lambda_i^A + \lambda_j^B + \lambda_k^C + \lambda_l^D + \lambda_{it}^{AX} + \lambda_{jt}^{BX} + \lambda_{kt}^{CK} + \lambda_{lt}^{DX} \quad (1)$$

where $i = 1,2,\ldots,\mathrm{I}$; $j = 1,2,\ldots,\mathrm{J}$; $k = 1,2,\ldots\mathrm{K}$; $l = 1,2,\ldots\mathrm{L}$; and $t = 1,2,\ldots,\mathrm{T}$.

For convenience in counting distinct parameters and without loss of generality, we choose the following "dummy coding" restrictions to identify the parameters:[1]

$$\lambda_1^X = \lambda_1^A = \lambda_1^B = \lambda_1^C = \lambda_1^D = 0$$

$$\lambda_{i1}^{AX} = \lambda_{j1}^{BX} = \lambda_{k1}^{CX} = \lambda_{l1}^{DX} = 0 \quad \text{for} \quad i = 1,2,\ldots,\mathrm{I}; j = 1,2,\ldots,\mathrm{J};$$

$$k = 1,2,\ldots,\mathrm{K}; l = 1,2,\ldots\mathrm{L};$$

$$\text{and} \quad \lambda_{1t}^{AX} = \lambda_{1t}^{BX} = \lambda_{1t}^{CX} = \lambda_{1t}^{DX} = 0 \quad \text{for} \quad t = 2,3,\ldots,\mathrm{T}.$$

As can be seen, the LC model described in equation (1) has the form of a log-linear model for the five-way frequency table cross-classifying the four observed variables and the latent variable—that is, the table with cell entries $\mathrm{F}_{\mathrm{ijklt}}$. The assumed model contains one-variable terms ("main effects") associated with the latent variable *X* and the four observed indicators *A*, *B*, *C*, and *D*, as well as all two-variable "interaction" terms that involve *X* which pertain to the association between *X* and each of the observed indicators. The one-variable effects are included because we do not wish to impose constraints on the univariate marginal distributions. The assumption that the observed responses to *A*, *B*, *C*, and *D* are mutually independent given $X = t$ ("local independence") is imposed by the omission of all interaction terms pertaining to the associations between the indicators. As shown in Appendix A, this set of conditional independence assumptions can also be formulated in another way, yielding the probability formulation for the LC model.

Note that for the one-class model, since $\mathrm{T} = 1$, the model described in equation (1) reduces to the usual log-linear model of mutual independence between the four observed variables:

$$\ln(F_{ijkl}) = \lambda + \lambda_i^A + \lambda_j^B + \lambda_k^C + \lambda_l^D. \qquad (2)$$

More generally, for models with any number of variables, we will denote the model of mutual independence as H_0, and use it as a baseline to assess the improvement in fit to the data of various LC models. The number of

[1]See Haberman (1979) for an alternative set of identifying restrictions based on ANOVA effects coding.

distinct parameters in the model of independence as described in equation (2) is as follows:[2]

$$\text{NPAR(indep)} = (\text{I} - 1) + (\text{J} - 1) + (\text{K} - 1) + (\text{L} - 1)$$

Expressing the number of distinct parameters in the model described in equation (1) as a function of NPAR(indep), yields:

$$\begin{aligned}\text{NPAR(T)} &= (\text{T} - 1) + \text{NPAR(indep)} \times [1 + (\text{T} - 1)] \\ &= (\text{T} - 1) + \text{NPAR(indep)} \times \text{T}\end{aligned}$$

The number of degrees of freedom (DF) associated with the test of model fit is directly related to the number of distinct parameters in the model tested.[3]

$$\begin{aligned}\text{DF(T)} &= \text{IJKL} - \text{NPAR(T)} - 1 \\ &= \text{IJKL} - [1 + \text{NPAR(indep)}] \times \text{T}\end{aligned}$$

Beginning with this baseline model (T = 1), each time the number of latent classes (T) is incremented by 1 the number of distinct parameters increases by 1 + NPAR(indep), and, as a consequence, the degrees of freedom are reduced by 1 + NPAR(indep). The first additional parameter is the main effect for the additional latent class, and the NPAR(indep) further parameters correspond to the effects of each observed (manifest) variable on this additional latent class.

2.2. *The Latent Class Factor Model*

Certain LC models can be interpreted in terms of two or more component latent variables by treating those components as a joint variable (Goodman 1974b; McCutcheon 1987; Hagenaars 1990). For example, a four-category latent variable $X = \{1, 2, 3, 4\}$ can be re-expressed in terms of two dichotomous latent variables $V = \{1, 2\}$ and $W = \{1, 2\}$ using the following correspondence:

[2]By convention, we do not count λ as a distinct parameter because of the redundancy to the overall sample size, and we subtract 1 from the number of cells when computing degrees of freedom.

[3]It is customary when one or more distinct parameters are unidentified or not estimable (a boundary solution), to adjust the DF, increasing it by the number of such unidentified or not estimable parameters.

	$W=1$	$W=2$
$V=1$	$X=1$	$X=2$
$V=2$	$X=3$	$X=4$

Thus $X = 1$ corresponds with $V = 1$ and $W = 1$, $X = 2$ with $V = 1$ and $W = 2$, $X = 3$ with $V = 2$ and $W = 1$, and $X = 4$ with $V = 2$ and $W = 2$.

The LC cluster model given in (1) with T = 4 classes can be re-parameterized as an *unrestricted* LC factor model with two dichotomous latent variables V and W as follows:

$$\ln(F_{ijklrs}) = \lambda + \lambda_r^V + \lambda_s^W + \lambda_{rs}^{VW} + \lambda_i^A + \lambda_j^B + \lambda_k^C + \lambda_l^D + \lambda_{ir}^{AV} + \lambda_{jr}^{BV} + \lambda_{kr}^{CV} + \lambda_{lr}^{DV} + \lambda_{is}^{AW} + \lambda_{js}^{BW} + \lambda_{ks}^{CW} + \lambda_{ls}^{DW} + \lambda_{irs}^{AVW} + \lambda_{jrs}^{BVW} + \lambda_{krs}^{CVW} + \lambda_{lrs}^{DVW}. \tag{3}$$

The correspondence between the two representations is that the one-variable terms pertaining to X are now written as $\lambda_{2(r-1)+s}^X = \lambda_r^V + \lambda_s^W + \lambda_{rs}^{VW}$, and the two-variable terms involving X as $\lambda_{i,2(r-1)+s}^{AX} = \lambda_{ir}^{AV} + \lambda_{is}^{AW} + \lambda_{irs}^{AVW}$, $\lambda_{j,2(r-1)+s}^{BX} = \lambda_{jr}^{BV} + \lambda_{js}^{BW} + \lambda_{jrs}^{BVW}$, etc. It is easy to verify that this reparameterization does not alter the *number* of distinct parameters in the model.

We define the *basic R*-factor LC model as a *restricted* factor model that contains R mutually independent, dichotomous latent variables, containing parameters ("factor loadings") that measure the association of each latent variable on each indicator. Specifically, the basic R-factor model is defined by placing two sets of restrictions on the unrestricted LC factor model. The resulting two-factor LC model is a restricted form of the four-class LC cluster model. Without these restrictions, the two-factor model would be unconstrained and would be equivalent to a four-cluster model.

The first set of restrictions sets to zero each of the three-way and higher-order interaction terms. For the basic two-factor model, we have $\lambda_{irs}^{AVW} = \lambda_{irs}^{BVW} = \lambda_{irs}^{CVW} = \lambda_{irs}^{DVW} = 0$. After imposing these restrictions, the two-variable terms in the basic two-factor model become

$$\lambda_{i,2(r-1)+s}^{AX} = \lambda_{ir}^{AV} + \lambda_{is}^{AW}, \quad \lambda_{j,2(r-1)+s}^{BX} = \lambda_{jr}^{BV} + \lambda_{js}^{BW}, \quad \text{etc.}$$

For variable A, λ_{ir}^{AV} represents the loading of A on factor V and λ_{is}^{AW} denotes the loading of A on factor W, etc. By fixing the three-variable terms to be equal to zero, we obtain a model that is conceptually similar to standard exploratory factor analysis: Each of the factors may have an effect on each indicator, but there are no higher-order interaction terms. Constraints of this form are necessary to allow the four latent classes to be expressed as a cross-tabulation of two latent variables and thus are essential for distinguishing the LC factor model from the LC cluster model.

The second set of restrictions imposes mutual independence between the latent variables. For the two-factor model, this latter restriction imposes independence in the two-way table ⟨VW⟩. This restriction makes the model more similar to standard *exploratory* factor analysis. We relax this assumption in Section 4, when we present *confirmatory* LC factor models.

Although the basic R-factor model is a special case of an LC *cluster* model containing 2^R classes, we show in Appendix A that because of the restrictions of the type given above, the basic R-factor LC model is actually comparable to an LC cluster model with only T = R + 1 clusters in terms of parsimony. This large reduction in number of parameters will be sufficient to achieve model identification in many situations. That is, in practice, it will frequently be the case that the basic R-factor will be identified when the LC cluster model with 2^R classes is not.

Table 1 verifies the equivalence in number of parameters (and the associated degrees of freedom) between the various identified LC cluster models and the corresponding basic LC factor models in the case of five dichotomous indicator variables. From this table we can also calculate, for example, that the basic LC two-factor model requires 23 − 17 = 6 fewer parameters than the four-class LC cluster model. This

TABLE 1
Equivalency Relationship Between LC Cluster and Basic LC Factor Models
(Example with Five Dichotomous Variables)

LC Cluster Models			Basic LC Factor Models		
Number of Latent Classes	Number of Parameters	DF	Number of Factors	Number of Parameters	DF
1	5	26	0	5	26
2	11	20	1	11	20
3	17	14	2	17	14
4	23	8	3	23	8
5	29	2	4	29	2

reduction corresponds to the five restrictions $\lambda_{irs}^{AVW} = \lambda_{irs}^{BVW} = \lambda_{irs}^{CVW} = \lambda_{irs}^{DVW} = \lambda_{irs}^{EVW} = 0$, plus the restriction that V and W are independent. (See Appendix A for a simple formula for calculating the number of such restrictions in the more general case.)

We conclude this section by noting an important difference between our LC factor model and the LC models with several latent variables proposed by Goodman (1974b), Haberman (1979), McCutcheon (1987), and Hagenaars (1990, 1993). The basic LC factor model described above includes all factor loadings between the latent variables and the indicators. This means that no assumptions need be made about which indicators are related to which latent variables. This makes this LC factor model better suited for exploratory data analysis than the LC models with several latent variables described in the literature.

Thus far we have described two alternative approaches for exploratory LC analysis, one involving the fitting of LC cluster models, the other fitting basic LC factor models. In the next section we consider some examples to illustrate and compare their performance on real data and introduce graphical displays that facilitate the interpretation of the obtained results.

3. EXAMPLES AND GRAPHICAL DISPLAYS

Comparison of the two approaches for exploratory LC analysis across several data sets found that the factor approach resulted in a more parsimonious and easier to interpret model almost every time. Since our selection of data sets was not random, we do not present those results here. Rather, for purposes of illustration, this section considers the analysis from two data sets where a basic two-factor model fits the data. In the first example, the comparable cluster model also provides an acceptable (but not as good) fit to the data; in the second example, the comparable cluster model provides a *much* worse fit, one that is not acceptable for these data.

This section also introduces graphical displays useful in displaying results from LC cluster and factor models. Details on the computation of the conditional probabilities appearing in the plots are given in Appendix B.

3.1. *Example* 1: 1982 *General Social Survey Data*

Our first example, taken from McCutcheon (1987) and reanalyzed by Van der Heijden, Gilula, and Van der Ark (1999) involves four categorical variables from the 1982 General Social Survey. Two items are evaluations of surveys by white respondents and the other two are evaluations of these

TABLE 2
Cross-Tabulation of Observed Variables for White Respondents to the 1982 General Social Survey

			(A) COOPERATION		
(C) PURPOSE	(D) ACCURACY	(B) UNDERSTANDING	Interested	Cooperative	Impatient/ Hostile
Good	Mostly true	Good	419	35	2
		Fair, poor	71	25	5
	Not true	Good	270	25	4
		Fair, poor	42	16	5
Depends	Mostly true	Good	23	4	1
		Fair, poor	6	2	0
	Not true	Good	43	9	2
		Fair, poor	9	3	2
Waste	Mostly true	Good	26	3	0
		Fair, poor	1	2	0
	Not true	Good	85	23	6
		Fair, poor	13	12	8

respondents by the interviewer (see Table 2). A summary of various LC models fit to these data is given in Table 3.

Model H_0 is the baseline model given in equation (2), which specifies mutual independence between all four variables. Model H_0 is a one-class LC model (a one-cluster model) which can also be interpreted as the equivalent 0-factor LC model. Since $L^2 = 257.26$ with DF = 29, this model is rejected. Next, consider the two-class model (H_1) that can be interpreted as either a two-cluster model or the equivalent one-factor model where the factor is dichotomous. The L^2 is now reduced to 79.34, a 69.1%

TABLE 3
Results from Various LC Models Fit to Data in Table 2

Model	Model Description	BIC	L^2	DF	p-value	% Reduction in $L^2(H_0)$
H_0	1-class	51.6	257.26	29	2.0×10^{-38}	0
H_1	2-class	−76.7	79.34	22	2.1×10^{-8}	69.1
H_{2C}	3-class	−98.7	21.89	15+2*	0.19	91.5
H_{2F}	basic 2-factor	−109.6	10.93	15+2*	0.86	95.7
H_3	4-class	−72.0	6.04	8+3*	0.87	97.7
H_{R2F}	restricted 2-factor	−140.9	22.17	22+1*	0.51	91.4
H_{1F3}	1-factor (3 levels)	−71.7	77.25	21	2.3×10^{-8}	70.0

*DF is increased by these boundary solutions.

reduction from the baseline model, but too high to be acceptable with DF = 22.

Next, consider the two 15-DF models[4]—H_{2C}, the 3-cluster model and H_{2F}, the basic 2-factor model. Each of these models provide an adequate fit to the data, although the factor model fits better, the L^2 being half that of the comparable cluster model. For comparison, Table 3 also provides results for the four-cluster model (H_3). Among the first five models listed in Table 3, H_{2F} is preferred according to the BIC criteria. The last two models in Table 3 are extended models that will be discussed in the next section.

Table 4 compares results obtained from the three-cluster Model (H_{2C}) with that from the basic 2-factor model (H_{2F}). The cell entries in the leftmost columns are "rescaled parameter estimates" suggested by Van der Heijden, Gilula, and Van der Ark (1999), and represent the estimated *conditional* probabilities of being a member of one of the three clusters. The rightmost columns contain corresponding quantities for the basic two-factor model, representing the estimated probabilities of being at level 1 for each of the two factors. *Unconditional* membership probabilities for the clusters and for level 1 of the factors are given in the last row of the table.

Graphical displays of the conditional probabilities reported in Table 4 are useful in comparing results between the two models. For the three-cluster model H_2, Van der Heijden, Gilula, and Van der Ark (1999, fig. 4) present a ternary diagram for visualizing the results and show the close relationship to two-dimensional plots produced by joint correspondence analysis (JCA). A slightly modified graphic, referred to here as a "barycentric coordinate" display is given in Figure 1 for the three-cluster model H_{2C}. The shaded triangle in Figure 1 with lines emanating to the sides represents the overall sample, which is plotted at the

[4]For both models H_{2C} and H_{2F}, the maximum-likelihood solution contains two boundary solutions and hence, by convention (see note 3) we increased the DF by 2. Adding the number of parameters estimated on the boundary to the number of degrees of freedom is a convention in LC analysis (for instance, see McCutcheon 1987). In our opinion, there is no good reason to do so, but it is outside the scope of this paper to present alternative testing methods for situations in which boundary estimates occur. For model H_{2C}, McCutcheon (1987) reported an adjusted DF of 16, increasing the usual DF by only 1 because the solution reported was not fully converged and contained, therefore, only one boundary solution. The solution presented in Van der Heijden et al. (1999) is the same solution as that presented here (containing two boundary solutions), but they also misreport the DF to be 16 instead of 17.

TABLE 4
Comparison of Results from the Three-Cluster Model with the Basic Two-Factor Model Conditional Membership Probability of Being in Cluster j = 1,2,3 (for Model H_{2C}) or Level 1 of Factor k = 1,2 (for Model H_{2F})

	Model H_{2C}			Model H_{2F}	
	Cluster 1	Cluster 2	Cluster 3	Factor1 (1)	Factor2 (1)
Indicators					
PURPOSE					
Good	0.72	0.25	0.03	0.83	0.71
Depends	0.38	0.17	0.45	0.65	0.28
Waste	0.24	0.02	0.73	0.59	0*
ACCURACY					
Mostly true	0.73	0.26	0.01	0.83	0.83
Not true	0.50	0.15	0.35	0.71	0.28
UNDERSTAND					
Good	0.76	0.08	0.16	0.89	0.53
Fair, poor	0*	0.77	0.23	0.28	0.71
COOPERATE					
Interested	0.70	0.17	0.13	0.86	0.58
Cooperative	0.27	0.40	0.33	0.38	0.51
Impatient/hostile	0*	0.39	0.61	0*	0.35
Overall Probability	0.62	0.21	0.17	0.78	0.57

*Indicates a boundary solution.

point corresponding to the unconditional membership probabilities for the clusters.

A different display for LC factor-models called the "bi-plot"[5] (Vermunt and Magidson, 2000) is given in Figure 2 for the two-factor model H_{2F}. For comparability to the barycentric coordinate plot where cluster 1 is assigned to the top vertex, we take factor 1 to be the *vertical* axis and

[5] In the context of correspondence analysis, the term "biplot" refers to a particular joint display of points representing both the rows and columns of a frequency table (Greenacre 1993). On the other hand, Gower and Hand (1996) stress that the "bi" in biplots arises from the fact that cases and variables are presented in the same plots. In Vermunt and Magidson (2000), we chose the term "bi-plot" because of the similarity of our plots to the plots used in correspondence analysis. However, despite the fact that in most of our examples we depict only variable categories, it is also possible to depict cases (or answer patterns) in our plots as we illustrated in our Figures 4, 6 and 8. For more detail about our plots, see Appendix B.

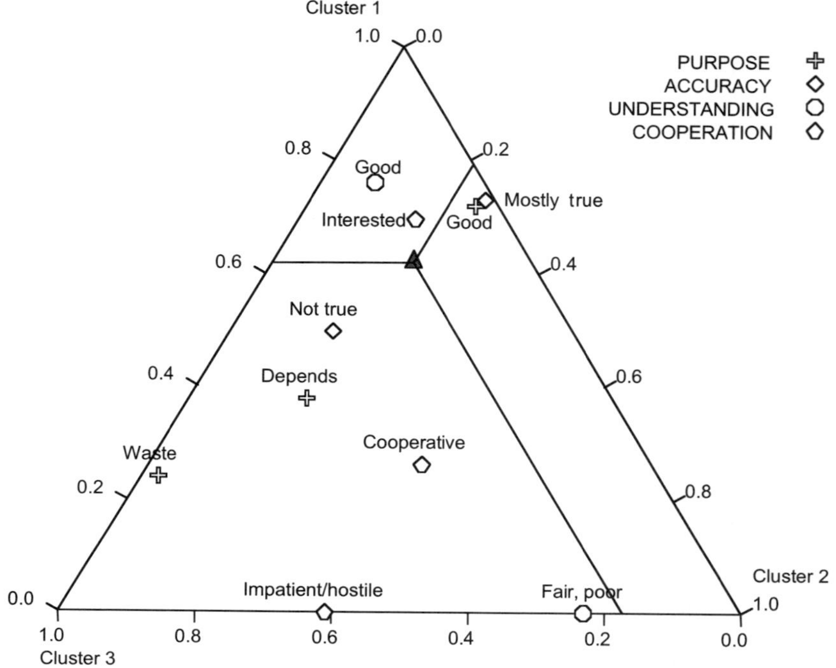

FIGURE 1. Barycentric coordinate display of results reported in Table 4 for model H_{2C}.

factor 2 the horizontal. By comparing these plots, we can see the large degree of similarity between the models, the primary difference being the relative positioning of COOPERATION = Impatient/hostile and UNDERSTANDING = Fair, poor.

Lines connecting the categories of a variable can make it easier to see to which factor the variables are most related. For example, Figure 3 shows that separation between the categories of the two respondent evaluation variables, PURPOSE and ACCURACY, occurs primarily along Factor 2 (the horizontal axis in Figure 3) while for the two interviewer evaluation variables, UNDERSTANDING and COOPERATION, separation occurs primarily along Factor 1 (the vertical axis). This makes clear that Factor 1 pertains primarily to the interviewer valuation while Factor 2 pertains primarily to the respondent valuation. These two factors are not only distinct (i.e., the one-factor model H_1 does not fit these data) but according to model H_{2F}, they are mutually independent.

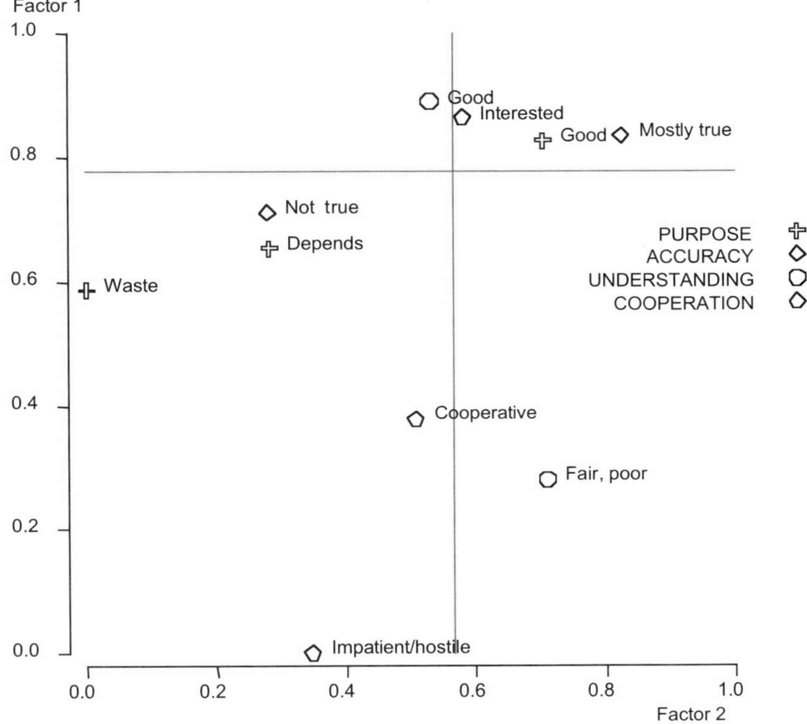

FIGURE 2. Bi-plot of results reported in Table 4 for model H_{2F}.

Since our models yield estimated membership probabilities for each individual case, both displays can easily be extended to include points for individual cases and covariate levels as well as any other desired groupings of the cases (see Appendix B). Our methodology is unified in the sense that the same methods and models that yield our displays for LC cluster models also yield the bi-plots for the LC factor models. Our barycentric coordinate display can be more easily extended in this manner than the methods proposed by Van der Heijden, Gilula, and Van der Ark (1999) with the ternary diagram. In our next example we will illustrate the inclusion in our plots of cases by including specific cases with selected response patterns. Then in Section 4, we show how the display of *all* response patterns can be used to identify a natural ordering between the classes (when such an ordering exists), and we describe two different approaches for overlaying covariate values (levels) onto the displays.

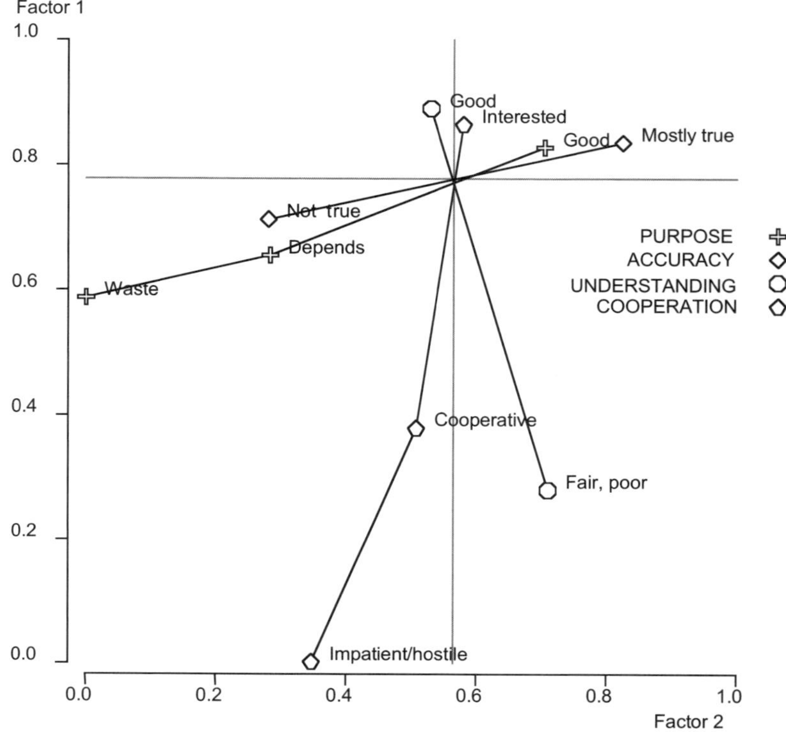

FIGURE 3. Bi-plot for Model H_{2F} with lines connecting categories of a variable.

The bi-plots offer several advantages over the related plots produced in correspondence analysis (CA) even when the data justifies a two-dimensional CA solution.[6] That is because the 2-dimensional CA solution is closely related to the 3-cluster solution (Gilula and Haberman 1986; De Leeuw and Van der Heijden 1991) which we have found typically does not fit the data as well as the 2-factor solution. As suggested in this paper, the LC factor models generally provide simpler explanations of data than

[6] An extensive comparison between the LC cluster model and (joint) correspondence analysis is given by Van der Heijden, Gilula and Van der Ark (1999). They showed that (joint) correspondence analysis is very similar to what we labeled the LC cluster model. More precisely, a two-dimensional joint correspondence analysis can describe exactly the results—the estimated frequencies in all two-way tables—of a three-cluster model.

LC cluster models and the related canonical models used in CA and principal components analysis.

Our LC factor model is more closely related to traditional factor analysis than to CA. There are several advantages over traditional factor analysis: (1) the variables can include different scale types—nominal, ordinal, continuous and/or counts, (2) solutions are typically uniquely identified and interpretable without the need for a rotation—there is no rotational indeterminacy, and (3) factor scores can be obtained for each case without the need for additional assumptions. Like traditional factor analysis, LC factor analysis can be used as a first step in a more confirmatory analysis. Later in this paper (Section 4) we describe a more confirmatory analysis of the data analyzed above.

3.2. *Example* 2: *Rheumatoid Arthritis Data*

Our second example consists of five dichotomous responses obtained from a mail survey regarding various musculoskeletal symptoms (see Table 5). Specifically, persons were asked whether they had any of the following symptoms today: back pain, neck pain, joint pain, joint swelling, and joint stiffness. For further details, see Wasmus, et al. (1989).

The traditional LC cluster approach, as applied by Kohlmann and Formann (1997) to these data, rejects the one-, two-, and three-class models in favor of the four-class model, which provides an acceptable fit to the data ($L^2 = 8.4$ with 8 degrees of freedom; $p = .39$). The BIC statistic also selects the four-class model as the one to be preferred among the LC cluster models listed in Table 6.

The close relationship between the latent class *cluster* model and the canonical model (Gilula and Haberman 1986; De Leeuw and Van der Heijden 1991) justifies a two-dimensional display such as that produced in joint correspondence analysis (JCA) when the three-cluster model is true (Van der Heijden, Gilula, and Van der Ark 1999). On the other hand, when the three-class model must be *rejected* as not providing an adequate fit to data, as in the present example, the two-dimensional JCA display cannot provide a complete description of these data because a third dimension is also needed. However, as we show below, a *different* two-dimensional display obtained from the LC factor model *does* provide a complete description of these data.

Table 7 provides a closer look at the differences between the three- and four-class solutions to these data. We see that for the most part, the

TABLE 5
Rheumatoid Arthritis Mail Survey Data

BACK	NECK	JOINT	SWELL	STIFF	Frequency
No	No	No	No	No	3,634
No	No	No	No	Yes	73
No	No	No	Yes	No	87
No	No	No	Yes	Yes	10
No	No	Yes	No	No	440
No	No	Yes	No	Yes	89
No	No	Yes	Yes	No	106
No	No	Yes	Yes	Yes	75
No	Yes	No	No	No	295
No	Yes	No	No	Yes	25
No	Yes	No	Yes	No	15
No	Yes	No	Yes	Yes	5
No	Yes	Yes	No	No	137
No	Yes	Yes	No	Yes	42
No	Yes	Yes	Yes	No	35
No	Yes	Yes	Yes	Yes	39
Yes	No	No	No	No	489
Yes	No	No	No	Yes	37
Yes	No	No	Yes	No	23
Yes	No	No	Yes	Yes	7
Yes	No	Yes	No	No	255
Yes	No	Yes	No	Yes	116
Yes	No	Yes	Yes	No	71
Yes	No	Yes	Yes	Yes	65
Yes	Yes	No	No	No	306
Yes	Yes	No	No	Yes	48
Yes	Yes	No	Yes	No	16
Yes	Yes	No	Yes	Yes	11
Yes	Yes	Yes	No	No	229
Yes	Yes	Yes	No	Yes	162
Yes	Yes	Yes	Yes	No	44
Yes	Yes	Yes	Yes	Yes	176
TOTAL					7,162

four-class solution maintains classes 1 and 2 from the three-class solution but splits class 3 into two separate clusters. One way to visualize the close relationship between these two solutions is to combine classes 3 and 4 of the four-class solution and compare the resulting barycentric coordinate display (presented in Figure 5) with the original one from the three-

TABLE 6
Results from Various LC Models Fit to Data in Table 5

Model H_m	Model Description	BIC	L^2	DF	p-value	% Reduction in $L^2(H_0)$
H_0	1-class	4592.8	4823.6	26	3.0×10^{-101}	0
H_1	2-class	376.6	554.2	20	1.3×10^{-104}	88.5
H_{2C}	3-class	38.2	162.4	14	2.3×10^{-27}	96.6
H_{2F}	Basic 2-factor	−110.5	13.7	14	0.5	99.7
H_{3C}	4-class	−62.6	8.4	8	0.4	99.8
H_{3F}	Basic 3-factor	−85.1	3.7	8+2*	1.0	99.9

*DF is increased by these boundary solutions.

cluster model (Figure 4). As can be seen, these plots are almost identical, adding visual support to our conclusion (based on inspection of Table 7) that the primary difference between the two solutions is the splitting of class 3 into separate clusters. However, these plots do not describe the significant differences that exist between clusters 3 and 4 of the four-cluster solution.

Results from fitting various basic factor models to these data are also included in Table 6. In particular, we see that despite the fact that the

TABLE 7
Comparison of Results Obtained Under Models H_{2C} and H_{3C} Conditional Membership Probabilities

	Three-Class Solution (H_{2C})			Four-Class Solution (H_{3C})			
Variables	Class 1	Class 2	Class 3	Class 1	Class 2	Class 3	Class 4
BACK							
No	0.94	0.32	0.37	0.93	0.31	0.60	0.09
Yes	0.06	0.68	0.63	0.07	0.69	0.40	0.91
NECK							
No	0.96	0.48	0.50	0.96	0.44	0.77	0.15
Yes	0.04	0.52	0.50	0.04	0.56	0.23	0.85
JOINT							
No	0.91	0.63	0.07	0.93	0.60	0.10	0.05
Yes	0.09	0.37	0.93	0.07	0.40	0.90	0.95
SWELL							
No	0.97	0.96	0.49	0.98	0.96	0.55	0.44
Yes	0.03	0.04	0.51	0.02	0.04	0.45	0.56
STIFF							
No	0.98	0.89	0.39	0.99	0.88	0.58	0.08
Yes	0.02	0.11	0.61	0.01	0.12	0.42	0.92
Overall probabilities	0.62	0.21	0.17	0.61	0.21	0.12	0.06

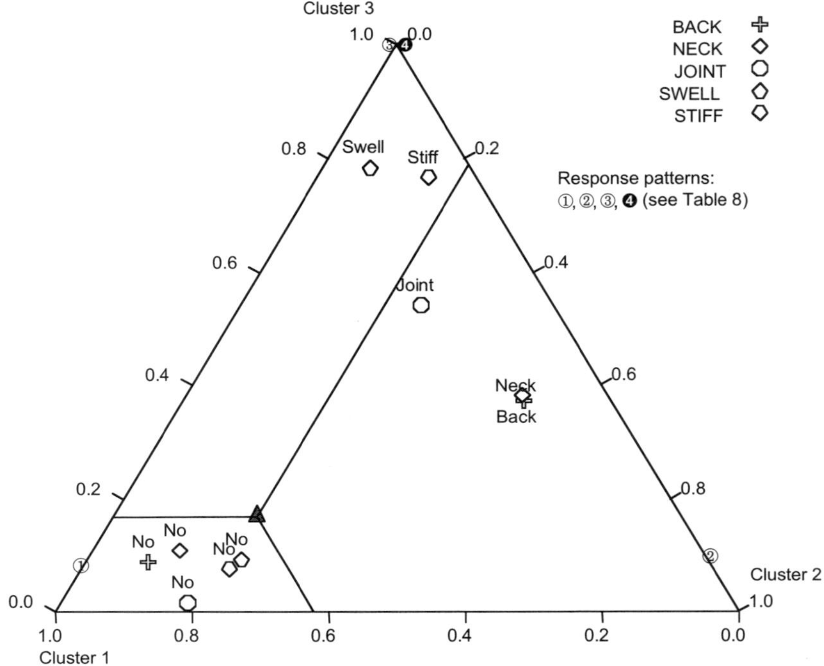

FIGURE 4. Barycentric coordinate display for model H_{2C} and four selected response patterns.

three-cluster model H_{2C} does *not* provide an adequate fit to these data, the comparable LC factor model H_{2F}, which posits two dichotomous factors, provides an excellent fit. Although the traditional exploratory approach yields the four-class LC cluster model H_{3C}, this model requires three dimensions for a display of the results. On the other hand, the alternative approach yields factor model H_{2F}, which justifies a valid two-dimensional display without the necessity of collapsing or otherwise reducing the variables in the model. The resulting bi-plot presented in Figure 6 shows that JOINT, SWELL and STIFF are more strongly related to factor 1 (the arthritis factor), and BACK and NECK to factor 2 (the pain factor).

In most cases where models suggest that at least two dimensions are needed to provide an adequate fit to the data, it seems reasonable to expect there to be two underlying factors and hence at least four different classes to take into account both the "low" and "high" levels of each

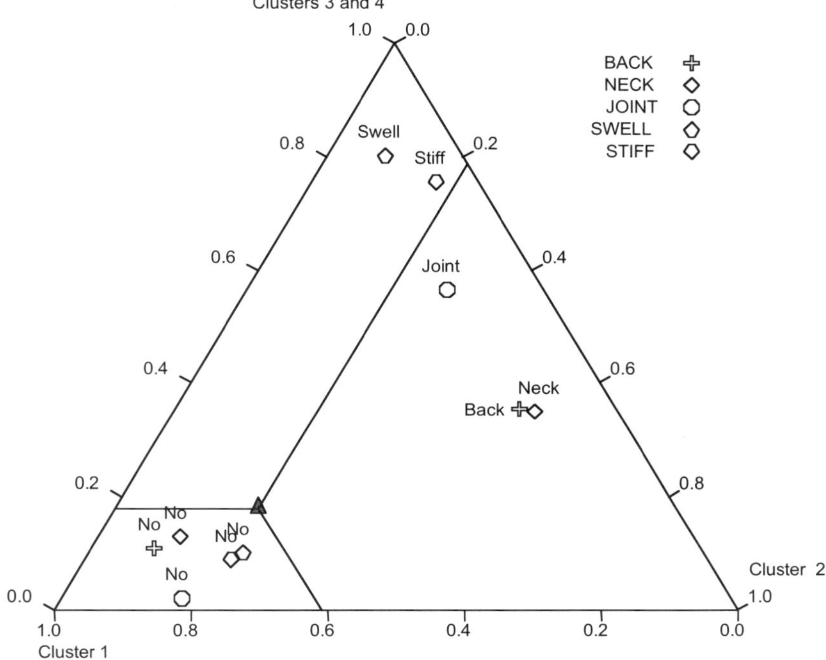

FIGURE 5. Barycentric coordinate display for model H_{3C} where clusters 3 and 4 are combined.

factor—i.e., (low, low), (high, low), (low, high), and (high, high). If this speculation is true, it would explain why the factor approach typically provides a better fit to real data. Closer inspection of the results of the four-cluster model parameters reported in Table 7 shows that, actually, the four-cluster model also suggests a two-dimensional solution: the four clusters correspond to the (low, low), (high, low), (low, high), and (high, high) combinations of the same two dimensions encountered in the two-factor model.

Using BACK and NECK as proxies for factor 2 and the other variables for factor 1, we selected four response patterns as proxies for the four classes. Table 8 compares the estimates of the expected frequency counts obtained from models H_{2C}, H_{3C}, and H_{2F} for these four selected response patterns. We see that the three-class cluster model fails to provide a good estimate for respondents who reported having all five pain symptoms—the (high, high) group.

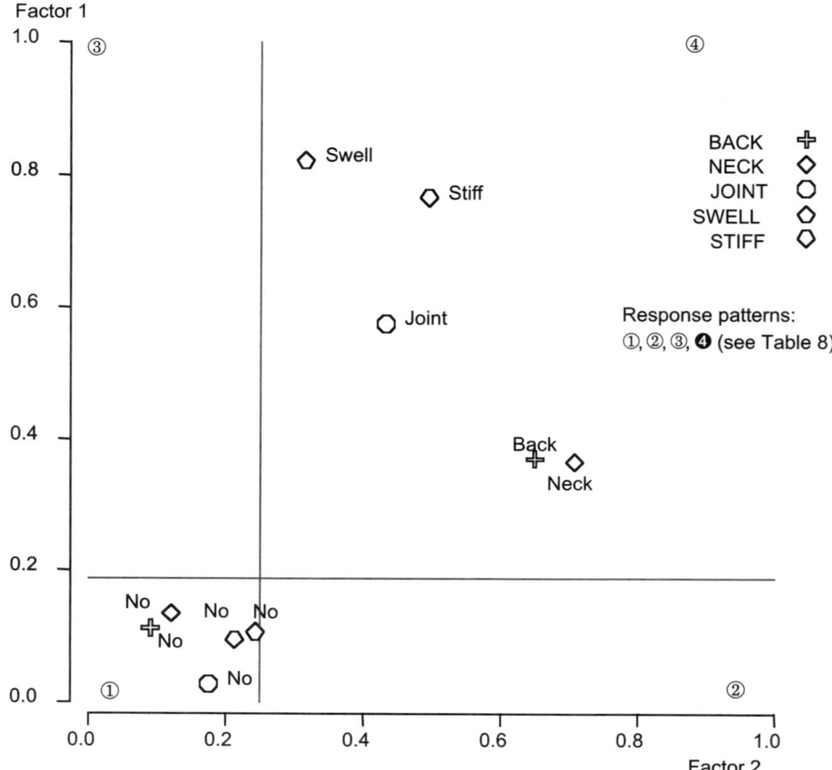

FIGURE 6. Bi-plot for model H_{2F} and four selected response patterns.

Overall, the expected frequencies estimated under the three-cluster model differ significantly from the observed frequencies for seven of the 32 response patterns, while the other two models provide good estimates for *all* response patterns. The four selected response patterns (or cases) are plotted in Figures 4 and 6 using the symbols ①, ②, ③, and ④. The symbol ④ appears in reverse shading as ❹ in Figure 4 to indicate the lack of fit. Figure 6 shows that these four response patterns appear in the four corners of the bi-plot, suggesting that they are in fact good indicators of the (low, low) . . . (high, high) levels of the joint factor. Figure 4 on the other hand shows that three clusters are inadequate to separate cases with response patterns 3 and 4, and indicates that the estimate of the expected count for response pattern 4 is poor.

TABLE 8

Comparison Between Models H_{2C}, H_{3C}, and H_{2F} Observed Versus Expected Frequencies for Four Response Patterns

						Frequency Counts			
							Expected		
Response Pattern	BACK	NECK	JOINT	SWELL	STIFF	Observed	H_{2C}	H_{3C}	H_{2F}
1	No	No	No	No	No	3,634	3,621.4	3,633.8	3,630.2
2	Yes	Yes	No	No	No	306	304.5	304.8	307.6
3	No	No	Yes	Yes	Yes	75	65.4	70.8	73.0
4	Yes	Yes	Yes	Yes	Yes	176	112.0*	173.7	174.9

*Significantly different from observed.

4. SOME EXTENSIONS OF THE BASIC LC FACTOR MODEL

In this section we consider some modifications and extensions of the basic LC factor model that may be of interest in certain situations. First, although in example 1 we treated the trichotomous variables COOPERATE (A) and PURPOSE (C) as nominal, they can be treated as ordinal in several different ways. The most straightforward approach is to assume the middle category to be equidistant from the others and modify the log-linear model described in equation (3) by using the uniform scores v_i^A and v_k^C

$$v_i^A = \{0 \text{ if i} = 1, 0.5 \text{ if i} = 2, 1 \text{ if i} = 3\}$$

$$v_k^C = \{0 \text{ if k} = 1, 0.5 \text{ if k} = 2, 1 \text{ if k} = 3\}$$

for the categories of variables A and C. Second, analogous to confirmatory factor analysis, we may wish to allow the two factors V and W to be correlated (with association parameter γ_{rs}^{VW}) and restrict the variables COOPERATION (A) and UNDERSTANDING (B) to load only on factor 1 and PURPOSE (C) and ACCURACY (D) to load only on factor 2. The log-linear representation for a confirmatory model of this type as compared with the basic two-factor model in Appendix A is as follows:

$$\gamma_{rs}^{VW} \neq 0;$$

$$\lambda_{ir}^{AV} = \lambda_r^{AV} v_i^A;\ \lambda_{ks}^{CW} = \lambda_s^{CW} v_k^C; \quad \text{where} \quad i, k = 1,2,3; j, l, r, s = 1,2;$$

$$\lambda_{is}^{AW} = \lambda_{js}^{BW} = \lambda_{jr}^{CV} = \lambda_{ks}^{DV} = 0.$$

The results of fitting this restricted two-factor model (H_{R2F}) are reported in Table 3. These suggest that this model fits the data very well (L^2 = 22.17, DF = 23; $p = .51$). The corresponding bi-plot is shown in Figure 7.

Our examples thus far utilized only dichotomous factors. To extend the factor model so that any factor may contain more than two ordered levels, we assign equidistant numeric scores between 0 and 1 to the levels of the factor. Clogg (1988) and Heinen (1996) used the same strategy for defining LC models that are similar to certain latent trait models. The use of fixed scores for the factor levels in the various two-way interaction terms guarantees that each factor captures a single dimension. For factors with more than two levels, we display in the bi-plot conditional means

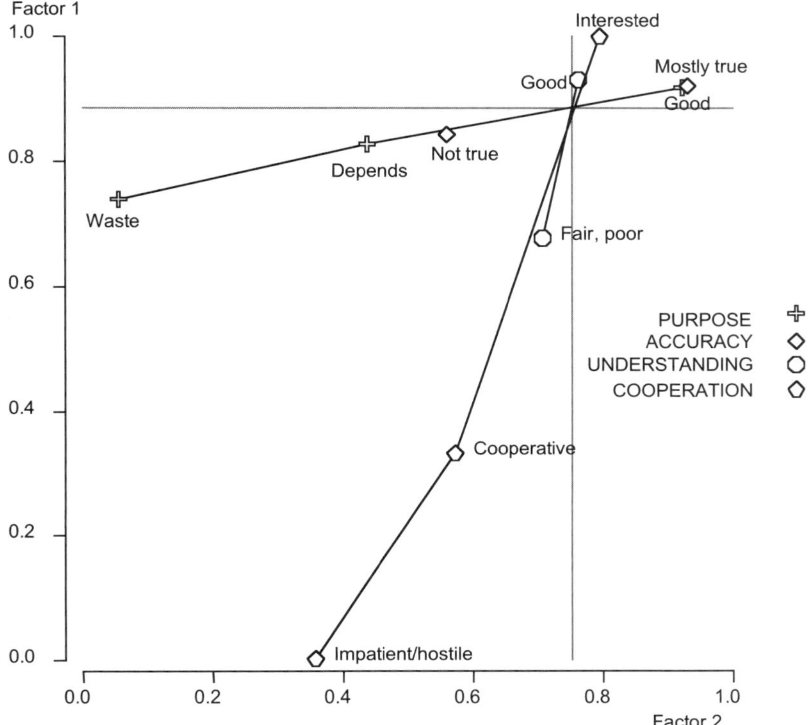

FIGURE 7. Bi-plot for model H_{R2F} with lines connecting the categories of a variable.

rather than conditional probabilities (see Appendix B). Note that if we assign the score of 0 to the first level and 1 to the last level (or vice versa), for dichotomous factors the conditional mean equals the conditional probability of being at level 2 (or level 1).

Finally, the extension to include covariates in a log-linear LC model is straightforward. To illustrate the use of covariates and the extension to a three-level factor, we will use the depression scale data for white respondents from the problems of everyday life study (Pearlin and Johnson 1977) as reported separately for males and females (Schaeffer 1988). Persons who reported having the symptom during the previous week were coded 1, all others 0. The symptoms measured were lack of enthusiasm, low energy, sleeping problems, poor appetite, and feeling hopeless.

GENDER was included in the model as an *active* covariate (see the discussion in Appendix B on active versus inactive covariates). Note that

TABLE 9
Results from Various LC Models Fit to the Depression Data

Model	Model Description	BIC	L^2	DF	p-value	% Reduction in $L^2(H_0)$
H_0	1-class	672.8	1097.1	57	2.3×10^{-192}	0
H_1	2-class	−233.7	138.5	50	3.1×10^{-10}	87.4
H_{2C}	3-class	−260.5	59.6	43	0.05	94.6
H_{2F}	Basic 2-factor	−274.6	45.5	43+1*	0.37	95.9
H_{1F3}	1-factor (3-levels)	−297.8	67.0	49	0.05	93.9

*DF is increased by these boundary solutions.

in the case of a single covariate, the log-linear LC model is identical whether GENDER is treated as a covariate or as another indicator (Clogg 1981; Hagenaars 1990).

Table 9 shows the results from fitting various LC models to these data. The traditional strategy required three classes as neither the 1- or 2-class models provided adequate solutions. We see again that the basic two-factor model fits the data better than the comparable three-cluster model. The results for the three-cluster solution are shown in Table 10 in terms of conditional response probabilities. Notice that those probabilities conditional on cluster 2 are ordered between the corresponding probabilities conditional on clusters 1 and 3, a pattern that is consistent with the depression scale being unidimensional, and suggests that we consider fitting a three-level one-factor model to these data.

Table 10 shows that the three-level factor solution is very similar to that given by the three-class solution. Both suggest that 10 percent of the population are in the "depressed" group (cluster 3 in the cluster model and level 3 in the factor model), and the rest are about equally distributed among the "healthy" (cluster 1) and the "troubled" cluster 2. The three-level model provides an acceptable fit to these data and contains only one parameter more than the two-class model (see Table 9). Unlike the three-class extension to the two-class model which requires seven additional parameters, the three-level model provides an attractive alternative to the three- (unordered) class model. The BIC suggests that the three-level one-factor model should be preferred over all models including the basic two-factor model.

In our experience with various data, increasing the number of levels in a factor does often provide a significant improvement in fit. This is,

TABLE 10
Conditional Probabilities Estimated Under the Three-Cluster Model and the One-Factor Three-Level Model

	Three-Cluster Model			One-Factor Three-level Model		
	Cluster 1	Cluster 2	Cluster 3	Level 1	Level 2	Level 3
Cluster Size	0.46	0.44	0.10	0.45	0.45	0.10
ENTHUS						
Lack of enthusiasm	0.26	0.82	0.96	0.26	0.81	0.98
No	0.74	0.18	0.04	0.74	0.19	0.02
ENERGY						
Low energy	0.03	0.63	0.95	0.03	0.61	0.99
No	0.97	0.37	0.05	0.97	0.39	0.01
SLEEP						
Sleeping problem	0.10	0.37	0.78	0.09	0.38	0.79
No	0.90	0.63	0.22	0.91	0.62	0.21
APPETITE						
Poor appetite	0.04	0.22	0.73	0.04	0.24	0.72
No	0.96	0.78	0.27	0.96	0.76	0.28
HOPELESS						
Hopeless	0.03	0.10	0.67	0.02	0.13	0.61
No	0.97	0.90	0.33	0.98	0.87	0.39

however, not always the case. For example, with our first data set we found that two distinct factors were required to provide an adequate fit to the data. In that situation, increasing the number of levels from 2 to 3 in the single-factor solution provides no benefit. Table 3 shows only a slight, nonsignificant reduction in the L^2 due to the inclusion of the additional parameter—from 79.34 for the one-factor two-level solution to 77.25 for the one-factor three-level solution. On the other hand, in the present example, the addition of this single parameter causes a reduction of the L^2 from 138.5 for the one-factor two-level solution to 67.0 under the one-factor three-level model (see again Table 9).

An informative graph can provide an attractive alternative to a table (such as Table 10) when the goal is to determine whether a natural ordering exists among a set of clusters. For example, a standard profile plot will show immediately that the conditional probabilities associated with cluster 2 always fall between the corresponding conditional probabilities associated with clusters 1 and 3.

As an alternative to the profile plot, we will now examine the implications obtained from a barycentric coordinate display (Figure 8) of the

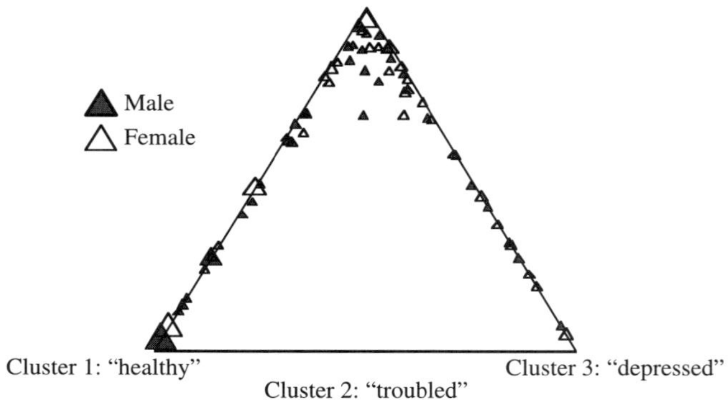

FIGURE 8. Barycentric coordinate display of the 64 response patterns for males and females based on the three-class model (H_{2c}).

Note: The area of each triangle is proportional to the estimated expected frequency associated with the corresponding response pattern (subject to a minimum size).

three-cluster solution, which includes a point for each observation (i.e., each observed response pattern). Note the obvious pattern that the points appear primarily along the left and right sides of the triangle, not along the base. This visual pattern can be interpreted as follows: Among persons who are likely to be "troubled" (those with response patterns plotted near the top vertex, associated with cluster 2), there is a substantial amount of overlap with the other clusters. Some of these cases also have a substantial probability of belonging to the "healthy" cluster and some have a substantial probability of belonging to the "depressed" cluster. However, there is virtually *no* overlap between those likely to be "healthy" and those likely to be "depressed" (the inner part of the base of the triangle contains no points). This asymmetric pattern suggests that cluster 2 ("troubled") is the middle cluster.

In both the three-cluster model and the three-level one-factor model, we find that GENDER has a significant relationship with the latent variable, females being more likely to be in the depressed group. Figure 9 displays two one-dimensional plots resulting from the three-level factor model (the bi-plot reduces to one dimension in the case of a single factor). The top plot was obtained using GENDER as an active covariate. For comparison, the plot at the bottom of Figure 9 was obtained using GENDER as an inactive covariate (its effect is not included in the model). Being "inactive" implies that if the "male" and "female" symbols were

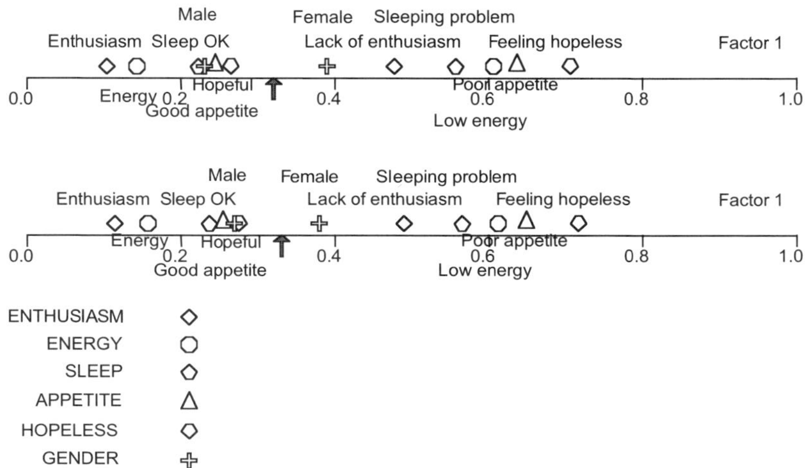

FIGURE 9. One-dimensional plots associated with the three-level factor model. *Note*: Gender is treated as "Active" in the top plot and "Inactive" in the bottom plot.

removed from the latter, it would be equivalent to the plot that would be obtained using a three-level model that *excludes* GENDER from the model (see Appendix B). The lessor distance between the "male" and "female" symbols in the latter plot (as compared with that displayed at the top of Figure 9) reflects the reduced association between GENDER and the latent variable, which is the result of the well-known attenuation phenomenon. In general, inclusion of covariates in a model can provide useful descriptive information on the latent variable(s). The decision to treat a covariate as active or inactive is largely a matter of personal preference.

5. IDENTIFICATION ISSUES

In some situations, LC models may not be identified. Two well-documented examples of LC models that are not identified without further constraints are the unrestricted three-class model for four dichotomous items (Goodman 1974a) and the unrestricted two- and three-class models for two polytomous items (Gilula and Haberman 1986; De Leeuw and Van der Heijden 1991; Clogg 1995; Van der Ark, Van der Heijden and Sikkel 1999).

The formal method to check for identification of a LC model is by means of the expected information matrix (Goodman 1974a, Formann

TABLE 11
Number of Unidentified Parameters in Various LC Cluster and Factor Models

Model	$2 \times 2 \times 2 \times 2$ table	$2 \times 2 \times 2 \times 2 \times 2$ table	4×5 table
2 clusters/1 factor	0	0	2
3 clusters	1	0	6
4 clusters	*	0	*
5 clusters	*	0	*
2 factors	0	0	4
3 factors	*	0	*
4 factors	*	0	*

*Situations that we did not consider because they are not very relevant.

1992).[7] If all model parameters are identified, this information matrix will be full rank; that is, all its eigenvalues will be larger than zero. On the other hand, if k model parameters are not identified, k eigenvalues will be equal to zero. To get more insight in the identifiability of the LC factor model, we determined the rank of the information matrix for various hypothesized LC cluster and LC factor models.[8] In particular, we studied three situations in which there might be identification problems—that is, tables of four and five dichotomous items, and of two polytomous items with four and five categories. The results are reported in Table 11.

As can be seen, in all situations in which the LC cluster model with $R + 1$ clusters is identified, the LC factor model with R factors is also identified. However, in two situations, we see that the LC factor model has *fewer* unidentified parameters than the corresponding LC cluster model having the same number of distinct parameters. For example, we see that while the three-cluster model for four dichotomous items is *not* identified (it has one unidentified parameter), the two-factor model is exactly identified and hence requires no identifying restrictions. Also, we see that while the three-cluster model for a 4×5 table has six unidentified parameters,

[7] The expected information matrix is the negative of the expected value of the matrix of second-order derivatives to all model parameters.

[8] As an extra check, we estimated the models of interest using the assumed (constructed) population distributions as observed data. For models that are identified, the parameter estimates should perfectly reproduce the population parameters. This result was obtained in all situations.

TABLE 12
Classification of School Children According to Eye and Hair Color

	Hair Color				
Eye Color	Fair	Red	Medium	Dark	Black
Blue	326	38	241	110	3
Light	688	116	584	188	4
Medium	343	84	909	412	26
Dark	98	48	403	681	85

the two-factor model has only four. These results on identification show that all models presented in the foregoing examples are identified.

Consider the classic 4×5 table given by Fisher (1940) classifying schoolchildren according to their hair and eye colors (Table 12). Table 13 provides results from various LC models. Gilula and Haberman (1986) showed that the one-component canonical model does not fit these data but a two-component model does ($L^2 = 4.73$ with DF = 2). They also showed that this model is equivalent to the three-class LC model (H_{2C} in Table 13), with the same DF if we take into account the fact that there are six unidentified parameters (see Table 11).[9] From the test results reported in Table 13, it can be seen that the basic two-factor model (H_{2F}) is saturated for these data (DF = 0), and hence provides a perfect fit ($L^2 = 0$).

The bi-plot and barycentric coordinate displays obtained from the three-class LC model and the basic two-factor LC model are not unique since the posterior classification (membership) probabilities are dependent upon the particular identifying restrictions used to identify the parameters (four distinct restrictions are needed for the basic two-factor model). However, the specification of restrictions is typical of a confirmatory rather than exploratory analysis. Rather than specifying restrictions (or using a particular set of boundary or other nonunique parameter estimates) to obtain a unique solution, one can alternatively apply some prior information to the parameters. Table 13 provides the results of fitting the LC cluster and factor models (H_{2C+} and H_{2F+}), and Figures 10 and 11 present the

[9] We assume that six identifying restrictions are made to identify these parameters. These restrictions need not be the same as those used to identify the two-component canonical model.

TABLE 13
Results from Various LC Models Fit to Fisher Data

Model	Model Description	L^2	DF*	p-value	% Reduction in $L^2(H_0)$
H_0	1-class	1218.31	12	2.0×10^{-253}	0
H_1	2-class	166.91	6	4.8×10^{-35}	86.3
H_{2C}	3-class	4.73	2	.094	99.6
H_{2F}	Basic 2-factor	0.00	0		100.0
H_{2C+}	3-class (alpha = 1)	4.73	2	.094	99.6
H_{2F+}	Basic 2-factor (alpha = 1)	0.35	0		100.0

*DF is increased by the number of unidentified parameters (see Table 11).

associated displays that occur when a slight departure from noninformative Dirichlet prior distributions are assumed for the model probabilities.[10]

From the bi-plot (Figure 11), we see that factor 1, the more prominent factor, is a "lightness-darkness" dimension. Factor 2 serves primarily as a contrast of black hair and dark eyes with medium and red hair color and lighter eye colors, (with fair and dark hair and blue eyes somewhere in between).

6. FINAL REMARKS

This paper presented a new method for performing exploratory LC analysis. Rather than increasing the number of classes, we proposed increasing the number of latent variables. We showed that because of the imposed constraints, the basic LC factor model with R latent variables has the same number of parameters as the LC cluster model with $R + 1$ classes. This is an important result because it shows that in terms of parsimony, increasing the number of factors is equivalent to increasing the number of clusters.

The examples showed that in most cases the LC factor model provides a more parsimonious and easier to interpret description of the data. There is a simple explanation for this phenomenon. When applying a LC

[10]The influence of the priors is equivalent to adding one fictitious observation for which the independence model holds to the data. As a result, the priors will smooth the estimates slightly to the independence model. For more details on the use of priors to prevent boundary solutions and to obtain identifiability, see Vermunt and Magidson (2000).

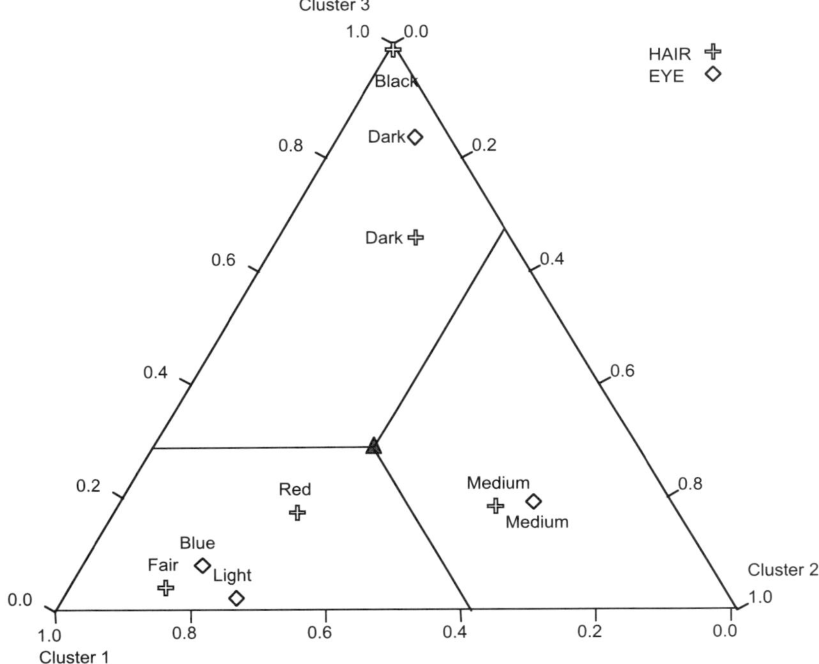

FIGURE 10. Barycentric coordinate display of results from model $H_{2C}(+)$ fit to Fisher data.

cluster model, it is not known how many dimensions the solution will capture: A three-cluster model may describe either one or two dimensions, while a four-cluster model may describe either one, two, or three dimensions. When a three-cluster model describes *one* dimension, it is very probable that a one-factor model with three or more levels will describe the data almost as well (see the depression example in Section 4). When a three-cluster model describes *two* dimensions, it has the disadvantage that it cannot capture all four basic combinations—(low, low), (high, low), (low, high), and (high, high)—of the two latent dimensions. Therefore, the two-factor model will fit better than the three-cluster model in these cases. In situations in which the four-cluster model gives a two-dimensional solution (as in the rheumatic arthritis data set where the four clusters represent the four possible latent combinations), it can be expected

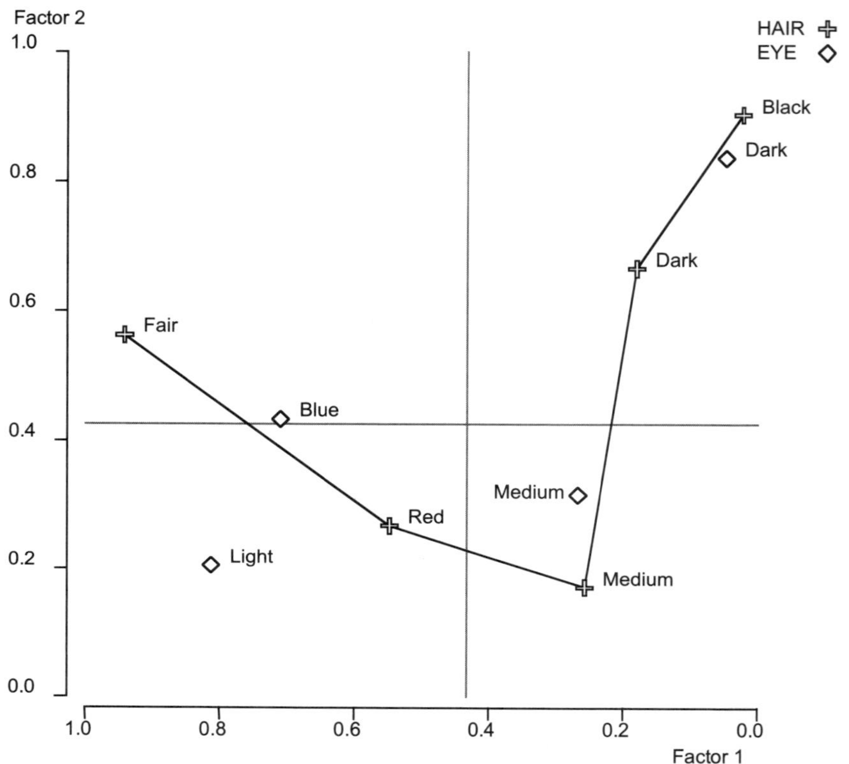

FIGURE 11. Bi-plot of results from model $H_{2F}(+)$ fit to Fisher data.

that a restricted four-cluster model (the two-factor model) will fit the data almost as well (and may be better in terms of BIC or *p*-value).

The above explanation yields strong arguments for using the two approaches in combination with one another, as we have been doing in the examples. There are two things that can happen when switching from the cluster to the factor model. First, the factor model may give a simpler description of the data than the cluster model. This occurs when the three-cluster solution is one-dimensional or when the four-cluster solution is two-dimensional, both of which are situations where the LC cluster model is overparametrized. Second, the factor model may give a better fit. We saw that this occurs when the three-cluster model is two-dimensional.

APPENDIX A: THE LC CLUSTER AND FACTOR MODELS FORMULATED USING CONDITIONAL PROBABILITIES

In this paper we used Haberman's (1979) log-linear formulation of the LC model because that made it easy to explain the similarities and differences between LC cluster and unrestricted LC factor models. However, in the case of the restricted two-factor model, a more general formulation is required. This appendix describes these two types of LC models using the more general probability formulation, and explains the relationship between the two formulations.

An alternative expression for the LC cluster model described in equation (1) is

$$\pi_{ijklt} = \pi_t^X \pi_{it}^{A|X} \pi_{jt}^{B|X} \pi_{kt}^{C|X} \pi_{lt}^{D|X},$$

which is the formulation used by Goodman (1974a, 1974b) and Clogg (1981, 1995). As was shown by several authors (see, for instance, Haberman 1979; Formann 1992; and Heinen 1996), there is a simple relationship between the conditional response probabilities appearing in the above equation and the log-linear parameters of equation (1), i.e.,

$$\pi_{it}^{A|X} = \frac{F_{i+++t}}{F_{++++t}} = \frac{\exp(\lambda_i^A + \lambda_{it}^{AX})}{\sum_{i'=1}^{I} \exp(\lambda_{i'}^A + \lambda_{i't}^{AX})}.$$

Similar expressions apply to the other three indicators. The probability of being in class t, π_t^X, can, however, not be written in terms of the log-linear parameters λ_t^X appearing in equation (1). These latent probabilities can be obtained by

$$\pi_t^X = \frac{F_{++++t}}{F_{+++++}} = \frac{\exp(\gamma_t^X)}{\sum_{t'=1}^{T} \exp(\gamma_{t'}^X)},$$

where the symbol γ is used to denote a log-linear parameter of the marginal distribution of the latent variable(s).

The two-factor LC model can be written as

$$\pi_{ijklrs} = \pi_{rs}^{VW}\pi_{ijklrs}^{ABCD|VW} = \pi_{rs}^{VW}\pi_{irs}^{A|VW}\pi_{jrs}^{B|VW}\pi_{krs}^{C|VW}\pi_{lrs}^{D|VW} \tag{4}$$

whereas, in the case of the *unrestricted* model we have

$$\pi_{rs}^{VW} = \frac{F_{++++rs}}{F_{++++++}} = \frac{\exp(\gamma_r^V + \gamma_s^W + \gamma_{rs}^{VW})}{\sum_{r'=1}^{R}\sum_{s'=1}^{S}\exp(\gamma_{r'}^V + \gamma_{s'}^W + \gamma_{r's'}^{VW})}$$

$$\pi_{rst}^{A|VW} = \frac{F_{i+++rs}}{F_{++++rs}} = \frac{\exp(\lambda_i^A + \lambda_{ir}^{AV} + \lambda_{is}^{AW} + \lambda_{irs}^{AVW})}{\sum_{i'=1}^{I}\exp(\lambda_{i'}^A + \lambda_{i'r}^{AV} + \lambda_{i's}^{AW} + \lambda_{i'rs}^{AVW})}, \text{ etc.,}$$

while, for the *basic* two-factor model, the conditional response probabilities in (4) are restricted by the following logit models

$$\pi_{rs}^{VW} = \frac{\exp(\gamma_r^V + \gamma_s^W)}{\sum_{r'=1}^{R}\sum_{s'=1}^{S}\exp(\gamma_{r'}^V + \gamma_{s'}^W)}$$

$$\pi_{irs}^{A|VW} = \frac{\exp(\lambda_i^A + \lambda_{ir}^{AV} + \lambda_{is}^{AW})}{\sum_{i'=1}^{I}\exp(\lambda_{i'}^A + \lambda_{i'r}^{AV} + \lambda_{i's}^{AW})}, \text{ etc.}$$

Note that this latter formulation excludes the marginal association between the latent variables, as well as the higher-order interaction terms.

The number of distinct parameters in the basic R-factor model is:

$$\begin{aligned}\text{NPAR(basic R-factor)} &= \text{R} + \text{NPAR(indep)} \times (1 + \text{R})\\ &= \text{R} + (\text{R}+1) \times \text{NPAR(indep)},\end{aligned}$$

while the number of distinct parameters in the LC cluster model was shown to be

$$\begin{aligned}\text{NPAR(T-cluster)} &= (\text{T} - 1) + \text{NPAR(indep)}\,(1 + (\text{T} - 1))\\ &= (\text{T} - 1) + \text{T} \times \text{NPAR(indep)}\,.\end{aligned}$$

Hence, it is seen that the degree of parsimony in the LC R-factor model is the same as that of a cluster model with T = R + 1 classes.

As shown in this paper, the *unrestricted* LC two-factor model is equivalent to the LC cluster model with four classes. Hence the number of restrictions that are placed by the basic two-factor model given above can be computed as the difference between the number of distinct parameters in the LC cluster model with T = 4 classes and the number in the basic LC two-factor model. More generally, the number of restrictions placed by the R-factor model can be computed as the difference between the number of distinct parameters in the LC cluster model with $T = 2^R$ classes and the basic LC R-factor model as follows:

$$\begin{aligned} \text{NRES} &= \text{NPAR}(2^{\text{R}}\text{-cluster}) - \text{NPAR}(\text{basic R-factor}) \\ &= [2^{\text{R}} - \text{R} - 1] \times [\text{NPAR}(\text{indep}) + 1]. \end{aligned}$$

APPENDIX B: FUNCTIONS OF CLASS-MEMBERSHIP PROBABILITIES APPEARING IN THE PLOTS

The quantities depicted in the various plots presented in this paper are functions of class-membership probabilities. This appendix explains how these quantities are computed. For the types of LC models considered by Van der Ark and Van der Heijden (1998) and Van der Heijden, Gilula, and Van der Ark (1999), our measures coincide with the rescaled parameters that they plotted, but for more general LC models this need not be the case.

Let us take the basic two-factor model with four indicators described in equations (3) and (4) as an example. The estimated probability of being in level r of the first factor V given a person's observed scores on the four indicators A, B, C, and D is defined as

$$\hat{\pi}_{rijkl}^{V|ABCD} = \frac{\hat{\pi}_{ijklr+}}{\hat{\pi}_{ijkl++}}.$$

Once the LC model of interest is estimated, these class-membership probabilities can be computed for each individual in the sample or, equivalently, for each observed response pattern.

A common quantity that we use to position each point in each of our plots is the conditional probability of being at a certain level of a latent variable given a certain response to one or more items. In the bi-plot associated with the LC factor model, we will, for instance, use the estimated conditional probability of being at level r of factor V given that $A = i$, denoted as $\hat{\pi}_{ri}^{V|A}$. Note that the more these probabilities differ between levels of A, the stronger A is related to factor V.

The probabilities $\hat{\pi}_{ri}^{V|A}$ can be obtained by aggregating the estimated class-membership probabilities $\hat{\pi}_{rijkl}^{V|ABCD}$. There are, however, two possible ways to perform the aggregation. Method 1 utilizes the *observed* cell probabilities p_{ijkl}^{ABCD} as weights. This yields

$$\hat{\pi}_{ri}^{V|A}(1) = \frac{\sum_{j=1}^{J}\sum_{k=1}^{K}\sum_{l=1}^{L} \hat{\pi}_{rijkl}^{V|ABCD}\, p_{ijkl}^{ABCD}}{\sum_{r=1}^{R}\sum_{j=1}^{J}\sum_{k=1}^{K}\sum_{l=1}^{L} \hat{\pi}_{rijkl}^{V|ABCD}\, p_{ijkl}^{ABCD}}.$$

Alternatively, method 2 utilizes the *estimated* cell probabilities as weights; that is,

$$\hat{\pi}_{ri}^{V|A}(2) = \frac{\sum_{j=1}^{J}\sum_{k=1}^{K}\sum_{l=1}^{L} \hat{\pi}_{rijkl}^{V|ABCD}\, \hat{\pi}_{ijkl}^{ABCD}}{\sum_{r=1}^{R}\sum_{j=1}^{J}\sum_{k=1}^{K}\sum_{l=1}^{L} \hat{\pi}_{rijkl}^{V|ABCD}\, \hat{\pi}_{ijkl}^{ABCD}}.$$

Method 1 was used to obtain the plots presented in Figures 1–7 and Figures 9–11. In Figures 4, 6, and 8 we also included the individual response patterns, including those not observed in the sample.

In the case of *unrestricted* models, if the model provides a good fit to the data, the estimated proportions should provide good approximations to the observed proportions so that both methods will yield very similar plots. However, for certain *restricted* models, where the estimated proportions satisfy the restrictions exactly but the observed proportions do not, the alternative displays may contain clear discernible differences, even when the model provides a good fit to the data.

For example, the restrictions for model H_{R2F} imply that the basic bi-plot should consist of two intersecting straight lines, one formed by connecting the points corresponding to the categories of the variables

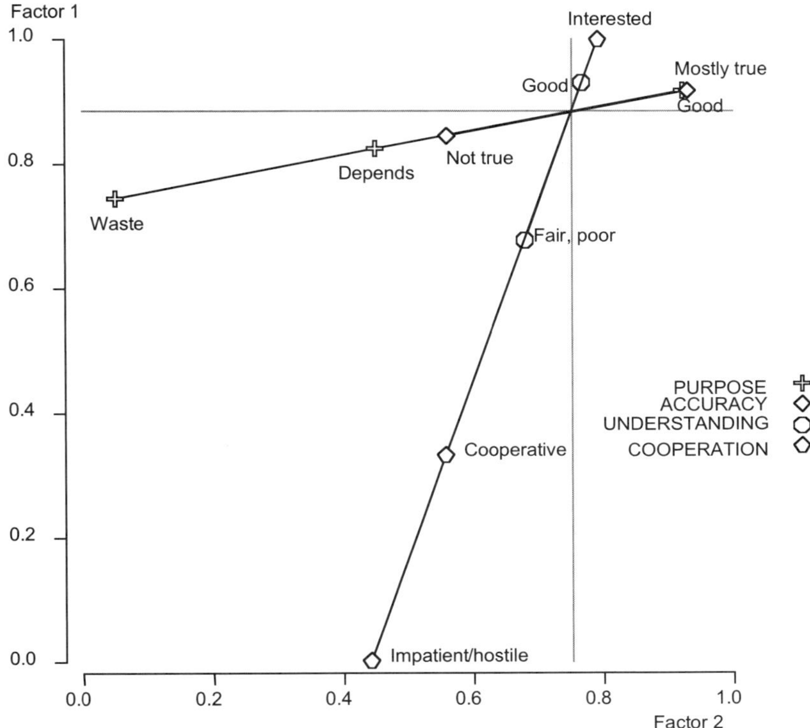

FIGURE 12. Bi-plot for model H_{R2F} obtained using aggregation method 2.

(C) PURPOSE and (D) ACCURACY, and the second formed by connecting the points corresponding to the categories of (A) COOPERATION and (B) UNDERSTANDING. .

Figure 12 shows the resulting bi-plot for model H_{R2F} when method 2 is used to compute the conditional probabilities. We see the two straight lines with an acute angle between them suggesting positive correlation between the latent variables *V* and *W* (labeled Factor 1 and Factor 2 in Figure 12).[11] On the other hand, the plot obtained in Figure 7 showed

[11] In a companion paper (Magidson and Vermunt 2000), we show how to derive the equations for the straight lines. Moreover, in it we demonstrate that the angle between these lines has meaning—for example, to the extent to which this angle is less than 90°, the two latent variables *V* and *W* exhibit positive correlation—and show how the magnitude of the correlation can be determined from the plot.

only the *approximation* of two straight lines since the observed proportions for these data do not satisfy exactly the restrictions imposed by the model.

In LC factor models with factors having more than two levels such as Model H_{1F3},[12] the results of which were displayed in Figure 9, we plot the factor means

$$\hat{E}_i^{V|A} = \sum_{r=1}^{R} \hat{\pi}_{ri}^{V|A} \cdot \upsilon_r^V,$$

where R is the number of levels of factor V, and υ_r^V denotes the fixed score assigned to level r of factor V.

In the case of a LC cluster model, we would plot $\hat{\pi}_{ti}^{X|A}$, which is the estimated conditional probability of being in a certain category of the single latent variable X. Van der Ark and Van der Heijden (1998), who called these quantities *rescaled parameters*, proposed computing them as follows:

$$\hat{\pi}_{ti}^{X|A}(3) = \frac{\hat{\pi}_{it}^{AX}}{\hat{\pi}_i^A} = \frac{\hat{\pi}_t^X \hat{\pi}_{it}^{A|X}}{\sum_{t'=1}^{T} \hat{\pi}_{t'}^X \hat{\pi}_{it'}^{A|X}}.$$

It can easily be shown that in a standard LC model with a single latent variable and no restrictions on the model probabilities, all three methods yield the same results; that is,

$$\hat{\pi}_{ti}^{X|A}(1) = \hat{\pi}_{ti}^{X|A}(2) = \hat{\pi}_{ti}^{X|A}(3).$$

The difference between our method and that of Van der Ark and Van der Heijden is that we derive and plot quantities that are defined for each individual in the sample—namely, the probability $\hat{\pi}_{rijkl}^{V|ABCD}$. A category-specific marginal conditional probability like $\hat{\pi}_{ri}^{V|A}$ is, therefore, just one of the several types of measures that can be depicted in the same plot. Other possibilities are depicting the location of specific

[12] In the case of dichotomous latent variables, the relationship between the expected value and the conditional probability provides a "true score regression" interpretation of the lines plotted in Figure 12.

response patterns (as in Figure 4 and Figure 6 of this paper),[13] the marginal probabilities for a subset of observed variables (for instance, $\hat{\pi}_{rij}^{V|AB}$), or the marginal probabilities for categories of variables that are not included in the LC model. We labeled the latter application the inactive-covariate method (Vermunt and Magidson 2000) since it yields information on the association of a covariate with each of the latent variables without including the covariate concerned in the LC model.[14]

To illustrate the inactive-covariate method, assume that there is a variable E whose levels are indexed by m. The probability of being in level r of latent variable V given that E equals m, $\hat{\pi}_{rm}^{V|E}$, is obtained as follows:

$$\hat{\pi}_{rm}^{V|E}(1) = \frac{\sum_{i=1}^{I}\sum_{j=1}^{J}\sum_{k=1}^{K}\sum_{l=1}^{L} \hat{\pi}_{rijkl}^{V|ABCD} p_{ijklm}^{ABCDE}}{\sum_{r=1}^{R}\sum_{i=1}^{I}\sum_{j=1}^{J}\sum_{k=1}^{K}\sum_{l=1}^{L} \hat{\pi}_{rijkl}^{V|ABCD} p_{ijklm}^{ABCDE}}.$$

Note that in this case we must use the observed cell probabilities as weights (method 1) because we do not have estimated probabilities for the joint distribution including E.

Another important advantage of our way of computing the plotted measures is that it can easily be extended to variables of other scale types, such as continuous dependent or independent variables. This is something that is used in the new computer program LatentGOLD (Vermunt and Magidson 2000), which implements the graphical displays discussed in this paper.

APPENDIX C: ESTIMATION OF THE LC CLUSTER AND LC FACTOR MODELS

The standard estimation method for LC models is the maximum-likelihood (ML) method under the assumption that the data come from a multi-

[13] It should be noted that Van der Heijden, Gilula, and Van der Ark (1999) already mentioned the possibility of incorporating information on individual cases in their ternary plots. They, however, did not explicitly discuss the relationship between the individual posterior membership probabilities and the rescaled probabilities nor the possibility of collapsing the individual posterior membership probabilities in ways other than to form categories of individual variables.

[14] In correspondence analysis, it is quite common to plot levels of inactive covariates. There they are called *passive variables*.

nomial distribution. ML estimation of the model parameters of the LC Factor model described in equation (4) involves finding the parameter values that maximize the following likelihood function:

$$L \propto \prod_{ijkl} \left(\sum_{rs} \pi_r^V \pi_s^W \pi_{irs}^{A|VW} \pi_{jrs}^{B|VW} \pi_{krs}^{C|VW} \pi_{lrs}^{D|VW} \right)^{Np_{ijkl}},$$

where N denotes the sample size and p_{ijkl}^{ABCD} the proportion of the sample belonging to the cell entry concerned. Maximization of the likelihood is a quite standard task that can be performed with an EM or a Newton-Raphson algorithm, or some combination of the two. Software packages that can be used to obtain ML estimates of the parameters of LC factor models are Newton (Haberman 1988), LEM (Vermunt 1997), and Latent-GOLD (Vermunt and Magidson 2000).

REFERENCES

Clogg, Clifford C. 1981. "New Developments in Latent Structure Analysis." Pp. 215–46 *Factor Analysis and Measurement in Sociological Research*, edited by D. J. Jackson and E. F. Borgotta. Beverly Hills, CA: Sage.

———. 1988. "Latent Class Models for Measuring." Pp. 173–205 in *Latent Trait and Latent Class Models*, edited by R. Langeheine and J. Rost. New York: Plenum.

———. 1995. "Latent Class Models." Pp. 311–59 in *Handbook of Statistical Modeling for the Social and Behavioral Sciences*, edited by G. Arminger, Clifford C. Clogg, and M. E. Sobel. New York: Plenum.

De Leeuw, Jan, and Peter G. M. Van der Heijden. 1991. "Reduced Rank Models for Contingency Tables." *Biometrika* 78:229–32.

Fisher, Ronald A. 1940. "The Precision of Discriminant Functions." *Annals of Eugenics*, London 10:422–29.

Formann, Anton K. 1992. "Linear Logistic Latent Class Analysis for Polytomous Data." *Journal of the American Statistical Association* 87:476–86.

Fraley, Chris, and Adrian E. Raftery. 1998. "How Many Clusters? Which Clustering Method?—Answers via Model-Based Cluster Analysis." Technical Report No. 329, Department of Statistics, University of Washington.

Gilula, Zri, and Shelby J. Haberman. 1986. "Canonical Analysis of Contingency Tables by Maximum Likelihood." *Journal of the American Statistical Association* 81:780–88.

Goodman, Leo A. 1974a. "Exploratory Latent Structure Analysis Using Both Identifiable and Unidentifiable Models." *Biometrika* 61: 215–31.

———. 1974b. "The Analysis of Systems of Qualitative Variables When Some of the Variables are Unobservable. Part I: A Modified Latent Structure Approach." *American Journal of Sociology* 79:1179–259.

Gower, John C., and David J. Hand. 1996. *Biplots*. London: Chapman and Hall.

Greenacre, Michael J. 1993. *Correspondence Analysis*. New York: Academic Press.

Haberman, Shelby J. 1979. *Analysis of Qualitative Data*. Vol. 2, *New Developments*. New York: Academic Press.

———. 1988. "A Stabilized Newton-Raphson Algorithm for Log-Linear Models for Frequency Tables Derived by Indirect Observations." Pp. 193–211 in *Sociological Methodology 1988*, edited by Clifford Clogg. Washington: American Sociological Association.

Hagenaars, Jaques A. 1990. *Categorical Longitudinal Data—Loglinear Analysis of Panel, Trend and Cohort Data*. Newbury Park, CA: Sage.

———. 1993. *Loglinear Models with Latent Variables*. Newbury Park, CA: Sage.

Heinen, T. 1996. *Latent Class and Discrete Latent Trait Models: Similarities and Differences*. Thousand Oaks, CA: Sage.

Hunt, Lyn, and Murray Jorgensen. 1999. "Mixture Model Clustering Using the MULTIMIX Program." *Australian and New Zeeland Journal of Statistics* 41: 153–72.

Kohlmann, Thomas, and Anton K. Formann. 1997. "Using Latent Class Models to Analyze Response Patterns in Epidemiologic Mail Surveys." Ch. 33 in *Applications of Latent Trait and Latent Class Models in the Social Sciences*, edited by J. Rost and R. Langeheine. New York: Waxmann.

Lawrence, C. J., W. J. Krzanowski. 1996. "Mixture Separation for Mixed-Mode Data." *Statistics and Computing* 6:85–92.

Lazarsfeld, Paul F., and Neal W. Henry. 1968. *Latent Structure Analysis*. Boston: Houghton Mifflin.

Magidson, Jay, and Jeroen K. Vermunt. 2000. "Bi-Plots and Related Graphical Displays Based on Latent Class Factor and Cluster Models." Proceedings of the RC33 Conference, University of Cologne, Cologne, Germany.

McCutcheon, Allan L. 1987. *Latent Class Analysis*, Newbury Park, CA: Sage Publications.

McLachlan, Geoffrey J., and Kaye E. Basford. 1988. *Mixture Models: Inference and Application to Clustering*. New York: Marcel Dekker.

Moustaki, Irini. 1996. "A Latent Trait and a Latent Class Model for Mixed Observed Variables." *British Journal of Mathematical and Statistical Psychology* 49:313–34.

Pearlin, Leonard I., and Joyce S. Johnson. 1977. "Marital Status, Life-Strains, and Depression." *American Sociological Review* 42:104–15.

Schaeffer, Nora C. 1988. "An Application of Item Response Theory to the Measurement of Depression." Pp. 271–308 in *Sociological Methodology 1988*, edited by C. Clogg. Washington: American Sociological Association.

Uebersax, J. S. 1993. "Statistical Modeling of Expert Ratings on Medical Treatment Appropriateness." *Journal of the American Statistical Association* 88:421–27.

Van der Ark, L. Andries, and Peter G. M. Van der Heijden. 1998. "Graphical Display of Latent Budget and Latent Class Analysis." Pp. 489–509 in *Visualization of Categorical Data*, edited by J. Blasius and M. Greenacre. Boston: Academic Press.

Van der Ark, L. Andries, Peter G. M. Van der Heijden, and D. Sikkel. 1999. "On the Identifiability in the Latent Budget Model." *Journal of Classification* 16:117–37.

Van der Heijden, Peter G. M., Z. Gilula, and L. Andries Van der Ark. 1999. "On a Relation Between Joint Correspondence Analysis and Latent Class Analysis."

Pp. 147–86 in *Sociological Methodology 1999*, edited by Michael E. Sobel and Mark P. Becker.

Vermunt, Jeroen K. 1997. "LEM: A General Program for the Analysis of Categorical Data. User's Manual." Tilburg University, The Netherlands.

Vermunt, Jeroen K., and Jay Magidson. 2000. *Latent GOLD 2.0 User's Guide*. Belmont, MA: Statistical Innovations.

———. 2001. "Latent Class Cluster Analysis." Ch. 3 in *Applied Latent Class Analysis*, edited by J. A. Hagenaars and A. L. McCutcheon. Cambridge, England: Cambridge University Press.

Wasmus, A., P. Kindel, S. Mattussek, and H. H. Raspe. 1989. "Activity and Severity of Rheumatoid Arthritis in Hannover/FRG and in One Regional Referral Center." *Scandinavian Journal of Rheumatology*, Suppl. 79:33–44.

Wolfe, John H. 1970. "Pattern Clustering by Multivariate Cluster Analysis." *Multivariate Behavioral Research* 5:329–50.

6

COVARIANCE MODELS FOR LATENT STRUCTURE IN LONGITUDINAL DATA

*Marc A. Scott**
Mark S. Handcock†

We present several approaches to modeling latent structure in longitudinal studies when the covariance itself is the primary focus of the analysis. This is a departure from much of the work on longitudinal data analysis, in which attention is focused solely on the cross-sectional mean and the influence of covariates on the mean. Such analyses are particularly important in policy-related studies, in which the heterogeneity of the population is of interest. We describe several traditional approaches to this modeling and introduce a flexible, parsimonious class of covariance models appropriate to such analyses. This class, while rooted in the tradition of mixed effects and random coefficient models, merges several disparate modeling philosophies into what we view as a hybrid approach to longitudinal data modeling. We discuss the implications of this approach and its alternatives especially on model interpretation. We compare several implementations of this class to more commonly employed mixed effects models to describe the strengths and limitations of each. These alternatives are compared in an application to long-term trends in wage inequality for young work-

This research was partially supported by the Russell Sage Foundation and the Rockefeller Foundation. The authors acknowledge gratefully the support of the National Science Foundation through grants SES-0087179 and SES-0088061. The authors thank Annette D. Bernhardt and Martina Morris, whose discussions and insights over the years are deeply embedded in this paper, and the anonymous reviewers, whose helpful comments have improved this paper.
*New York University
†University of Washington, Seattle

ers. The findings provide additional guidance for the model formulation process in both statistical and substantive senses.

1. INTRODUCTION AND MOTIVATION

An increasing number of social and behavioral science studies collect information from subjects at several points in time. These longitudinal studies enable researchers to study changes in the phenomena of interest over the life-course of the subjects. At each observation time, at least one response, such as wages earned or the occurrence of a meaningful event, such as graduation from college, is recorded. As with regression, one may collect explanatory covariates in the hope that differences in these inputs will be associated with different levels of response. Each subject is thus associated with his or her own time series of responses and a corresponding set of potentially time-varying explanatory covariates. Models for longitudinal data attempt to relate those individual time series to an overall group process.

The focus on either individual or group processes plays a key role in how one models longitudinal data. For example, if we are modeling a continuous response, Y, in terms of explanatory covariates, X, then the familiar linear model, for individual i,

$$Y_i = X_i\beta + \epsilon_i \tag{1}$$

could be adopted, but Y_i and ϵ_i would be n_i-vectors, where n_i is the number of observations on individual i. Similarly, X_i would be of dimension $n_i \times p$, where p is the number of explanatory covariates. Note that we are modeling a response *vector*, yet this distinction is not made explicitly with our notation. Alternatively, the model may be written

$$Y_i(t) = X_i(t)\beta + \epsilon_i(t),$$

where the index t identifies a specific element of the response vector Y_i. If we were to proceed with a classical multiple regression, stacking the responses by individual and then by observation within individual, we would obscure an important feature of longitudinal data; namely, we know that some set of observations come from the same individual. And observations within the same individual may be correlated due to unobserved individual characteristics. To see this, let us return to the notation in (1), but now

$$Y_i = X_i\beta + \alpha_i + \epsilon_i^*, \tag{2}$$

where α_i is an unobserved scalar trait for subject i, the residual variation is mean zero and uncorrelated with the unobserved process, and $E(\epsilon_i^*(t)\epsilon_i^*(t')) = 0$ for $t \neq t'$. Since we do not observe α_i, we tend to use (1) when the underlying process is accurately described by (2), so the residual variation structure ϵ_i is really $\alpha_i + \epsilon_i^*$. The unobserved trait induces a correlation within individual i, since

$$E(\epsilon_i(t)\epsilon_i(t')|\alpha_i) = E((\alpha_i + \epsilon_i^*(t))(\alpha_i + \epsilon_i^*(t'))|\alpha_i) = \alpha_i^2,$$

and $\alpha_i^2 \neq 0$ in general. Note that the unobserved α_i may not correspond to a single measurable characteristic; instead it proxies for all unobserved characteristics.

There are several different ways to think about the correlation structure in longitudinal data. The different perspectives are induced by the nature of the unobserved trait and its relationship to the covariates and residual variation. If substantive interest is on the effects of the covariates on the response averaged over the population, then models are usually formulated for the mean response averaged over the unobserved traits. Broadly speaking, the correlation structure is modeled as a nuisance parameter, and regression coefficients represent *population-average* effects (Liang and Zeger 1986; Zeger and Liang 1986; Prentice 1988). Alternatively, individual differences may be of interest and can be modeled directly as latent variables; for these *individual-specific* models, regression parameters are to be interpreted conditionally on the value of the subject's latent variable. We will discuss these different approaches, certain variations thereof, and their implications in subsequent sections. Along the way, we will introduce a class of models for longitudinal data that merges these two approaches in a new hybrid form, which is conceptually linked to principal components and factor analysis. First, we introduce the substantive problem that motivates this new formulation.

In labor market economics, a rise in cross-sectional measures of wage inequality that began in the 1970s and has persisted into the 1990s is well-documented (Levy and Murnane 1992; Danziger and Gottschalk 1993; McMurrer and Sawhill 1998). This means that there are greater numbers of workers making more and making less than ever before. And for many groups of workers, wages have remained stagnant over time. This stagnation is due in part to a disproportionate growth in the lower tail of the wage distribution. Using data from two young adult cohorts in the National Longitudinal Survey (NLS), we find, for example, that 30- to

35-year-old white men have a mean wage of $17.78 in 1979, while this figure is $14.27 per hour for a similarly aged group in 1992 (inflation adjusted, 1999 dollars). A measure of inequality is the variance in outcomes; the variance of the logged wages increased 44 percent over the same period.

This dramatic rise has prompted researchers to look more closely at trends in inequality over the life-course of a worker. Cross-sectional data can document a rise in inequality, but since each cross-section is a random sample from the population, one cannot conclude that the same people are making the higher wages in each period. Statements such as "the rich are getting richer while the poor are getting poorer" cannot be definitively made. But longitudinal data can be used to address this type of question. To couch this in labor economic terms, we would like to examine two competing hypotheses that explain the growth in inequality:

I. Wages have become more volatile.
II. Wages have become more stratified over time, indicating a reduction in economic mobility.

The scenarios are illustrated in the three figures below. Figure 1 represents an economy in which individual "profiles" fan out over time, but not excessively. This is our stylized image of a past economy; in Figures 2 and 3, we change the covariance structure to reflect at least a

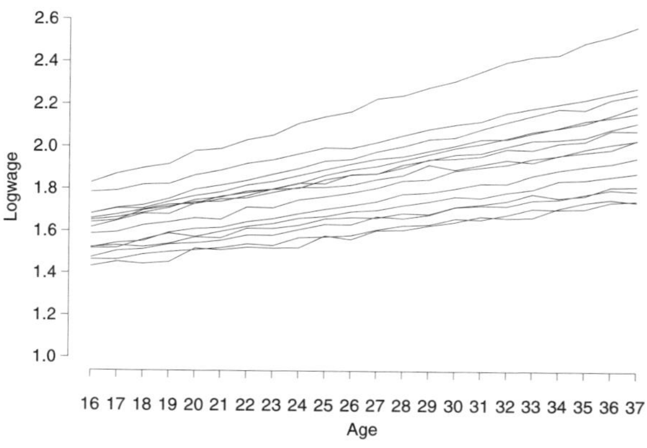

FIGURE 1. Stylized wage trajectories for a less stratified economy.

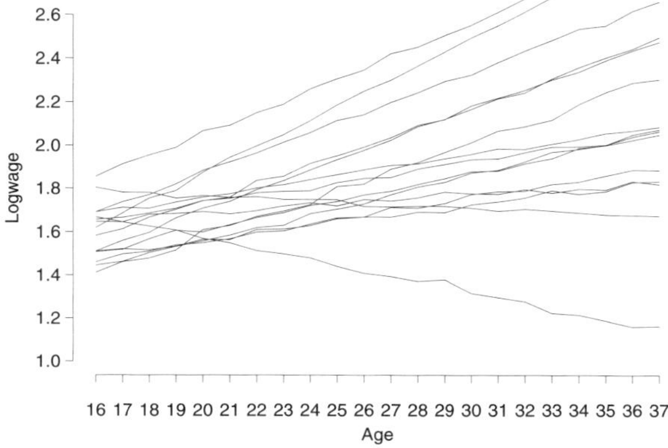

FIGURE 2. Stylized wage trajectories for a more stratified economy.

doubling of process variance, but we do this in very different ways. In Figure 2, the structured variation has become more stratified, but the residual process is left unchanged. In Figure 3, the structured variation is identical to that used in Figure 1, but the residual variance of the process has been greatly increased. This last figure may seem exaggerated, but the average variation between individuals is actually a bit smaller than in Figure 2.

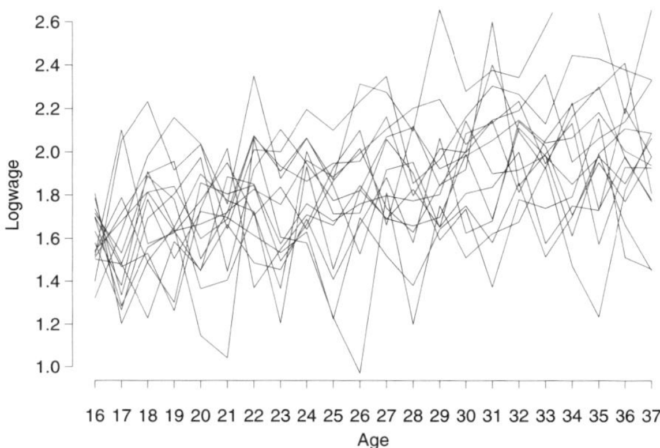

FIGURE 3. Stylized wage trajectories for a more volatile economy.

Based on the figures, the difference between increased stratification (Figure 2) and increased volatility (Figure 3) seems transparent, but in a real application, both hypotheses may be true and the differences may be more subtle. Each possibility has a different substantive interpretation, so sorting out the extent to which each hypothesis describes the changes in wage structure is very important and will have different implications in terms of policy.

To investigate the two hypotheses, Bernhardt et al. (1997), Gottschalk and Moffitt (1994), Haider (1996), and Baker (1997) decompose the wage into permanent and transient components as follows. Let

$$w(t) = p(t) + u(t), \tag{3}$$

where w is the wage, p is its permanent portion, and u is a residual variation term, capturing short-term, or transient, variation. For a specific worker, $p(t)$ can be thought of as his or her mean wage at time t, with residual variation $u(t)$. Assuming independence of $p(t)$ and $u(t)$, we see that

$$\text{Var}(w(t)) = \text{Var}(p(t)) + \text{Var}(u(t)),$$

and that the two hypotheses can be differentiated through this variance decomposition: a rise in wage variance must involve a rise in at least one of the two variance components. Greater stratification implies an increase in the first term, while greater volatility involves the second. If we had a substantial number of observations for each individual, we could estimate $p(t)$ using separate regressions for each. The distribution of these predicted curves would represent permanent variation, while the residuals represent transient variation. The hypotheses of interest describe differences in wage trajectories without any socioeconomic controls, so the only explanatory covariates we include in this analysis are functions of time.

This last point warrants further explanation. Socioeconomic variables such as level of schooling, parent's education, and industry of employment, capture expected returns to individual (supply-side) and employer (demand-side) characteristics. For example, there may be changes in the mean return to obtaining a high school degree that reflects the value of that set of skills in the labor market. Including socioeconomic covariates also controls for compositional shifts in the labor market. The growth in a specific sector of the economy could induce growing inequality if that sector is typically associated with lower wages. But all of these explanations are necessarily focused on the permanent portion of the wage trajectory, since volatility is associated with residual rather than mean effects. The first stage in any analysis of wage inequality is the accurate documentation of the growth in inequality, and how it is apportioned with regard to permanent and transient components. Thus our focus is first on covariance structure, not on the socioeconomic covariates that might "explain" the structure.

In many longitudinal studies, there are a relatively small number of observations per individual, so estimating separate regressions to assess wage inequality is infeasible. A variance components model (Searle et al. 1992) using (3) can partition the variance into long-term, permanent variation and short-term, transitory variation. We note that the distinction between long- and short-term trends is fundamentally about economic mobility. The variation between the individuals' permanent components is a measure of mobility relative to one's peers, and a variance components analysis allows one to evaluate this important economic issue.

In matters with such strong policy implications, proper specification of a model that describes the components of variation is crucial. What may be less apparent is the role of the covariance structure in such an analysis. If we generalize the basic model (2) for longitudinal data to allow for more complex individual characteristics, we get the standard mixed effects model (Diggle, Liang, and Zeger 1994),

$$Y_i = X_i \beta + Z_i \delta_i + \epsilon_i. \tag{4}$$

We have introduced a random-effects component, $Z_i \delta_i$, in which Z_i is an $n_i \times q$ known design matrix, and δ_i is a q-vector of unknown (latent) variables. It is often assumed that δ_i are mean zero multivariate Gaussian. Under this assumption, it is seen that $E(Y_i) = X_i \beta$, while $E(Y_i | \delta_i) = X_i \beta + Z_i \delta_i$. This distinction is important. The latter approach asserts that individuals differ from the population average response in a systematic manner, which is dependent on some latent characteristics. In our application, the growth in wage inequality and evidence for the two competing hypotheses are features of the latent process, $Z_i \delta_i$, not the population-average process $X_i \beta$. If $\delta_i \sim N_q(0, G)$ and $\epsilon_i \sim N_{n_i}(0, R)$, independently, then

$$\text{Cov}(Y_i(t), Y_i(t')) = \{Z_i G Z_i' + R\}_{tt'}.$$

Note that the $X_i \beta$ term is not included. In other words, the covariance structure of the responses, rather than the mean structure, captures the nature of individual differences, and thus inequality, in the labor market. Strictly speaking, the covariance structure captures all extra-mean variation. Since we employ only time as an explanatory covariate for the mean, all of the contributions to inequality are expressed in the covariance. This establishes a baseline level of inequality that we can later use additional covariates (such as education) to explain.

Models for this covariance structure that can differentiate between hypotheses 1 and 2 will be developed in subsequent sections.

1.1. *Data*

As alluded to above, we will anchor our presentation by using an example from labor market economics, where proper modeling of covariance structure is of paramount importance. We will be investigating two datasets from the NLS. The first, or original cohort, is a representative sample of young men aged 14–21 first interviewed in 1966 and interviewed annually for the next 15 years (with the exception of 1972, 1974, 1977, and 1979). The second dataset began with a comparable sample of young men in 1979 who have been interviewed yearly since then for 15 additional years. For comparability between cohorts, we selected only non-Hispanic whites, with resulting sample sizes of 2614 and 2373 respectively for the original and recent cohorts. For a detailed description of these datasets and their comparability, see Bernhardt et al. (1997). According to Topel and Ward (1992), "the first ten years of a career will account for 66 percent of lifetime wage growth for male high school graduates and almost exactly the same fraction of lifetime job changes," so it is important to understand trends manifesting themselves in this early period.

In this paper, we present several different ways to model covariance structure with the ultimate goal of addressing questions such as those posed in hypotheses 1 and 2. One of these methods is novel in the literature, so it is to be developed in some depth. We begin by discussing several different philosophical perspectives to longitudinal data modeling in Section 2. To address hypotheses like the ones just presented, we argue that a different modeling philosophy is necessary; we develop a hybrid framework with this in mind in Section 3 and illustrate it in Section 4. We apply more traditional models to our labor market data in Section 5 and discuss the strengths and weaknesses of each approach, including the substantive implications of each choice. Section 6 summarizes the discussion and suggests future directions of research.

2. ALTERNATIVE MODELING PHILOSOPHIES

The choice of modeling framework should depend on the substantive question of interest. For example, in many medical applications, one may be focused on how a treatment affects the population as a whole. However, if there are potentially serious risks involved in treatment, the distribution of outcomes, including information about the extremes, may be of importance. Along with many modeling paradigms comes a modeling philosophy, focused on the primary goals of the research. We now describe several philosophies in longitudinal data modeling.

2.1. *Population-Average Analysis*

Population average models focus on describing the population, rather than individuals within it. Much as in classical regression, the mean response is modeled conditional on the observed covariates. In a linear model, $E(Y|X) = X\beta$, the parameter β describes how changes in the components of X affect the overall population. With longitudinal data, we have seen that the covariance of the responses within an individual influences the response trajectory. For some problems, that covariance structure is effectively a nuisance parameter—it must be included in the model but is of no intrinsic interest in and of itself. Generalized Estimating Equations (GEE) is a methodology that produces consistent estimates of population-average parameters even when the covariance structure is misspecified (Liang and Zeger 1986; Zeger and Liang 1986; Prentice 1988). This technique allows one to pursue the population-average approach to modeling, while accounting for the dependencies due to the longitudinal nature of the data. Since the covariance is viewed as secondary, the method does not yield a variance components analysis, which one might use to address our labor market hypotheses, for example.

2.2. *Individual-Specific Analysis*

Individual-specific effect models consist of two key components: (1) the fixed effects, which capture gross differences between individuals based on differences in their explanatory covariates; and (2) the random effects, which reflect the influence of unobserved covariates. These so-called "unobserved" covariates are just a device to capture unexplained but systematic variation in outcomes. Typically there is no single covariate, such as "motivation," that would replace the individual effects in our model, were we able to measure it. Rather, after controlling for what was measured, some systematic differences between individuals are likely to exist for a variety of reasons. Because we are looking at longitudinal data, we can verify that some differences seem to persist throughout an individual's life-course, and that these are not simply random disturbances.[1]

Under model (4), the fixed effects are captured by the $X_i\beta$ term, while the random effects are modeled via $Z_i\delta_i$. The δ_i vector is indexed with an i to reflect the fact that every individual is expected to have their own value for this "parameter." These models are also referred to as random coefficient models (Longford 1993) because the coefficient on the Z_i terms is allowed to vary. These coefficients introduce extra-mean variation into the response in a systematic manner mediated by the design matrix Z_i.

We interpret these models conditional on the individual specific effects, so we are modeling $E(Y_i|X_i, Z_i, \delta_i)$, rather than $E(Y_i|X_i)$. Using model (4), the interpretation of the fixed effects parameters shifts to the following. Given the individual specific effect δ_i, the expected response for individual i is $X_i\beta + Z_i\delta_i$. We are making statements about individuals, not populations; the regression coefficients reflect this distinction and should be interpreted in this conditional manner. In the standard linear mixed effects model in which all random components are assumed Gaussian, the distinction between population average and individual specific modeling is more philosophical, as the models and their parameter estimates are identical. This is not the case for a generalized linear mixed model (GLMM; see McCulloch 1997; Hu et al. 1998; Crouchley and Davies 1999).

What may be less immediately apparent about this shift toward an individual-specific perspective is that the parameters that define the distribution of the effects often represent meaningful components of variation. For example, if δ_i is a scalar and Z_i is a column of ones, then the individual differences are being modeled as shifts in the intercept. This implies that the differences between individuals are constant over the life-course. The variance of the random effect δ_i is an important model parameter. If it is large, then large differences between individuals exist and persist throughout the life-course; if it is small, they do not. The ability to

[1]Note that this modeling philosophy is agnostic toward the substantive interpretation assigned to the systematic differences.

interpret a variance component in terms of a substantive question is a key feature of individual-specific modeling.

Note that not all mixed effects models are oriented toward meaningful variance components analyses. Beyond the fixed effects, the variation is modeled in the random effects and in the residual variation structure. In model (4), $\delta_i \sim N_q(0, G)$ and $\epsilon_i \sim N_{n_i}(0, R)$, and the residual variation structure, R, can be made arbitrarily complex. There is often a tension, in terms of modeling, between these two components. ARMA models (Box and Jenkins 1976) can capture a substantial portion of the within-individual correlation, but they do so via parameters that do not take on individual-specific values. For example, the correlation between observations may be given by ρ, but ρ does not vary between individuals. So we know how variation occurs, but we cannot directly use it to position a curve above or below the mean trajectory.

Jones (1990) discusses this model formulation issue by comparing a classical random growth curve model to an AR(1) model for that same structure. He finds that these two approaches typically compete with each other in terms of explaining the variation in the data. We tend to favor models that emphasize structured variation in the $Z_i\delta_i$ term, because these provide direct summaries of differences between individuals.

In sum, mixed effects models may be based on an individual-specific philosophy, but they are not required to do so. Thus care must be given in the model formulation process as to which philosophical perspective to adopt.

2.3. *Latent Curve Models*

A related but philosophically different approach to modeling longitudinal trajectories was developed by Meredith and Tisak (1990).[2] They outline a framework in which each response is a weighted average of a fixed set of curves:

$$Y_i(t) = \sum_k \omega_{ik}\phi_k(t) + \epsilon_i(t), \tag{5}$$

where $Y_i(t)$ represents the response for the ith individual, ω_{ik} is the individual-specific coefficient associated with the kth latent curve $\phi_k(t)$,

[2] We also refer the reader to Raykov (2000), in which latent curve modeling is developed using the structural equation modeling (SEM) approach. SEM emphasizes covariance structure in the model formulation.

and $\epsilon_i(t)$ is the residual process. The ϕ_k capture the shape and magnitude of the variation, and the ω_{ik} allow individuals to differ systematically, much in the same way that random coefficients do in mixed effects models. In the above formulation, the mean process will be a specific weighted sum of the latent curves, but it could just as well be parameterized separately, as in the fixed effects portion of a mixed model. For the remainder of this discussion, we will ignore the mean of the process, or assume it is identically zero.

If the latent curves are known, then the formulation is similar to a mixed effects model. If we stack the ϕ_k as columns of a design matrix $Z(t) = \{\phi_1(t), \phi_2(t), \ldots, \phi_K(t)\}$ at T design points $t_1, t_2, \ldots, t_T$, then we can estimate a model:

$$Y_i(t) = Z(t)\delta_i + \epsilon_i(t),$$

again, ignoring the mean process. But when model (5) was originally presented, it was assumed that the latent curves were not known and would be estimated directly from the data. With a few additional assumptions, this would be a factor analysis, which is a particular decomposition of the covariance into structured and residual variation. The former are captured in the factor loadings, while the latter are summarized by the specific variances. The large variability inherent in covariance estimation prompted researchers to impose smoothness constraints on the curves (Rice and Silverman 1991). A basic premise of the new model that we will propose is that smooth latent curves can go a long way toward describing systematic variation in longitudinal data.

In practice, the latent curve model described above cannot be estimated without further assumptions. If the ϕ_k are known, then this can be estimated as a random growth curve mixed effects model. If they are left completely unspecified, we have a factor analysis formulation. Both of these model-based approaches avoid some technical problems that arise when an estimate of the full unspecified covariance matrix is required.[3]

[3]Missing data at the individual-record level is a key challenge in direct estimation of the covariance matrix but is surmountable. Many algorithms have been developed to estimate pairwise covariances, $\sigma_{tt'} = E((Y_t - \overline{Y}_t)(Y_{t'} - \overline{Y}_{t'}))$, from all available observations. Unfortunately, the resulting full covariance matrix may not be positive semidefinite (Jolliffe 1986). Beale and Little (1975) impose a multivariate normality assumption and estimate the covariance parameters using the method of maximum likelihood. But it is uncertain how robust these methods are to violations of the normality assumption. Other methods have been developed, with similar limitations. For further discussion see Devlin et al. (1981), Locantore et al. (1999), and Arminger and Sobel (1990).

Moving beyond these traditional models will actually open up a whole new way to think about longitudinal data modeling, and we develop this alternative approach at length in Section 3.

2.4. *Latent Class Models*

So far, we have discussed models for which differences between individuals are expressed as an offset from the mean value in shifts that come from a continuous distribution. For example, the random coefficients in mixed effects models come from a multivariate Gaussian distribution, yielding a wide (actually, infinite) variety of outcomes. If the differences "clump" together in a natural way, then it might make sense to restrict the variation to a finite set of possibilities, in which each represents a clump or cluster of similar outcomes in the population. This is the approach taken by latent class analysis (Clogg 1995).[4] The analyst divides the population into K distinct classes, and typically any variation that exists within a class is of secondary interest.[5] The model can be represented as

$$Y_i(t) = X_i(t)\beta_k + \epsilon_i(t), \text{ when } C_i = k, \tag{6}$$

where the random variable C_i captures the latent class membership, and β_k represents the regression coefficient for class k.[6] By allowing the regression coefficients to take on several different values, a set of distinct trajectories can be captured, assuming that the data support them. In formulating such models, one typically models membership in one of the K classes as a random process following a multinomial distribution, so individuals are members of exactly one class. Several features of the population are documented in this approach: the shape of the different trajectories, and the probability of membership in each. Exten-

[4] Strictly speaking, latent class models capture discrete outcomes, while latent trait models are employed with continuous responses. We view latent class modeling conceptually as a form of mixture modeling (Banfield and Raftery 1993, Muthén and Shedden 1999), and thus make no distinction as to response type for these models.

[5] The model-based clustering work of Banfield and Raftery (1993) is an exception; they try to capture the within-class variation using several different forms for the covariance.

[6] Comparing this to a standard mixed effects model, it is interesting to note that one can view the β_k as random coefficients governed by a multinomial distribution, in which case $E(\beta_k)$ may be different from zero, and $X_i(t)$ assumes the role of both mean and random effects design matrices ($X_i(t)$ and $Z_i(t)$ in (4)). Such random coefficients follow a discrete, rather than the more classical continuous, distribution. We thank an anonymous reviewer for suggesting this interpretation.

sions of this approach by Muthén and Shedden (1999) and Roeder et al. (1999) involve estimating a multinomial "choice" model for class membership. For example, we might assume that membership is based on a multinomial logit model in which some subset of the explanatory covariates play a role:

$$\text{logit}[P(C_i = k|X_i)] = \theta_k + X_i\beta_k, \quad k = 1, \ldots, K,$$

where X_i are explanatory variables influencing membership and θ_k are scalars (for identifiability, we would fix $\theta_1 = 0$ and $\beta_1 = 0$). The full model combines this choice model with a model for the response, conditional on the class membership and the explanatory covariates.

This modeling philosophy focuses on identifying subgroups in the data with similar mean structures. However, there are close links to approaches that model the covariance. To see this, consider the model as the number of latent classes increases. If there is only one latent class, then this approach is equivalent to regression and is not modeling covariance at all. As the number of classes increases, more of the covariation in profiles is attributed to the classification. If there are a large number of classes, then the covariation in the profiles is largely explained by the classification and the within-class variation will be reduced. There is a clear tradeoff between mean and covariance modeling as the number of classes increases. However, the present latent class models do not attempt to identify features shared by the entire population (the features are by definition disjoint), and we do not consider them here.

2.5. *Discussion*

In sum, there are several different ways to think about modeling longitudinal data. One can concentrate on the population average and represent the covariance structure as a foil. Or, one can model individual differences directly by imposing a strict structure on how these differences arise. A relatively general framework is to decompose variation into the sum of curves with different weights. This could be in the form of a factor analysis, but a model-based approach to this is preferred over analyses based on the directly estimated covariance matrix. In some instances, one can separate the variation into similar clusters, with an explicit model for how these are determined by explanatory covariates.

All of these are good ideas, depending on the substantive issues to be addressed. We would use the second and third to explicitly model variation in populations that is quite general in form and consider the fourth when natural clusters are apparent.

3. A HYBRID MODEL

The theoretical approaches of Section 2 each have their value and place. In our labor economic example, we wish to extract permanent and transient variance components. We want the permanent component to reflect features of the whole population while still allowing the expression of individual differences. A modeling class that identifies a common, population-level pattern as distinct from short-term effects requires a hybrid modeling philosophy, since both population-average and individual-specific approaches are being employed. When used to address hypotheses 1 and 2, such an approach will provide a highly interpretable and novel variance components decomposition.

3.1. *The Proto-Spline Model Class*

In Scott (1998) and Scott and Handcock (2001), we introduced the hybrid proto-spline class of heterogeneity models. Motivated by a longitudinal study of wage growth, we formulated a class of models that capture long- and short-term features of the covariance structure. The models use a latent curve formulation to identify long-term patterns of variation, and they yield a meaningful variance components decomposition. The proto-spline class is distinguished by the data-adaptive manner in which the curves are estimated. We will now describe this class in detail.

The proto-splines class is derived from the model class (5) of Meredith and Tisak (1990),

$$Y_i(t) = \mu_i(t) + \sum_{k=1}^{K} \omega_{ik}\phi_k(t) + \epsilon_i(t). \tag{7}$$

We have added a general mean process and changed the approach to modeling ω_{ik} as follows. What was formerly an unconstrained individual specific weight, we will now view as a random coefficient from some known distribution. In addition, we will specify a functional form for the $\phi_k(t)$. However, only a functional *form* and not a specific function is necessary for estimation of the proto-spline class.

We restrict the ϕ_k to be orthonormal.[7] This parallels the orthogonality employed in principal components analysis and allows us to interpret each curve's contribution as mathematically distinct from the others. We assume that the random coefficients, ω_{ik} are independent (for different k), which further uncouples the latent curves. This formulation mirrors many psychological and behavioral models in which a response is the combination of several orthogonal shocks to the system. For the proto-spline class, the way the orthogonality of the ϕ_k is maintained is a departure from techniques used in principal component analysis and in Rice and Silverman (1991), in that no external constraints are placed on the estimation procedure.

Consider first the case where the stochastic variation can be described by one curve, ϕ_1 (this is a single latent curve model). We must specify the functional form of ϕ_1, and this is done by choosing an appropriate functional space.[8] For example, we can assume that ϕ_1 is a cubic spline with knots at four equispaced time points. Cubic splines are smooth functions that have a tremendous degree of flexibility in terms of the possible set of shapes that they describe (see Green and Silverman 1994 for details). In our theoretical development (Scott and Handcock 2001), we employed the cubic spline function space because of its smoothness features and flexibility, and this is where the "spline" portion of the proto-spline class is derived. We are not restricted to the class of cubic splines; for example, we can specify that ϕ_1 has the form of a jump process, well-described by wavelets (Ogden 1996). To keep the discussion on familiar ground, ϕ_1 will come from the function space of all quadratic curves for most of the remainder of this paper.

We denote the chosen function space by $\mathcal{H}$, and proceed with the specification of the proto-spline model class. Let $\psi_1(t), \ldots, \psi_T(t)$ be an orthogonal basis for $\mathcal{H}$. Then $\phi_1 \in \mathcal{H}$ is a specific linear combination of those bases, just as is an element of a vector space:

$$\phi_1(t) = \sum_{j=1}^{T} \eta_j \psi_j(t), \tag{8}$$

[7]Orthonormal means that $\int_{-\infty}^{\infty} \phi_j(t)\phi_k(t)\,dt = \mathcal{I}(j = k)$. For a discussion of orthogonality and spline bases, see De Boor (1998).

[8]Function spaces have properties similar to vector spaces and are collections of curves that share a set of well-defined properties. We use them to limit the set of possible shapes that define the structured variation in a process (see Jain et al. 1995 for details of function space theory).

where the η_j are T *nonrandom* parameters that define the curve. If $\mathcal{H}$ is smooth, then so is $\phi_1(t)$. Extending this to the response variable, for the full model, we have

$$Y_i(t) = \mu_i(t) + \omega_{i1}\phi_1(t) + \epsilon_i(t) \tag{9}$$

$$= \mu_i(t) + \omega_{i1}\sum_{j=1}^{T} \eta_j \psi_j(t) + \epsilon_i(t), \tag{10}$$

where ω_{i1} is a mean zero random coefficient with variance one and $\epsilon_i(t)$ are i.i.d. Gaussian random variables with variance σ_ϵ^2.[9]

Our model has two variance components, the variance of ω_{i1} and the residual variance, σ_ϵ^2, and it is a *parametric* covariance model that defers specification of the curve $\phi_1(t)$ to the estimation phase. The uncertainty in the form of $\phi_1(t)$ (until estimation) is a distinguishing feature of proto-spline models. Note that the parameters η_j define the shape of ϕ_1, which is fixed. These parameters do not represent the variance of a random coefficient, but taken as a whole, they determine the magnitude of the random curve ϕ_1 and thus the variance in the process.

The uncertainty allowed in the proto-spline class deserves further attention. In a standard mixed effects model, the random effects design matrix is fixed. Systematic variation takes a known form mediated by that design. The proto-spline class is a departure from this paradigm because it allows the shape of the design, given by ϕ_1 in our example, to be determined from all of the information in the data. In this sense, the curve ϕ_1 is a population-average value—the whole population influences its shape, and it can be considered a population "feature." Individual-specific differences are directly modeled using the random coefficient ω_{i1}. So this model is a hybrid between population-average and individual-specific philosophies and it belongs to the latent curve class of models.

In fact, the only philosophy not employed here is that of latent class modeling. As previously discussed, there is always a tension between modeling the covariance and modeling the mean, and since our emphasis is on covariance modeling, we do not utilize the latent class modeling philosophy, in which mean processes dominate.

[9] Note that the magnitude of the variation associated with ϕ_1 is contained in its norm, and the residual variation structure $\epsilon_i(t)$ can be made more complex.

3.2. *Extensions*

In this section we extend the development of the single proto-spline model in (7) through (10) to the general multiple proto-spline model. We note that the choice of our function space implies that ϕ_1 has a nonparametric interpretation, since it is a curve lying in a potentially smooth, continuous function space. Note that the model is not restricted to the space of any particular functions. Any finite-dimensional function space (or vector space) can be employed. An advantage to the proto-spline class of models is that the bases may be chosen to reflect the form expected in the substantive process without knowing which specific version of that form is present. If we choose models that result in latent curve estimates with a functional interpretation, features such as the derivative become available.

We define the full proto-spline class by extending the single curve example to more than one curve without introducing additional parameters. The main idea is to use only a subset of the T bases ψ_j to construct each curve ϕ_k. For this development, we let $\mathcal{H}$ be a basis for cubic splines with an appropriate set of knots. Let $\mathcal{I}_k$ be an indexing function defined on the integers $1, \ldots, T$, which selects the basis functions used to construct the kth curve. In our simple example, ϕ_1 uses all T basis functions, so $\mathcal{I}_1 = \{1, \ldots, T\}$. We construct latent curves as a deterministically weighted sum of the basis functions specified by the indexing function $\mathcal{I}$ so

$$\phi_k(t) = \sum_{j \in \mathcal{I}_k} \eta_j \psi_j(t). \tag{11}$$

In order to ensure orthogonality of the ϕ_k, the index sets given by $\mathcal{I}_k$ must be disjoint. This restriction implies that once we decide to estimate more than one latent curve, the curves are highly constrained elements from the class $\mathcal{H}$, using only a subset of the bases for each. Since in the theoretical development $\mathcal{H}$ was chosen to be the natural cubic splines, we named the resulting ϕ_k *proto-splines*, because they are *partial* versions of a full spline fit. This method requires T parameters to build all K curves; if we do not normalize the curves, then for identifiability the random coefficients ω_{ik} are all presumed to have variance one.

To place this model in the context of those previously developed, we examine it for two extreme cases. First, if $K = T$, then each proto-spline is just a rescaled version of the basis function. This is essentially the model proposed in Brumback (1996) and Brumback and Rice (1998), although the form of their model was chosen to produce cubic spline *predictions* for individual curves. If $K = 1$, then we are estimating a smooth principal component in the presence of noise, and it is constrained to be a natural cubic spline.[10]

A more useful approach is to choose K to be small in relation to T, so that for equal-sized index sets, T/K bases are available for each latent curve. Equations (7) and (11) still apply, but the "proto-spline" nature of the curve estimates becomes more apparent. This intermediate case is similar to a principal functions analysis (Ramsay and Silverman 1997), in which we expect that most of the variation in the process is captured in a few of the largest principal functions. We are enforcing a small number of these by our choice of K, and we maintain the orthogonality requirement by the way the model is constructed. Note that this model differs from a principal functions analysis in that we can choose our function spaces with substantive features in mind, rather than simple smoothness constraints. We then build our model directly around these structures.

3.3. *Link to Mixed Effects Models*

The standard mixed effects model can be expressed in the following form:

$$Y_i(t) = X_i(t)\beta + Z_i(t)\delta_i + \epsilon_i(t). \tag{12}$$

A key feature of this model is that $X_i(t)$ and $Z_i(t)$ are *prespecified* designs. The single latent curve proto-spline model is precisely the above model, with $Z_i(t) = \phi_1(t)$ and $\delta_i = \omega_{i1}$, only $Z_i(t)$ is *specified from the data*. This illustrates a conceptual distinction between proto-spline models and other mixed effects models.

To explore the conceptual difference, we will consider three random quadratic models. For Model I, we assume that we know the exact quadratic curve that describes the structured covariation about the mean. Let $Z_i(t) = t + \frac{1}{2}t^2$, so $Z_i(t)$ is a scalar-valued function describing a *particular* growth structure. Further, let the random effect, δ_i, be a Gaussian random variable with unknown variance (the variance is one of the model's variance components). For a specific individual,

[10]Another name for smooth principal components, principal functions, comes from the functional data analyses arena and is discussed at length in Ramsay and Silverman (1997). The reader is also referred to Lindstrom (1995), who uses splines to model a population of curves.

$$Y_i(t) = X_i(t)\beta + \left(t + \frac{1}{2}t^2\right)\delta_i + \epsilon_i(t). \tag{13}$$

Every subject gets some random multiple of the fixed curve $t + \frac{1}{2}t^2$.

For Model II, we consider a mixed effects model in which each individual has their own quadratic perturbation as follows. Let the elements forming the three columns of $Z_i(t)$ be given by the vector $(1, t, t^2)$, and let $\delta_i = (\delta_{1i}, \delta_{2i}, \delta_{3i})$ be a vector of random coefficients, with a multivariate Gaussian distribution. Then for an individual specific curve,

$$Y_i(t) = X_i(t)\beta + \delta_{1i} + \delta_{2i}t + \delta_{3i}t^2 + \epsilon_i(t). \tag{14}$$

While this is quite flexible, the variance components analysis requires a full description of the estimated covariance structure of the random effects, which is contained in a 3×3 matrix that includes important covariance as well as variance components. We must use all of this information when describing any variance partitioning.

Model I is highly inflexible in that we must impose an exact form for growth beyond the mean. However, the variance component for δ_i is highly interpretable—it is the variance of the coefficient of precisely determined shocks to the system, so a larger variance means that there is greater dispersion in individual growth and that all structured growth follows the same form. It would be difficult to make a similar statement about Model II.

For Model III we consider a single latent curve proto-spline model, which offers the interpretability of the simpler model (I), and the flexibility of the more complex model (II). Let $\phi_1(t) = \eta_1\psi_1(t) + \eta_2\psi_2(t) + \eta_3\psi_3(t)$, where $\psi_1(t) = 1$, $\psi_2(t) = t$ and $\psi_3(t) = t^2$.[11] While this might resemble model II, the vector (η_1, η_2, η_3) is common to each individual and does not represent individual-specific random effects. Every individual curve has the following form:

$$Y_i(t) = X_i(t)\beta + \delta_i(\eta_1 + \eta_2 t + \eta_3 t^2) + \epsilon_i(t), \tag{15}$$

with the parameters (η_1, η_2, η_3) fixed and identical across individuals; this is a reparameterization of (10) that keeps the notation consistent. Each of these models is different, and we claim that the proto-splines offer an effective compromise between the rigidity and flexibility of Models I and II, respectively, while remaining highly interpretable from a variance components perspective.

[11] We are ignoring the orthogonality requirement in this example for illustrative purposes.

To understand the link between proto-splines and other mixed effects models it is important to understand their technical distinctions. Scott and Handcock (2001) discuss estimation for the proto-spline model and show that there is a likelihood-equivalent but *nonstandard* mixed effects model corresponding to the proto-spline class. In this section we describe the ways in which the proto-spline model is nonstandard.

For notational convenience we suppress reference to time in the functions, representing $\psi_j(t)$ and $Z_i(t)$ as ψ_j and Z_i, respectively. Let $Z_i = \{\psi_1, \psi_2, \ldots, \psi_T\}$ be a design matrix constructed using the basis functions for the space $\mathcal{H}$. The coefficients η_j are assumed to be ordered so that if there are K different groups used in the model, with the kth group given as $\gamma_k = (\eta_{k1}, \ldots, \eta_{kn_k})^T$, then the coefficients can be stacked into a $T \times K$ matrix $\Gamma = \bigoplus_{k=1}^{K} \gamma_k$. The difference between these two models can be understood by examining their representations. Our proto-spline model class is

$$Y_i = X_i\beta + Z_i\Gamma\delta_i + \epsilon_i, \tag{16}$$

where $\delta_i \sim N_K(0, I_K)$. The likelihood-equivalent mixed effects model is

$$Y_i = X_i\beta + Z_i\delta_i^* + \epsilon_i, \tag{17}$$

where $\delta_i^* \sim N_T(0, \Gamma\Gamma')$.

The proto-spline formulation (16) has K random effects, while (17) has T. In (16), the random effect distribution is completely known ($N(0,1)$), while in (17) the parameters governing the effects (the γ_k's), must be estimated for us to know the structure of the random effects. In (16), the design $Z_i\Gamma$ represents the latent curve ϕ_1 and is estimated, while in (17), the design Z_i is prespecified. These distinctions are convenient ways to interpret the components of the models; they have the same likelihood and set of unknown parameters. In principal, the likelihood equivalence means that any software that can estimate a mixed effects model can be used to estimate the parameters of the proto-spline class. However, the covariance structure associated with model (17) would not be implemented in standard statistical software for mixed effects models, such as `SAS PROC MIXED` or `lme` in `Splus`.

While we have some evidence that these are different models, is this really the case? Restricting our attention to the *single* proto-spline model, formulation (16) contains a scalar random effect, δ_i, while the vector δ_i^* defined in (17) contains T effects. It is interesting to note that the covariance structure $\Gamma\Gamma'$ governing δ_i^* is degenerate, since $\Gamma\Gamma'$ is not positive definite. This does not introduce problems with estimation, however, because the degeneracy is removed in the full likelihood, once residual variation is included. If one examines the structure $\Gamma\Gamma'$ more closely, it is apparent that each element of the vector δ_i^* is linearly dependent on each of the others, so in essence only *one* random effect is generated by this covariance structure.[12] So the likelihood-equivalent model (17) is a nonstandard mixed effects model, which is equivalent to our proto-spline model, even in terms of the observations that would be generated from it, if we consider the limit of its degenerate covariance matrix.

What this means is that our proto-spline formulation effectively "corrects" the degeneracy in (17) by modeling the random effects in a simpler manner, without direct reference to the relationships indicated by the latter model's $\Gamma\Gamma'$ covariance structure. The γ_k parameters contained in the Γ matrix are essential to each formulation of the model but should not be confused with what is actually random in the process. By viewing the design as estimated, rather than prespecified, our formulation (16) correctly separates the model into a portion driven by *population* features contained in the γ_k and individual features represented by δ_i.

In sum, the proto-spline class provides an interpretation for an interesting class of nonstandard mixed effect models.[13] This interpretation is a philosophically distinct, hybrid modeling approach, and thus not only generates new knowledge with its use, but also establishes a new way to "allocate" the information provided in longitudinal data. The parameters contained in γ_k partition the variance as follows: they set the overall level of variation, since this is given by the sum of the components' squared values; and they describe the correlation structure because they define a shape which relates observations at different points in time. This formulation thus captures two things simultaneously in a full modeling class—orienting a modeling class to have these philosophical properties is to our knowledge novel in the literature.[14] By develop-

[12]Due to the degeneracy, this analysis involves taking the limit as the covariance structure approaches $\Gamma\Gamma'$ from a "nearby" positive definite structure. The dependent relationships correspond to the relative magnitudes of the components η_{kj} of γ_k.

[13]Given their degeneracies, it is unclear if they can truly be labeled as mixed effects models; they are certainly nonstandard.

[14]The proto-spline class is closely linked to a factor analysis model, which could be interpreted similarly, but we have not seen a formulation that explicitly attempts to guide the shape of the factors using something as flexible as a function space. The work of Rice and Silverman (1991) was pioneering by constraining principal components to be smooth, but it was not presented as a modeling class, and inferential properties were not fully developed.

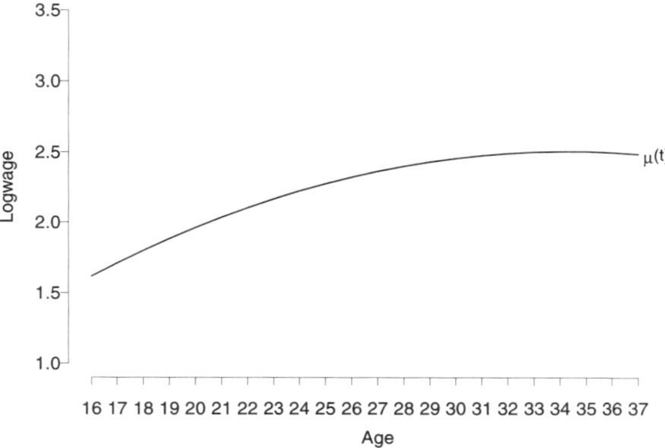

FIGURE 4. Mean curve for single proto-spline model.

ing this class using likelihood-based procedures, a complete set of inferential tools is at the analyst's disposal. Scott and Handcock (2001) establish the asymptotic properties of this class and discuss inferential techniques. Being able to differentiate between population and individual effects is crucial to the formation of comparative statements in the policy domain.

4. Illustration

For ease of exposition, we illustrate our model class by fitting a single latent quadratic curve proto-spline model to longitudinal wage data from the NLS. For the fixed effects, $X_i(t)$, we use a simple quadratic in age; this yields Model III of Section 3.3. In Figure 4, we display the cross-sectional mean of the process.[15] It provides the center from which the curves deviate. In Figure 5, we superimpose 4 simulated realizations from the proto-spline model fit, with the residual process $\epsilon_i(t)$ suppressed. The fitted curve $\hat{\phi}_1$ used in that simulation is presented in Figure 6. From this figure, one can see that the growth of wages near the college years of 18 to 22 sets the extent of growth for the later years as well. The shape of the single latent curve describes the long-term trend in variation—strong growth in the twenties, followed by steady but diminished growth in the

[15] As discussed, there is no choice for the mean that does not depend on the choice of covariance structure. We found the mean to be fairly robust to alternative formulations, and chose a quadratic mean for ease of exposition.

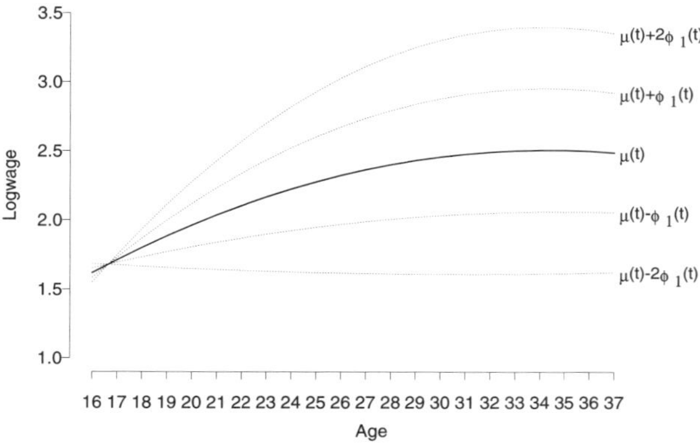

FIGURE 5. Curves for random coefficients one and two standard deviations from the mean for a single proto-spline model.

thirties. Each realization is simply the mean curve plus some random multiple (positive or negative) of the latent curve $\hat{\phi}_1$.

One might be concerned that imposing a quadratic latent curve is overly restrictive and essentially forces the decomposition into the shape indicated above. However, within the class of quadratic curves there are pure linear and constant curves; if there were no change in the *growth rate* at early and later ages, then we would expect a different fitted latent curve. By forming a single latent curve spanning all ages, we are specifying that

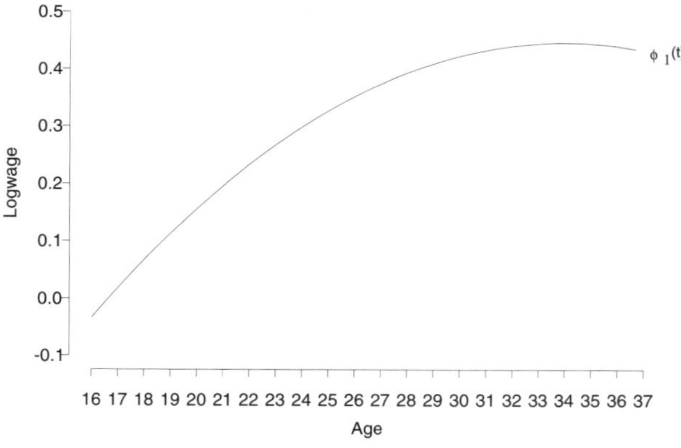

FIGURE 6. Fitted latent curve for a single proto-spline model.

we want this curve to represent long-term structure, within the quadratic class. This is in part how we can model the covariance structure for the entire age span even though only segments of the full trajectory are observed for a specific individual.[16] More complex spaces may reveal more complicated dependencies, should they exist, and they should be considered in the model formulation process.

In Figure 5, we see that the effect of the single latent curve crosses the mean at age 17. The zero value for $\hat{\phi}_1$ near this age corresponds to a negligible amount of permanent variance, but even this is not predetermined by our choice of basis. If below-mean wages at those ages were to lead to much larger gains later on, the "crossover" would be at some later age. Random quadratics do limit us to a single change in the direction of growth (positive or negative), while higher-order polynomials would not. Finally, note an important difference between this model and Model II. In the latter, each individual has a uniquely shaped quadratic curve, so it may rise quickly and not level off, or it may level off quickly. In our model, which is basically Model III, every individual's variation beyond the mean has the same shape, given by $\hat{\phi}_1$—with only the magnitude of that variation allowed to vary.

5. APPLICATION AND COMPARISON OF MODELS

To illustrate how the models differ in practice, we apply several different covariance models to labor market data from the NLS. After a preliminary analysis, we found that the mean structure in this data resembles a quadratic curve. We thus set the columns of the fixed effects design matrix to correspond to constant, linear and quadratic growth over time.[17] More complex mean structures can describe the influence of additional covari-

[16] Longitudinal data are often unbalanced or incomplete, sometimes by design. For example, the NLS cohort aged 14–21 during the initial survey year is tracked for 16 years, so complete individual records would span ages 14–30 and 21–37 in the extremes. No information on the correlation between responses at age 14 and 37 is available at the individual level. Estimating the covariance between ages 14 and 37 without making further assumptions about the covariance is not possible. This concern and others noted by Jolliffe (1986) and Beale and Little (1975) are sufficient to warrant a model-based approach; the gains in precision associated with the imposition of a model (Altham 1984) further justify this. For a more sophisticated treatment of missing data issues in covariance structure estimation, the reader is also referred to Arminger and Sobel (1990).

[17] Note that we orthogonalize and normalize these basis vectors; so instead of a vector of ones, the first column is a vector consisting entirely of $1/\sqrt{22}$, based on the 22 ages from 16 to 37.

ates on aggregate wage growth; our goal in this study is to understand the degree of long-term wage stratification, so the overall divergence of these curves over time in comparable samples yields important substantive information. Next, we must select a form for the structured portion of the variation. For wage data, the structured portion consists of long-term, or permanent, differences between wage trajectories.

We will compare three models. The first is a random quadratic mixed effects model similar to Model II and to that used by Bernhardt et al. (1997) in their analyses. The second is a single latent curve proto-spline model, similar to Model III, and the third is an extension of proto-spline models that includes a second nonorthogonal latent curve. Beyond the structural variation just described, the residual variation is modeled simply as independent with constant variance.

5.1. *Random Quadratics*

The strength of a random quadratic model such as that given by (14) is the flexibility provided by the three random coefficients, δ_{1i}, δ_{2i}, and δ_{3i}. Note that the quadratic basis we use is an orthogonalized and normalized version of $(1, t, t^2)$, which is also the fixed effects basis. The random coefficients are globally constrained to come from a multivariate Gaussian density. This choice yields a broad range of curves of various shapes and intensities. This distributional form does, however, require that there are no clusters of curves, or other multimodalities.

We assume that the δ_i are distributed as $N(0, G)$, where G is a completely unspecified 3×3 covariance matrix defined by six distinct parameters. We fit the model on data from the recent NLS cohort using maximum likelihood estimation,[18] and find that

$$\hat{G} = \begin{pmatrix} +2.019 & +0.899 & -0.265 \\ +0.899 & +1.312 & +0.096 \\ -0.265 & +0.096 & +0.529 \end{pmatrix}$$

and $\hat{\sigma}_\epsilon^2 = 0.0719$.[19] Unfortunately, these results are somewhat hard to interpret. The structured portion of the covariance is given by $Z_i \hat{G} Z_i^T$,

[18] All of the following results are based on recent cohort data; we make cross-cohort comparisons in Section 5.4.

[19] Differences in these findings and those presented by Bernhardt et al. (1997) are due to a different choice for the quadratic basis, but they are otherwise comparable.

where Z_i is the random effects design matrix. Since the rows of Z_i correspond to the subject's age, this matrix product describes individual wage differences at each age and how they relate to each other. For example, the diagonal of $Z_i \hat{G} Z_i^T$ represents the structured, or permanent, wage variance at each age. These values are plotted against age in Figure 7 below. The initially larger variance at the earliest ages indicates some initial stratification between individual trajectories that seems to diminish by age 20, only to increase substantially from that point forward, with a dramatic rise after age 32. Had permanent differences in trajectories been limited to an intercept shift, this graph would have consisted of a horizontal line some distance above the axis. The result above indicates that wages fan out quite dramatically as individuals age, and it gives some indication of how the process accelerates. We can infer that the trajectory fans out as a whole because the partition is based on a model employing a continuous curve for the permanent portion of the trajectory.

5.2. *Single Latent Curve proto-spline*

In this model, we assume that most of the structured variation takes a specific form, but we let the exact shape be determined by the data. The explicit model is

$$Y_i(t) = X_i(t)\beta + \delta_i \phi_1(t) + \epsilon_i(t), \tag{18}$$

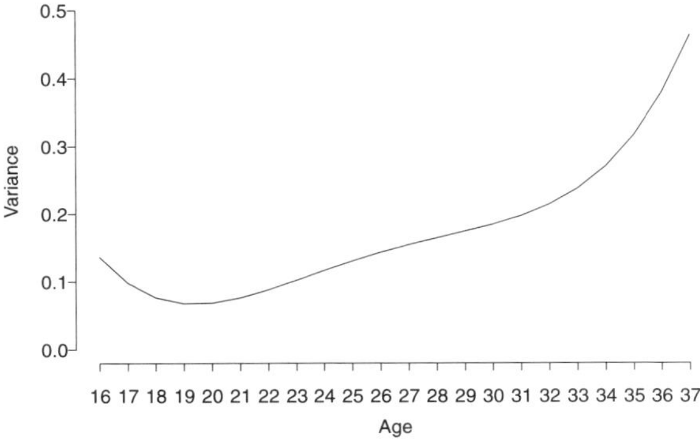

FIGURE 7. Permanent wage variance for random quadratic model.

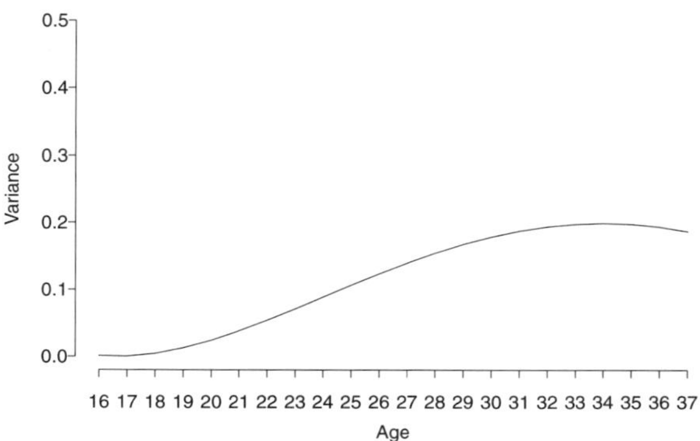

FIGURE 8. Permanent wage variance for single latent curve model.

where ϕ_1 is the single latent curve, assumed to lie in the space of quadratic curves, and δ_i is the random coefficient for the ith individual. This is the same model as the one used for our illustrative example in Section 4. A look again at Figure 5 reveals the strength of this model. A wide range of outcomes are easily represented by the mean plus a random multiple of the single latent curve, $\hat{\phi}_1$.

Figure 6 displays this curve for the recent cohort. In this figure, the interpretability of this class of longitudinal data models becomes apparent. The single latent curve reveals most of what we need to know about structured variation. Contrast this to the covariance matrix $\hat{G}$, which along with design matrix Z_i provides the equivalent information in a less accessible form. The random coefficient on our proto-spline model is standard Gaussian, so we have an immediate sense of the range of impact of the single latent curve.

The restriction to a single latent curve does limit our ability to model more complex structured variation. In Figure 8, we see that the permanent variation, the squared version of $\hat{\phi}_1$, describes a very simple growth structure.[20] Two features stand out in comparison to random quadratic models: the permanent variation starts out lower at the youngest ages and it does not grow as dramatically as individuals age. We believe that the initial variation is less important from a likelihood perspective, so it is effectively being ignored in the estimation process. Had we used a higher order

[20]The permanent variance calculation is straightforward in this case because the random coefficient δ_i is standard Gaussian.

polynomial, we might have discovered persistent initial wage differences. If this were the case, we would expect $\hat{\phi}_1$ to begin higher, possibly decrease somewhat and then increase again, in a shape similar to the permanent variance graph from the random quadratic model.

5.3. *Double Latent Curve Model*

The limitations of a single curve model prompts us to explore a model with two latent curves. Fitting such a model under the pure proto-spline formulation would require the fitted curves to be orthogonal, and this restricts the function spaces in which each may lie. We propose a new model that effectively "reuses" the basis for each latent curve. The model, abstractly, is given by

$$Y_i(t) = X_i(t)\beta + \delta_{1i}\phi_1(t) + \delta_{2i}\phi_2(t) + \epsilon_i(t), \tag{19}$$

where ϕ_1 and ϕ_2 are latent curves and δ_{1i} and δ_{2i} are i.i.d. standard Gaussian random coefficients. We construct each curve from the same basis.

$$\phi_k(t) = \sum_{j=1}^{T} \eta_{kj}\psi_j(t), \tag{20}$$

with $k = 1$ or 2, effectively doubling the number of parameters used by the single latent curve model. After adding some identifiability constraints to our estimation procedure, we were able to fit this more complex model.

The double latent curve model can best be understood as the combination of a common mean process and two independent "shocks" taking some functional form. We choose to continue to employ the space of quadratic polynomials for ease of exposition. Looking at Figure 9, we find that the fitted curves are quite different from each other. These are the forms for the two shocks, $\hat{\phi}_1$ and $\hat{\phi}_2$. We see that $\hat{\phi}_1$ is quite similar to its counterpart in the single latent curve model, although it starts out further below the origin. The latter feature will induce greater permanent variation at the youngest ages, and then this will subside, as the curve crosses the origin between ages 18 and 19 (contrast this to the crossing at age 17 in the single curve model). The second curve introduces a whole new feature to the covariation. It appears that individuals who start out earning more are penalized as they age. This is indicated by $\hat{\phi}_2$'s initially positive level of about 0.2 at age 16, which sinks to -0.3 by age 37. Of course, negative random coefficients are just as likely as positive ones, so this

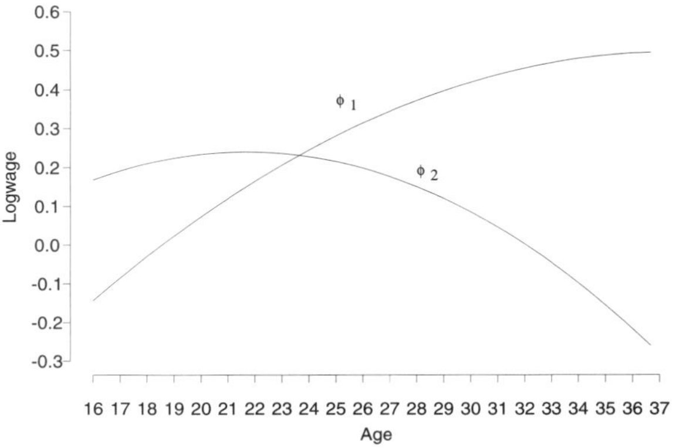

FIGURE 9. Fitted proto-splines for double latent curve model.

curve could also represent later growth for young workers who initially accept lower wages. There is mild evidence that this is capturing an "education effect," in which individuals who defer fully entering the labor market (and possibly pursue education or training) benefit with larger wage growth in the long run.[21]

Note also the similarities and differences of our fitted model to a principal components analysis (PCA). The proto-spline restriction to a smooth function space means that short-term variability is definitely removed, and each curve represents a permanent component of variation. With a model-based approach, we can precisely describe how the latent curves are added to the response process. This is less immediate with the components in a PCA, because the PC scores have no predetermined distributional form. Further, the proto-spline process is well-defined under the entire age range of interest without either the use of an ad hoc procedure or the need for a balanced design.

The permanent variance partitioning for this model is given in Figure 10. By including two curves additively and independently, this model allows for larger early and later year variation. The effects are permanent, in that they persist over the lifetime of a worker, but their independence points to a subtlety of these variance decompositions. Two curves, along with their coefficients, describe the systematic portion of a trajectory, but

[21] This effect was based on an analysis of the final level of education attained by each individual and the predicted value of the coefficient $\hat{\delta}_{2i}$ of $\hat{\phi}_2$.

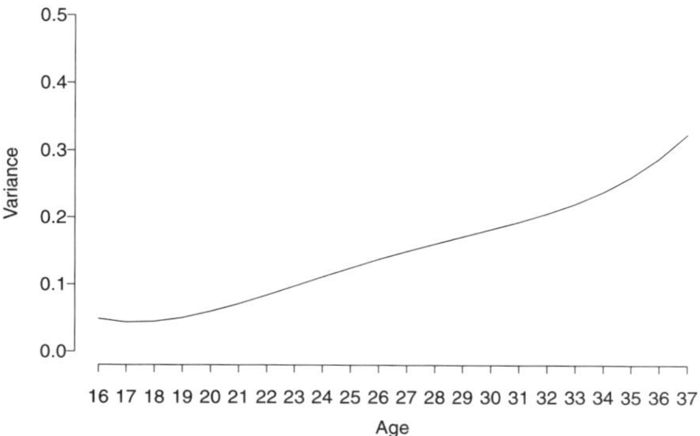

FIGURE 10. Permanent wage variance for double latent curve model.

the independence of the coefficients severs any link between the two. In terms of generating mechanisms, this makes sense only if two different features of the wage growth process are being captured, such as an overall growth (often attributed to returns to job tenure and experience) and an education effect.

The above comment also points to a limitation of the random quadratic model. Namely, it is hard to describe an underlying process (often thought of as a latent characteristic) that is driving the three coefficients forming the curves. One would have to propose a social or economic generating mechanism that involves intercept, slope, and acceleration components. The latent curve models provide simpler explanations, which is an advantage in this case.

5.4. *Comparing Variance Partitions*

Although related, these three models provide different variance decompositions. We display the permanent variation plots in Figure 11 and include 95 percent confidence intervals at each age. We discuss the construction of those intervals in the appendix. Notable differences exist for the youngest and oldest ages, with strong agreement in the middle range. The single latent curve model does not pick up much structured wage variation at the youngest ages. If initial differences in wages persist during the youngest ages but then diminish, then this model will have to choose between the initial and later year effects—and since the latter are larger, they tend

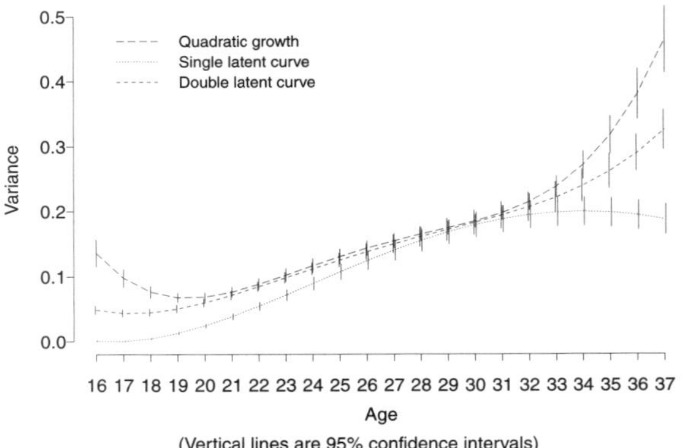

FIGURE 11. Permanent wage variance for all three models.

to dominate. The double proto-spline model picks up this extra variation in $\hat{\phi}_2$, and this is reflected in larger permanent variance for the younger ages. The random quadratic model picks up more variation in both younger and older ages and labels it permanent. We contend that the additional flexibility of the random quadratic model allows it to follow the raw data more closely, capturing less rigid forms of variation. This is indirectly confirmed by examining the residual variation, which is 0.072 for random quadratics, and 0.078 and 0.098 for double and single latent curve models, respectively.

Below we present the variance decomposition for each cohort to address an important question. While each model partitions the variance differently, do these differences have substantive impact? That is, how sensitive are the answers to the substantive questions to the choice of model? In our application, the question of interest is whether or not the permanent wage variance between the cohorts differs, and if so, by how much. Any model we use will be only an approximation, but if the answer to our question is consistent across models, we can have more confidence in any conclusions we draw.

In Figures 12 through 14, we make a cross-cohort comparison and display the model-based permanent variance for each model along with 95 percent confidence intervals at each age. All of the models indicate a significantly larger permanent variance in the recent cohort, starting sometime in the mid-twenties. The difference is most dramatic in the random quadratic model and least so in the single latent curve model. There is

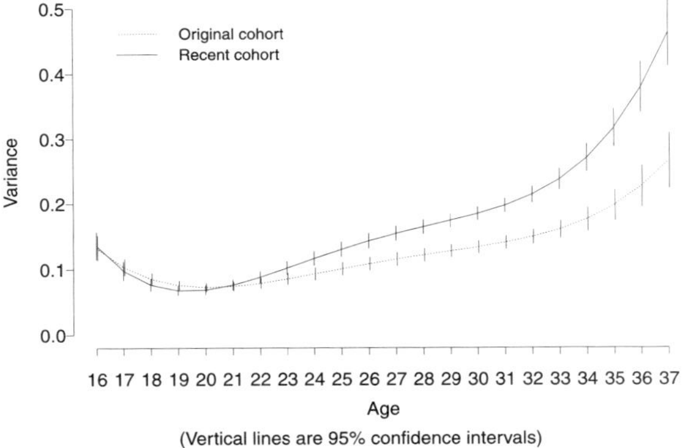

FIGURE 12. Permanent wage variance for random quadratic model.

some between-model discrepancy in what portion of the variance is permanent at the youngest ages, and in how the cohorts differ. Both latent curve models contain a crossover, in which the original cohort starts out more stratified until the early twenties, at which point the opposite is true. In contrast, the random quadratic model posits that both cohorts are more permanently stratified initially and to a comparable extent. If we are interested in the absolute magnitude of permanent wage stratification, we must look more closely at all of these models and determine which is more

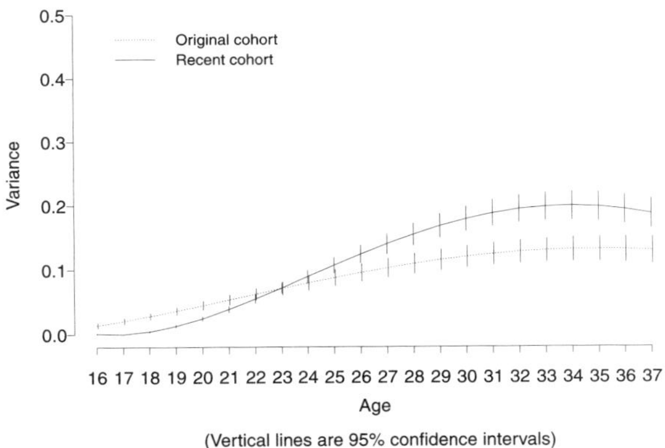

FIGURE 13. Permanent wage variance for single latent curve model.

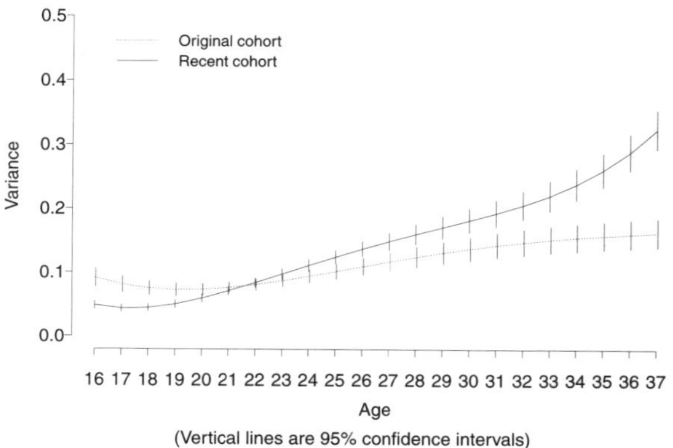

FIGURE 14. Permanent wage variance for double latent curve model.

justified on substantive grounds. If we were concerned about wage stratification at the younger ages, a deeper understanding of each model's characteristics is warranted, since these models tell three different stories.

5.5. *Discussion of Findings*

All three of these models indicate a significant increase in permanent wage variation in the recent cohort for the older ages. But the magnitude of these differences varies greatly between models, and strong differences in the partitions exist at the younger ages.

Since the random quadratic model labeled more variation as permanent, it may be overfitting that feature in some sense. The flexibility of random quadratics admits even a U-shaped curve, but is it desirable to use such a shape to describe *permanent* wage gains? U-shaped curves, in which initial and final wages are nearly identical, involve a shift in the direction of wage change, from loss to gain. So in what sense is this indicative of a permanent, or lasting, trend? We must understand how the choice of model is reflected in the variance partition if we intend to make an informed assessment of social phenomena.

Latent curve models stand out as a philosophically mixed approach to creating variance partitions. They are highly interpretable, with independent components acting as shocks to the process. The shocks may be readily interpretable in the context of the generating mechanisms for the social processes under study. They offer a handy form of rigidity compared to random quadratic models, yet they are inherently adaptive to overall patterns of structured variation. The hybrid nature of this model class provides a new type of analysis to which results from other classes can be compared. Thus these models can be viewed as excellent foils to the classical random quadratic model.

All three of the models describe the structured portion of variance in such a way that "permanent" is a reasonable label to apply. That is, the model describes smooth versions of the curves in space that are reasonable attempts to separate the analyst-defined signal from noise; and the signal is nonstochastic, conditional on the parameters that describe it. The differences in these definitions allow different aspects of variation to be identified.

6. CONCLUSION

We embarked on this analysis to determine how different models for covariance affect variance component partitioning. Along the way, we introduced a new, hybrid class of latent curve models, proto-splines, that offer an interpretable paradigm for describing covariation, which is well-suited to formulating substantive questions directly. These models locate population-level persistent covariance structure and reflect it in the shape and size of latent curves. We view proto-splines as covariance function smoothers; they are nonparametric in the sense that the estimated curve lies in a function space, yet the model formulation provides a straightforward interpretation of the curves that is often missing in other nonparametric techniques. In the model formulation, the researcher imposes a class of functions to capture substantively meaningful structure. The restriction to a particular class of functions forces proto-spline models to be conservative in the way they fit the data—being less susceptible to outliers, which in other models may influence both prediction and fit. This makes them invaluable in comparisons with more traditional models; the ways in which they differ point out characteristics of each, with the clearly defined behavior of our models acting as a foil for the others.

In future work, we will consider relaxing the independence assumption for the proto-spline model class. For example, our double latent curve model could include a term for the correlation between curves. This extension would open up the possibility of very different latent curves, since the independence constraint ultimately lowers the likelihood of certain shapes for the fitted curves. Including more complex residual structures, such as age-specific variances, as a check on the homogeneous variance assumption could prove useful.

In many socio-economic processes, there are jump points that are not smooth but have important substantive meaning. Adapting the proto-spline class to allow for uncertainty in the timing of the change-point could prove useful. Raftery (1994) explores this issue; integrating his approaches with ours is a research direction of interest.

Relaxing the Gaussian assumption is worth investigating, but we would limit this to forms that remain interpretable, such as parametric forms. One approach that has been suggested by several researchers is a latent class, or mixture formulation (see Clogg 1995, Banfield and Raftery 1993, Muthén and Shedden 1999, Roeder et al. 1999, Verbeke and Lesaffre 1997, Xu et al. 1996). Under this paradigm described earlier, individuals belong to *one* latent class, and then conditional on class membership they follow a certain structure. An important point is that the remaining structure could be flexibly captured in the proto-spline models just introduced; most models currently in use do not offer such directly interpretable covariance formulations.

In work in progress, we are examining diagnostics for these models in greater detail. Model selection criteria such as AIC (Akaike 1974) and BIC (Schwarz 1978) can be applied here. These are discussed in Vonesh and Chinchilli (1997) and Pinheiro et al. (1994). Recent extensions to the AIC discussed in Simonoff and Tsai (1999) appear to be especially promising in the context of these variance component models. An alternative to model selection is the use of Bayesian model averaging (Hoeting et al. 1999). A developed set of diagnostic techniques will add to our understanding of how each model captures and partitions variation.

APPENDIX: CONSTRUCTION OF CONFIDENCE INTERVALS

Confidence intervals for the model-based variances, such as the permanent variation, are constructed from the asymptotic covariance matrix of the model parameters. For proto-spline models, explicit forms for these covariance matrices are given in Scott and Handcock (2001). The construction begins by finding the variance associated with each point on the latent curve. Each curve is a linear combination of a set of basis functions, with the coefficients specified by the model parameters. If these coefficients are given by column vector $\ell_k = (\eta_{k1}, \ldots, \eta_{kT})^T$, the basis functions by matrix $Z = [\psi_1, \ldots, \psi_T]$, and the asymptotic covariance matrix of ℓ_k by H_k, then the resulting latent curve is given by $\phi_k = Z\ell_k$ and the covariance of $Z\ell_k$ is ZH_kZ^T. So the variance of the estimate of the curve $\hat{\phi}_k$ at each time point (and their covariances) are contained in the diagonals (and off-diagonal elements) of ZH_kZ^T. Confidence intervals for the permanent variance (the squared value of the curve estimate) at a particular time point can be constructed via a delta-method approximation involving that same asymptotic covariance matrix.[22]

REFERENCES

Akaike, Hirotugu. 1974. "A New Look at the Statistical Model Identification." *IEEE Transactions on Automatic Control* 19:716–23.

Altham, Patricia M. E. 1984. "Improving the Precision of Estimation by Fitting a Model." *Journal of the Royal Statistical Society*, Ser. B, 46:118–19.

Arminger, Gerhard, and Michael E. Sobel. 1990. "Pseudo-Maximum Likelihood Estimation of Mean and Covariance Structures with Missing Data." *Journal of American Statistical Association* 85:195–203.

Baker, Michael. 1997. "Growth-Rate Heterogeneity and the Covariance Structure of Life-Cycle Earnings." *Journal of Labor Economics* 15:338–75.

Banfield, Jeffrey D., and Adrian E. Raftery. 1993. "Model-Based Gaussian and Non-Gaussian Clustering." *Biometrics* 49:803–21.

Beale, E., and Roderick Little. 1975. "Missing Values in Multivariate Analysis." *Journal of the Royal Statistical Society*, Ser. B, 37:129–45.

Bernhardt, Annette, Martina Morris, Mark Handcock, and Marc Scott. 1997. "Work and Opportunity in the Post-Industrial Labor Market. Final report to the Russell Sage and Rockefeller Foundations." Institute on Education and the Economy, Columbia University, New York.

Box, George, and Gwilym Jenkins. 1976. *Time Series Analysis: Forecasting and Control*. San Francisco: Holden-Day.

Brumback, Babette A. 1996. "Statistical Models for Hormone Data." Ph.D. dissertation, University of California, Berkeley.

Brumback, Babette A., and John A. Rice. 1998. "Smoothing Spline Models for the Analysis of Nested and Crossed Samples of Curves." *Journal of American Statistical Association* 93:961–76.

Clogg, Clifford C. 1995. Latent Class Models. Pp. 311–59 in Gerhard Arminger, Clifford C. Clogg, and Michael E. Sobel, eds., *Handbook of Statistical Modeling for the Social and Behavioral Sciences*. New York: Plenum Press.

[22]Confidence intervals for extra-mean variation for random quadratic models involve a slightly different calculation and will not be discussed in this paper.

Crouchley, R., and R. B. Davies. 1999. "A Comparison of Population-Averaged and Random-Effect Models for the Analysis of Longitudinal Count Data with Baseline Information." *Journal of the Royal Statistical Society*, Ser. A, 162:331–47.

Danziger, Sheldon, and Peter Gottschalk, eds. 1993. *Uneven Tides: Rising Inequality in America.* New York: Russell Sage Foundation.

De Boor, Carl. 1998. *A Practical Guide to Splines*, vol. 27. New York: Springer-Verlag.

Devlin, Susan J., and Ramanathan Gnanadesikan, and Jon R. Kettenring. 1981. "Robust Estimation of Dispersion Matrices and Principal Components." *Journal of the American Statistical Association* 76:354–62.

Diggle, Peter J., Kung-Yee Liang, and Scott L. Zeger. 1994. *Analysis of Longitudinal Data*. Oxford, England: Oxford University Press.

Gottschalk, Peter, and Robert Moffit. 1994. "The Growth of Earnings Instability in the US Labor Market." *Brookings Papers on Economic Activity* 2:217–72.

Green, Peter J., and Bernard W. Silverman. 1994. *Nonparametric Regression and Generalized Linear Models: A Roughness Penalty Approach.* London: Chapman and Hall.

Haider, Steven. 1996. "Earnings Instability and Earnings Inequality in the United States: 1967–1991." University of Michigan unpublished manuscript.

Hoeting, Jennifer A., David Madigan, Adrian E. Raftery, and Chris T. Volinsky. 1999. "Bayesian Model Averaging." *Statistical Science* 14, no. 4:382–417.

Hu, Frank B., Jack Goldberg, Donald Hedeker, Brian R. Flay, and Mary A. Pentz. 1998. "Comparison of Population-Averaged and Subject-Specific Approaches for Analyzing Repeated Binary Outcomes." *American Journal of Epidemiology* 147, no. 7:694–703.

Jain, Pawan K., Om P. Ahuja, and Khalil Ahmad. 1995. *Functional Analysis*. New York: Wiley.

Jolliffe, Ian T. 1986. *Principal Component Analysis*. New York: Springer-Verlag.

Jones, M. C. 1990. "Serial Correlation or Random Subject Effects?" *Communications in Statistics*, Ser. B, 19, no. 3:1105–23.

Levy, Frank, and Robert Murnane. 1992. "U.S. Earnings Levels and Earnings Inequality: A Review of Recent Trends and Proposed Explanations." *Journal of Economic Literature* 30:1333–81.

Liang, Kung-Yee, and Scott L. Zeger. 1986. "Longitudinal Data Analysis Using Generalized Linear Models." *Biometrika* 73:13–22.

Lindstrom, Mary J. 1995. "Self-modelling with Random Shift and Scale Parameters and a Free-knot Spline Shape Function." *Statistics in Medicine*, 14, 2009–2021.

Locantore, N., J. S. Marron, D. G. Simpson, N. Tripoli, J. T. Zhang, and K. L. Cohen. 1999. "Robust Principal Component Analysis for Functional Data." *Test* 8:1–73.

Longford, Nicholas T. 1993. *Random Coefficient Models*. New York: Oxford.

McCulloch, Charles E. 1997. "Maximum Likelihood Algorithms for Generalized Linear Mixed Models." *Journal of the American Statistical Association* 92:162–70.

McMurrer, Daniel, and Isabel Sawhill. 1998. *Getting Ahead: Economic and Social Mobility in America*. Washington: Urban Institute Press.

Meredith, William, and John Tisak. 1990. "Latent Curve Analysis." *Psychometrika* 55:105–22.

Muthén, Bengt, and Kerby Shedden. 1999. "Finite Mixture Modeling with Mixture Outcomes Using the EM Algorithm." *Biometrics* 55:463–69.

Ogden, R. Todd. 1996. *Essential Wavelets for Statistical Applications and Data Analysis*. Boston: Birkhäuser.

Pinheiro, José C., Douglas M. Bates, and Mary J. Lindstrom. 1994. "Model Building for Nonlinear Mixed Effects Models." Technical Report 931, Department of Statistics, University of Wisconsin, Madison.

Prentice, Ross L. 1988. "Correlated Binary Regression with Covariates Specific to Each Binary Observation." *Biometrics* 44:1033–48.

Raftery, Adrian E. 1994. "Change Point and Change Curve Modeling in Stochastic Processes and Spatial Statistics." *Journal of Applied Statistical Science* 1:403–24.

Ramsay, James O., and Bernard W. Silverman. 1997. *Functional Data Analysis*. New York: Springer.

Raykov, Tenko. 2000. "Modeling Simultaneously Individual and Group Patterns of Ability Growth or Decline." Pp. 127–46 in *Modeling Longitudinal and Multilevel Data*, edited by Todd D. Little, Kai U. Schnabel, and Jürgen Baumert. Mahwah, NJ: Lawrence Erlbaum.

Rice, John A., and Bernard W. Silverman. 1991. "Estimating the Mean and Covariance Structure Nonparametrically When the Data Are Curves." *Journal of the Royal Statistical Society*, Ser. B, 53:233–43.

Roeder, Kathryn, Kevin G. Lynch, and Daniel S. Nagin. 1999. "Modeling Uncertainty in Latent Class Membership: A Case Study in Criminology." *Journal of the American Statistical Association* 94:766–76.

Schwarz, Gideon. 1978. "Estimating the Dimension of a Model." *Annals of Statistics* 6:461–64.

Scott, Marc A. 1998. "Statistical Models for Heterogeneity in the Labor Market." Ph.D. dissertation, New York University.

Scott, Marc A., and Mark S. Handcock. 2001. "Latent Curve Covariance Models for Longitudinal Data." Working Paper, Center for Statistics and the Social Sciences, University of Washington, Seattle.

Searle, Shayle R., George Casella, and Charles E. McCulloch. 1992. *Variance Components*. New York: Wiley.

Simonoff, Jeffrey S., and Chih-Ling Tsai. 1999. "Semiparametric and Additive Model Selection Using an Improved AIC Criterion." *Journal of Computational and Graphical Statistics* 8:22–40.

Topel, Robert H., and Michael P. Ward. 1992. "Job Mobility and the Careers of Young Men." *Quarterly Journal of Economics* 107:439–79.

Verbeke, Geert, and Emmanuel Lesaffre. 1997. "A Linear Mixed-Effects Models with Heterogeneity in the Random-Effects Population." *Journal of American Statistical Association* 91:217–21.

Vonesh, Edward F., and Vernon M. Chinchilli. 1997. *Linear and Nonlinear Models for the Analysis of Repeated Measurements*. New York: Marcel Dekker.

Xu, Weichun, Donald Hedeker, and Viswanathan Ramakrishnan. 1996. "Mixtures in Random-Effects Regression Models." Unpublished manuscript, School of Public Health, University of Illinois at Chicago.

Zeger, Scott L., and Kung-Yee Liang. 1986. "Longitudinal Data Analysis for Discrete and Continuous Outcomes." *Biometrics* 42:121–30.

7

THE COHESIVENESS OF BLOCKS IN SOCIAL NETWORKS: NODE CONNECTIVITY AND CONDITIONAL DENSITY

*Douglas R. White**
Frank Harary†

This study shows several ways that formal graph theoretic statements map patterns of network ties into substantive hypotheses about social cohesion. If network cohesion is enhanced by multiple connections between members of a group, for example, then the higher the global minimum of the number of independent paths that connect every pair of nodes in the network, the higher the social cohesion. The cohesiveness of a group is also measured by the extent to which it is not disconnected by removal of 1, 2, 3, ..., k actors. Menger's Theorem proves that these two measures are equivalent. Within this graph theoretic framework, we evaluate various concepts of cohesion and establish the validity of a pair of related measures:

This paper was prepared under NSF grant #BCS-9978282, "Longitudinal Network Studies and Predictive Cohesion Theory" (White 1999), and revised with Santa Fe Institute support from John Padgett. It provides the foundational theoretical basis on which the hypotheses of the large-scale longitudinal network studies of the research grant are based. We thank James Moody and anonymous *American Journal of Sociology* reviewers of Moody and White (2000) and White et al. (2001) for a great many useful comments and suggestions made in early revisions of this paper. Two anonymous reviewers of *Sociological Methodology* made extensive suggestions for intermediate and final revisions, and we are indebted to Phil Bonacich and Santa Fe Institute participants in the Working Group on Co-Evolution of Markets and the State—John Padgett, Michael Heaney, Walter Powell, David Stark, Sander van der Leeuw and Sanjay Jain—for useful commentary.

*University of California, Irvine
†New Mexico State University

1. *Connectivity—the minimum number k of its actors whose removal would not allow the group to remain connected or would reduce the group to but a single member—measures the social cohesion of a group at a general level.*
2. *Conditional density measures cohesion on a finer scale as a proportion of ties beyond that required for connectivity k over the number of ties that would force it to k* + 1.

Calibrated for successive values of k, these two measures combine into an aggregate measure of social cohesion, suitable for both small- and large-scale network studies. Using these measures to define the core of a new methodology of cohesive blocking, we offer hypotheses about the consequences of cohesive blocks for social groups and their members, and explore empirical examples that illustrate the significance, theoretical relevance, and predictiveness of cohesive blocking in a variety of substantively important applications in sociology.

Solidarity is a generic concept encompassing multiple ways that individuals coalesce into groups. We can distinguish several kinds of bonds that contribute to solidarity: *members to group*; *members to group norms*; *members to leaders*; and *members to members*. We can conceive of these bonds as having *forms* such as moral rules, norms, incentives, or contexts, and *contents* such as various types of relationships. Form and content, social "facts" of relationships versus norms that might govern them, and other oppositions are not removed from one another. Rather, they are performed, enacted, and understood in networks of interactions. Hence, it is useful to partition solidarity into its *ideational* and *relational* components (Fararo and Doreian 1998), the former referring to the psychological identification of members within a collectivity,[1] and the latter to the connections among the collectivity's members, which can be visualized as graphs.

Within the relational component of solidarity, we can further distinguish two aspects of the form of relations of a group that help to hold it together. What we call *cohesion* is the contribution made by (adding or subtracting) individual members of a group, together with their ties, to

[1]What we call *attachment* of members to groups often involves complex interactions among psychological, dispositional, moral, normative, and contextual concerns, and they are often for this reason difficult to measure and to depict as graphs. To simplify measurement, researchers often try to elicit from individuals indicators of their attachments to groups. The same is true of what we call *adherence to leadership*. Common research questions in this domain are: What are the attractive or charismatic qualities of leaders (or attractions *to* their followers) that create weaker or stronger many-to-one ties or commitments?

holding it together. What we call *adhesion* (edge cohesion) is the contribution made to holding a group together—keeping membership constant—by (adding or subtracting) ties between its members.[2] We ask one of the fundamental questions of sociology: How and when do groups, norms, leaders, and commitments emerge out of cohesive clusters? Alternatively, we can ask: How and when does the formation of groups and the emergence of leaders lead to the transformation of cohesive clusters? Because cohesion often spills over the boundaries of formal groups, dynamic reconfiguration of groups and alliances can be studied in the interplay between these two questions.[3] Alternately, as different groups emerge and overlap, and groups interact at another level of organization, dynamic reconfigurations of cohesiveness can be studied, oscillating between different levels involving questions about top-down and bottom-up effects.[4]

The *content* of ties is also important to how we view the dynamics of cohesion and group transformations. At the simplest level (Harary 1953), negative ties tend to repel and positive ties attract. We are principally concerned here with positive dyadic bonds and the concept and measurement of cohesion as a relational component of social solidarity, where the ties in question are ones that can bond pairs of people in nonexclusive ways that could constitute a basis for positive relations that hold a group together. We do not try to deal here with more subtle refinements of content as they might affect solidarity, but we try to isolate the contribution of different structural forms of connection, given the simplifying assumption of relatively homogeneous "positive" content of ties. The model of cohesion presented here would not be appropriate, for example, if the relation under study was that of conflict or antagonism, where "negative" ties occur (see Harary 1953).

Section I develops a series of assertions of increasing precision that provide intuitive foundations for sociological models of cohesion

[2]In the way we will operationalize these two concepts, they will be closely related, but cohesion will turn out to be the stronger measure since removal of individuals from a group automatically removes their ties, while removal of ties does not entail removal of individuals.

[3]In heterarchic systems, such as a government that derives its legitimacy from "We the people" to guarantee empowerment against intrusions at intermediate levels (Morowitz 2000:11–12), multiple relations contend for and oscillate in their salience for regulatory processes. Such oscillations include centralized systems that are hierarchically organized from upper to lower levels. Alternatives include decentralized systems that are emergent, often hierarchically, from lower to upper levels.

[4]Powell, White, Koput, and Owen-Smith (2001) develop analysis for bottom-up effects in the emergence of new structural forms in collaborative networks among biotechnical firms, for example, as distinct from the top-down effects of co-evolving government policies and agencies affecting the biotech industry.

and, secondarily, adhesion. Sections I.B and I.C provide some general expectations and hypotheses about cohesion and adhesion in terms of their sociological antecedents and consequences. We show the significance of defining structural cohesion as resistance-to-taking-a-group-apart and path cohesion as stick-togetherness (our definitions 1.1.2. and 1.2.2) and discuss the sociological implications of these two facets of cohesion, and similarly for two parallel aspects of adhesion. We show how these two aspects meld in each case into a single equivalent concept that defines the boundaries of social groups at different levels of cohesion or adhesion. Section I.D shows the utility of defining density and closeness of ties within bounded cohesive blocks, which will lead to a later section (III) on conditional density. Section II provides the graph theoretic foundations for concepts and measurements of cohesion and adhesion, and gives the definitions needed for the proofs of equivalence of the twin aspects of structural and path cohesion or adhesion. Section III defines conditional density and a scalable measure of cohesion that combines connectivity and conditional density within nested patterns of subgroup cohesion and subgroup heterogeneity. Section IV examines a case study of a factional dispute in a karate club to exemplify our measures of both cohesion and adhesion, and shows how it is useful as well to take into account relative density and closeness within the bounded context of connectivity subsets. Section V describes how the proposed measures of cohesion have been tested in larger scale sociological studies than the karate example, and Section VI summarizes and concludes our study.

I. TOWARD SOCIOLOGICAL MODELS OF COHESION AND ADHESION

A. Some Basic Intuitions and Concepts

The following series of sociological assertions may help to give the reader some intuitive underpinnings for the models of cohesion and adhesion that follow in Section II. Intuitively, cohesion begins with the role of individuals in holding a group together:

1. *A group is cohesive to the extent that its members possess connections to others within the group, ones that hold it together.*

If cohesion begins with individuals who are connected, higher levels of group cohesiveness should entail that the removal of some one (two, three. . .) actor(s) should not disconnect the group. Simmel (1908 [1950:123]) noted the fundamental difference in this respect between a solitary dyad and a triad:

> The social structure [of the dyad] rests immediately on the one and on the other of the two, and the secession of either would destroy the whole . . . as soon, however, as there is a sociation [clique] of three, a group continues to exist even in case one of the members drops out.

We identify this as the first of two facets of cohesion:

1.1. *A group is cohesive to the extent that it is resistant to being pulled apart by removal of its members.*

Generalizing Simmel's intuition as a structural feature of cohesion, we introduce the following definition:

1.1.1. A group is *structurally cohesive* to the extent that it is resistant to being pulled apart by the removal of a subset of members.

The concept of the robustness of connections under removal of members of a group is closely related to the graph theoretic concept of connectivity given in Section II. There we review the graph theoretic foundations of cohesion and adhesion. Harary et al. (1965) anticipated the approach of utilizing connectivity as a measure of cohesiveness. Wasserman and Faust (1994:115–17) cite his definition of connectivity (Harary 1969) as one way to measure the cohesion of a graph, but they do not apply it to finding cohesive subgroups. White (1998; White et al. 2001) develops the latter idea, and Moody and White (2000) provide and apply an algorithm for measuring maximal subsets of nodes in a graph at different levels of connectivity. We implement this approach here, defining the structural aspect of the cohesion of a group in quantitative terms as follows (the formal exposition here parallels Moody and White):

1.1.2. A group's *structural cohesion* is equal to the minimum number of actors who, if removed from the group, would disconnect the group.

This is the minimum number k of its actors whose removal would not allow the group to remain connected or would reduce the group to a single member. It allows hierarchies of cohesive blocks to be identified. At the highest level, for a clique with n members, all but one member must be removed to get an isolate, so the structural cohesion is defined as $n - 1$. Cohesiveness may be viewed as "the resistance of a group to disruptive forces" (Gross and Martin 1952:553), and structural cohesion provides a relational basis for a group to resist disruption by defection or removal of members.

If resistance to being pulled apart is an aspect of cohesiveness, however, we must pay equal attention to a second, more integrative aspect of cohesion commonly discussed in the literature.[5] This integrative aspect is emphasized in such definitions of cohesiveness as "the forces holding the individuals within the groupings in which they are" (Moreno and Jennings 1937:371); "the total field of forces that act on members to remain in the group" (Festinger et al. 1950:164); and "a dynamic process that is reflected in the tendency for a group to stick together and remain united in pursuit of its goals and objectives" (Carron 1982:124).

This second aspect of the cohesive integration of a social group can be defined and measured—independently of robustness to disruption by removal or defection of members—by the number of distinct ways that members of a group are related. Cohesion increases, for example, when members have multiplex bonds, such as two people who are classmates, friends, and neighbors. Two people may also be connected by multiple independent paths that have no intermediate members in common. We identify such possibilities in the second of two related facets of cohesion:

1.2. *A group is cohesive to the extent that pairs of its members have multiple social connections, direct or indirect, but within the group, that pull it together.*

The integrative aspect of group cohesion that we will examine is the number of independent paths linking pairs of members. We define this aspect of cohesion as follows:

1.2.1. A group is *path cohesive* to the extent that its members have a multiplicity of independent paths between them, *within the group*, that pull it together.

[5]French (1941:370), for example, discussed how a group exists as a balance between "cohesive" and "disruptive" forces, including responses to disruptive forces.

This can be defined quantitatively as follows:

1.2.2. A group's *path cohesion* is equal to the minimum number of its independent paths taken over all pairs of members.

When we define structural and path cohesion formally, as we do in Section II, one of the purposes of the formal language of graphs is to derive as a theoretical result or mathematical proof that the two graph theoretic concepts of path (1.2.2: stick-togetherness) and structural (1.1.2: won't-pull-apart) cohesion are equivalent. This is important to sociological theory, and the mathematics can contribute at the conceptual level to sociological explanation, because it demonstrates that two measurement constructs—each of which is central to the study of social cohesion—can be reduced to one by virtue of their formal equivalence. We do not claim that these are the only constructs relevant to understanding cohesion, but simply that when our substantive and intuitive sociological conceptions converge on these two constructs of structural and path cohesion, they are formally equivalent. Both measures that are thereby unified are highly relevant to the relational component of group solidarity. Although the measurement of connectivities or node-independent paths in social networks is a complex problem computationally, accurate approximation techniques are now available (e.g., White and Newman 2001) for large networks.

Besides the removal of members, the only other way in which a group is vulnerable to disconnection is by removal of ties between members. This possibility defines what we call *adhesion* within a group (which is thus a logically weaker concept than cohesion because removal of individuals is excluded). We arrive at a definition of adhesion by elaborating a series of sociological assertions that run parallel to those about cohesion, except that here the members of a group are held constant, and we consider, between group members, only the ties, whose removal can separate the group:

2. *A group is adhesive to the extent that its members' ties hold it together.*

Facet 1

2.1. *A group is adhesive to the extent that it is resistant to being pulled apart by removal of ties between members.*

2.1.1. A group is *structurally adhesive* to the extent that it is resistant to being pulled apart by removal of a subset of its ties between members.

Facet 2

2.2. *A group is adhesive to the extent that the ties between its members or indirect connections within the group pull it together.*

To count the number of such ties or indirect connections, we refer in this context to paths between two members within a group as being disjoint (technically speaking: edge-disjoint) if none of the dyadic ties that make up the respective paths are the same:

2.2.1. A group is *path adhesive* to the extent that it is held together by (edge-) disjoint paths between each pair of members.

Our two facets of adhesion can be precisely defined as follows:

2.1.2. A group's *structural adhesion* is equal to the minimum number of direct links between group members that, if removed, would disconnect the group.
2.2.2. A group's *path adhesion* is equal to the minimum number of (edge-) disjoint paths among different pairs of members.

Thus we define group adhesion to refer to stick-togetherness/don't-pull-apart in relation to the edges or paths that connect the group but holding constant the members of the group itself.

High adhesion may be obtained without a concomitant rise in cohesion by subgroups that link through one or a few central nodes. Figure 1 gives two examples where in each case the cohesion is minimal (each group is vulnerable to disconnection by removal of a single member) but adhesion is significantly higher (three ties must be removed to disconnect any of the members of these two groups). In the first example there is a structure of many small cliques that have one member in common (e.g., a common "leader" unifying the cliques). In the second, there is the same number of small cliques, but the central member who links them is not a member of the cliques. The examples differ in the structure of cohesion in the subgroups (overlapping versus nonoverlapping cohesive subgroups). The converse, high cohesion with low adhesion, is impossible by defini-

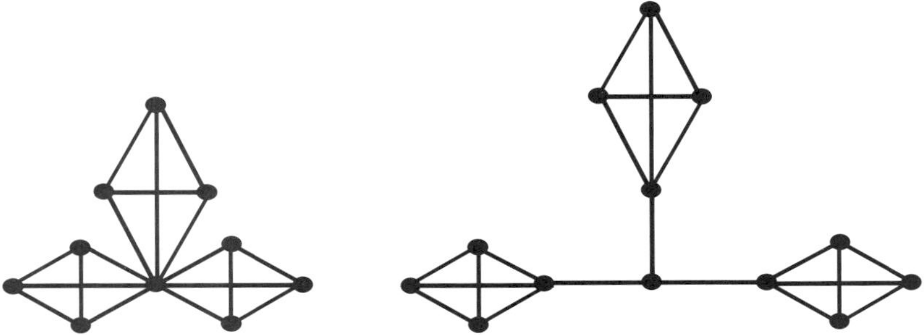

FIGURE 1. Two graphs with low cohesion (one node-removal separates each graph) but high adhesion (a minimum of three edge-removals separates each graph).

tion, which conveys the sense in which adhesion is a weaker measure of cohesion, or perhaps a measure of something quite different, necessary but not sufficient for cohesion.

Our graph theoretic formalization in Section II takes up the two facets of structural and path cohesion, then those of adhesion, shows the mathematical equivalence of these two facets for both cohesion and adhesion and how cohesion and adhesion are mathematically related. Before doing so, under the heading of hypotheses, we examine some of the implications of these two concepts for group structure and social processes. We will not consider the concepts of attachment-to-group, adherence to leadership, or adherence to norms, but these themes might be developed by treating the group, leader, or normative elements and constructs, as distinguished nodes, and investigating individual-to-group or follower-to-leader ties within the broader network, or one- and two-mode networks of individual and normative elements.

B. Hypotheses About Cohesion

Once we develop a graph theoretic methodology that provides formal measures for the intuitive concepts of cohesion, it will be possible in the long run and over many studies to evaluate the social consequences at the group and individual level that are thought to follow from different aspects of cohesion. Differences in cohesiveness, including finer levels of differences in density within each group (see Section I.D), should have recurrent antecedents and/or predictive consequences for social groups and their members across different social contexts.

Our goal here is to develop methodology and not to test hypotheses, so we will not attempt to define relevant measures for possible consequences, at the group or individual level, of our measures of cohesion, but some relevant ideas and examples may be briefly sketched. At the level of formal theory, for example, if the relevant units of time or cost are normalized for the networks of two groups (such as longevity of group members, time-decay of ties, etc.), it is a testable hypothesis that the network with higher structural cohesion (other things being equal) will, in a set period of time, be less likely to separate into two disconnected groups. Formal theory might be developed to predict outcomes such as relative stability of groups, or the relative duration of a group as a social configuration.

Similarly, if information transmission in a network is noisy or unreliable, then compensatory gains in path cohesion should give an initial rapid benefit from higher capacity to transmit redundant information. Further benefits will at some point begin to have diminishing marginal returns, analogous to the declining marginal benefits to reliable measurement of averaging more independent measures of the same variable. This, and the fact that adding links in a network typically has a cost, leads to the hypotheses that, when transmission is unreliable (or quality decays with distance), measurable benefits to gains in connectivity will be high initially, but growth of cohesion at higher levels will tend to be self-limiting because of a rising cost/benefit ratio. As compared to suboptimal levels of cohesion in a network in this context, near-optimal levels are hypothesized to occur at very low densities for large networks and, given sufficient stability, to predict higher congruence in information transmittal, higher levels of consensus among group members, more rapid emergence of group norms, and higher levels of effective coordination in mobilizing group action or exerting group-level influence. Relations for which path cohesion might be especially predictive of relevant outcome variables are those that serve as conduits for items that are transmitted in social networks, such as information, gossip, disease, or favors or goods exchanged.

Engineering applications of network concepts of transmission generally emphasize designing networks so that distance decay in signal transmission is compensated by intermittent amplifiers that dampen noise and boost coherent signals. It is often assumed by social theorists who utilize concepts of transmission or flow in social networks that such amplifiers are absent in naturally occurring social interactions. The feedback circuits required for amplification, however, are found in cohesive blocks. Path cohesive blocks of such networks thus might be hypothesized to serve as natural amplifiers in social networks, boosting signal by creating internal patterns of coherence. For the phenomenon of network externalities in which a product's value is enhanced by additional users, the early exponential rise in adoption may be accelerated by path cohesion, or intermittently decelerated if the cohesion is concentrated in distinct pockets.[6]

The Internet is an example of a type of network in which redundancies facilitate transmission and the emergence of cohesive pockets and hierarchies of users and sites. Cohesion, not adhesion, was the object of the packet-switching transmission design through multiple pathways.[7] The physical elements of the ARPANET/Internet system, such as links among servers, also required cohesion and not just adhesion. At a third level, links between Web pages, cohesion has been an emergent phenomenon of potential benefit to users.

Path cohesion also operates as resistance to a group's being pulled apart through bonding effects that are independent of distance rather than subject to distance decay. It is k times more difficult to break apart two nodes if they have k independent chains of connections than it is to break them apart if they have a single chain of connections. Hence higher path cohesion is an indicator of a group's resistance to being pulled apart even with transmission decay or its absence altogether.

Long-range bonding effects may operate through chains of connectivity even in sparse networks. Grannis (1998), for example, found that the best predictor of contiguous zones of homogeneity in urban neighborhoods is not closeness of ties or walking or driving distance, but chaining of neighbor relations along residential streets. These bonding chains do not imply that members of the homogeneous sets have a high density of neighbor relations, or high door-to-door transmission rates, but that they have chains of neighboring by which members of the homogeneous group

[6] In this case, however, connectivity theory would suggest a critical threshold where the rise in added value goes from linear (because component sizes grow linearly with adoption up to this threshold) to exponential (because after the threshold is reached, sizes of component and/or cohesive sets begin to grow exponentially), to dampened marginal returns.

[7] If the designers of ARPANET, the military forerunner of the multiple-path Internet packet technology, had only been concerned with adhesion, the system might have been designed around a single central hub that would have left it vulnerable to attack.

are neighbors of neighbors of neighbors, etc., without constraint on path length. Homogeneity tends to be transitive through these local bonds rather than decaying with distance. Grannis (personal communication) hypothesized that structural cohesion contributes to neighborhood homogeneity but did not test the hypothesis directly.

For individuals, membership in one or more groups with differing levels of structural and path cohesion might also have predictive consequences for levels of attachment and participation in the group or the larger community in which the individual is embedded.

Are cohesive blocks in social networks equivalent to what Granovetter (1973, 1983) identified as "strong" as opposed to "weak" ties—namely, ties of high multiplexity where dyadic interaction is frequent? If strong ties tend to cluster due to greater transitivity than weak ties, structural cohesion within clique-like structures would follow as a consequence. The two concepts are not equivalent, however, and structural cohesion does not imply such transitivity. It is an open question as to whether the relevant circumstances in which weak ties are more effective than strong ones for network reachability include effects of structural cohesion.

C. Hypotheses About Adhesion

Structural and path adhesiveness in social networks is not our primary concern here, but hypotheses about the effects of adhesion should be considered alongside those concerning cohesion. Higher levels of adhesion imply more channels of connections between pairs of members of a group, even if the channels are not strictly parallel but may run through the same (e.g., central) nodes. High adhesion networks with low cohesion (e.g., Figure 1), like graph centralization, may lead to vulnerability of strategic points of control in social networks.[8] Hence, adhesion is a direct measure of the potential for flow between nodes, without considering the potential for congestion or vulnerability through central nodes. Centralized polities and

[8] When adhesion and cohesion in a graph are minimal, but the graph is connected, and the maximum distance in the graph is two, the graph is maximally centralized as an egocentric star. In general, high adhesion relative to low cohesion within a social group implies that the network is relatively centralized, but the pattern of centralization may be one of a central node connecting a number of cohesive outliers. The relation between centrality measures and graph theoretic measures of adhesion and cohesion (edge and node connectivity) is complex and deserves separate treatment.

bureaucracies, for example, may require high adhesion networks if the latter entail the potential for establishing control points internal to social groups.

Social fragmentation is a domain where adhesive groupings have been used to hypothesize about lines of cleavage, given the presence of internal conflict within a previously solidary group. Zachary (1975, 1977) argued that when conflicts between rival leaders within a group are sufficiently intense, the group would segment through dissolution of the minimum number of links needed to separate into two. Anticipating our analysis of this case in Section IV, we take issue with this adhesion-based hypothesis for several reasons. First, the idea that a minimum number of edges can be removed to disconnect a graph does not imply that a unique set of edges will be identified by this criterion. The graph in Figure 2, where nodes 1 and 2 represent two leaders in conflict, helps to illustrate the critique. The removal of pairs of edges a, b will disconnect 1 from 2, but so will removal of the two edges c, d, or the edges e, f, or e, h. Second, we would argue that the persons who are more cohesively linked to leaders, with closeness of ties as a secondary factor, are more likely to remain as members of their respective factions. Hence in Figure 2 persons 3 and 5 will be more likely to remain with 1 and persons 4 and 6 with leader 2. This illustrates that minimum edge-removal is not the only way to effectively divide the group. Further, there is a single node in Figure 2 whose removal would disconnect the graph. Hence the social pressure to take sides might be greatest for this person, node 4, who is also the only member of the two most cohesive sets, 1-3-4-5 versus 2-4-6, each of which is circled in Figure 2. On the basis of cohesiveness and tie density, we would expect that person 4 would remain in leader 2's faction, hence expected to decouple from 3 and from 5 rather than from 2 and 6. The end result is the same as edge

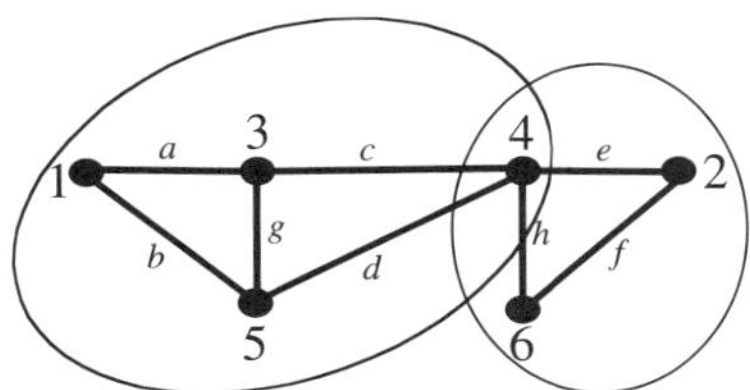

FIGURE 2. Cohesive blocks in a factional dispute between leaders 1 and 2.

removal, in which nodes remain and edges are removed. We would argue, however, that the underlying social dynamics of segmentation are more likely to involve the agency of individual decision-makers, hence favoring hypotheses about effects of cohesion, closeness, and the density of cohesive blocks rather than effects of adhesion, or minimum removal of edges. Since edges do not autoregulate independently of the agents they connect, we might hypothesize that while cohesive blocks are likely to influence the development of norms and sanctions about what kinds of edges with outsiders are favored or disfavored, adhesive subsets that are not also cohesive are less likely to do so.

D. Hypotheses that Integrate Other Aspects of Cohesion: Conditional Density and Other Variables

Given a first level of structural and path cohesion at which graphs can be ordered by their invulnerability to disruption (connectivity) and inversely to the ties that hold them together (equivalent definitions 1.1.2 and 1.2.2), additional finer levels of cohesion can be ordered by density, closeness of ties, and other factors.[9] We can define a strict measure of conditional density (Section III) because a certain density and minimum number of ties within a group are already implied by its level of connectivity.[10] Within the boundaries of cohesive blocks established by structural and path cohesion, our graph theoretic formalization in Section II allows us to describe a finer level of cohesion reflecting aspects such as density, that make a secondary contribution to cohesion.[11] At this second level of cohesion, a *conditional definition* related to cohesion is one based on a feature of cohesion that lends itself to a finer level of measurement, where the feature has a necessary minimum and maximum value associated with the level of structural and path cohesion, and is measured within the bounded cohesive set associated with that level.

Conditional density will be a primary focus of our development of a scalable measure of cohesion that takes an integer value k for a certain

[9] We shift here to refer to the equivalent concepts of structural cohesion and path cohesion simply as "cohesion." Our assertion in doing so is that these concepts capture two of the most important facets of many-to-many ties among clusters of individuals as they form into cohesive blocks. Throughout this section, we are concerned with how other variables also contribute to cohesion, with density as a case in point.

[10] This is not the case for multiplexity (multiple types of ties between group members) or for frequency of interaction between members of a group, which can vary independently of structural and path cohesion.

[11] This could also be done for diameter, closeness of connections, or adhesion as secondary aspects of cohesion.

level of structural and path cohesion for a uniquely defined subgroup of a social network, plus a decimal value (between 0 and 1) for an added contribution to the robustness of cohesion within the group made by within-group density. It provides a useful example of how complementary aspects of cohesion can be measured. These ideas toward a general methodology for the cohesive blocking of social networks must remain intuitive until conditional density is given formal explication in Section III.

One purpose of our graph theoretical formalization of the concepts of structural and path cohesion and conditional density is to show the advantages of a scalable aggregate measure of cohesion in social groups over other approaches that use relative densities of different clusters of nodes in social networks to try to identify the boundaries of cohesive social groups. Clique-finding algorithms, for example, give a unique inventory of cohesive clusters whose relative density is maximal, but the denser regions of social networks will often exhibit many intersecting cliques. The intersections among cliques form a lattice that typically defines a welter of intersecting social boundaries (Freeman 1996). As a density threshold for overlapping subgroups is relaxed, the overlap of subgroups rises exponentially. Forcing social group detection into a framework of mutual exclusion, on the other hand, makes little substantive sense when the concept of structural cohesion provides a meaningful framework for detecting and interpreting multiple group memberships. Structural and path cohesion are also able to detect more distributed patterns of cohesion in social networks than the unions of intersecting cliques.

In contrast to approaches that use a density criterion alone, different levels of structural and path cohesion will typically define hierarchical nesting of relatively few bounded cohesive subgroups, with severe limits on the overlap between hierarchical clusters, and the lower the level of cohesion, the less the overlap, hence high coherence of structure. Without offering detailed hypotheses,[12] but judging from case studies presented in Section IV or reviewed in Section V, along with those in Moody

[12]"Invisible colleges" in intellectual and citation networks, for example, are likely to be predicted from cohesive blocks and conditional densities, with downstream predictions from measures of cohesion to other group and individual level sociological effects. Similar models of effects might be applied to the idea of cohesive blocks of infectious sites in epidemiology. Identification of cohesive blocks and conditional densities in networks of economic exchange may provide a means of identifying cores and hierarchies in economic systems, or intensive markets for particular product clusters. In analysis of distributed cohesion in large networks such as these, the study of overlapping cliques will usually fail to identify cohesive sets that are anywhere near as large as those identified by structural and path cohesion.

and White (2000), we have reason to think that structural and path cohesion, along with additional density criteria within cohesive blocks, will be found to have important consequences for many different types of social groups, and that the graph theoretic concepts of cohesion and conditional density will find a useful explanatory niche in sociological theorizing. We would insert a caveat, however—namely, that consideration of the type of social relations being studied ought to guide how the concepts of adhesion and cohesion might be used, either separately or in combination with conditional density or other measures such as distance on shortest paths.

The emergence of trust in social groups, for example, might depend on both level of structural cohesion and the relative compactness of cohesive blocks—in terms of interpersonal distances on shortest paths—in the following way. In such groups, each individual A might receive information concerning each other group member B through a variety of paths that flow through distinct sets of intermediaries, and if the distances from A to B are sufficiently short, then A will be able to interpret these multiple independent sources of information about B's characteristics or identity as a person but as seen or filtered by a variety of others. This ability to compare independent perspectives on each of the others in the group is conducive to discriminations concerning trust and distrust. Not everyone in such groups will necessarily be trusted, but the conditions fostered by comparisons within such groups would provide a reliable basis for informed judgments as to trust. Hence more elaborated discriminations about trust (and hence the emergence of high-trust networks) might be expected to be more frequent within such groups.

As a hypothesized basis for interpersonal trust, the model of connectivity plus conditional density is one in which conditional distance also needs to be taken into account. As in the case of density, we can determine the minimum and maximum possible diameter of a group (the largest shortest-path distance for any two members) and the corresponding minimum and maximum average shortest-path distances between members, if we know the number of its members and the structural cohesion of the group. Watts (1999a, b) defines a "small world" as a large network with local clustering of ties but relatively low average distance between members.[13] We do not develop here a model of conditional distance analogous

[13] He shows that, for model networks with many nodes, high local clustering, and very high average distances between nodes, successive random rewiring of edges produces a small world rather quickly by creating shortcuts that shorten the average internode distances. Small worlds and conditional distance are well worth further investigation in relation to structural and path cohesion.

to that of conditional density, although it would be possible to do so. Rather, we note that within our model of conditional density, as edges are added randomly to a graph at a certain level of structural and path cohesion (thereby adding to conditional density), average internode distances will also fall quickly, resulting in the closeness of a "small world." Assuming that increases to conditional density for groups at a given level of structural cohesion occur by random addition of edges, conditional density becomes a proxy for conditional distance. Precise measures of conditional distance could be constructed to develop further the methodology of cohesive blocking, and our conditional density measure is instructive as to how one might proceed to do so.

II. THE GRAPH THEORETIC FOUNDATIONS OF COHESION AND ADHESION

For clarity of presentation in formalizing definitions and theorems about social cohesion and adhesion, a social relation hypothesized or assumed to contribute to cohesion or adhesion is considered as a graph. This allows us to equate the sociological definitions 1.1.2 and 1.2.2 for cohesion and 2.1.2 and 2.2.2 for adhesion with corresponding graph theoretic definitions of node and edge connectivity and, using the theorems of Menger (1927), to establish the equality between the two fundamental properties of cohesion and adhesion: resistance to being pulled apart (definitions 1.1.2 and 2.1.2), and stick-togetherness (1.2.2 and 2.2.2). Our goal in this section is to provide a formal methodology with appropriate graph theoretic terminology for the cohesive (or adhesive) blocking of social networks.

A *graph* $G = (V, E)$ consists of a set V of n *nodes* or *vertices* and a set E of m *edges* each joining a pair of nodes. We say G has *order* n and *size* m. The two nodes in each unordered pair (u,v) in E are said to be *adjacent* and constitute an edge that is *incident* with nodes u and v.[14] A *path* in G is an alternating sequence of distinct nodes and edges, beginning and ending with nodes, in which each edge is incident with its preceding and following node. A graph is *connected* if every pair of nodes is joined by a path. The *distance* between two nodes in G is the minimum

[14] A group with nonsymmetric relations is representable by a digraph $D = (V, A)$ consisting of a set V of *nodes* and a set A of *arcs* (directed edges) consisting of ordered pairs of nodes in V. A more complex but also more general derivation of our results regarding measures of cohesion, applicable to digraphs, was done by Harary, Norman and Cartwright (1965, ch. 5).

FIGURE 3. A disconnected graph with two components and three cliques, each a K_3.

size of a path of G that connects them. A *subgraph* of a graph G is a graph having all of its nodes and edges in G.

Since we regard a social group with nondirected interpersonal relations as part of a social network—as a subgraph of a larger graph—it is useful to provide some definitions about subgraphs. A set S is *maximal* (*minimal*) with respect to some property if no proper superset (subset) of S, containing more (fewer) elements than S, has the property but S does. A *component* of G is a maximal connected subgraph. A *complete graph* K_n of order n has every pair of nodes adjacent. A *clique* of a graph G is a maximal complete subgraph of G of order at least 3, hence a maximal subgraph K_n of G of order $n \geq 3$. Figure 3 shows a disconnected graph with two components and three cliques, each a K_3.

A. *Connectivity and Resistance to Pulling Apart by Removal of Nodes*

Two primary references on the node and edge connectivities of G, denoted by κ (kappa) and κ', respectively, are Harary (1969, ch. 5) and Tutte (1966). The *removal of a node* v from G leaves the subgraph $G - v$ that does not contain v or any of its incident edges. The (*node-*) *connectivity* $\kappa(G)$ is defined as the smallest number of nodes that when removed from a graph G leave a disconnected subgraph or a trivial subgraph.[15] The connectivity of a disconnected graph is zero as no nodes need to be removed; it is already not connected. Our definition 1.1.2 (section I.A) corresponds, in the terminology of graph theory, to that of the (node) connectivity of a graph. The *trivial graph* K_1 of one node and no edges ($n = 1$ and $m = 0$), or a disconnected graph, has cohesion 0. A solitary dyad has cohesiveness 1, a triad has 2, and a 4-clique has 3.

[15]This two-part definition is needed because no matter how many nodes are removed from a complete graph, the remaining subgraph remains complete and hence connected until the trivial graph with one node is obtained, and we do not remove it since its removal leaves emptiness. Thus connectivity is defined as $n - 1$ for the complete graph K_n.

FIGURE 4. A graph G that is a star.

A *cutnode* of a connected graph G is one whose removal results in a disconnected graph. A set S of nodes, edges or nodes and edges *separates* two nodes u,v in a connected graph G if u and v are in different components of $G - S$. A *node cut set* (*cutset*) is a set of nodes that separates a connected graph into two components. An *endnode* is one with a single incident edge. Its removal does not separate a graph. A *cycle* of order n nodes, designated C_n, is obtained from a path P_n with $n \geq 3$ by adding an edge joining its two endnodes. Two paths are (node-) *disjoint* or *node-independent* if they have no nodes in common other than their endnodes. A cycle containing nodes u,v entails that u and v are joined by two (node-) disjoint paths. A *tree* is a connected graph with no cycles, as in Figure 4. It is easy to see that each node in a tree is either an endnode or a cutnode.

A connected graph has connectivity 1 if and only if it has a cutnode. Thus a tree has connectivity 1 but a cycle does not; it has $\kappa = 2$. In Figure 5, which shows the eleven graphs of order 4, the first five graphs are disconnected (the first graph is *totally disconnected*), while the remaining six are connected and thus consist of a single component. The first two connected graphs are the trees of order four. The last is the complete graph K_4. The second of size 4 is the cycle C_4. The graph before C_4 has a cutnode and hence connectivity 1.

A maximal connected subgraph of G with connectivity $k > 0$ is called a *k-component* of G, with synonyms *component* for 1-component, *bicomponent* for 2-component (called a *cyclic component* by Scott 2000:105) and *tricomponent* for 3-component (called a *brick* by Harary and Kodama 1964). In Figure 5 graphs 5 and 8 have bicomponents of order 3—namely, triangles; the three graphs from C_4 to K_4 have bicomponents of order 4; and the complete graph K_4 is itself a tricomponent.

	Graph	Size	Number of Components	Connectivity	Type
1	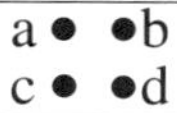 a• •b c• •d	0	4	0	
2		1	3	0	
3		2	2	0	
4		2	2	0	
5		3	2	0	
6	P_4 	3	1	1	Path (tree)
7	$K_{1,3}$ 	3	1	1	Star (tree)
8		4	1	1	
9	C_4 	4	1	2	Cycle
10	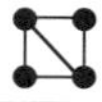	5	1	2	
11	K_4 	6	1	3	Complete graph

FIGURE 5. The eleven graphs of order 4.

A *block* of G is a maximal connected subgraph with no cutnodes (Harary 1969; Even 1979; Gibbons 1985).[16] The blocks of a graph give a partition of its edges. In Figure 5 there are three graphs that are single blocks: C_4 and the last two graphs. Graphs 2 and 5 contain a single block plus isolated nodes. There are two K_2 blocks in graphs 3 and 4 and two blocks in the graph before C_4. Three blocks are contained in each of the two trees of order 4, since each edge is a block. A block may contain a solitary dyad (not contained in a cycle) whereas a bicomponent is a block in which there are 3 or more nodes.

[16] Scott (2000:108,187 fn. 9), owing to the fact that block has another meaning in network analysis, uses the unnecessary and unfortunate term *knot*, easily confounded with the established term with another meaning in topology. Everett (1982a, 1982b) deals separately with both types of block.

A *cohesive block* of a graph G (a term we define here for use in sociological analyses of cohesion) is a k-component of G where the associated value of connectivity defines the cohesion of the block. We use *cohesivity* to refer to cohesive blocks of $\kappa = 2$ or more.[17] Some of the most commonly used network measures of cohesion, as we will show below, lack a guarantee of cohesivity, or even of connectedness. Within blocks of connectivity 1 will be nested more cohesive blocks, if any, of higher connectivity.[18] We may use the term *cohesive groups* to refer to substantive contexts where this concept has been applied to identify social groups on the basis of their network connectivities. We use *cohesive subsets* to refer to subgraphs of a graph G that may be cohesive in some respects but do not necessarily correspond to cohesive blocks defined by connectivities of subgraphs.

B. Edge Connectivity, and Resistance to Pulling Apart by Removal of Edges

As distinct from node removal, the *removal of an edge e* from G leaves the subgraph $G - e$ that contains all the nodes of G. Edge removal presents a lesser vulnerability to a graph being pulled apart than node removal, which removes all incident edges. An edge of a connected graph whose removal results in a disconnected graph is called a *bridge*.[19] The *removal of a set of edges* in G is the successive removal of each edge e in the set. An *edge-cutset* (or *edge-cut*) of a connected graph G is a set of edges whose removal results in a disconnected graph. The *edge connectivity* κ'

[17]The motivation for coining the technical term *cohesivity* is that blocks with $\kappa = 1$ are connected but easily disconnected by removal of single nodes, and thus only weakly structurally cohesive (Moody and White 2000). They are not really cohesive if we mean by that term "difficult to break apart" and "held together by coordinate bonds" rather than by adherence to single connecting nodes. Thus a group in which everyone was connected only to a single leader would lack cohesivity.

[18]To clarify the subtle difference between the graph theoretic and our sociological vocabulary once again, the *blocks* of order $n \geq 3$ are 2-component *cohesive blocks* (which may contain higher order k-components) while *blocks* of order $n = 2$ (single edges that are not contained in cycles) are contained within 1-component blocks that lack cohesivity. The *blocks* of a 1-component consist either of dyads not contained in cycles, or of proper subgraphs of the 1-component that have cohesivity (connectivity 2 or more). A 2-component is both a *block* and a *cohesive block*.

[19]Another characterization of a tree is that it is connected and that each edge is a bridge. A connected graph has $\kappa' = 1$ if and only if it has a bridge. Connected graphs 6, 7, and 8 in Figure 5 have bridges.

FIGURE 6. The bow tie graph. The lowest order of graph ($n = 5$) at which edge and node connectivities ($\kappa = 1$, $\kappa' = 2$) differ.

(G) of G is the smallest number of edges in an edge-cutset. Thus a disconnected graph has $\kappa' = 0$. Our definition 2.1.2 (Section I.A) corresponds to that of edge connectivity.

Edge connectivity does not differ from node connectivity for the graphs in Figure 5, where both types of connectivity are equal: zero for the first five graphs; one for the next three; two for the ninth and tenth, and three for K_4. Only at order 5 do node and edge connectivity of graphs begin to diverge, as exemplified in Figure 6, where the edge connectivity is 2 but the connectivity is 1.[20]

An *adhesive block* of a graph G is a k-edge-component of G where the associated value of edge connectivity defines the adhesion of the block. Figure 6 contains a single adhesive block with $\kappa' = 2$, but two overlapping cohesive blocks with $\kappa = 2$. Adhesive blocks may also overlap: An adhesive block with edge connectivity κ' may have at most $\kappa' - 1$ edges in common with a second block of equal or higher connectivity. Borgatti et al. (1990) define LS and lambda sets based on edge connectivity but restrict them to mutually exclusive subsets of adhesive blocks. This does not assure that such sets are cohesive, however, as they may contain cutnodes.

Two paths are *edge-independent* if they have no edges in common. Nodes 1 and 2 in Figure 6 are joined by just one node-independent path but two edge-independent paths. Graph G_1 in Figure 7 also illustrates the difference between node and edge connectivity: Nodes 1 and 2 are joined by two node-independent and three edge-independent paths, and five nodes (all but nodes 1, 2, and 3) are separable by either two edges or two nodes. Node and edge connectivity both equal 2 for the total graph (adhesive and cohesive blocking of $\kappa' = \kappa = 2$), but there is a greater surplus of path adhesion between nodes 1 and 2 than path cohesion.

[20]Node and edge connectivity are equal for any graph in which the minimum degree $\delta(G)$ is sufficiently large so that $\delta(G) \geq n/2$ (Harary 1969:44).

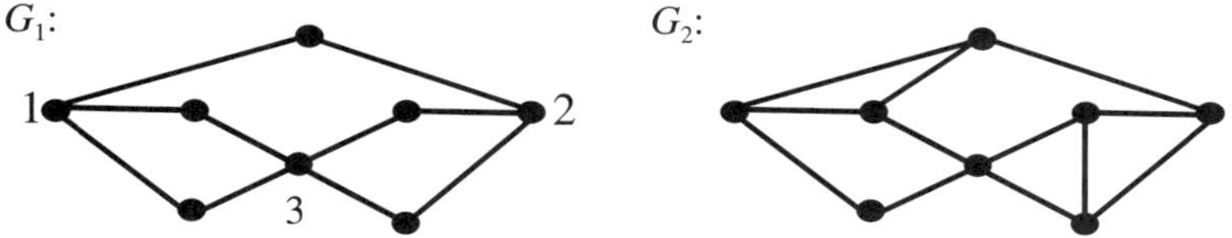

FIGURE 7. Two graphs with the same cohesion but different levels of adhesion.

C. *Egocentric (Degree), Dyadic (Size), and Density Criteria as Partial but Insufficient Indicators of Cohesion, and Their Relation to Node and Edge Connectivity*

The *degree* of a node u, denoted deg u, is the number of nodes to which u is adjacent. The *minimum degree* $\delta(G)$ is the smallest degree of a node in G. In an attempt to define cohesive subsets, Seidman (1983) defines a *k-core* of graph G as a maximal subgraph with $\delta \geq k$. Doreian and Woodward (1994) prove that k-cores form hierarchical series—i.e., for $k' > k$, a k'-core is a subgraph (possibly empty) of a k-core. The k-core, however, is no guarantee of cohesivity. The graphs in Figure 1 have $\delta = 3$ and thus are 3-cores, but are minimally cohesive because each has a cutnode (connectivity $\kappa = 1$) and lack cohesivity ($\kappa \geq 2$), (connectivity 0). For larger k, the same observation holds: There is no necessary concomitant increase in cohesion. The bow tie graph in Figure 6 is a similar example, with $\delta =$ 2—hence a 2-core, lacking cohesivity.

The *density* $\rho(G)$ is the ratio of m edges of a graph G of order n and the number m_1 of edges of the complete graph K_n. As $m_1 = m(K_n) = n(n-1)/2$ we have

$$\rho(G) = m/m_1 = 2\mathrm{m}/\mathrm{n}(\mathrm{n}-1). \tag{1}$$

Increases in size (number of edges, implying increased density) for a fixed n do not necessarily increase connectivity, and connectivity can vary independently of them. For example, the graph in Figure 3 has $n = 7$, $m = 8$, and connectivity 0. Other graphs with the same order and size have connectivity 1 or 2. There are, however, some dependencies between connectivity, degree, size, and density. We will make use of these dependencies later, in defining conditional density.

Whitney's Theorem (1932; cf. Harary 1969:43) states the inclusion relations between connectivity $\kappa(G)$ at the stronger end of a scale

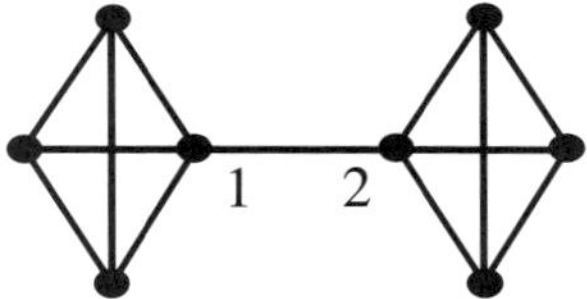

FIGURE 8. Graph with $\delta(G) = 3$ (a 3-core and 5-plex) that lacks both 3-connectivity and 3-edge connectivity. It is not even 2-connected, and thus lacks cohesivity ($\kappa \geq 2$), nor is it 2-edge-connected ($\kappa = \kappa' = 1$).

of cohesiveness, edge connectivity $\kappa'(G)$ at the middle, and minimum degree $\delta(G)$ at the weaker end (more inclusive, but less or at best equally cohesive):

Whitney's Theorem: For any graph G, $\kappa(G) \leq \kappa'(G) \leq \delta(G)$. (2)

From Whitney's Theorem it follows that every k-component is nested in a k-edge-component that is contained in a k-core, but not conversely. It follows that $\delta/(n-1)$, $\kappa'/(n-1)$, and $\kappa/(n-1)$ are the minimum densities, respectively, given δ and the connectivities κ' and κ of a graph G.[21]

Seidman and Foster (1978) attempted another measure of cohesion that is inadequate for similar reasons as the k-core. A *k-plex* is a maximal subgraph of order n where every node has degree $n-k$ or greater. Not every k-plex is an $(n-k)$-component. Figure 4 contains a 3-plex of order 5 (hence $n-k=2$) that lacks cohesivity ($\kappa \geq 2$) because it contains a cutnode. For increases in $k \geq 2$, a k-plex may still have a cutnode or even be disconnected and thus there is no necessary concomitant increase in cohesion. In general, k-plexes and k-cores do not entail either respective $n-k$ or k node or edge connectivity. Figure 8 shows a graph of order 8 with a bridge between nodes 1 and 2. This graph is a 3-core and 5-plex that lacks both connectivity 3 and edge connectivity 3. Because of the bridge, the graph has edge (and node) connectivity 1. A connected graph

[21] In 1736, Euler proved the first theorem in graph theory, that the sum of the degrees of the nodes of any graph G is $2m$, twice the size of the graph (see Harary 1969:14). Letting $\underline{d}$ denote the average degree, this shows that $\underline{d} = 2m/n$. Since the smallest degree cannot be bigger than the average degree—i.e., $\delta \leq \underline{d}$, we have $\delta \leq 2m/n$ so $2m \geq n\delta$. Given the ordering of values $\delta \geq \kappa' \geq \kappa$ of G, Whitney's Theorem implies that $2m \geq n\delta \geq n\kappa' \geq n\kappa$. Recall that the density of a graph G is $\rho(G) = 2m/n(n-1)$. It follows that the minimum density $\rho(G)$ of a graph with minimum degree δ, substituting the inequality $m \geq n\delta/2$, and canceling, is $\delta/(n-1)$. Similarly, it follows that $\kappa'/(n-1)$ and $\kappa/(n-1)$ are the minimum densities, respectively, given connectivities κ' and κ of a graph G.

with no bridges (e.g., graphs 9–11 in Figure 5) has κ' at least 2. We shall not refer to a k-core or a k-plex further, as neither lend themselves to useful theorems or measures relating to cohesion in groups.[22]

D. Connectivity and Multiple Independent Paths as Cohesion, Menger's First Equality

Some of the deepest theorems in graph theory concern the equivalence between structural properties of graphs, such as connectivity (based on cutnodes), and how graphs are traversed. A graph G is *k-connected* if its connectivity is at least k. It is *k-edge-connected* when its edge connectivity is at least k. Karl Menger (1927) proved the equality of k-connectedness and the minimum number of node-independent paths between every pair of nodes,[23] which is a property of how a graph can be traversed. Consider graph G_1 in Figure 7: There is no pair of nodes with fewer than two node-independent paths, such as join nodes 1 and 2. The graph also cannot be disconnected by removal of fewer than 2 nodes. The proof of Menger's Theorem is found in Harary (1969:47), but its relevance to connectivity as a measure of cohesion (Wasserman and Faust 1994:115–17; Scott 2000:100–20) does not seem to be recognized in current sociological literature.[24] Menger's formulation and characterization of k-connected graphs, given below, is one of the most useful results in all of graph theory in that it establishes an equivalence between a structural and a traversal property of graphs, properties that happen to be the two most salient attributes of cohesion. Hence the structural cohesion in a group (definition 1.2.1) is equivalent to the path cohesion of the group (1.2.2).[25]

[22]The unions of intersecting cliques are another attempt to define cohesive sets (Freeman 1996), but the unions of cliques that have only one node in common also lack cohesivity.

[23]He accomplished this as an abstract result in the study of point-set topology. Note that by definition a graph of connectivity k is k-connected, but a k-connected graph may have connectivity k or greater. Likewise for edge connectivity k and k-edge-connected.

[24]Scott (2000:13) notes that "Harary developed powerful models of group cohesion" but does not develop what these ideas were in his chapter on cohesion.

[25]Alba and Kadushin (1976) define the cohesion of two nodes as the number of cycles in which they are contained. Since two cycles may differ but have edges in common, k cycles containing two nodes do not imply $k - 1$ (node-) disjoint paths between them, so this measure of cohesion does not identify clear boundaries of cohesive subsets. As noted, Harary, Norman, and Cartwright (1965) were the first to propose the connectivity of a graph (for the digraph case) as the primary measure of cohesiveness.

The *local connectivity* of two nonadjacent nodes u,v of a graph G is written $\kappa(u,v)$ and is defined as the minimum number of nodes needed to disconnect u and v. When u and v are adjacent they cannot be separated by removal of any number of nodes. Therefore local connectivity $\kappa(u,v)$ is not defined when u and v are adjacent. A complete graph, in which every pair of nodes is adjacent, does not have any local connectivities, and its (global) connectivity is defined as $n-1$, which corresponds to the number of node-independent paths that join each pair of nodes. But when G is not complete, the connectivity $\kappa(G)$ is the minimum value of the local connectivity taken over all nonadjacent pairs of nodes. Local and global edge connectivities are similarly defined, but with no exception for adjacent nodes.

Local Menger's Theorem A: The minimum node cut set $\kappa(u,v)$ separating a nonadjacent u,v pair of nodes equals the maximum number of node-independent u-v paths.[26]
Global Menger's Theorem A: A graph is k-connected if and only if any pair of nodes u,v is joined by at least k node-independent u-v paths.

Hence, for sociology, Menger's Theorem states the equivalence of our two parallel series of definitions of cohesion: connectivity (structural cohesion) and number of independent paths (path cohesion), which can be combined into a single concept of cohesion. Algorithms for computing numbers of node-independent paths between all pairs of nodes are given in White and Newman (2001). We now begin to expand on these two aspects of cohesion and reach a fuller appreciation of their sociological interpretation and implications.

E. (Edge-) Flow Connectivity and Node-Flow Connectivity

A *multigraph M* is obtained from a graph G when some of the edges are converted to two or more edges. An (integer valued) *network* is obtained from a graph G by assigning natural numbers, called *weights*, *values*, or *capacities*, to the edges of G. Therefore, when each edge with value t in a network is replaced by t edges joining u and v, we have a multigraph. Multigraphs are especially useful when the number of edges between two nodes (or corresponding values of the weighted graph or network) repre-

[26] The local and global theorems of Menger are examples of minimax theorems in mathematics.

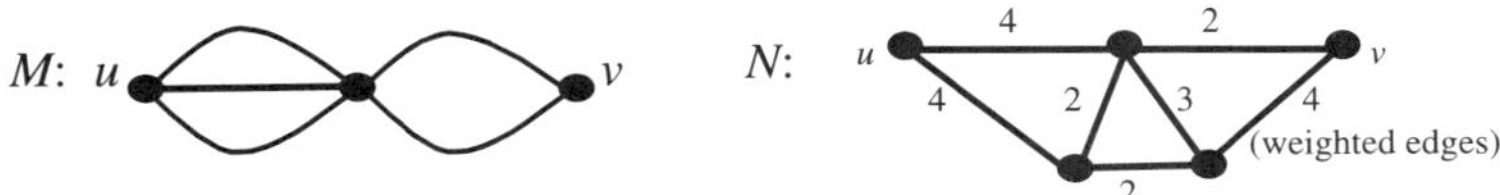

FIGURE 9. Multigraph M illustrating node-flow connectivity $\kappa''(u,v) = \kappa''(M) = 2$, where the connectivity is $\kappa(u,v) = \kappa(M) = 1$, and a network N (weighted graph) where node-flow connectivity $\kappa''(u,v) = 4$ but $\kappa'(u,v) = 6$.

sent flow capacities such as an ordinal limit on how much of some item can be transmitted from one node to another. The flow along a u-v path in which there are multiple edges in a multigraph is the minimum number of multiple edges joining adjacent pairs of nodes in the path. More generally, in a multigraph M, the flow from u to v is the number of edge-independent single-edge u-v paths. In the first graph of Figure 9, for example, there are two edge-independent single-edge u-v paths.

Extrapolating from Menger's Theorem, the local *(edge-) flow* from u to v in a multigraph M equals $\kappa'(u,v)$, the minimum number of edges in a cutset that separates u and v. This result illustrates how the concept of adhesion can be extended to graphs with weighted edges to capture the idea of differential strengths or capacities of edges. The (edge-) flow measure is widely used in the study of capacitated networks and flows (Ford and Fulkerson 1956), and will be discussed shortly.

We now consider only node-independent u-v paths: The local u-v *node-flow* (i.e., node-independent flow) is the maximum sum for a set of u-v flows for node-independent u-v paths. For graphs, this is simply the number of node-independent paths and by Local Theorem A is equal to $\kappa(u,v)$, the minimum number of nodes that must be deleted to disconnect u and v. To capture the idea of node-flow for a multigraph (equivalently, for a network), we expand the concept of connectivity to consider node-independent flow through multiple edges. The local *node-flow connectivity, $\kappa''(u,v)$*, in a multigraph M is the smallest number of edges in a set of node-independent u-v paths whose removal disconnects u and v.[27] The (global) *node-flow connectivity, $\kappa''(M)$*, is the smallest number of edges in a set of node-independent paths connecting any pair of nodes, whose removal disconnects M. This is not edge connectivity, because we consider only at the edges on node-independent paths. Figure 9 shows a mul-

[27] Two or more edges are *parallel* in a multigraph M if they join the same two nodes u,v. To disconnect a connected multigraph, one or more sets of parallel edges must be removed.

tigraph M where $\kappa(u,v) = \kappa(M) = 1$ but $\kappa''(u,v) = \kappa''(M) = 2$. The networks M and N (with weighted edges) in Figure 9 show $\kappa''(u,v) = 2$ and $\kappa''(u,v) = 4$, respectively.

By restatement of Menger's Local and Global Theorems,[28] we derive new corollaries of the celebrated Ford-Fulkerson Theorem (1956):

Local Ford-Fulkerson (Node-Flow Edge-Cut) Corollary. The *u-v* node-flow in a multigraph M equals the minimum number of edges in a cutset $\kappa''(u,v)$, within a set of node-independent paths, that separates u and v.
Global Ford-Fulkerson (Node-Flow Edge-Cut) Corollary. The minimum of the (maximum) *u-v* node-flows for all u,v pairs in a multigraph M equals $\kappa''(M)$, the minimum number of edges in a cutset, within a set of node-independent paths, whose removal disconnects M.

Because removing a node v of a connected G removes deg v edges and deg v is 1 or more, we also obtain the equivalent of Whitney's Theorem:

$$\kappa''(u,v) \leq \kappa'(u,v) \leq \min(\deg(u), \deg(v)). \tag{3}$$

Network N of Figure 9 (a graph with weighted edges), for example, shows flow or edge connectivity $\kappa'(u,v) = 6$, compared with node-flow connectivity $\kappa''(u,v) = 4$.

The concept of node-flow, as defined for the first time here, is not a single minimum value over a graph or multigraph but defines instead a matrix of values between each pair of nodes. Hence it provides a more detailed account of how cohesion is distributed in a group or network.[29] Flows through multiple node-independent paths are especially important in considering influences or effects as they spread through a network, and in compensating for distance decay. Higher redundancy—i.e., node independence—in flow may compensate for transmission decay at larger distances, and blocks of actors connected by node-independent flows may act as amplification systems for boosting the coherent signals transmitted in social interactions.

[28] Insofar as we know, the definition of node-flow is a new concept, and the restatements are new, but its proof is obvious from Menger's Theorem and the definition of node-flow.

[29] Scaling techniques applied to node-flow matrices should give a more detailed analysis of differential cohesion in a group, but node-flow has been more difficult to compute for large networks than connectivity, hence White and Newman's (2001) results will provide a fruitful avenue of research.

F. Edge Connectivity and Edge-Independent Paths as Adhesion, Menger's Second Equality

Like cohesion, we defined social adhesion both in terms of resistance to disconnection through edge removal (2.1.2—structural adhesion) and of multiple paths (2.2.2—path adhesion). These two definitions are also unified as equivalents by the edge version of Menger's Global and Local Theorems:

Local Menger's Theorem B: The minimum number of edges in a cutset separating u and v equals the maximum number of edge-independent paths that join u and v.
Global Menger's Theorem B: A graph G is k-edge-connected if and only if every pair of nodes u,v in G are joined by at least k edge-independent u-v paths.

When the edges of graphs are weighted, or we convert a weighted graph to an equivalent multigraph, we can make use of Ford and Fulkerson's (1956) maximum flow–minimum cut theorem, one of the most widely used results in all of operations research:[30]

Local Ford-Fulkerson (Edge-Cut) Theorem. The maximum flow u-v in a multigraph M equals the minimum edge-cut $\kappa'(u,v)$ that separates u and v.
Global Ford and Fulkerson (Edge-Cut) Theorem. The minimum flow between any pair of nodes in a multigraph M (equivalently, a network or integer-weighted graph) equals the minimum number of edges $\kappa'(M)$ whose removal disconnects M.

It is this theorem that Zachary (1975, 1977) uses to partition his karate club network, whose leaders are in conflict, into two halves: those who are most adhesively connected (by the greatest number of edge-independent paths = the least-edge cutset) with the club's administrator and those most adhesively connected to the club's karate instructor. We discussed this case in Section I.C, in which our critique of Zachary's adhesion-based minimum

[30] Dirac (1960) showed that this result, in which each edge e has a numerical weight $w(e)$, is a straightforward corollary of Menger's Theorem B. Several variations on Theorems A and B are presented in Harary (1969, ch. 5).

edge-cut method began with its weakness as a sociological basis for identifying the relational component of solidarity as compared with a cohesion-based minimum removal of nodes. Our critique noted that it is easier to assert mechanisms whereby social pressures operate on individuals—due to their agency—to take sides in disputes, than to understand why group segmentation should occur along a minimum edge-cut.[31] In Section IV, following Section III where we develop the measure of conditional density, we exemplify and compare the two methods (adhesive edge connectivity and cohesive node connectivity) for the Zachary karate club study.

G. The Hierarchical Properties of Cohesive and Adhesive Blocks

At the first level of analysis of structural and path cohesion and adhesion, which reduce to the concepts of node and edge connectivities in graphs, we can complete the series of intuitive assertions of Section I as follows:

1.3. Relationally cohesive groups can be regarded as multiply nested in terms of connectivity values in the following sense: a connected graph can contain several 2-components, each of which can contain 3-components, and so forth. Likewise for a multigraph or graph in which edges are weighted: cohesive groups are multiply nested in terms of their node-flow-connectivity values.

2.3. Relationally adhesive groups are multiply nested in terms of edge connectivity values in the sense that a connected graph can contain several 2-edge-components, each of which contain 3-edge-components, etc. Likewise for a multigraph or weighted graph: adhesive groups are multiply nested in terms of their flow-connectivity values.

Graphs and social groups at the same levels of connectivity can be further ordered at a second level, according to conditional density, taken up in the next section.

[31] Ties have no autonomous agency, so that if a social network has a certain edge-flow between two conflicting individuals (and there may be many edge-flow equivalent edge-cuts that will partition the group into disconnected factions), how would the "network" know to partition along an edge-cut? Alternatively, where a cutnode or cutset of individuals exists whose removal would disconnect the graph, social pressure to choose sides is likely to fall on this individual or set of individuals, who have the agency to alter their ties according to principles of cohesion, density, and closeness of ties to the leaders and their cohesively closer faction members, agency which is lacking to the network as a whole.

III. CONDITIONAL DENSITY

The idea of conditional density is that if some property of a graph is held constant—such as connectivity—then density may vary only within a limited range and can be rescaled from zero to some maximum within that range. Since connectivity is an integer number, a minimum value for a group, and density above the minimum required for connectivity at that level makes an additional contribution to cohesion, a rescaling of density as a fractional number allows us to add the two together to get an aggregate measure of cohesion. By adding conditional density in such a measure, we can account for additional cohesion that connectivity cannot capture alone.

To define precisely the conditional density of a graph G with respect to some structural property, we need some preliminary definitions. Let P be a generic property of graphs, such as connected, or bipartite, etc. We always denote the order of G by n (nodes) and its size by m (edges). Let $m_0(G{:}P)$ be the minimum size of a graph G of order n that has property P, and let $m_1(G{:}P)$ be the maximum size. Then the *conditional P-density*, $\rho(G{:}P)$, is defined by

$$\rho(G{:}P) = (m - m_0)/(m_1 - m_0).$$

If m_1 is the maximum m in a graph of order n with a given κ, and m_2 is the smallest m that forces that graph to surpass property P of connectivity κ, then $m_2 = m_1 + 1$ is the *upper size limit* on the number of edges at which a less than complete graph G of order n cannot retain property P, but below which G has property P. The *conditional P-density*, $\rho_2(G{:}P)$, of an (n, m) graph, which is always less than one, is defined within the lower and upper size limits m_0 and m_2:[32]

$$\rho_2\,(G{:}P) = (m - m_0)/(m_2 - m_0) < 1. \quad (4)$$

If P is omitted from either of these formulas, so that $m_0 = 0$ and we let $m_1 = m_2 = m(K_n) = n(n-1)/2$, the size of a complete graph K_n, then ρ_2 and ρ reduce to the usual graph density formula:

$$\rho(G) = \rho_2(G) = m/m_1 = m/(n(n-1)/2) = 2m/n(n-1).$$

[32]The notation for m_0 and m_1 designates that density normally varies between 0 and 1; conditional P-density ρ_2 approaches but never reaches 1 unless $m_1 = m(Kn)$. This latter characteristic will be useful when we define cohesion as an aggregate measure consisting of the sum of connectivity κ plus conditional κ-density $\rho_2(G{:}\kappa)$.

For graph 8 in Figure 5, for example, the ordinary density $\rho(G) = .67$, and where the property P is that of connectivity ($\kappa = 1$), graph 8 has a surplus of one edge beyond those needed for $\kappa = 1$, while the maximum such surplus is two edges for a connected graph with 4 nodes, hence the conditional P-density of this graph is ρ_2 $(G{:}\kappa = 1) = 0.5$. Three surplus edges beyond those required for $\kappa = 1$ are needed to force a graph with 4 nodes to have $\kappa = 2$, as in graph 10. In general, conditional P-density ρ_2 is the ratio of surplus edges, beyond those minimally needed for a graph of order n to have property P, to the upper size limit m_2 at which a graph with order n *cannot* still retain property P.[33]

A. Connectivity and Conditional Density: A Unified Approach to Measuring Cohesion

Graph connectivity and density are two aspects of cohesion that are tightly bound together. We take advantage of their interdependence to combine and unify them into a single measure of cohesion.

To apply conditional density to the property of connectivity requires the values of $m_0(G{:}\kappa)$ and $m_1(G{:}\kappa)$ or $m_2(G{:}\kappa)$ for a graph G of size m and order n with connectivity κ.[34] These are known from extremal graph theory.[35] Let $\lceil x \rceil$ be the fraction x rounded up to the nearest integer, and for conciseness, let $m^* = m(K_{n-1})$, the size of the complete graph of order $n - 1$. The limiting size $m_2(G{:}\kappa)$ of a graph of order n with connectivity κ, where $0 \leq \kappa < n - 1$, is $1 + \kappa + m^*$. For $\kappa = n - 1$ we define $m_2(G{:}\kappa) = n(n - 1)/2$, the maximum size of a graph, giving maximum conditional density of 1 only for K_n. The minimum numbers of edges m_0 of G with connectivity $\kappa = 0$, 1, and >1 are 0, $n - 1$, and $\lceil n\kappa/2 \rceil$, respectively. In general, $m_0 = \lceil \mathrm{n}\kappa/2 \rceil$ rises linearly with n, while m_1 and m_2 rise quadrat-

[33] Conditional P-densities ρ and ρ_2 differ in that the denominator of the former limits density to an interval [0,1] relative to the number of edges at which property P cannot be retained. Conditional P-density, $\rho(G{:}P)$, is the number of surplus edges divided by the maximum number of surplus edges at which a graph with order n can still retain property P.

[34] See also Harary (1983) on conditional connectivity, and Harary and Cartwright (1961) on the number of arcs in each connectedness category of a digraph.

[35] See Harary (1969:17–19) for an introduction to extremal graphs. The result $(m{:}n,\ \kappa > 1) = \lceil n\kappa/2 \rceil$ agrees with a minimum density of $\kappa/(n - 1)$ for a graph of connectivity $\kappa > 1$. A problem opposite to that of conditional density, covered in extremal graph theory, is *conditional connectivity*: What are the minimum and maximum connectivities for a graph of order n and size m? A 4-node graph with 5 edges, for example, must be 2-connected.

ically, so that conditional densities are more tightly limited when there are fewer nodes and higher values of κ.

When $\rho_2(G{:}\kappa)$ is close to zero, the connectivity structure is fragile, in that the removal of a randomly chosen edge is likely to reduce the connectivity of G. The minimum size of a graph G of order n for $\kappa = 2$, for example, is n, realized only by the cycle C_n. The removal of any one of these n edges reduces the connectivity to $\kappa = 1$. If G contains one surplus edge, the chance that random removal of an edge will reduce the connectivity of G to 1 is $n/(n+1)$. As the surplus density $\rho_2(G{:}P = \kappa)$ increases, more nodes will have extra edges, and the graph becomes less vulnerable to a lowered connectivity with the removal of a random edge. As conditional density approaches 1, the connectivity structure is more robust: Many randomly chosen edges can be removed with less chance of reducing connectivity.

B. Cohesion: A Scalable Aggregate Measure (Connectivity κ Plus ρ_2 Density)

The sum of the connectivity κ and the conditional density $\rho_2(G{:}\kappa)$ of a graph G is not the only possible measure of its cohesion but is a better measure than any of the other cohesive subset algorithms discussed in Sections II.C and I.D (k-plex, k-core, and intersecting cliques) because none of the higher values on these measures is a guarantee of our minimum criterion of cohesivity ($\kappa \geq 2$; for any value of k, a k-core or k-plex may even have $\kappa = 0$). Connectivity and conditional density each contribute independently to cohesion, according to the two criteria reviewed earlier: the structural cohesion integer and the conditional density fraction. We now consider how density plays into the criteria for cohesion.

For the first criterion of cohesion—namely, that a cohesive block stays together—the value k of $\kappa(G)$ is the guarantee that a graph G cannot be disconnected without removal of at least k nodes. In addition, higher values of conditional density reduce the likelihood that removal of a random edge will diminish the value of κ.

For the second criterion of cohesion, that the nodes of a cohesive block should be strongly tied, the value k of κ is also the guarantee, by Menger's Theorem A, that every pair of nodes in a graph with $\kappa(G) = k$ has k or more independent paths connecting them. In addition, the higher the value of conditional density, $\rho_2(G{:}\kappa)$, the less the likelihood that the removal of a random edge will diminish the minimum number k of independent paths that join every pair of nodes.

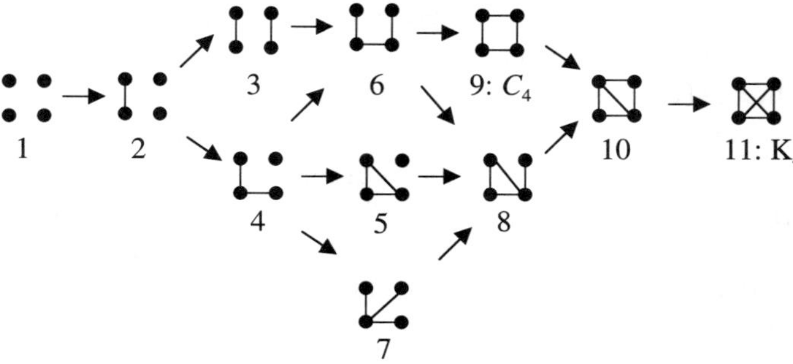

FIGURE 10. The 11 graphs of order 4 showing transitions by graph evolution (addition of edges).

The probabilistic framework for considering the contributions of conditional density to cohesion—invoking the *expected* impact of edge removal as a supplement to the *greatest* impact as measured by connectivity (structural cohesion)—provides one of the major advantages of this approach over alternatives such as conditional distance or conditional adhesion.[36]

C. A Well-Constructed Measure of Cohesion

A well-constructed measure requires a demonstration of the *unit* of measurement that gives a monotone increase in magnitude of the quantity measured. The unit for which the aggregate measure of cohesion is monotone increasing is the addition of an edge within a connected graph of order *n*. Hence an essential criterion for measurement is satisfied. The aggregate cohesion measure is monotonically increasing in any sequence of graphs of a given order (n) in which edges are successively added. The sequences of graphs of order 4 shown in Figure 10, for example, satisfy this criterion. These are the same 11 graphs as in Figure 5, along with directed arrows showing which graphs are transformed to another by addition of

[36]Future developments in the theory of random graphs (Palmer 1985; Kolchin 1999) might also help to establish whether the distribution of distances between nodes in a graph with connectivity κ and conditional density $\rho_2(G{:}\kappa)$ is less than, equal to, or greater than expected in a "random" distribution. Approximation methods have not yet been developed to answer these questions within random graph theory, although a simulation approach might be useful to bring the emergence of small world cohesivity into the kind of simulation framework developed by Watts (1999a).

an edge; their aggregate cohesion measures are given in the fourth row of Table 1: For each successive graph under edge addition, there is an increase in aggregate cohesion.

Only certain sequences of adding edges will give maximum increases in aggregate cohesion. Cohesion is increased maximally in the sequences in Figure 10, for example, that lead from the totally disconnected graph (1) to the graph with all nodes connected by a single path (6), to one with all nodes connected by a single cycle (9), to the graph consisting of a single clique (11). The principle of attaining successive maximum cohesion by adding edges in a graph of any order n is always to build first a single connecting path, then a cycle (C_n of connectivity 2), then to place in a distributed way the minimum edges needed to build connectivity 3, similarly for connectivity 4, and so forth.

Adding edges so as to build cliques of maximum order as a subgraph, in contrast, does not maximize increase in overall connectivity or aggregate cohesion, although it does increase subgroup density and heterogeneity. Nor does adding an edge to a graph increase cohesion if one or two new nodes are also added incident to the edge. Unless cohesion was initially zero, this will decrease the cohesion of the graph.

Table 2 shows in columns 2 and 3, for the various values of n and κ given in column 1, the values m_0 and m_2 for graphs of order $n > 1$ with

TABLE 1

Connectivity κ, Conditional Density $\rho_2(G{:}\kappa)$, and Aggregate Cohesion $\kappa + \rho_2(G{:}\kappa)$, for the 11 Graphs in Figure 5

Graph G	1	2	3	4	5	6	7	8	9	10	11
Size (edges)	0	1	2	2	3	3	3	4	4	5	6
κ	0	0	0	0	0	1	1	1	2	2	3
$\rho_2(G{:}\kappa)$	0.0	.25	0.5	0.5	.75	0.0	0.0	.5	0.0	0.5	0.0
$\kappa + \rho_2(G{:}\kappa)$	0.0	.25	0.5	0.5	.75	1.0	1.0	1.5	2.0	2.5	3.0
Component S		a, c	a, c	a, c, d		G	G	G	G	G	G
κ		1	1	1		1	1	1			
$\rho_2(S{:}\kappa)$		0.0	0.0	0.0		0.0	0.0	0.5			
$\kappa + \rho_2(S{:}\kappa)$		1.00	1.00	1.00		1.0	1.0	1.5			
Bicomponent S					a, c, d			a, c, d	G	G	G
κ					2			2	2	2	
$\rho_2(S{:}\kappa)$					0.0			0.0	0.0	0.5	
$\kappa + \rho_2(S{:}\kappa)$					2.0			2.0	2.0	2.5	
Tricomponent S											G
κ											3
$\rho_2(S{:}\kappa)$											0.0
$\kappa + \rho_2(S{:}\kappa)$											3.0

TABLE 2
Ranges of m_0 and m_2 for Computing Conditional Density $\rho_2(G{:}\kappa)$ at Connectivity κ

Graph Sizes Given: Order n, Connectivity κ	At κ min $m_0 = [n\kappa/2]^+$	Forcing $\kappa + 1$ $m_2 = 1 + \kappa + m^*$ for $\kappa < n - 1$
$n > 1$, $\kappa = 0$ Fig. 3	0	$1 + \kappa + m^*$
$n > 1$, $\kappa = 1$ Figs.1,2,4,6,8 and 5.8	$n - 1$	$1 + \kappa + m^*$
$n = 4$, $\kappa = 2$ Fig. 5.9	4	6
$\kappa = 3$ Fig. 5.11	6	6
$n = 5$, $\kappa = 2$	5	9
$\kappa = 3$	8	10
$\kappa = 4$	10	10
$n = 6$, $\kappa = 2$	6	13
$\kappa = 3$	9	14
$\kappa = 4$	12	15
$\kappa = 5$	15	15
$n = 7$, $\kappa = 2$ Fig. 7	7	18
$\kappa = 3$	11	19
$\kappa = 4$	14	20
$\kappa = 5$	18	21
$\kappa = 6$	21	21
$n = 40$, $\kappa = 2$	40	744
$\kappa = 3$	60	745
$\kappa = 4$	80	756
$\kappa = 5$	100	757
$\kappa = 6$	120	758
$\kappa = 39$	780	780

$m^* = m(K_{n-1})$, the size of the complete graph of order $n - 1$.

$\kappa = 0$ or 1, and for graphs with $4 \leq n \leq 7$ and $n = 40$ nodes for various values of $\kappa > 1$. Illustrative graphs from Figures 1–8 are referenced in the table. The bow tie graph ($n = 5$, $\kappa = 1$) in Figure 6, for example, has a conditional density of (6-4)/(8-4) = 0.5 and an ordinary density of 0.6.

As noted above, the denominator of conditional density $\rho_2(G{:}\kappa)$ ensures that it cannot reach 1.0 for a given κ. This allows the aggregate measure of cohesion—as a connectivity integer plus a conditional density decimal (<1)—to correctly distinguish between the case of maximum density at connectivity κ and minimum density at connectivity $\kappa + 1$, where the aggregate cohesiveness of the former is always less than that of the latter.[37]

[37]This is not the case for the sum of connectivity and $\rho(G, \kappa)$ conditional density, which does not give a measure of cohesion because the sum $\kappa + \rho(G, \kappa)$ for a graph with connectivity κ and size $m_1(G, \kappa)$ is the same as the sum for a graph with connectivity $\kappa + 1$ and size $m_0(G, \kappa) = 0$.

D. Subgroup Cohesion

The boundaries and measures of each of the *k*-components of a graph provide a convenient way to study the structure of social cohesion. One of the problems in previous measures of social cohesion such as intersecting cliques, *k*-cores, and *k*-plexes—apart from the fact that they are no guarantee of cohesivity ($\kappa \geq 2$; or even that $\kappa > 0$)—is that there is so much overlap in the cohesive subsets they identify. The measure of cohesion based on the sum of the connectivity $\kappa(S)$ of a subgraph S and its conditional density $\rho_2(S{:}\kappa)$ typically yields more interpretable cohesive subgroups, with very little overlap, and a hierarchy of nested *k*-components, each with successively higher levels of cohesion.

To illustrate measurement of subgroup cohesion, relationships among the cohesion measures are shown in Table 1 for each *k*-component of the eleven 4-node graphs in Figure 5. Rows two to four of the table show the connectivity κ, conditional density $\rho_2(G{:}\kappa)$, and aggregate cohesion $\kappa + \rho_2(G{:}\kappa)$ for each of the graphs in their entirety. The second, third, and fourth sets of four rows each show these values for the largest component, bicomponent, and tricomponent, if any, of each of the 11 graphs.

E. Subgroup Inhomogeneities

Social groups with networks of high connectivity have high cohesion, but they may be highly inhomogeneous if they have high conditional densities as well. Groups with low conditional densities have relatively fewer surplus edges with which to create local subgroup inhomogeneities. Thus some of the problems in the study of nested subgroups, their relative homogeneities and inhomogeneities, and the relation between cohesion and social solidarity (Markovsky and Lawler 1994; Markovsky and Chaffee 1995; Markovsky 1998) can be studied by means of connectivity and conditional density.

IV. AN EMPIRICAL EXAMPLE: ZACHARY'S KARATE CLUB

Zachary's (1975, 1977) two-year ethnographic network study of 34 members of a karate club is a good proving ground to examine concepts, measures and hypotheses involving relational aspects of social solidarity. This section provides an illustration of how measures of cohesion are used to predict the outcome variable of sides taken in a factional dispute from the boundaries of nested cohesive sets. The disputants were the karate teacher (T, #1, Mr. Hi) and the club administrator (A, #34, John) and the dispute was about whether to improve the solvency of the club by raising fees (teacher) or by holding costs down (as A insisted). This resulted in each calling meetings at which they hoped to pass self-serving resolutions by encouraging attendance of their own supporters. The formation of factions was visible to the ethnographer and evident in meeting attendance, which varied in factional proportions according to the convener. Ultimately Mr. Hi (T) was fired, set up a separate club, and the factional split became the basis for each student's choice of which of the new clubs they would join. The prediction tested here is that when two "sociometric centers" of a group force a division into two, the cohesion measure will predict how members of the old group will distribute among the new ones.

A. Global View of the Karate Network

Figure 11 shows the network of friendships among the 34 members. Zachary weighted the strength of each friendship by the number of con-

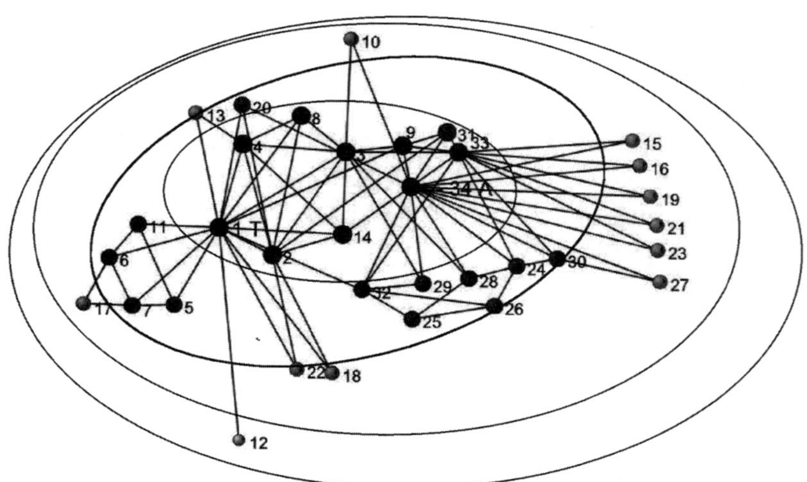

FIGURE 11. Nested adhesive sets for edge connectivities of 1, 2, 3, and 4. This and the following figures are drawn with Batagelj and Mrvar's (1997, 1998) Pajek software.

TABLE 3
Edge Connectivity Sets for the Karate Club

Sets	Members [1,34 leaders]	Nested in Set	n	κ'
1	1–34		34	1
2	1–11,13–34	1	33	2
3	1–9,11,14,20,24–26,28–34	2	22	3
4	1–4,8–9,14,31,33–34	3	10	4

texts (karate and other classes, hangouts, tournaments, and bars) in which the pair met, but the weights are not shown in the figure. Instead, concentric rings of adhesive subsets are circled in Figure 11 according to their 1-, 2-, 3-, and 4-edge connectivity. Table 3 lists the members and gives the number (n) in each set, the concentric nesting of the sets, and the edge connectivity κ' of each. The set with highest adhesion, which consists of 10 members and includes A and T, is separable by four edges ($\kappa' = 4$) but A and T are separated by a minimum of 10. There are, however, many different edge-cuts of size 10 that separate A and T. Hence unweighted edge-cuts, as well as adhesive sets, fail to predict faction membership. Each of the nested 1-, 2-, 3-, and 4-edge-connected subsets contains a cutnode (T) and lacks cohesivity since $\kappa < 2$.

Zachary used weighted minimum edge-cuts between A and T (the Local Ford-Fulkerson max flow–min cut theorem) to predict the separation of the two factions. Except for three persons who did not take sides, this gave a near-perfect prediction of the split. The particular distribution of weights on the edges, however, contributed to a unique-cut solution, pushed somewhat away from T since weights were highest for those close to him. Zachary did not utilize criteria for subgroup cohesion, but the dynamics of the dispute gives us the opportunity to examine cohesive blocks before the split and the role they played in mobilizing the taking of sides.

Looked at in terms of cohesion (Figure 12) the network has five cohesive blocks of connectivity 2 or greater, each enclosed in Figure 12 by one of the concentric circles. Only node T is common to them all. Two exclude node A (a 3-component within a 2-component) and three (a 4-component within a 3- within a 2-component) include node A. Table 4 shows the cohesive blocks 1–5 circled in Figure 12, their members, number of nodes, the hierarchical nesting of each block, its connectivity, conditional density, and aggregate cohesion. An additional

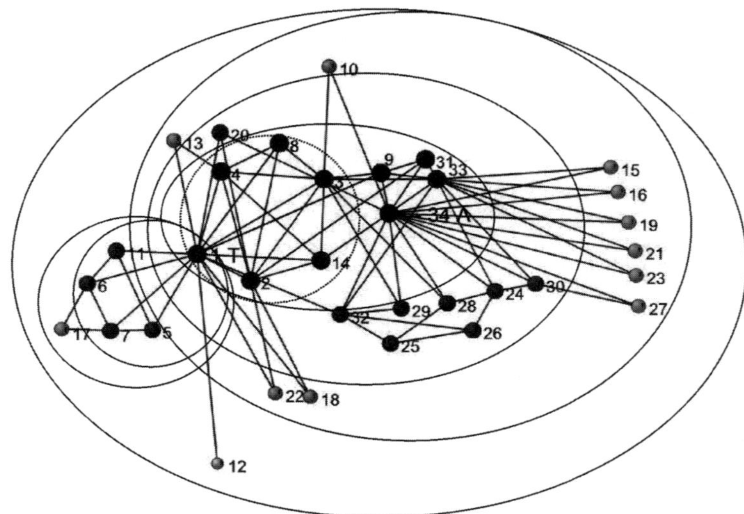

FIGURE 12. Cohesive blocks hierarchically ordered by connectivity into two nests (the outer dotted circle nests them all in a connected graph with connectivity 1).

subset with the highest aggregate cohesion of 4.75 is also shown—the six people within the dotted circle in Figure 12—which is not a maximal cohesive block but part of block 5 (with cohesion 4.24). This subset forms the core of support for Mr. Hi, while the remnants of block 5

TABLE 4
Connectivity Block and Subset Characteristics for Karate Club

Blocks and Sets	Members [1,34 leaders]	Nested in Set	n	κ	ρ_2	Aggregate Cohesion
1	1,5–7,11,17		6	2	.2	2.20
2	1,5–7,11	2	6	3	.54	3.54
3	1–4,8–10,13–16,18–34		28	2	.12	2.12
4	1–4,8–9,14,20,24–26,28–34	3	18	3	.12	3.12
5	1–4,8–9,14,31,33,34	4	10	4	.24	4.24
6*	1–4,8,14	5	6	4	.75	4.75
7*	9,31,33,34	5	4	3	.00	3.00

*Sets 1–5 are cohesive blocks; set 6 is the densest cohesive subblock within 5 and set 7 is the residual within 5 after taking out set 6.

after removing this subset, shown as set 7 in Table 4, are supporters of A.

A first and approximate prediction of factions uses the number of node-independent paths (node-flow) joining pairs of nodes, and then takes the maximum spanning tree of the edges in the original network selected in order of largest number of node-independent paths (White and Newman 2001: the spanning tree portion of the algorithm, in general, breaks ties in favor of pairs of nodes separated by least distance). The result is depicted in Figure 13, in which the vertical line is a good predictor of the initial factional alignment, with followers of T to the left and those of A to the right. Person 9, on A's side of the prediction line, initially aligns with A but later switches to T. After removal of the cutnode between T and A, which is also person 9 (which also removes the two dotted lines in the figure), two trees remain with T and A at their respective centers. Except for those who do not take sides (three nodes labeled with a question mark), and two others, 28 and 29, the trees predict the factional alignments. The spanning tree algorithm, however, introduces some noise to Figure 13 as

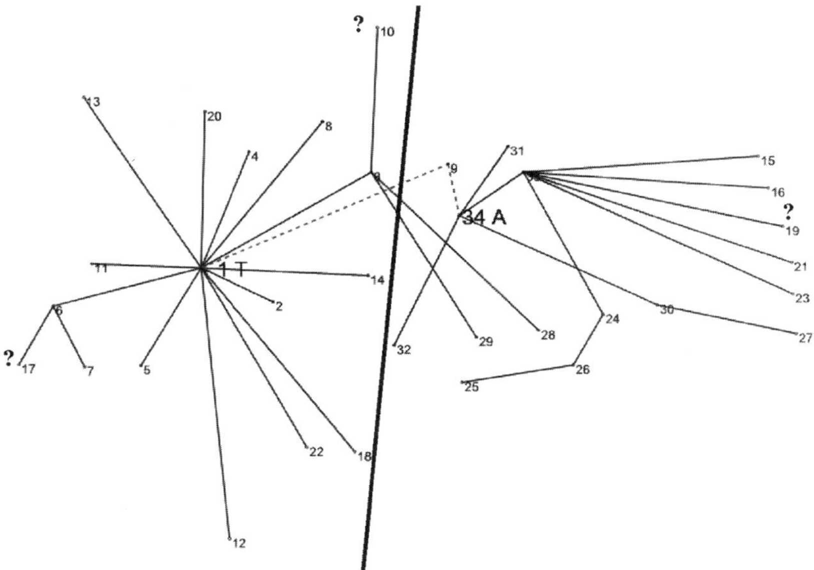

FIGURE 13. Maximum spanning tree of the numbers of node-independent paths between pairs of nodes, where solid lines predict faction members except for 28 and 29 and those nodes labeled with a question mark.

a predictor variable because choice is arbitrary among edges that are equally well qualified for the spanning tree. Persons 28 and 29 are an example, and could equally well be linked by the algorithm to A, thereby improving the prediction.

B. Closeup of Cohesion in the Karate Network

Because cohesive blocking is a deterministic procedure, it makes more precise predictions than White and Newman's approximation algorithm. If we situate the problem of determining factional divisions in the context of the opposition between leaders, as Zachary did, there are four persons—9, 14, 20, and 32—who had friendships with both leaders and thus had to make up their minds which leader to follow as the club split. Their membership in cohesive blocks and subsets provides a determinate prediction as to their decisions about which leader to follow. The choices they made corresponded not to the number of contexts in which they had friendships with T (Mr. Hi) or A (John), as Zachary would suggest, but to the pull of cohesive ties with others in core group of T (set 6 in Table 4) versus A (set 7). For each of these four people, who must decide between T and A, Table 5 contains four labeled rows: In the three columns under Mr. Hi's faction are the subset size (n), number of edges (e), and aggregate cohesion ($\kappa + \rho_2$) within Mr. Hi's faction (set 6); and similarly for A's faction, set 7. In the center of the table is a column that shows whether cohesion is greater with T ($>$) or A ($<$). In the rightmost columns are each person's predicted and actual choice of faction, showing that each of these people chose to align with the faction in which they have highest cohesion.

TABLE 5
Aggregate Cohesion (AC) with Leadership Factions for Persons Tied to Both Leaders and Obliged to Choose Between Them

Member	Mr. Hi's Faction		AC_1	AC_1	A's Faction		AC_2	Predicted Choice of Faction	Actual Choice of Faction
	n	e	$\kappa + \rho_2$	AC_2	n	e	$\kappa + \rho_2$		
14	6	14	4.75	$>$	5	7	1.75	Mr. Hi	Mr. Hi
20	4	5	2.5	$>$	5	7	1.75	Mr. Hi	Mr. Hi
9	2	1	2.0	$<$	4	6	4.0	A	A
32	2	1	2.0	$<$	5	8	2.83	A	A

Students 14 and 20, for example, had more cohesion with Mr. Hi's group than with A's, and they aligned with Mr. Hi's faction in attendance at meetings. Students 9 and 32, on the other hand, had more cohesion with A's group and aligned with his faction. Each of these four people had to make a choice to drop a tie with the leader whose faction they rejected. If we remove the line connecting 14 to 34 (A) because 14 chose to join T's faction, for example, we observe in Figure 14 that even this one edge-removal results in a smaller 4-connected cohesive block of six persons {1, 2, 3, 4, 8, 14}, out of the original 10 in block 5, nested within a larger 3-cohesive block. All six persons in this 4-block align with T, as predicted from cohesion. If we allocate the remaining nodes in the 3-block according to their cohesion with T versus A, person 20 is predicted to go with T and the remainder with A. Allocating those in the 2- and 1-components by the same procedure, only person 10's alignment is indeterminate, and 10 was one of the three not factionally aligned.

The results of this test of the global predictions of faction membership from our connectivity measures are summarized in Table 6 ($r = .969$, $p < .000001$). The columns indicate whether cohesion is greater, equal, or less with Mr. Hi (T) than with John (A). This correlation is nearly identical to Zachary's prediction using the Ford-Fulkerson maximum flow–

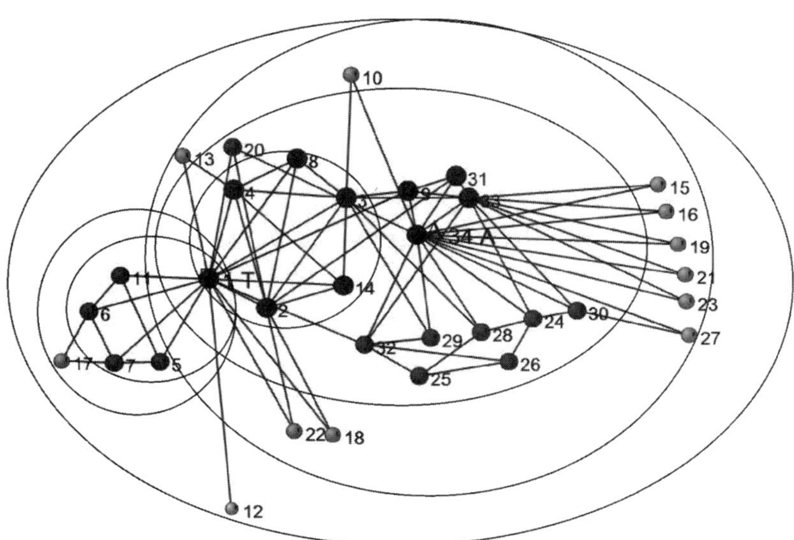

FIGURE 14. Nested cohesive sets by k-connectivity after person 14 affiliates with T.

TABLE 6
Predictions of Faction Membership from Structural Cohesion ($r = .969$)

Cohesion Faction	Mr. Hi (T)	Equal for T and A	John (A)	Members by ID number
Mr. Hi's (T)	15			1–8,11–14,18,20,22
None	1	1	1	17, 10, 19
John's (A)			16	9,15,16,21,23–34

minimum cut algorithm on weighted edges, as shown in Table 7 ($r = .955$). Zachary's prediction, however, contains an unwarranted postulate of some kind of network "agency" that "finds" an optimal edge-cut without any explanation as to mechanism.

C. Evaluation of Results

Alignment of factions in the karate club is predicted by structural and path cohesion as well as by Zachary's adhesive weighted edge-cuts. The results shows the contribution of conditional density, in addition to cohesion measured by connectivity, to identifying localized high-density subgroups within cohesive blocks. The high-density subgroup (set 6) that was the core of T's support group was a very compact group with minimum distances among members, which may have contributed to leader T's retention of so many followers in the breakup of the club. Zachary had the right result as well, but possibly for the wrong reasons.[38] Although both models make near-perfect predictions, the cohesion argument has advantages over the capacitated flow and possibly other arguments in the karate study on the grounds of parsimony (use of unweighted over weighted edges) and a process model of agency as the mechanism involved in segmentation.[39]

[38] Another reason that Zachary's capacitated flow argument does so well is that flow, in the unweighted case, is highly correlated with number of independent paths.

[39] The fact that Mr. Hi is the cutnode in a bifurcated network might help to explain—in sociological terms—why he is the instigator of the dispute in the first place: He has a set of at least five potential students who were never integrated into the larger cohesive block containing the administrator (#34), and for Mr. Hi it was clear from the beginning that they would follow his leadership. He was also a strong figure for many of his other adherents.

TABLE 7
Predictions of Faction Membership from Zachary's Minimum Weighted Edge-Cut ($r = .955$)

Edge-Cut Faction	Mr. Hi (T)	John (A)	Members by ID number
Mr. Hi's (T)	15		1–8,11–14,18,20,22
None	1	2	17, 10, 19
John's (A)		16	9,15,16,21,23–34

V. TESTING PREDICTIVENESS OF COHESION MEASURES ON A LARGER SCALE

The evidence of the karate data is useful in evaluating connectivity as a measure of ohesion. The aggregate cohesion measure makes correct predictions about the consequences of cohesion for individual behavior and the emergence or division of social groups, but it does so on a relatively small scale in which different measures and approaches to cohesion might give similar results. Everett (1996) analyzed the overlap of cliques in Zachary's data, and got similar results concerning cohesive subsets that predicted faction membership. Large high-connectivity groups will not in general, however, be constructed out of intersecting cliques. We do not presume that connectivity is the only measure of cohesion, only that it is a fundamental component of interpersonal cohesion in social groups, large or small.

In our computation of factional groups for the karate club, we used the measure of node-flow (number of node-independent paths) to compute pairwise cohesion (White and Newman 2001). Pairwise cohesion is computed separately for each pair of nodes in a group, whereas connectivity is the minimum of these values over all pairs. Pairwise flow, which measures the number of edge-independent paths, is always the same or greater than node-flow. Johansen and White (forthcoming) successfully used the maximum flow measure, equivalent to an unweighted version of Zachary's method, in predicting large-scale political factions in a nomadic society. The use of pairwise measures of cohesive strength (both flow and node-flow) may be widely useful in studying patterns of social cohesion and adhesion, but it is still an open research question as to which measures make better predictions, and why.

Moody and White (2000) characterize the respective graphs of socially cohesive friendship groups in 12 American high schools, and again of 57 financially cohesive business groups, by computing k-components. They find that embeddedness in k-connected groups is a strong predictor of school attachment and is the only predictor of attachment among diverse network variables that replicates significantly across all schools. Using data from a study of business unity by Mizruchi (1992), they also show that cohesion or level of connectivity applied to the network of corporate interlocks among 57 firms, controlling for other network measures, predicts similarity in business behaviors. They illustrate the fundamental importance of connectivity and its hierarchical embedding,[40] and argue for a wide range of applications in sociology. Moody and White's (2000) algorithm successively removes sets of nodes with the lowest connectivity. By combining several algorithms of low complexity, the algorithm makes connectivity computations feasible for relatively large graphs. Studies using connectivity to measure social cohesion, such as surmised but not actually employed by Grannis (1998), however, are still quite rare.[41]

Brudner and White (1997) and White et al. (2001), for example, identified sociologically important cohesive blocks in two large (n = 2332 and 1458 respectively), sparse networks using the concept of cohesion measured by connectivity. The first of these studies showed that membership in a cohesive block, defined by marital ties among households in an Austrian farming village, was correlated with stratified class membership, defined by single-heir succession to ownership of the productive resources of farmsteads and farmlands. In the second study, they found that the cohesive block defined by marital ties of Mexican villagers was restricted to a bicomponent that included families with several generations of residence and excluded spatial outliers and recent immigrants and families in adjacent villages. The cohesive block defined by *compadrazgo*,[42] on the other hand, crosscut this village nucleus and integrated spatial outliers and recent immigrants. In contrast to the first study, the Mexican case established a network basis for the observed cross-village egalitarian class structure.

[40] In both their analyses, they define two measures, one the highest k-connected subgraph to which each node belongs, and the other a measure of cohesive embeddedness, discussed above. The two measures will typically be highly correlated.

[41] NSF grant #BCS-9978282, "Longitudinal Network Studies and Predictive Cohesion Theory," Principal Investigator Douglas R. White and consultant Frank Harary, is focused on comparative studies of this type.

[42] Ritual kinship established between parents and godparents.

To illustrate how structural and path cohesion might be combined with a conditional distance approach, our example of cohesiveness structures in the Internet might be extended to study whether cohesive blocks of Web sites that exceed a certain conditional density (or effective diameter) may define the user communities and content or functional clusters on the Web. Like density and distance, diameter within cohesive sets—what we would call "conditional diameter"—is one of the other predictive measures that could be developed within a methodology for analysis of cohesive blocks, although we will not do so here. As a further example, "invisible colleges" in intellectual and citation networks are likely to be predicted both from cohesive blocks and conditional densities or diameters.

VI. SUMMARY AND CONCLUSION

In arguing for a distributed and scalable conception and measurement of cohesion, our purpose is to provide a theoretical foundation for asking some empirical questions about social cohesion that logically lie at the heart of sociology and social anthropology. It is clear that cohesion is an important concept fundamental to defining social groups and their boundaries as emergent phenomena. Work carried out by Watts (1999a,1999b) on the small world problem tied network structure to an important global characteristic of networks, their "connectedness," but like Wasserman and Faust (1994:115–17) he did not utilize the graph theoretic measurement of connectivity.[43] Small-scale "social psychological" cohesion based on the model of cliques and attachment-to-group makes a difference because social psychological cohesion affects the strength of group norms, how much individuals are willing to sacrifice for the groups, and so forth. But in a large network what difference does subgroup cohesion at a macro-level make when defined by *k*-component connectivity?[44] This is an empirical problem of considerable significance. Suppose we have two large groups both equal in the density of choices, both connected and similar in other specific structural features as well, but one being more cohesive

[43] Graph theoretic terminology has the advantage of distinguishing simple connectedness from connectivity, with its higher-order properties of structural and path cohesion. Watts uses the two terms interchangeably, thereby ignoring one of the major contributions of graph theory to the study of group cohesion. Wasserman and Faust are aware of the graph theoretic concept of connectivity as an indicator of cohesion but do not discuss methods or algorithms to apply to social networks to compute levels of connectivity.

[44] Another common use of the term connectivity is for the distribution of number of ties for each node, synonymous with the graph theoretical concept of degree.

than the other in the sense defined here. What would be the concomitant differences in the behavior of the groups and their members?

This paper goes back to a fundamental problem for network theory to establish a solid theoretic and measurement basis by which macrolevel questions of this sort can be examined in large-scale social networks. It is the foundational paper for a series of empirical studies addressing such issues. A subsequent paper in this series (Moody and White 2000) contains literature reviews and empirical analyses of case studies that examine the consequences of cohesion defined as *k*-component connectivities in large-scale social groups.

Within a social group, high connectivity plus a modest additional density of randomly distributed ties that reduce average path length within the group (Watts 1999b) is capable of generating large-scale group cohesion, as we showed in Section I.D. Our hypotheses (I.B) suggested how such cohesion might affect coordinated social action, social homogeneity, the emergence of group norms at the macro level and, in sufficiently compact groups (I.C), the emergence of interpersonal trust. Watts (1999a, 1999b) has alerted sociologists to reconsider the problem of "distributed social phenomena" in terms of his models and parameters of "small worlds"—large networks with local clustering of ties but relatively low average distance between members. Connectivity plus conditional density is another model of distributed social phenomena that defines a measure of cohesion not in terms of local clustering but of node-independent paths and invulnerability to disconnection by node removal.[45] The identification of bounded connectivity subgroups in a network is an ideal means of finding the boundaries of cohesive worlds ("small" in the sense of low average path lengths but not necessarily locally clustered) and measuring the degree of cohesiveness in each of their embedded subgroups.[46]

[45] A typical critique of connectivity-based measures of cohesion might run like this: "a cycle of 1000 people (connectivity 2) running from the United States to China and back does not constitute a cohesive group." Surely not, but a group of 1000 people with connectivity 5 (or higher, each a higher embedded level of cohesion), conditional density of 10 percent, and first and second shortest average path lengths of 3.5 and 4.0 (a "small world" as defined by Watts 1999a, b) is a large-scale group with considerable cohesiveness.

[46] Future research can combine the "small world" approach that takes as key variables the average path length of the first and second shortest independent paths between pairs of nodes (Watts 1999a, b) with our connectivity approach. When the average path lengths of the first and second shortest independent paths in a network are short, the logical implication is that the average cycle length between any two pairs of nodes is also relatively short (approximated by the sum of the two shortest independent path-length averages), and thus measuring the average cycle length of

A potential bias in favor of defining social cohesion as existing "only" in face-to-face groups may well have accumulated from the past century of small-group research, reinforced by "common sense" about primary groups. We have shown step by step, within both an intuitive and a graph theoretic framework, giving concrete hypotheses and sample results, the limitations of such a bias. Using the data of social networks we examined cohesion as the network component of a more inclusive concept of solidarity, which includes individual psychological attachments to a group, but does not stop at the boundaries of primary groups. We offered an alternative methodological perspective and detailed hypotheses as to how network cohesion may exist in large-scale groups as easily as in small.

Our precise and scalable method for measuring cohesion in networks and subgroups of any size has the advantage of detecting boundaries of subgroups, finding hierarchies of embedded subgroups, and measuring cohesiveness at each level of embedding. No other method of measuring cohesiveness has these advantages (most give an overwhelming welter of overlapping subgroups that introduce a second intervening level of analysis and interpretation), and our review of graph theoretic concepts (see also White 1998) shows no other method to possess equal validity in terms of the construct criteria that cohesive groups are "resistant to breaking apart" (see our definition 1.1.2) and are weaker or stronger in proportion to the "multiplicity of bonds" that hold them together (1.2.2). When combined with conditional density, the connectivity-based measure of cohesion has measurement validity in that our measure of cohesion increases with each additional edge added to a graph of fixed size. In the karate club example we showed how cohesive blocks and their conditional density contribute to a process of group division.

A fundamental intuition involved in the concept of social cohesion, we argue, is consistent with the idea that the greater the minimum number of actors whose removal disconnects a group, the greater the cohesion. Equivalently, as demonstrated by Menger's Theorem (1927), the greater the number of multiple independent paths, the higher the cohesion. The level of cohesion is higher when members of a group are connected as opposed to disconnected, and further, when the group and its

biconnectivity in the network. Similarly, the sum of the averages for first, second, and third shortest independent paths give an approximation of the average cycle length of triconnectivity, and so forth. In the case of triconnectivity, there are two independent "shortest cycles" between pairs of nodes. The relationship of average path length in k-connected structures needs to be investigated both in simulations and large-scale empirical network studies.

actors are not only connected but also have redundancies in their interconnections. Overlapping circles of friends increase social cohesion, for example, although our operationalization of the cohesion is not the same as the "intersecting social circles" concept of Simmel.[47] The higher the redundancies of independent connections between pairs of nodes, the higher the cohesion, and the more social circles in which any pair of persons is contained.[48]

To give a brief synopsis of the arguments behind the methodology presented here, given that the cohesiveness of a group is greater when there are higher redundancies of interconnections by multiple independent paths, the cohesion of a graph or subgraph is measured by its connectivity and, on a finer scale, by surplus density conditional on connectivity. Measurements of social cohesion by connectivity and conditional density are constructed by the following two sets of definitions derived from graph theory:

1. The *connectivity* $\kappa(G)$ of a graph G is the smallest number k of nodes whose removal disconnects any component of G or reduces the order of any component to a single node. A graph G is *k-connected* if $\kappa(G) \geq k$. A *k-component* is a maximal k-connected subgraph of G. A graph G is *k-cohesive*, to coin a new sociological term, if $\kappa(G) = k$. Hence, for each value of k, the k-components of a social network represented by a graph G define empirical social groups with a corresponding level k of cohesion. Subgroups with higher levels of cohesion are embedded in those with lower cohesion since the k-components of a graph form hierarchies by inclusion. According to Menger's Theorem, a graph is k-connected if and only if every pair of nodes is connected by at least k independent paths. The redundancy of multiple independent paths connecting actors is fundamental to measuring group cohesion as distinct from the proximities of actors in a network. The *structural cohesion* of a group is thus the minimum num-

[47] In Simmel's (1908) conception, zones around each ego or ego-memberships in groups simply overlap or intersect to form extensive connected networks (cf. Blau 1964; Kadushin 1966), but without necessarily forming higher-order cycles or connectivity sets (see footnote 25 regarding Alba and Kadushin's unsuccessful attempt to operationalize the higher-order cycles concept of cohesion).

[48] The widely used "social circles" approach to large-scale cohesion as webs of overlapping cliques (Alba 1972, 1973, 1982; Alba and Moore 1978) has the same defect as Freeman's (1996) intersecting cliques: pairs of nodes connected at some distance by multiple independent paths are not necessarily detected as part of the same cohesive subset.

ber k of its actors whose removal would not allow the group to remain connected or would reduce the group to but a single member. Hence a k-cohesive block is not only k-connected but every pair of actors is connected by at least k node-independent paths.

2. *Conditional density* measures cohesion on a finer scale, that of surplus density beyond that implied by connectivity. For each of the k-components of a graph, these two measures may be combined into an aggregate measure of social cohesion, suitable for both small- and large-scale network studies.

As a distributive phenomenon with emergent properties—such as might define the boundaries of social groups—connectivity is of crucial importance to the study of social networks. Many types of large-scale cohesive sets not detectable by other measures are identifiable from k-component connectivities. Correlations between hierarchical embeddedness in cohesive blocks and potential effects of cohesion—such as school attachment, or similarities in business behaviors, as in the studies of Moody and White (2000)—underscore the conceptual and substantive importance of connectivity as the primary measure of cohesiveness. In the study of social networks, both large and small, node connectivities and conditional densities are fundamental measurement concepts for social cohesion. Yet, one of the preconceptions about cohesion that is most resistant to change is the idea that in social networks, social interaction has only proximal effects, and that indirect effects quickly decay as we move from direct effects to effects along paths of distance 2 or 3, beyond which indirect effects are regarded as minimal.

It is worth stressing once more that what this bias in preconceptions of social cohesion omits are the two fundamental properties of the redundancies created by multiple independent pathways and multiple-node cut sets. First, independent pathways are convergent in their indirect effects, even at a distance. Independent paths between every pair of nodes in a cohesive block defined by connectivity at level k (which necessarily equals the minimum number of such paths) may more than compensate for the decay of effects of cohesive interaction along long paths. Studies of large-scale social diffusion, for example, typically rest upon and demonstrate the fact that long paths matter. What connectivity provides in terms of transmission effects within the internal networks of cohesive groups is the possibility for repetition along multiple independent pathways of rumor, information, material item, and influence transmission. Second, multiple independent pathways (equinumerous to minimum cuts) necessarily imply stronger bonding between pairs of nodes, regardless of distance decay. It is k times as hard to break apart a network tying nodes together by k node-independent pathways than it is to break apart a single chain that connects them.

The effects of multiple bonding and redundancy or repetition along convergent independent pathways are crucial in the formation of social coherence, social norms, sanctions and solidarities, and the emergence of socially or culturally homogeneous groups, and thus should be of focal interest to the study of social cohesion, including cohesion on a very large scale.

REFERENCES

Alba, Richard D. 1972. "COMPLT—A Program for Analyzing Sociometric Data and Clustering Similarity Matrices." *Behavioral Science* 17:566.

———. 1973. "A Graph Theoretic Definition of a Sociometric Clique." *Journal of Mathematical Sociology* 3:113–26.

———. 1982. "Taking Stock of Network Analysis: A Decade's Results." Pp. 39–74 in *Research in the Sociology of Organizations* 1, edited by Samuel B. Bacharach. Greenwich, CN: JAI Press.

Alba, Richard. D., and Charles Kadushin. 1976. "The Intersection of Social Circles: A New Measure of Proximity in Networks." *Sociological Methods and Research* 5:77–102.

Alba, Richard D., and Gwen Moore. 1978. "Elite Social Circles." *Sociological Methods and Research* 7:167–88.

Batagelj, Vladimir and Andrej Mrvar. 1997. "Networks/Pajek: A Program for Large Networks Analysis." University of Ljubljana, Slovenia. http://vlado.fmf.uni-lj.si/pub/networks/pajek/.

———. 1998. "Pajek: A Program for Large Networks Analysis." *Connections* 21:47–57.

Blau, Peter. 1964. *Crosscutting Social Circles*. Orlando, FL: Academic Press.

Borgatti, Stephen P., Martin G. Everett, and Paul Shirley. 1990. "LS Sets, Lambda Sets and Other Cohesive Sets." *Social Networks* 12:337–57.

Brudner, Lilyan A., and Douglas R. White. 1997. "Class, Property, and Structural Endogamy: Visualizing Networked Histories." *Theory and Society* 26:161–208.

Carron, Albert V. 1982. "Cohesiveness in Sport Groups: Implications and Considerations." *Journal of Sport Psychology* 4:123–38.

Dirac, Gabriel A. 1960. "Généralisations du Théorème de Menger." *Comptes Rendus de Académie des Sciences. Paris* 250:4252–53/405–09.

Doreian, Patrick, and Katherine L. Woodward. 1994. "Defining and Locating Cores and Boundaries of Social Networks." *Social Networks* 16:267–93.

Even, Shimon. 1979. *Graph Algorithms*. Potomac, MD: Computer Science Press.

Everett, Martin G. 1982a. "Graph Theoretic Blocking of k-plexes and k-cutpoints." *Journal of Mathematical Sociology* 9:75–84.

———. 1982b. "A Graph Theoretic Blocking Algorithm for Social Networks." *Social Networks* 5:323–46.
———. 1983. "An Extension of EBLOC to Valued Graphs." *Social Networks* 5:395–402.
———. 1984. "An Analysis of Cyclically Dense Data using EBLOC." *Social Networks* 6:97–102.
———. 1996. "Cohesive Subgroups." http://www.analytictech.com/networks/chapter_4_cohesive_subgroups.htm.
Fararo, Thomas, and Patrick Doreian. 1998. "The Theory of Solidarity: An Agenda of Problems." Pp. 1–31 in *The Problem of Solidarity: Theories and Models*, edited by Patrick Doreian and Thomas Fararo. Amsterdam: Gordon and Breach.
Festinger, Leon, Stanley Schachter, and Kurt Back. 1950. *Social Pressures in Informal Groups*. New York: Harper.
Ford, Lester R., and David R. Fulkerson. 1956. "Maximal Flow Through a Network." *Canadian Journal of Mathematics* 8: 399–404.
Freeman, Linton C. 1992. "The Sociological Concept of 'Group': An Empirical Test of Two Models." *American Journal of Sociology* 98:55–79.
———. 1996. "Cliques, Galois Lattices, and the Structure of Human Social Groups." *Social Networks* 18:173–87.
French, John R. P., Jr. 1941. "The Disruption and Cohesion of Groups." *Journal of Abnormal and Social Psychology* 36:361–77.
Gibbons, Alan. 1985. *Algorithmic Graph Theory*. Cambridge, England: Cambridge University Press.
Granovetter, Mark S. 1973. "The Strength of Weak Ties." *American Journal of Sociology* 78:1360–80.
———. 1983. "The Strength of Weak Ties: A Network Theory Revised." *Sociological Theory* 1:203–33.
Grannis, Richard. 1998. "The Importance of Trivial Streets: Residential Streets and Residential Segregation." *American Journal of Sociology* 103:1530–64.
Gross, Neal, and William E. Martin. 1952. "On Group Cohesiveness." *American Journal of Sociology* 52:546–54.
Harary, Frank. 1953. "On the Notion of Balance of a Signed Graph." *Michigan Mathematics Journal* 2:143–46
———. 1969. *Graph Theory*. Reading, MA: Addison-Wesley.
———. 1983. "Conditional Connectivity." *Networks* 13:347–57.
Harary, Frank, and Dorwin Cartwright. 1961. "The Number of Lines in a Digraph of Each Connectedness Category." *SIAM Review* 3:309–14.
Harary, Frank, and Yuji Kodama. 1964. "On the Genus of an n-connected Graph." *Fundamenta Mathematicae* 54:7–13.
Harary, Frank, Robert Norman, and Dorwin Cartwright. 1965. *Structural Models: An Introduction to the Theory of Directed Graphs*. New York: Wiley.
Johansen, Ulla C., and Douglas R. White. Forthcoming. "Collaborative Long-Term Ethnography and Longitudinal Social Analysis of a Nomadic Clan in Southeastern Turkey." In *Chronicling Cultures: Long-Term Field Research in Anthropology*, edited by Robert V. Kemper and Anya Royce. Walnut Creek, CA: Altamira Press.
Kadushin, Charles. 1966. "The Friends and Supporters of Psychotherapy: On Social Circles in Urban Life." *American Sociological Review* 31:786–802.

Kolchin, Valentin F. 1999. *Random Graphs*. Cambridge, England: Cambridge University Press.

Laumann, Edward O., Peter V. Marsden, and David Prensky. 1989. "The Boundary Specification Problem in Network Analysis." Pp. 61–87 in *Research Methods in Social Network Analysis*, edited by Linton C. Freeman, Douglas R. White and A. Kimball Romney. Fairfax, VA: George Mason University Press.

Libo, Lester M. 1953. *Measuring Group Cohesiveness*. Ann Arbor: Research Center for Group Dynamics, Institute for Social Research, University of Michigan.

Markovsky, Barry. 1998. "Social Network Conceptions of Solidarity." Pp. 343–72 in *The Problem of Solidarity: Theories and Models*, edited by Patrick Doreian and Thomas Fararo. Amsterdam: Gordon and Breach.

Markovsky, Barry, and Mark V. Chafee. 1995. "Social Identification and Solidarity: A Reformulation." Pp. 249–70 in *Advances in Group Processes*, vol. 12, edited by Barry Markovsky, Jodi O'Brien and Karen Heimer. Greenwich, CT: JAI Press.

Markovsky, Barry, and Edward J. Lawler. 1994. "A New Theory of Social Solidarity." Pp. 113–37 in *Advances in Group Processes*, vol. 11, edited by Barry Markovsky, Jodi O'Brien and Karen Heimer. Greenwich, CT: JAI Press.

Menger, Karl. 1927. "Zur Allgemeinen Kurventheorie." *Fundamenta Mathematicae* 10:96–115.

Mizruchi, Mark S. 1992. *The American Corporate Network, 1904–1974*. Beverly Hills, CA: Sage Publications.

Moody, James, and Douglas R. White. 2000. "Social Cohesion and Connectivity: A Hierarchical Conception of Social Groups." *Santa Fe Institute Working Paper* 00-08-049, submitted to the *American Journal of Sociology*.

Moreno, Jacob L., and Helen H. Jennings. 1937. "Statistics of Social Configurations." *Sociometry* 1:342–74.

Morowitz, Harold. 2000. "Emergence and the Law." *Complexity* 5(4):11–12.

Mudrack, Peter E. 1989. "Defining Group Cohesiveness: A Legacy of Confusion?" *Small Group Behavior* 20:37–49.

Palmer, Edgar N. 1985. *Graphical Evolution: An Introduction to the Theory of Random Graphs*. New York: Wiley.

Powell, Walter W., Douglas R. White, Kenneth W. Koput, and Jason Owen-Smith. 2001. "Evolution of a Science-Based Industry: Dynamic Analyses and Network Visualization of Biotechnology." Working paper, Santa Fe Institute.

Scott, John. 2000. *Social Network Analysis: A Handbook*. 2d ed. London: Sage.

Seidman, Stephen B. 1983. "Internal Cohesion and LS Sets in Graphs." *Social Networks* 5:97–107.

Seidman, Stephen B., and Brian L. Foster. 1978. "A Graph-theoretic Generalization of the Clique Concept." *Journal of Mathematical Sociology* 6:139–54.

Simmel, Georg. 1908. *Soziologie: Untersuchungen uber die Formen der Vergesellschaftung*. 2d ed. Munich, Germany: Duncker and Humbolt. Partly translated [1950] in *The Sociology of Georg Simmel*, edited by K. H. Wolf. New York: Free Press.

Skvoretz, John. 1998. "Solidarity, Social Structure, and Social Control." Pp. 373–402 in *The Problem of Solidarity: Theories and Models*, edited by Patrick Doreian and Thomas Fararo. Amsterdam: Gordon and Breach.

Tutte, William T. 1966. *Connectivity in Graphs*. Toronto: University of Toronto Press.

Wasserman, Stanley, and Katherine Faust. 1994. *Social Network Analysis: Methods and Applications*. Cambridge, England: Cambridge University Press.

Watts, Duncan J. 1999a. *Small Worlds: The Dynamics of Networks Between Order and Randomness*. Princeton Studies in Complexity. Princeton: Princeton University Press.

———. 1999b. "Networks, Dynamics, and the Small-World Phenomenon." *American Journal of Sociology* 105:493–527.

White, Douglas R. 1998. "Concepts of Cohesion, Old and New: Which Are Valid, Which Are Not?" Working paper, Department of Anthropology, University of California, Irvine.

———. 1999. "Longitudinal Network Studies and Predictive Cohesion Theory." NSF grant #BCS-9978282, http://eclectic.ss.uci.edu/~drwhite/nsf/nsf.htm

White, Douglas R., and Mark Newman. 2001. "Fast Approximation Algorithms for Finding Node-independent Paths." Working paper, Santa Fe Institute.

White, Douglas R., M. Schnegg, L. A. Brudner, and H. Nutini. Forthcoming. "Conectividad Múltiple y sus Fronteras de Integración: Parentesco y Compadrazgo en Tlaxcala Rural." In *Redes Sociales: Teoría y Aplicaciones*, edited by Jorge Gil and Samuel Schmidt. Mexico City: UNAM Press.

Whitney, Hassler. 1932. "Congruent Graphs and the Connectivity of Graphs." *American Journal of Mathematics* 54:150–68.

Zachary, Wayne W. 1975. *The Cybernetics of Conflict in a Small Group: An Information Flow Model*. M.A. thesis, Department of Anthropology, Temple University.

———. 1977. "An Information Flow Model for Conflict and Fission in Small Groups." *Journal of Anthropological Research* 33:452–73.

8

THE STATISTICAL EVALUATION OF SOCIAL NETWORK DYNAMICS

*Tom A. B. Snijders**

A class of statistical models is proposed for longitudinal network data. The dependent variable is the changing (or evolving) relation network, represented by two or more observations of a directed graph with a fixed set of actors. The network evolution is modeled as the consequence of the actors making new choices, or withdrawing existing choices, on the basis of functions, with fixed and random components, that the actors try to maximize. Individual and dyadic exogenous variables can be used as covariates. The change in the network is modeled as the stochastic result of network effects (reciprocity, transitivity, etc.) and these covariates. The existing network structure is a dynamic constraint for the evolution of the structure itself. The models are continuous-time Markov chain models that can be implemented as simulation models. The model parameters are estimated from observed data. For estimating and testing these models, statistical procedures are proposed that are based on the method of moments. The statistical procedures are implemented using a stochastic approximation algorithm based on computer simulations of the network evolution process.

1. INTRODUCTION

Social networks represent relations (e.g., friendship, esteem, collaboration, etc.) between actors (e.g., individuals, companies, etc.). This paper is concerned with network data structures in which all relationships within a given set of n actors are considered. Such a network can be represented by an $n \times n$ matrix $x = (x_{ij})$, where x_{ij} represents the relation directed

*University of Groningen, The Netherlands

from actor i to actor j $(i, j = 1, \ldots, n)$. Only dichotomous relations are considered here: the relation from i to j either is present, denoted $x_{ij} = 1$, or absent, denoted $x_{ij} = 0$. Self-relations are not considered, so that the diagonal values x_{ii} are meaningless. They are formally defined as $x_{ii} = 0$. This x is the adjacency matrix of the directed graph by which the network can be represented; it is also called the *sociomatrix*.

More specifically, we consider longitudinal data on entire networks. It is supposed that the data available are a time series $x(t), t \in \{t_1, \ldots, t_M\}$ of social networks for a constant set $\{1, \ldots, n\}$ of actors. The observation times are ordered—i.e., $t_1 < t_2 < \ldots < t_M$. The number M of time points is at least 2. The purpose of the statistical analysis is to obtain an insight in the evolution of the network, where the initial state $x(t_1)$ is taken for granted.

Longitudinal social network data are a complex data structure, requiring complex methods of data analysis for a satisfactory treatment. Holland and Leinhardt (1977a, 1977b) and Wasserman (1977) already proposed to use continuous-time Markov chains as a model for longitudinal social networks. In a continuous-time model, time is assumed to flow on continuously, although observations are available only at the discrete time points t_1 to t_M, and between the observations the network is assumed to change unobserved at random moments as time progresses. Continuous-time models offer, in principle, greater flexibility than the discrete-time Markov chain models elaborated—e.g., by Katz and Proctor (1959) and Wasserman and Iacobucci (1988).

A basic continuous-time Markov chain model for dichotomous social networks, the reciprocity model, was elaborated by Wasserman (1977, 1979, 1980) and further investigated by Leenders (1995a, 1995b) and Snijders (1999). This model is limited because it assumes *dyad independence*. A dyad is defined as the pair (x_{ij}, x_{ji}) of relations between two actors i and j. Dyad independence means that the dyads $(X_{ij}(t), X_{ji}(t))$ evolve as mutually independent Markov chains. This assumption effectively allows one to change the analysis from the level of the network to the level of the dyad. This is computationally attractive but does not leave much room for realistic statistical modeling. Effects related to dependence in the relations between sets of three or more actors—e.g., transitivity ("a friend of my friend is my friend")—cannot be represented by models with dyad independence. Other continuous-time models for social network evolution were proposed by Wasserman (1980) and Mayer (1984), but these models were also very restrictive in order to allow parameter estimation.

Markov chain Monte Carlo (MCMC) methods can be used to develop statistical procedures for quite general probability models for the evolution of social networks, provided that these models can be implemented as stochastic simulation models. This was proposed by Snijders (1996) for data defined by sociometric rankings. Snijders and Van Duijn (1997) sketched how this approach can be used for dichotomous social network data. They also indicated how such an actor-oriented model must be specified in order to obtain the dyad-independent models of Wasserman and Leenders. Empirical applications of these stochastic actor-oriented models were presented in Van de Bunt (1999) and Van de Bunt, Van Duijn, and Snijders (1999). The present paper extends this method to data observed at more than two time points, specifies a more efficient and simpler stochastic approximation algorithm, and presents a wider array of effects that can be included in the model.

The basic idea for our model for social network evolution is that the actors in the network may evaluate the network structure and try to obtain a "pleasant" (more neutrally stated, "positively evaluated") configuration of relations. The actors base their choices in the network evolution on the present state of the network, without using a memory of earlier states. However, they are assumed to have full knowledge of the present network. This represents the idea that actors pursue their own goals under the constraints of their environment, while they themselves constitute each others' changing environment (cf. Zeggelink 1994). It is immaterial whether this "network optimization" is the actors' intentional behavior; the only assumption is that the network can be modeled *as if* each actor strives after such a positively evaluated configuration. This evaluation is defined as a function of the network as regarded from the perspective of the focal actor, and depends on parameters that are to be estimated from the data. This approach to network evolution is in line with the theoretical sociological principle of methodological individualism and was referred to by Snijders (1996) as a *stochastic actor-oriented model.* The evaluation includes a random element to account for the deviation between theoretical expectation and observed reality, which leads to a kind of random utility model (cf. random utility models commonly used in econometrics and treated, e.g., in Maddala [1983]). The models can be implemented as stochastic simulation models, which is the basis for the MCMC procedure for parameter estimation. This is a frequentist procedure, using the method of moments. The MCMC implementation of the method of moments uses a stochastic approximation algorithm that is a descendant of the Robbins-Monro (1951) algorithm.

2. CONTINUOUS-TIME MARKOV CHAINS

This section gives a brief introduction to continuous-time Markov chains. Karlin and Taylor (1975) and Norris (1997) give general treatments of this kind of stochastic process model. More elaborate introductions to continuous-time Markov chain models for social networks are given by Leenders (1995b) and Wasserman (1979, 1980).

The available data are assumed to be two or more observations of social networks; but the present section is phrased, more generally, in terms of an arbitrary finite outcome space $\mathcal{Y}$. The finitely many observation times t_1 to t_M are embedded in a continuous set of time points $\mathcal{T} = [t_1, t_M] = \{t \in \mathbb{R} \mid t_1 \leq t \leq t_M\}$. Thus it is assumed that changes can take place unobserved between the observation moments. This is not unrealistic and allows a more versatile and natural mathematical treatment.

Suppose that $\{Y(t) \mid t \in \mathcal{T}\}$ is a stochastic process where the $Y(t)$ have a finite outcome space $\mathcal{Y}$ and the time parameter t assumes values in a bounded or unbounded interval $\mathcal{T} \subset \mathbb{R}$. Such a stochastic process is a Markov process or Markov chain if for any time $t_a \in \mathcal{T}$, the conditional distribution of the future, $\{Y(t) \mid t > t_a\}$ given the present and the past, $\{Y(t) \mid t \leq t_a\}$, is a function only of the present, $Y(t_a)$. This implies that for any possible outcome $x \in \mathcal{Y}$, and for any pair of time points $t_a < t_b$,

$$\begin{aligned} &\mathrm{P}\{Y(t_b) = x \mid Y(t) = y(t) \text{ for all } t \leq t_a\} \\ &\quad = \mathrm{P}\{Y(t_b) = x \mid Y(t_a) = y(t_a)\}. \end{aligned} \tag{1}$$

The Markov chain is said to have a stationary transition distribution if the probability (1) depends on the time points t_a and t_b only as a function of the elapsed time in between, $t_b - t_a$. It can be proved that if $\{Y(t) \mid t \in \mathcal{T}\}$ is a continuous-time Markov chain with stationary transition distribution, then there exists a function $q : \mathcal{Y}^2 \rightarrow \mathbb{R}$ such that

$$\begin{aligned} q(x, y) &= \lim_{dt \downarrow 0} \frac{\mathrm{P}\{Y(t + dt) = y \mid Y(t) = x\}}{dt} \quad \text{for } y \neq x \\ q(x, x) &= \lim_{dt \downarrow 0} \frac{1 - \mathrm{P}\{Y(t + dt) = x \mid Y(t) = x\}}{dt}. \end{aligned} \tag{2}$$

This function q is called the intensity matrix or the infinitesimal generator. The element $q(x, y)$ is referred to as the *rate* at which x tends to change into y. More generally, an event is said to happen at a rate r, if the probability that it happens in a very short time interval $(t, t + dt)$ is approximately equal to $r\,dt$.

The simultaneous distribution of the Markov chain $\{Y(t) | t \geq t_a\}$ with stationary transition distribution is determined completely by the probability distribution of the initial value $Y(t_a)$ together with the intensity matrix. Specifically, the transition matrix

$$P(t_b - t_a) = \big(\mathrm{P}\{Y(t_b) = y | Y(t_a) = x\}\big)_{x, y \in \mathcal{Y}}$$

is defined by

$$P(t) = e^{Qt},$$

where Q is the matrix with elements $q(x, y)$ and the matrix exponential is defined by

$$e^{Qt} = \sum_{h=0}^{\infty} \frac{Q^h t^h}{h!}.$$

The reasons for specializing the model to Markov processes with stationary transition distributions are that such models often are quite natural, and that they lend themselves well to computer simulation. The resulting dynamic computer simulation models can be regarded as a type of discrete event simulation model as discussed by Fararo and Hummon (1994).

3. STOCHASTIC ACTOR-ORIENTED MODELS FOR NETWORK EVOLUTION: SIMPLE SPECIFICATION

The specification of the model developed in this paper has three ingredients: the rate function, the objective function, and the gratification function. A simple specification is determined by only the objective function, with a constant rate function and a gratification function equal to zero. The model is explained first for this simple specification. The rate and gratification functions are treated in a later section.

3.1. *Basic Model Ingredients*

The class of all sociomatrices—i.e., of all $n \times n$ matrices of 0-1 elements with a zero diagonal—is denoted by $\mathcal{X}$. Note that $\mathcal{X}$ has $2^{n(n-1)}$ elements, a number that is so huge that analytical calculations based on the intensity matrix will be out of the question for most purposes.

It is assumed that all actors "control" their outgoing relations, which are collected in the row vector $(X_{i1}(t), \ldots, X_{in}(t))$ of the sociomatrix. Actors have the opportunity to change their outgoing relations at stochastic times; in the interval between the observation moments t_m and t_{m+1} these opportunities occur at a rate ρ_m. When actors change their outgoing relations, they are assumed to strive after a rewarding configuration for themselves in the network. This goal is modeled in the so-called *objective function f* discussed below, to which a random component is added, representing the actors' drives that are not explicitly modeled. The actors are assumed to have all information required to calculate their own objective function. This information can be extensive or limited, depending on the model.

At any single time point, at most one actor may change his outgoing relations. Furthermore, he may change only one relation at the time. Of course, many small changes between two observation times can result in a big difference between the two observed networks. The fact that the model specification focuses on changes of single relations is the major reason why continuous time modeling is relatively straightforward. (An example of a continuous-time model for social networks where more than one relation can change at one time point is given by Mayer [1984].) It should be noted that the fact that the actors take into account the present network structure that is common to them all, introduces a high degree of interdependence between them (when one marginalizes out, rather than conditions upon, the current network structure).

3.2. *Objective Function*

The objective function for actor i is denoted by

$$f_i(\beta, x), \quad x \in \mathcal{X}, \tag{3}$$

and indicates the degree of satisfaction for actor i inherent in the relational situation represented by x. This function depends on a parameter vector β. In the simple model specification of this section, the parameter of the statistical model is $\theta = (\rho, \beta)$, where $\rho = (\rho_1, \ldots, \rho_{M-1})$ is the vector of change rates during the time periods from t_m to t_{m+1} $(m = 1, \ldots, M-1)$.

Suppose that at some moment t, actor i has the opportunity to change her outgoing relations. At this moment, actor i determines the other actor j with whom she will change her relation x_{ij}. If immediately before time t actor i does have a relation to actor j, then a change implies withdrawing the relation; if immediately before time t actor i does *not* have a relation to actor j, then a change implies initiating the relation. Given the present state x of the network, the network that results when the single element x_{ij} is changed into $1 - x_{ij}$ (i.e., from 0 to 1 or from 1 to 0), is denoted by $x(i \rightsquigarrow j)$. Note that $x(i \rightsquigarrow j)$ refers to an entire adjacency matrix. When the current network is x, actor i has the choice between $x(i \rightsquigarrow j)$ for all possible $j = 1, \ldots, n, j \neq i$. It is assumed that actor i chooses the j that maximizes the value of her objective function $f_i(\beta, x(i \rightsquigarrow j))$ plus a random element,

$$f_i(\beta, x(i \rightsquigarrow j)) + U_i(t, x, j). \tag{4}$$

The term $U_i(t, x, j)$ is a random variable, indicating the part of the actor's preference that is not represented by the systematic component f_i. It is assumed that these random variables are independent and identically distributed for all i, t, x, j. The assumption that the actor tries to maximize (4), which refers to the state obtained immediately after making this single choice, can be regarded as an assumption of myopia: the actor does not consider the longer-term, or indirect, effects of her choices.

3.3. *Markov Chain with Random Utility Component*

These functions are used in the following way to define a continuous-time Markov chain $X(t)$ with the finite outcome space $\mathcal{X}$.

Events—i.e., changes of the network structure—take place at discrete time points; in between these points, the network structure remains constant. The process is modeled as being right-continuous: If a change takes place from state x_0 to state x_1 at time t_0, then there is an $\epsilon > 0$ such that $X(t) = x_0$ for $t_0 - \epsilon < t < t_0$, while $X(t) = x_1$ for $t_0 \leq t < t_0 + \epsilon$.

The actions of the n actors depend only on the current state of the network, not on the history of how this network came into being. All actors change their relations one at a time at stochastic moments at a rate ρ_m. This means that at each time point $t \in (t_m, t_{m+1})$, the time until the next change by *any* actor has the negative exponential distribution with parameter $n\rho_m$ and the expected waiting time until the next change by any actor is $1/(n\rho_m)$. When an event occurs, all actors have the same probability $1/n$ to be the one to change one of their outgoing relations. Given that actor i may change an outgoing relation, she chooses to change her relation to that actor j $(j \neq i)$ for whom the value of (4) is highest.

It is convenient to let the $U_i(t, x, j)$ have the type 1 extreme value distribution (or Gumbel distribution) with mean 0 and scale parameter 1 (Maddala 1983). This assumption is commonly made in random utility modeling in econometrics. When this distribution is used, the probability that the given actor i chooses the other actor j for changing the relation x_{ij} is the multinomial logit expression (cf. Maddala [1983, p. 60]),

$$p_{ij}(\theta, x) = \frac{\exp(f_i(\beta, x(i \rightsquigarrow j)))}{\sum_{h=1, h\neq i}^{n} \exp(f_i(\beta, x(i \rightsquigarrow h)))} \quad (j \neq i). \tag{5}$$

3.4. *Intensity Matrix*

It was mentioned in Section 2 that stationary transition distributions of continuous-time Markov chains are characterized by their intensity matrix. In our case, where relations are allowed to change only one at a time, the intensity matrix can be represented by functions $q_{ij}(x)$, indicating the change rates of x to $x(i \rightsquigarrow j)$ for $j \neq i$. All other change rates are 0. These functions are defined for $i, j = 1, \ldots, n$, $i \neq j$ as

$$q_{ij}(x) = \lim_{dt \downarrow 0} \frac{\mathrm{P}\{X(t + dt) = x(i \rightsquigarrow j) | X(t) = x\}}{dt}. \tag{6}$$

The intensity matrix $q(x, y)$ defined in (2) is related to $q_{ij}(x)$ by

$$q(x, y) = \begin{cases} q_{ij}(x) & \text{if } y = x(i \rightsquigarrow j) \\ 0 & \text{if } x \text{ and } y \text{ differ in more than one element} \\ -\sum_{i \neq j} q_{ij}(x) & \textit{if } x = y. \end{cases} \tag{7}$$

Note that directed graphs x and y differ in exactly one element (i, j) if and only if $y = x(i \rightsquigarrow j)$ and $x = y(i \rightsquigarrow j)$.

For the Markov chain in the simple model specification of the present section, $q_{ij}(x)$ is given for time period (t_m, t_{m+1}) by

$$q_{ij}(x) = \rho_m p_{ij}(\theta, x). \tag{8}$$

3.5. *Specification of the Model*

The objective function must contain the substantive ingredients of the model, including, for example, actor attributes and structural properties of the directed graph. Since actors have direct control only of their outgoing relations, only the dependence of f_i on row i of the adjacency matrix has an influence on the behavior of the model.

A convenient choice for the objective function is to define it as a sum

$$f_i(\beta, x) = \sum_{k=1}^{L} \beta_k s_{ik}(x), \tag{9}$$

where the weights β_k are statistical parameters indicating the strength of the corresponding effect $s_{ik}(x)$, controlling for all other effects in the model, and the $s_{ik}(x)$ are relevant functions of the digraph that are supposed to play a role in its evolution. All formulas given below for possible components s_{ik} refer to a contribution to the objective function of actor i, while the other actors to whom i could be related are indicated by j.

Effects can be distinguished according to whether they depend only on the network x—in which case they can be regarded as endogenous network effects—or also on covariates, which are supposed to be determined exogenously. Covariates can be of two kinds: (1) actor-dependent covariates V with values v_i for actor i, or (2) pair-dependent (dyadic) covariates W with values w_{ij} for the ordered pair (i, j). Only constant (i.e., time-independent) covariates are considered.

The following list is a collection of network effects, as possibilities for the functions s_{ik} in (9).

1. *Density effect*, defined by the out-degree

$$s_{i1}(x) = x_{i+} = \sum_j x_{ij};$$

2. *Reciprocity effect*, defined by the number of reciprocated relations

$$s_{i2}(x) = \sum_j x_{ij} x_{ji};$$

3. *Popularity effect*, defined by the sum of the in-degrees of the others to whom i is related,

$$s_{i3}(x) = \sum_j x_{ij} x_{+j} = \sum_j x_{ij} \sum_h x_{hj};$$

4. *Activity effect*, defined by the sum of the out-degrees of the others to whom i is related,

$$s_{i4}(x) = \sum_j x_{ij} x_{j+} = \sum_j x_{ij} \sum_h x_{jh};$$

5. *Transitivity effect*, defined by the number of transitive patterns in i's relations (ordered pairs of actors (j, h) to both of whom i is related, while also j is related to h),

$$s_{i5}(x) = \sum_{j,h} x_{ij} x_{ih} x_{jh};$$

6. *Indirect relations effect*, defined by the number of actors to whom i is indirectly related (through one intermediary—i.e., at sociometric distance 2),

$$s_{i6}(x) = \#\{j \mid x_{ij} = 0, \max_h(x_{ih} x_{hj}) > 0\};$$

7. *Balance*, defined by the likeness between the out-relations of actor i to the out-relations of the other actors j to whom i is related,

$$s_{i7}(x) = \sum_{j=1}^{n} x_{ij} \sum_{\substack{h=1 \\ h \neq i,j}}^{n} (b_0 - |x_{ih} - x_{jh}|), \tag{10}$$

where b_0 is a constant included for convenience. If the density effect is included in the model (which normally will be the case), the number b_0 can be chosen so as to obtain the clearest interpretation without essentially changing the model specification.

For example, to have a balance effect that is not too strongly correlated with the density effect, the number b_0 in (10) can be chosen so that the average of the second sum in this equation over all actors and over the first $M - 1$ time points is 0. In other words,

$$b_0 = \frac{1}{(M-1)n(n-1)(n-2)} \sum_{m=1}^{M-1} \sum_{i,j=1}^{n} \sum_{\substack{h=1 \\ h \neq i,j}}^{n} |x_{ih}(t_m) - x_{jh}(t_m)|. \tag{11}$$

This list can be extended, in principle, indefinitely. Potentially important additional types of effect are *nonlinear effects*—i.e., nonlinear functions of s_{ik} defined above, the out-degree x_{i+} being the primary candidate for such a nonlinear transformation; and other *subgraph counts* in which actor i is involved, of which the reciprocity and transitivity effects are examples.

In practically all applications it will be advisable to include the density effect, because the other effects listed above should be controlled for this effect. The reciprocity effect is so fundamental in social relations that it is advisable also to include this effect in most applications.

The transitivity and balance effects, and the indirect relations effect when it has a negative weight, all are different mathematical specifications of the intuitive idea that actor i has a "closed" or transitive personal network—i.e., the others to whom i is related tend to have comparatively many relations among themselves. Verbal theories will not often be detailed enough to distinguish between these effects. It can be determined empirically if one or some of these three effects succeed better than the others in accounting for the observed degree of closure, or transitivity, in the data.

For each actor-dependent covariate V there are the following three basic potential effects. (The notation for the functions s_{ik} does not explicitly indicate their dependence on the covariate values v_j.)

8. *Covariate-related popularity*, defined by the sum of the covariate over all actors to whom i has a relation,

$$s_{i8}(x) = \sum_j x_{ij} v_j;$$

9. *Covariate-related activity*, defined by i's out-degree weighted by his covariate value,

$$s_{i9}(x) = v_i x_{i+};$$

10. *Covariate-related dissimilarity*, defined by the sum of absolute covariate differences between i and the others to whom he is related,

$$s_{i10}(x) = \sum_j x_{ij} |v_i - v_j|.$$

Positive covariate-related popularity or activity effects will lead to associations between the covariate and the in-degrees and out-degrees, respectively. A negative covariate-related dissimilarity effect will lead to relations being formed especially between actors with similar values on the covariate.

This list can be extended—for example, by including covariate values in the definitions of the network effects listed above. This represents interactions between the covariate and the network effect.

The main effect for a pair-dependent covariate is as follows:

11. *Covariate-related preference*, defined by the sum of the values of w_{ij} for all others to whom i is related,

$$s_{i11}(x) = \sum_j x_{ij} w_{ij}.$$

Here also, the list can be extended by including covariate values in the definition of network effects.

Theoretical insights into the relational process and experience with modeling this type of data have to determine the effects that are included.

4. MOMENT ESTIMATORS

Let the objective function be given by (9), so that the parameter of the statistical model is $\theta = (\rho, \beta)$. The dimensionality of β is denoted L and the total number of dimensions for θ is $K = M - 1 + L$. Analogous to what was proposed for a similar model by Snijders (1996), this parameter can be estimated by the method of moments (explained for general statistical models—for example, by Bowman and Shenton 1985). This means that a statistic $Z = (Z_1, \ldots, Z_K)$ is used, for which θ is determined as the solution of the K-dimensional moment equation

$$\mathcal{E}_\theta Z = z, \tag{12}$$

where z is the observed outcome. This moment equation will be specified further by certain ways of conditioning on the initial and intermediate outcomes $x(t_1)$ to $x(t_{m-1})$.

First the choice of the statistic Z is discussed, and then a MCMC algorithm that can be used to approximate the solution of the moment equation.

For the estimation, no assumptions whatsoever are made about the initial state $x(t_1)$. Therefore, the estimation is carried out conditional on this initial state, and this state is not used to obtain any information about the value of the parameter.

In the absence of a formal method such as a reduction to sufficient statistics, the statistics Z_k should be chosen so that they are relevant for the components of the parameter θ in the sense that the expected values of Z_k $(k = 1, \ldots, K)$ are sensitive to changes in the components of θ. One way to specify this is to require that for all k

$$\frac{\partial \mathcal{E}_\theta Z_k}{\partial \theta_k} > 0.$$

A more stringent specification is to require that this property hold not only for all separate coordinates of the parameter vector, but also for all linear combinations:

$$a' \left(\frac{\partial \mathcal{E}_\theta Z}{\partial \theta} \right) a > 0 \text{ for all } a \in \mathbb{R}^K, a \neq 0, \tag{13}$$

where $(\partial \mathcal{E}_\theta Z / \partial \theta)$ is the matrix of partial derivatives. This requirement is far from implying the statistical efficiency of the resulting estimator, but it confers a basic credibility to the moment estimator and it ensures the convergence of the stochastic approximation algorithm mentioned below.

The components of $\theta = (\rho, \beta)$ are the rates of change ρ_m in the time interval (t_m, t_{m+1}) and the weights β_k in the objective function (9). The motivation for the statistics Z_i, at this moment, is of a heuristic nature, based on their obvious connection to the parameters and supported by sufficiency considerations in certain special cases.

For ρ_m, a relevant statistic is the total amount of change in the mth time period measured by the number of differences between two consecutive observation moments,

$$C_m = \sum_{\substack{i,j=1 \\ i \neq j}}^{n} |X_{ij}(t_{m+1}) - X_{ij}(t_m)|. \tag{14}$$

This choice for the statistic relevant for ρ_m can be supported by noting that if $\beta = 0$, which reduces the model to the trivial situation where the $X_{ij}(t)$ are randomly changing 0-1 variables, C_m is a sufficient statistic for ρ_m.

For β_k, a relevant statistic is the sum over all actors i of the digraph statistics s_{ik}, observed at time t_{m+1},

$$S_{mk} = \sum_{i=1}^{n} s_{ik}(X(t_{m+1})). \tag{15}$$

This statistic has an immediate intuitive appeal: If β_k is larger, then the actors strive more strongly to have a high value of s_{ik}, so that it may be expected that S_{mk} will be higher for all m. The statistics S_{mk} are combined over the $M - 1$ time intervals by an unweighted sum.

Combining all these proposals, the moment estimator for θ is defined as the solution of the system of equations

$$\mathcal{E}_\theta\{C_m | X(t_m) = x(t_m)\} = c_m \; (m = 1, \ldots, M - 1) \tag{16}$$

$$\sum_{m=1}^{M-1} \mathcal{E}_\theta\{S_{mk} | X(t_m) = x(t_m)\} = \sum_{m=1}^{M-1} s_{mk} \; (k = 1, \ldots, L), \tag{17}$$

where c_m and s_{mk} are the observed outcomes of the statistics C_m and S_{mk}.

Although in our experience these equations mostly seem to have exactly one solution, they do not always have a solution. This can be seen as follows. For a fixed value of β, the left-hand side of (16) is an increasing function of ρ_m, tending to an asymptote which is lower than the maximum possible value of c_m, this maximum being $n(n - 1)$. This implies that the method proposed here is not suitable for observations $x(t_m)$ and $x(t_{m+1})$, which are too far apart in the sense of the metric (14). For such observations the dependence of $x(t_{m+1})$ on the initial situation $x(t_m)$ is practically extinguished, and it may be more relevant to estimate the parameters of the process generating $x(t_{m+1})$ without taking this initial situation into account.

For the trivial submodel where all $X_{ij}(t)$ are independent, the existence of maximum likelihood and moment estimators is discussed in Snijders and Van Duijn (1997).

4.1. *Covariance Matrix of the Estimator*

The delta method (e.g., see Bishop, Fienberg, and Holland 1975, sec. 14.6) can be used to derive an approximate covariance matrix for the moment estimator $\hat{\theta}$. (This holds generally for moment estimators; see Bowman and Shenton 1985, formula 5.) For a homogeneous notation for the parameters ρ_m and β, denote $C_{mm} = C_m$ and formally define $C_{mk} = 0$ for $k \neq m$, and denote

$$Z_m = (C_{m1}, \ldots, C_{m,M-1}, S_{m1}, \ldots, S_{mL}).$$

Then the moment equations (16, 17) can be written as

$$\sum_{m=1}^{M-1} \mathcal{E}_\theta\{Z_m \mid X(t_m) = x(t_m)\} = \sum_{m=1}^{M-1} z_m. \tag{18}$$

Further denote

$$\sum \theta = \sum_{m=1}^{M-1} \text{cov}\{Z_m \mid X(t_m) = x(t_m)\} \tag{19}$$

$$D_\theta = \frac{\partial}{\partial \theta} \sum_{m=1}^{M-1} \mathcal{E}\{Z_m \mid X(t_m) = x(t_m)\}. \tag{20}$$

Then it follows from the delta method, combined with the implicit function theorem and the Markov property for the $X(t)$ process, that the approximate covariance matrix of $\hat{\theta}$ is

$$\text{cov}(\hat{\theta}) \approx D_\theta^{-1} \sum \theta \, D_\theta'^{-1}. \tag{21}$$

It is plausible that these estimators have approximately normal distributions, although a proof is not yet available. Based on the assumption of normally distributed estimates, the parameters can be tested using the t-ratios defined as the parameter estimate divided by its standard error, referred to a standard normal null distribution. (In other words, the test is carried out as a t-test with infinite degrees of freedom; this test should be regarded as a rough approximation, since no definite results are yet available on the distribution of this test statistic.)

4.2. *Conditional Moment Estimation*

The method of moments can be modified by conditioning on the outcomes c_m of C_m ($m = 1, \ldots, M - 1$) rather than using moment equations involving these statistics. This provides a more stable and efficient algorithm and reduces the parameter estimated by the method of moments to the L-dimensional β. This can be helpful especially for larger values of M.

The modified method is based on the property that the distribution of a continuous-time Markov chain $X(t)$ remains invariant when the time parameter is divided by some constant value while the rate parameter is multiplied by the same value. Specifically, when the rate parameter ρ_m obtains for all $t \geq t_m$, then the distribution of $X(t_m + t)$, conditional on $X(t_m)$ and for $t > 0$, depends on ρ_m and t only through their product, $t\rho_m$. The modified method can be loosely described as follows. For each period m independently, the Markov chain is started at time $t = 0$ with the initial value $x^{[m]} = x(t_m)$ and a rate parameter equal to 1. The process is stopped at the first moment t when $\sum_{ij} |X_{ij}(t) - x_{ij}^{[m]}| = c_m$. This value of t is expected to be close to the product $\rho_m(t_{m+1} - t_m)$ and the statistics observed at this moment are compared with the statistics calculated from observation $x(t_{m+1})$.

To explain this more formally, denote by $X^{(1)}(t)$ a Markov chain evolving according to our model with a fixed and constant rate parameter $\rho = 1$ and a given value of β, and denote by $S_k^{(1)}(t)$ the corresponding statistics (15). Independent replications of this stochastic process, starting at $t = 0$ with $X^{(1)}(0) = x(t_m)$, are used as models for the $M - 1$ periods. Define the statistic

$$C^{(1)}(t) = \sum_{\substack{i,j=1 \\ i \neq j}}^{n} |X_{ij}^{(1)}(t) - X_{ij}^{(1)}(0)| \tag{22}$$

and the stopping time

$$T_m^{\text{fin}} = \min\{t \geq 0 \,|\, C^{(1)}(t) \geq c_m\}. \tag{23}$$

The conditional moment estimator for β is defined as the solution of

$$\sum_{m=1}^{M-1} \mathcal{E}_\beta\{S_k^{(1)}(T_m^{\text{fin}}) | X^{(1)}(0) = x(t_m)\} = \sum_{m=1}^{M-1} s_{mk} \; (k = 1, \ldots, L) \tag{24}$$

and, given the resulting estimate $\hat{\beta}$, ρ_m is estimated by

$$\hat{\rho}_m = (t_{m+1} - t_m)^{-1} \mathcal{E}_{\hat{\beta}}\{T_m^{\text{fin}} | X^{(1)}(0) = x(t_m)\}. \tag{25}$$

It follows from the general theory of Markov chains that for all possible values of c_m the stopping time T_m^{fin} is finite with probability 1, and even has a finite expected value. Therefore the difficulties with the definition of the estimator for large values of c_m, as discussed for the unconditional moment estimator, do not arise here. However, this consolation is only theoretical, because in practice, for large t the value of $C^{(1)}(t)$ fluctuates randomly about an asymptote lower than the maximum possible value of $n(n-1)$, and the stopping time T_m^{fin} is indeed finite but horribly large. The simulation-based algorithm, explained below, is not practically feasible for values of c_m larger than this asymptote.

5. STOCHASTIC APPROXIMATION

The moment equations for the two estimation methods are defined by (18) and (24), but the conditional expectations that are central in these equations cannot be calculated explicitly (except for some special and rather trivial cases, as discussed in Snijders and Van Duijn [1997]). However, it is rather straightforward to simulate random digraphs with the desired distributions. Therefore, stochastic approximation methods—in particular, versions of the Robbins-Monro (1951) procedure—can be used to approximate the moment estimates. Introductions to stochastic approximation and the Robbins-Monro algorithm are given, for example, by Ruppert (1991) and Pflug (1996).

The algorithm to solve the equation (12) is based on a sequence $\hat{\theta}_N$ generated according to the iteration step

$$\hat{\theta}_{N+1} = \hat{\theta}_N - a_N D_0^{-1}(Z_N - z), \tag{26}$$

where Z_N is generated according to the probability distribution defined by the parameter value $\hat{\theta}_N$. For a_N, a sequence is used that converges slowly to 0. D_0 is a positive diagonal matrix. In principle, the optimal choice of D_0 might be nondiagonal. However, Polyak (1990), Ruppert (1988), and Yin (1991) (as discussed also by Pflug [1996, sec. 5.1.3] and Kushner and Yin, 1997) showed that if all eigenvalues of the matrix of partial derivatives, $(\partial \mathcal{E}_\theta Z / \partial \theta)$, have positive real parts and certain regularity conditions are satisfied, then convergence at an optimal rate can be achieved when D_0 is the identity matrix, with a_N a sequence of positive numbers converging to 0 at the rate N^{-c}, where $0.5 < c < 1$. To obtain this optimal convergence rate, the solution of (12) must be estimated not by the last value $\hat{\theta}_N$ itself, but by the average of the consecutively generated $\hat{\theta}_N$ values. This algorithm is a Markov chain Monte Carlo algorithm because the iteration rule (26) indeed defines a Markov chain.

The convergence properties of this algorithm hold asymptotically for $N \to \infty$. To have good properties already for relatively low values of N, it is important to specify the algorithm in such a way that it quickly comes close to the target value. This can be achieved by applying a result due to Pflug (1990), who showed that the limiting first order autocorrelation of the sequence $(Z_N - z)$ generated by (26) is negative. This means that as long as the partial sums of successive values of the product $(Z_N - z)'(Z_{N-1} - z)$ are positive, it must be assumed that the sequence $\hat{\theta}_N$ still is drifting toward the limit point rather than wandering around the limit point, so that it is not desirable to decrease the step sizes a_N. Therefore a_N remains constant as long as there still seems to be such a drift going on, except that when N gets too large a_N is decreased anyway, in order to retain the convergence rate N^{-c} for the sequence a_N.

These ideas are combined in the specification of the algorithm as given in the appendix. The algorithm provides an arbitrarily accurate approximation to the solution of (12) as well as an estimate of the covariance matrix (21). It is available in the freeware PC program SIENA (see the discussion in Section 10).

6. AN EVOLVING NETWORK OF UNIVERSITY FRESHMEN

As an illustration, data are used from a study conducted by Van De Bunt (1999), which were analyzed also by Van De Bunt, Van Duijn, and Snijders (1999). For a more extensive description of this data set we refer to these publications. In the present paper, this data set is used only as an illustration without paying much attention to the theoretical interpretations.

The actors in this network are a group of 32 university freshmen who were following a common study program in a Dutch university. This group comprised 24 female and 8 male students. The number of observations used here is $M = 3$. The data used here are those for the time points labeled t_2, t_3, and t_4 in Van De Bunt, Van Duijn, and Snijders (1999). There are 3 weeks between time points t_2 and t_3, and also between t_3 and t_4. For the purpose of this illustration, the time points are relabeled t_1, t_2, and t_3. The relation studied is defined as "at least a friendly relationship," referred to here as a positive relation ($x_{ij} = 1$). The absence of a positive relation is referred to as a null relation ($x_{ij} = 0$).

There is missing data due to nonresponse, increasing from 9% at t_1 to 19% at t_3. This incompleteness of data is treated in the estimation procedure in the following ad hoc fashion. (It will be important to conduct further studies to evaluate this way of dealing with incomplete data, and compare it with potential alternatives.)

Missing data are treated in a simple way, trying to minimize their influence on the estimation results. The simulations are carried out over all $n = 32$ actors. In the initial observation $x(t_m)$ for each period, missing entries $x_{ij}(t_m)$ are set to 0. In the course of the simulations, however, these values are allowed to become 1 like any other values $x_{ij}(t)$. For the calculation of the statistics S_{mk} and C_m, the values of $x_{ij}(t_m)$ as well as of $X_{ij}(t_{m+1})$ are set to 0 whenever at least one of the two observations $x_{ij}(t_m)$ and $x_{ij}(t_{m+1})$ is missing.

To get a basic impression of the data, it may be noted that densities (calculated over the available data) at the three observation moments increase from 0.15 via 0.18 to 0.22. The number of observed changes between the observations at t_1 and t_2 was 60 (out of 744 directed pairs (i, j) for which the value of x_{ij} was observed at observations t_1 and t_2); between t_2 and t_3 this was 51 (out of 679 observations).

The first model estimated includes the basic effects of density and reciprocity, together with the three basic triadic effects: transitivity, indirect relations, and balance. The purpose of this stage in the analysis is to investigate which of these triadic effects are empirically supported by these network evolution data. The number b_0 in (10) is defined by (11). The conditional moment estimator was used and the algorithm was specified as described in the appendix, except that to increase precision 5 subphases were carried out in phase 2 and $n_3 = 1000$ steps were made in phase 3. The results are displayed as Model 1 in Table 1.

The estimated rate parameters, $\hat{\rho}_1 = 3.87$ and $\hat{\rho}_2 = 3.10$, indicate that on average the actors made 3.87 changes of relationships between the first two observations, and 3.10 changes between the last two observations. (This includes two-way changes between two observations that remained unobserved because they canceled each other.)

As suggested in Section 4.1, the effects are tested by t-statistics defined by the ratio of parameter estimate to standard error, referred to as standard normal distribution. There is a strongly significant reciprocity effect ($t = 1.98/0.31 = 6.39$). Of the three triadic effects, the indirect relations effect is significant ($t = -0.347/0.074 = -4.69$), but the other two are not significant at the 5 percent level, although the transitivity effect comes close. When the balance effect was deleted from the model, the t-value for the transitivity effect became 1.94 (results not shown

TABLE 1
Parameters and Standard Errors for Models Estimated Using Observations at t_1, t_2, t_3

	Model 1		Model 2		Model 3	
Effect	Par.	(s.e.)	Par.	(s.e.)	Par.	(s.e.)
Rate (period 1)	3.87		3.78		3.91	
Rate (period 2)	3.10		3.14		3.07	
Density	−1.48	(0.30)	−1.05	(0.19)	−1.13	(0.22)
Reciprocity	1.98	(0.31)	2.44	(0.40)	2.52	(0.37)
Transitivity	0.21	(0.11)	—		—	
Balance	−0.33	(0.66)	—		—	
Indirect relations	−0.347	(0.074)	−0.557	(0.083)	−0.502	(0.084)
Gender activity	—		—		−0.60	(0.28)
Gender popularity	—		—		0.64	(0.24)
Gender dissimilarity	—		—		−0.42	(0.24)

here), just short of significance at the 5 percent level. The results obtained when deleting the two nonsignificant effects from the model are shown as Model 2 in Table 1. The indirect relations effect becomes larger, and the density and reciprocity effects change, because these effects now must also represent the effects represented by transitivity and balance in Model 1. It can be concluded that there is evidence of a tendency to have closed networks in the sense of a relatively low number of indirect relations; controlling for this effect and for reciprocity, there is no significant tendency toward a high number of transitive triplets or toward balanced relationships. No significant evidence was found for other structural network effects (estimation results not shown here).

As a next step, the three basic effects of gender were included in the model. In the original data set, gender was represented by a dummy variable equal to 0 for women and 1 for men. The means were subtracted from this variable as well as from the dissimilarity variable $|v_i - v_j|$. Given that the proportion of women was 75 percent, this leads to the variable v_i being -0.25 for women and $+0.75$ for men, and the dissimilarity variable being -0.387 for equal-gender pairs and 0.613 for unequal-gender pairs. The results for the model including the structural effects of reciprocity and indirect relations as well as the three covariate effects of gender are presented in Table 1 as Model 3. It can be concluded that women are more active in creating positive relations than men ($t = -0.60/0.28 = -2.14$), while men receive more positive choices ($t = 0.64/0.24 = 2.67$), but there are no significant (dis)similarity effects associated with gender. The control for gender does not have an important influence on the reciprocity or indirect relations effects.

The results based on the observations at these three moments can be compared with results based on only two of these observations. This can be used to check the model assumption that the parameter values β_k in the time interval between t_1 and t_2 are the same as between t_2 and t_3. Furthermore, for the analysis of the evolution of the network from t_1 to t_3, this illustrates the greater precision obtainable by including the information about the network at t_2. The comparison is made only for Model 3 and reported in Table 2.

None of the estimates are significantly different between the periods t_1–t_2 and t_2–t_3. This supports the use of a common model for the entire period t_1–t_3.

To compare the Model 3 column of Table 1 with the t_1, t_3 column of Table 2, the estimates in the former column are called "three-observation" and those in the latter column "two-observation" estimates. It appears that the corresponding estimates differ at most by about one "two-observation" standard error; for all parameters but one, the three-observation estimates are closer than the two-observation estimates to the mean of the separate estimates for the t_1–t_2 and t_2–t_3 periods. The three-observation standard errors all are clearly smaller than the two-observation standard errors. This provides some support for the expected greater reliability of the three-observation as compared with the two-observation estimates.

TABLE 2
Parameter Estimates and Standard Errors for Model 3, Estimated from Two Observations

Observations	t_1, t_2		t_2, t_3		t_1, t_3	
Effect	Par.	(s.e.)	Par.	(s.e.)	Par.	(s.e.)
Rate	3.64		3.21		5.29	
Density	−0.99	(0.32)	−1.30	(0.28)	−0.78	(0.31)
Reciprocity	2.36	(0.52)	2.89	(0.67)	2.40	(0.48)
Indirect relations	−0.432	(0.113)	−0.653	(0.140)	−0.536	(0.146)
Gender activity	−0.75	(0.40)	−0.39	(0.42)	−0.77	(0.36)
Gender popularity	0.40	(0.31)	1.03	(0.44)	0.36	(0.26)
Gender dissimilarity	−0.35	(0.35)	−0.58	(0.43)	−0.22	(0.31)

7. EXTENDED MODEL SPECIFICATION

The general model specification contains, in addition to the objective function, two other elements: (1) the rate function, which shows that actors may differ in the rate at which they change their relations; and (2) the gratification function, which shows that various effects may operate differently for the creation of a relation (where x_{ij} goes from 0 to 1) than for its dissolution (x_{ij} changing from 1 to 0).

7.1. *Rate Function*

The rate function for actor i is denoted

$$\lambda_i(\rho, \alpha, x, m) \text{ for } x \in \mathcal{X}, \tag{27}$$

and indicates the rate at which actor i is allowed to change something in his outgoing relations in the time period $t_m \leq t < t_{m+1}$. In the simple specification given above, this rate function depended only on m and not on i or x, and was defined as $\lambda_i(\rho, \alpha, x, m) = \rho_m$. The roles of the statistical parameters ρ and α are discussed below.

These rate functions and the conditional independence of the actors imply that at each time point t, the time until the next change by *any* actor has the negative exponential distribution with parameter

$$\lambda_+(\rho, \alpha, x, m) = \sum_{i=1}^{n} \lambda_i(\rho, \alpha, x, m), \textit{for } x = x(t), t_m \leq t < t_{m+1} \tag{28}$$

(provided that this next change still is before time t_{m+1}). The parameter of the negative exponential distribution is taken here as the reciprocal of the expectation, so the expected waiting time until the next change after time t is $1/\lambda_+(\rho, \alpha, x(t), m)$ (where a possible change to the following time interval is not taken into account). Given that a change occurs, the probability that it is actor i who may change his out-relations is

$$\frac{\lambda_i(\rho, \alpha, x, m)}{\lambda_+(\rho, \alpha, x, m)}. \tag{29}$$

Nonconstant rate functions can depend, for example, on actor-specific covariates or on network statistics expressing the degree to which the actor is satisfied with the present network structure. Of course, the rate function must be restricted to positive values. In order not to burden the specification with too many complications, it is proposed that the rate function be defined as a product

$$\lambda_i(\rho, \alpha, x, m) = \lambda_{i1}\lambda_{i2}\lambda_{i3}$$

of factors depending, respectively, on period m, actor covariates, and the actor's personal network. The corresponding factors in the rate function are the following:

1. The dependence on the period can be represented by a simple factor

$$\lambda_{i1} = \rho_m$$

for $m = 1, \ldots, M - 1$.

2. The effect of actor covariates with values v_{hi} can be represented by the factor

$$\lambda_{i2} = \exp\left(\sum_h \alpha_h v_{hi}\right). \tag{30}$$

3. The dependence on the network can be modeled, for example, as a function of the actor's out-degree, in-degree, and number of reciprocated relations. Define these by

$$x_{i+} = \sum_j x_{ij},\ x_{+i} = \sum_j x_{ji},\ x_{i(r)} = \sum_j x_{ij}x_{ji}$$

(recalling that $x_{ii} = 0$ for all i).

Snijders and Van Duijn (1997) investigated how the rate function should be specified in order to obtain Wasserman's (1979) reciprocity model as a special case. Denoting the corresponding parameter by α_1, for the dependence on the out-degree this led to the factor

$$\lambda_{i3} = \frac{x_{i+}}{n-1}\exp(\alpha_1) + \left(1 - \frac{x_{i+}}{n-1}\right)\exp(-\alpha_1). \tag{31}$$

This defines a linear function of the out-degree, parametrized in such a way that it is necessarily positive.

For a general dependence on the out-degree, in-degree, and number of reciprocated relations, one can use an average of such terms, the second and third one depending on x_{+i} and $x_{i(r)}$, respectively.

It would be interesting to explore other specifications of the rate function, expressing in a theoretically more satisfactory way the circumstances and characteristics upon which it depends how quickly actors change their relations.

7.2. *Gratification Function*

The basic motivation for the third model ingredient, the *gratification function*, is that a given effect may operate more strongly, or less strongly, for the creation than for the dissolution of relations. For example, it is conceivable that although actors prefer to establish reciprocated relations, they are quite willing to initiate as yet unreciprocated relations; but that, once they have a reciprocated relationship, they are very reluctant to let it go—for example, because of the investments accumulated in this relation (cf. Van De Bunt [1999]). This would mean that the reciprocity effect is greater for dissolution than for creation of ties. Such a difference cannot be represented by the objective function alone. Therefore the model includes also a gratification function

$$g_i(\gamma, x, j), \quad \text{defined for } i, j = 1, \ldots, n,\ i \neq j,\ x \in \mathcal{X}, \tag{32}$$

which indicates the instantaneous gratification experienced by actor i when, from the given network configuration x, element x_{ij} is changed into its opposite, $1 - x_{ij}$.

When a gratification function is included in the model, expression (4) for the momentary objective function maximized by i is replaced by the sum of the actor's preference for the new state, the gratification experienced as a result of the change, and a random element:

$$f_i(\beta, x(i \rightsquigarrow j)) + g_i(\gamma, x, j) + U_i(t, x, j). \tag{33}$$

Using the same assumptions for the random term $U_i(t, x, j)$ as above, the probabilities of the various possible new states $x(i \rightsquigarrow j)$ are now given by

$$p_{ij}(\theta, x) = \frac{\exp(r(\theta, i, j, x))}{\sum_{h=1, h\neq i}^{n} \exp(r(\theta, i, h, x))} \quad (j \neq i), \tag{34}$$

where

$$r(\theta, i, j, x) = f_i(\beta, x(i \rightsquigarrow j)) + g_i(\gamma, x, j).$$

These probabilities do not change when a term is added to $r(\theta, i, j, x)$ that does not depend on j. It is often more convenient to work with

$$r(\theta, i, j, x) = f_i(\beta, x(i \rightsquigarrow j)) - f_i(\beta, x) + g_i(\gamma, x, j). \tag{35}$$

The instantaneous effect g_i is a more general model component than the objective function f_i, because the objective function depends only on the new state $x(i \rightsquigarrow j)$, whereas the gratification function depends arbitrarily on the new state as well as the old state x. The reason for not working with just the gratification function is that the objective function, attaching a value to each network configuration, often is conceptually more attractive and better interpretable than the instantaneous gratification effect.

The gratification function can be specified by a weighted sum,

$$g_i(\gamma, x, j) = \sum_{h=1}^{H} \gamma_h r_{ijh}(x) \tag{36}$$

for certain statistics $r_{ijh}(x)$, each containing either a factor x_{ij} (if it reflects the gratification involved in withdrawing a relation—i.e., changing x_{ij} from 1 to 0) or a factor $(1 - x_{ij})$ (if the effect is about the gratification involved in creating a relation). Some examples of such terms are the following:

1. $\gamma_1 x_{ij} x_{ji}$: Indicator of a reciprocated relation; a negative value of γ_1 reflects the costs associated with breaking off a reciprocated relation.
2. $\gamma_2(1 - x_{ij}) \sum_h x_{ih} x_{hj}$: The number of actors through whom i is indirectly related to j; a positive value of γ_2 reflects that it is easier to establish a new relation to another actor j if i has many indirect relations to j via others who can serve as an introduction.
3. $\gamma_3 x_{ij} w_{ij}$: The value w_{ij} for another actor to whom i has a relation; e.g., a negative value of γ_3 reflects the costs for i associated with breaking off an existing relation to other actors j with a high value for w_{ij}.

7.3. *Intensity Matrix and Simulation*

The model that includes an arbitrary rate function $\lambda_i(\rho, \alpha, x, m)$, an objective function, and a gratification function, still is a continuous-time Markov chain. The intensity matrix $q(x, y)$ is still given by (7), now with

$$q_{ij}(x) = \lambda_i(\rho, \alpha, x, m) p_{ij}(\theta, x), \tag{37}$$

where p_{ij} now is given by (34).

Note that it is straightforward to define an algorithm that simulates this stochastic process. Schematically, this can be done as follows. Suppose that the present time point is $t \in [t_m, t_{m+1})$. The time until the next change by any actor is generated by a negative exponential distribution with parameter (28), provided that the moment so determined is before time t_{m+1}. The actor who is to change a relation (i.e., the row of the adjacency matrix in which a change will occur) is actor i with probability (29). The other actor with whom actor i will change the relation (column of the adjacency matrix) is j with probability (34). When j is chosen, element x_{ij} is changed into its opposite, $1 - x_{ij}$.

7.4. *Choice of Statistics for Estimation*

The use of the method of moments requires also the selection of statistics that are relevant for the parameters included in the rate and gratification functions.

A tentative choice for statistics to estimate the parameters α_h in (30) is provided by the total amounts of change weighted by v_{hi},

$$C_{M+h-1} = \sum_{m=1}^{M} \sum_{\substack{i,j=1 \\ i \neq j}}^{n} |X_{ij}(t_{m+1}) - x_{ij}(t_m)| v_{hi}. \tag{38}$$

To estimate the parameter α_1 in (31) for the effect of out-degree on rate of change, the statistic

$$C_{M+H} = \sum_{m=1}^{M} \sum_{\substack{i,j=1 \\ i \neq j}}^{n} |X_{ij}(t_{m+1}) - x_{ij}(t_m)| x_{i+}(t_m) \tag{39}$$

can be used (where H is the total number of covariates used for modeling the rate function), and similarly for the effects of the in-degree and the number of reciprocated relations. These choices are intuitively plausible and have led to reasonable estimates in some trial data sets, but more research is required.

For the parameters γ_h included in the gratification function (36), a relevant statistic is

$$R_h = \sum_{m=1}^{M-1} \sum_{\substack{i,j=1 \\ i \neq j}}^{n} |X_{ij}(t_{m+1}) - x_{ij}(t_m)| r_{ijh}(x(t_m)), \tag{40}$$

which is the sum of the r_{ijh} values of newly formed relations if r_{ijh} contains a factor $(1 - x_{ij})$, and the sum of r_{ijh} values of disappeared relations if r_{ijh} contains a factor x_{ij}.

These statistics C_{M+h} and R_h are used in the method of moments in the same way as $\sum_m S_{mk}$ in (17) and (25).

8. CONTINUATION OF THE EXAMPLE

Continuing the example of the network of university freshmen, the effect (31) of the out-degrees on the rate of change is included, and the gratification function is defined as the sum of the effect of breaking reciprocated relations and the effect of gender difference on breaking a relation,

$$g_i(\gamma, x, j) = \gamma_1 x_{ij} x_{ji} + \gamma_2 x_{ij} |v_i - v_j|$$

where v_i indicates the gender of actor i.

The results are given as Model 4 in Table 3. It can be concluded that the tendency of actors with higher out-degrees to change their relations more often is close to significance at the 5 percent level ($t = 0.90/0.47 = 1.91$), and that relations with other actors of the opposite sex are terminated more quickly than those with others of the same sex ($t = 1.64/$

TABLE 3
Parameter Estimates and Standard Errors for Model with Rate and Gratification Effects

	Model 4	
Effect	par.	(s.e.)
Rate (period 1)	5.05	
Rate (period 2)	3.95	
Out-degree effect on rate	0.90	(0.47)
Density	−0.99	(0.20)
Reciprocity	2.82	(0.56)
Indirect relations	−0.508	(0.091)
Gender activity	−0.52	(0.31)
Gender popularity	0.55	(0.30)
Gender dissimilarity	0.08	(0.37)
Breaking reciprocated relation	−0.58	(1.06)
Breaking relation with different-gender other	1.64	(0.62)

$0.62 = 2.65$). The effect of reciprocity on breaking a relation is not different from what may be expected from the main reciprocity effect ($t = -0.58/1.06 = -0.55$). Comparing these results with those for Model 3 in Table 1, it can be concluded that the activity and popularity effect for gender now are somewhat weaker (having lost their significance at the 5 percent level), and the main gender dissimilarity effect has vanished due to the inclusion of the effect of gender dissimilarity on breaking a relation. Thus Model 4 suggests that friendly relations with actors of the opposite sex are less stable, and that there is no evidence (as one might erroneously conclude from Model 3) that friendly relations are initiated less with actors of the opposite sex than with those of the same sex.

9. ASYMPTOTIC DISTRIBUTION AND RELATION WITH THE p^* MODEL

If it is possible to reach every state from every given initial state in a finite number of steps (as is the case here), the distribution of a Markov chain with stationary intensity matrix on a finite outcome space tends to a unique limiting distribution as $t \to \infty$, independent of the initial distribution. For a certain specification of our model, this limiting distribution is the p^* model for social networks proposed by Wasserman and Pattison (1996), generalizing the Markov graph distribution proposed by Frank and Strauss (1986). The p^* model is a family of probability distributions for a single observation x on a stochastic directed graph X. The probability distribution for the p^* model is defined by

$$\mathrm{P}\{X = x\} = \frac{\exp(\beta' z(x))}{\kappa(\beta)} \tag{41}$$

where $z(x)$ is a vector of statistics of the digraph and $\kappa(\beta)$ is a normalization factor. The following proposition indicates a specification for the actor-oriented model that yields the p^* distribution as the limiting distribution.

Proposition 1. Define for all i the objective function by

$$f_i(\beta, x) = \beta' z(x) \tag{42}$$

and the gratification function by $g_i = 0$. Furthermore, define the rate function by

$$\lambda_i(x) = \sum_{\substack{h=1 \\ h \neq i}}^{n} \exp(\beta' z(x(i \rightsquigarrow h))). \tag{43}$$

Then the limiting probability distribution of $X(t)$ for $t \to \infty$ is the p^* distribution with probability function (41).

Proof. It follows from (34), (37), and (43) that

$$q_{ij}(x) = \exp(\beta' z(x(i \rightsquigarrow j))).$$

Note that the symbol $x(i \rightsquigarrow j)$ can be understood as the result of taking matrix x and applying the operation of changing x_{ij} into $1 - x_{ij}$. Applying this operation twice returns the original matrix x, which can be represented as $(x(i \rightsquigarrow j))(i \rightsquigarrow j) = x$. Therefore,

$$q_{ij}(x(i \rightsquigarrow j)) = \exp(\beta' z(x))$$

which implies

$$\exp(\beta' z(x)) q_{ij}(x) = \exp(\beta' z(x(i \rightsquigarrow j))) q_{ij}(x(i \rightsquigarrow j))$$

and, for Q defined by (7), that

$$\exp(\beta' z(x)) q(x, y) = \exp(\beta' z(y)) q(y, x)$$

for all x, y. In terms of the theory of Markov chains (e.g., Norris 1997, pp. 124–25), this means that the intensity matrix Q and the distribution (41) are in detailed balance, which implies that (41) is the stationary distribution for Q. Since all states communicate with one another, the stationary distribution is unique and (41) is also the limiting distribution. Q.E.D.

An interpretation of the rate function (43) is that actors for whom changed relations have a higher value, will indeed change their relations more quickly.

10. DISCUSSION

The procedure proposed in this paper provides a method for the analysis of two or more repeated observations on a social network, in which network as well as covariate effects are taken into account. In view of processes in the real-life evolution of social networks, in which endogenous network effects cumulate continuously over time, the continuous-time nature of this model will be attractive in many applications. The procedure is available in SIENA (Simulation Investigation for Empirical Network Analysis, available free of charge from http://stat.gamma.rug.nl/

snijders/siena.html), which runs under Windows, and is contained in the StOCNET package (http://stat.gamma.rug.nl/stocnet).

The present article provides the basic procedure, but this methodology could benefit from further elaborations and improvements, for example, along the following lines. The algorithm has been proved to work well in various applications, but it is rather time-consuming and improvements may be possible. A proof of the sufficient condition for its convergence (see the appendix: the eigenvalues of $[D_0^{-1}\partial\mathcal{E}_\theta Z/\partial\theta]$ should have positive real parts) is still lacking. The frequency properties of the standard errors and the hypothesis tests are based on large sample approximations and should be investigated. The robustness of the proposed estimates and tests to deviations from the model assumptions is an interesting point for further study. The method of moments was chosen because of its feasibility, but it may be possible to develop other estimation methods for this model. As additions to the toolbox, it would be useful to have measures for goodness of fit and some kind of standardized effect sizes. The present implementation contains an ad hoc way of dealing with missing data, which merits further investigation.

Although the model is presented as an actor-oriented model, it uses an extremely simple and myopic behavioral model for the actors. This simplicity is a strength because more complicated models for the behavior of actors in a relational network would be more restrictive and less general in their domain of applicability. On the other hand, for specific applications it could be interesting to develop statistical network evolution models incorporating a sociologically more interesting behavioral model.

Further extensions are possible. An extension to relations with ordered outcome categories would increase the scope of the model. One could also think of extending the model to include unobserved heterogeneity by means of random effects, but this would lead the model outside of the realm of complete observations of the state of a Markov process, and therefore require more complex estimation methods.

APPENDIX: STOCHASTIC APPROXIMATION ALGORITHM

The purpose of the algorithm is to approximate the solution of the moment equation (12). In this appendix, the solution is denoted by θ_0. As mentioned in the text above, the algorithm uses the idea of Polyak (1990) and Ruppert (1988) to employ a diagonal matrix D_0 in the iteration step (26) and estimate the solution by partial averages of $\hat{\theta}_N$ rather than the last value; and it uses the idea of Pflug (1990) to let the values of a_N remain constant if the average products of successive values $(Z_N - z)(Z_{N-1} - z)$ are positive, since this suggests that the process still is drifting toward its limit value. However, the specification used here deviates from Pflug's proposal by requiring, for the premature decrease of a_N, that for *each* coordinate the partial sum of the product of successive values be negative, rather than requiring this only for the sum over the coordinates. Furthermore, the number of steps for which a_N is constant is bounded between a lower and an upper limit to ensure that a_N is of order N^{-c}.

A crucial condition for the Polyak-Ruppert result about the optimal convergence rate of the partial sums of $\hat{\theta}_N$ to the solution of (12), is the assumption that all eigenvalues of the matrix of partial derivatives, $(D_0^{-1}\partial\mathcal{E}_\theta Z/\partial\theta)$, have positive real parts; see Yin (1991), Pflug (1996), or Kushner and Yin (1997). This condition is implied by condition (13) if D_0 is the identity matrix. For our model and the proposed statistics used in the moment estimators, we conjecture that this condition is satisfied, but the proof is still a matter of further research. Whether the algorithm yields an estimate that indeed solves the moment equation (12) to a satisfactory degree of precision is checked in the "third phase" of the algorithm below. The practical experience with the convergence of the algorithm is, for most models applied to most data sets, quite favorable.

The reason for incorporating the matrix D_0 is to achieve better compatibility between the scales of Z and of θ. The diagonal elements of D_0 are defined as the estimated values of the derivatives $\partial\mathcal{E}_\theta(Z_k)/\partial\theta_k$ where θ is at its initial value. To see that this leads to compatibility of the scales of Z and θ, note that in the extreme case where $\mathrm{var}(Z_k) = 0$ and the diagonal elements of D_0 are equal to $\partial\mathcal{E}_\theta(Z_k)/\partial\theta_k$, (26) for $a_N = 1$ is just the iteration step of the Newton-Raphson algorithm applied to each coordinate of Z separately. Thus, beginning the algorithm with a_N in the order of magnitude of 1 will imply that the initial steps have an approximately right order of magnitude.

The algorithm consists of three phases, which can be sketched as follows. The number of dimensions of θ and of Z is denoted by p and the initial value is denoted θ_1.

- **Phase 1:** In this phase a small number n_1 of steps are made to estimate $D(\theta_1) = (\partial\mathcal{E}_\theta(Z)/\partial\theta)|_{\theta=\theta_1}$, using common random numbers; the diagonal elements of this estimate are used to define D_0.

This is described formally as follows. Denote by e_j the j'th unit vector in p dimensions. In step N, generate $Z_{N0} \sim \theta_1$ and $Z_{Nj} \sim \theta_1 + \epsilon_j e_j$, where all the $p+1$ random vectors use a common random number stream to make them strongly positively dependent and where ϵ_j are suitable constants. For different N, the random vectors are generated independently. Compute the difference quotients

$$d_{Nj} = \epsilon_j^{-1}(Z_{Nj} - Z_{N0});$$

for small values of ϵ_j the expected value of the matrix $d_N = (d_{N1}, \ldots, d_{Np})$ approximates $D(\theta_1)$. However, ϵ_j must be chosen not too small because otherwise the variances of the d_{Nj} become too large.

At the end of this phase, estimate $E_{\theta_1} Z$ and $D(\theta_1)$ by

$$\bar{z} = \frac{1}{n_1} \sum_{N=1}^{n_1} Z_{N0} \text{ and } \hat{D} = \frac{1}{n_1} \sum_{N=1}^{n_1} d_N,$$

respectively, make one estimated Newton-Raphson step,

$$\hat{\theta}_{n_1} = \theta_1 - \hat{D}^{-1}(\bar{z} - z),$$

and use the diagonal matrix $\tilde{D} = \text{diag}(\hat{D})$ in Phase 2.

- **Phase 2:** This is the main phase, consisting of several subphases. The number of iteration steps per subphase is determined by a stopping rule, but bounded for subphase k by a minimum value n_{2k}^- and a maximum value n_{2k}^+. In each subphase, a_N is constant. The only difference between the subphases is the value of a_N.

  The subphase is ended after less than n_{2k}^+ steps as soon as the number of steps in this subphase exceeds n_{2k}^- while, for each coordinate Z_k, the sum within this subphase of successive products $(Z_{Nk} - z_k) \times (Z_{N-1,k} - z_k)$ is negative. If the upper bound n_{2k}^+ is reached, then the subphase is terminated anyway.

  In each iteration step within each subphase, Z_N is generated according to the current parameter value $\hat{\theta}_N$. After each step, this value is updated according to the formula

$$\hat{\theta}_{N+1} = \hat{\theta}_N - a_N \tilde{D}^{-1}(Z_N - z). \tag{44}$$

At the end of each subphase, the average of $\hat{\theta}_N$ over this subphase is used as the new value for $\hat{\theta}_N$.

The value of a_N is divided by 2 when a new subphase is entered. The bounds n_{2k}^- and n_{2k}^+ are determined so that $N^{3/4}a_N$ tends to a finite positive limit.

The average of $\hat{\theta}_N$ over the last subphase is the eventual estimate $\hat{\theta}$.

- **Phase 3:** Phase 3 is used only for the estimation of $D(\theta)$ and $\Sigma(\theta)$, using common random numbers for the estimation of the derivatives; and as a check for the (approximate) validity of (12). Therefore the value of $\hat{\theta}_N$ is left unchanged in this phase and is equal to the value obtained after the last subphase of Phase 2. The simulations and the estimation of $E_\theta Z$ and $D(\theta)$ are as in Phase 1. The covariance matrix of Z, required for the calculation of (21), is estimated in the usual way.

This algorithm contains various constants that can be adapted so as to achieve favorable convergence properties. Experience with various data sets led to the following values. The number of steps in Phase 1 is $n_1 = 7 + 3p$. The values of ϵ_i are chosen at least 0.1, in most cases 1.0, because the variability obtained by the use of small values of ϵ_i is more serious than the bias obtained by the use of this large value. The minimum number of steps in subphase 2.k is $n_{2k}^- = 2^{4(k-1)/3}(7 + p)$ and the maximum number is $n_{2k}^+ = n_{2k}^- + 200$. The initial value of a_N in Phase 2 is 0.2. The default number of subphases is 4, but fewer or more numerous subphases can be used to obtain smaller or larger precision. The default number of steps in Phase 3 is $n_3 = 500$. Phase 3 takes much time because each step requires $p + 1$ simulations; however, the variance estimate is rather unstable if the number of steps is much smaller.

REFERENCES

Bishop, Yvonne M., Stephen E. Fienberg, and Paul Holland. 1975. *Discrete Multivariate Analysis*. Cambridge, MA: MIT Press.

Bowman, K.O., and L.R. Shenton. 1985. "Method of Moments." Pp. 467–73 in *Encyclopedia of Statistical Sciences*, vol. 5, edited by S. Kotz, N. L. Johnson, and C. B. Read. New York: Wiley.

Doreian, Patrick, and Frans N. Stokman, eds. 1997. *Evolution of Social Networks*. Amsterdam: Gordon and Breach.

Fararo, Thomas J., and Norman P. Hummon. 1994. "Discrete Event Simulation and Theoretical Models in Sociology." *Advances in Group Processes* 11:25–66.

Frank, Ove, and David Strauss. 1986. "Markov Graphs." *Journal of the American Statistical Association* 81:832–42.

Holland, Paul, and Samuel Leinhardt. 1977a. "A Dynamic Model for Social Networks." *Journal of Mathematical Sociology* 5:5–20.

———. 1977b. "Social Structure as a Network Process." *Zeitschrift für Soziologie* 6:386–402.

Karlin, S., and H. M. Taylor. 1975. *A First Course in Stochastic Processes*. New York: Academic Press.

Katz, Leo, and Charles H. Proctor. 1959. "The Configuration of Interpersonal Relations in a Group as a Time-dependent Stochastic Process." *Psychometrika* 24:317–27.

Kushner, Herbert J. and George G. Yin. 1997. *Stochastic Approximation: Algorithms and Applications*. New York: Springer.

Leenders, Roger Th. A. J. 1995a. "Models for Network Dynamics: A Markovian Framework." *Journal of Mathematical Sociology* 20:1–21.

———. 1995b. *Structure and Influence. Statistical Models for the Dynamics of Actor Attributes, Network Structure, and Their Interdependence.* Amsterdam: Thesis Publishers.

Maddala, G. S. 1983. *Limited-dependent and Qualitative Variables in Econometrics.* Cambridge, England: Cambridge University Press.

Mayer, T. F. 1984. "Parties and Networks: Stochastic Models for Relationship Networks." *Journal of Mathematical Sociology* 10:51–103.

Norris, J. R. 1997. *Markov Chains*. Cambridge, England: Cambridge University Press.

Pflug, Georg Ch. 1990. "Non-asymptotic Confidence Bounds for Stochastic Approximation Algorithms with Constant Step Size." *Monatshefte für Mathematik* 110:297–314.

———. 1996. *Optimization of Stochastic Models*. Boston: Kluwer.

Polyak, B. T. 1990. "New Method of Stochastic Approximation Type." *Automation and Remote Control* 51:937–46.

Robbins, H., and S. Monro. 1951. "A Stochastic Approximation Method." *Annals of Mathematical Statistics* 22:400–407.

Ruppert, David. 1988. "Efficient Estimation from a Slowly Convergent Robbins-Monro Process." Technical Report No. 781, School of Operations Research and Industrial Engineering, Cornell University.

———. 1991. "Stochastic Approximation." In *Handbook of Sequential Analysis*, edited by B. K. Gosh, and P. K. Sen. New York: Marcel Dekker.

Snijders, Tom A. B. 1996. "Stochastic Actor-oriented Models for Network Change." *Journal of Mathematical Sociology* 21:149–72. Also published in Doreian and Stokman (1997).

———. 1999. "The Transition Probabilities of the Reciprocity Model." *Journal of Mathematical Sociology* 23:241–53.

Snijders, Tom A. B., and Marijtje A. J. Van Duijn. 1997. "Simulation for Statistical Inference in Dynamic Network Models." Pp. 493–512 in *Simulating Social Phenomena*, edited by R. Conte, R. Hegselmann, and P. Terna. Berlin: Springer.

Van de Bunt, Gerhard G. 1999. *Friends by Choice. An Actor-oriented Statistical Network Model for Friendship Networks Through Time.* Amsterdam: Thesis Publishers, 1999.

Van de Bunt, Gerhard G., Marijtje A. J. Van Duijn, and Tom A. B. Snijders. 1999. "Friendship Networks Through Time: An Actor-oriented Statistical Network Model." *Computational and Mathematical Organization Theory* 5:167–192.

Wasserman, Stanley. 1977. "Stochastic Models for Directed Graphs." Ph.D. dissertation, Department of Statistics, Harvard University.

———. 1979. "A Stochastic Model for Directed Graphs with Transition Rates Determined by Reciprocity." Pp. 392–412 in *Sociological Methodology 1980*, edited by K. F. Schuessler. San Francisco: Jossey-Bass.

———. 1980. "Analyzing Social Networks as Stochastic Processes." *Journal of the American Statistical Association* 75:280–94.

Wasserman, Stanley, and Katherine Faust. 1994. *Social Network Analysis: Methods and Applications*. New York: Cambridge University Press.

Wasserman, Stanley, and D. Iacobucci. 1988. "Sequential Social Network Data." *Psychometrika* 53:261–82.

Wasserman, Stanley, and Philippa Pattison. 1996. "Logit Models and Logistic Regression for Social Networks: I. An Introduction to Markov Graphs and p^*." *Psychometrika* 61:401–25.

Yin, George. 1991. "On Extensions of Polyak's Averaging Approach to Stochastic Approximation." *Stochastics* 36:245–64.

Zeggelink, Evelien P. H. 1994. "Dynamics of Structure: An Individual Oriented Approach." *Social Networks* 16:295–333.

NAME INDEX

Abbott, Andrew, 26, 29
Aghajanian, Akbar, 15
Agresti, Alan, 8, 18, 157
Ahmad, Khalil, 280n
Ahuja, Om P., 280n
Aitchison, John, 19
Akaike, Hirotugu, 149, 162, 163, 165, 167, 169, 300
Akerlof, George, 53n, 103
Alba, Richard D., 329n, 354n
Albert, James, 17
Allison, Paul, 15
Altham, Patricia M. E., 289n
Altschul, S. F., 29
Alwin, Duane F., 12
Amemiya, Takashi, 18
Anderson, Elijah, 51, 52
Anderson, Philip, 71, 71n
Ansell, C. K., 26
Appold, S. J., 30
Arminger, Gerhard, 14, 276n, 289n
Aronson, Elliot, 52
Arrow, Kenneth J., 92t
Arthur, W. Brian, 72
Axinn, W. G., 15

Back, Kurt, 310
Baker, Michael, 270
Baker, R. J., 16
Banfield, Jeffrey D., 30, 277n, 300
Barman, Emily, 29
Barnard, John, 25
Basford, Kaye E., 224
Batagelj, Vladimir, 342f
Bates, Douglas M., 300
Beale, E., 276n, 289n
Bearman, Peter S., 26, 29, 30
Beck, Nathaniel, 2
Becker, Gary, 50
Becker, Mark P., 8
Begg, Colin B., 18
Bénabou, Roland, 50
Benzécri, J.-P., 6
Bernhardt, Annette D., 10, 270, 272, 290, 290n
Besag, Julian E., 26, 27
Biblarz, Timothy J., 7
Bikhchandani, Sushil, 58n
Birch, M. W., 5, 6
Bishop, Yvonne M., 374
Blalock, Herbert, 55
Blalock, Hubert M., 12, 20, 24, 108n, 111, 119
Blau, Peter M., 4, 12, 12f, 94, 354n
Blume, Lawrence, 71
Boatwright, Peter, 21
Bock, R. D., 20, 21
Boguski, M. S., 29
Bollen, Kenneth A., 13, 30
Boomsma, A., 14
Borgatti, Stephen P., 326
Bosker, Roel J., 21

Bowles, Samuel, 94, 95, 96
Bowman, K. O., 372, 374
Box, George, 275
Boyd, L. H., 20
Bradlow, Eric T., 21
Brewster, Karen, 51n
Brock, William, 61, 62, 66, 74, 78, 79, 79n, 84, 107, 108n, 116
Brooks-Gunn, Jeanne, 51n
Brown, Roger, 52
Browne, Michael W., 2
Brudner, Lilyan A., 350
Brumback, Babette A., 282
Bryk, Anthony S., 21, 75n
Bucur, Alexander, 7
Bumpass, Larry, 114, 114n
Burt, Ronald S., 15

Calhoun, Craig, 117
Card, David, 50n
Carley, Kathleen M., 28, 29
Carlin, John B., 21
Carr, Deborah, 28
Carron, Albert V., 310
Cartwright, Dorwin, 309, 321n, 329n, 336n
Casterline, John B., 21
Celeux, Gilles, 9
Chafee, Mark V., 341
Chambers, Jack K., 62
Chamratrithirong, Aphichat, 114
Charles, Maria, 8
Chib, Siddartha, 17
Chickering, D. Maxwell, 9
Chilès, Jean-Paul, 27
Chinchilli, Vernon M., 300
Clogg, Clifford C., 2, 6, 9, 224, 244, 246, 249, 255, 277, 300
Coale, Ansley J., 113n
Cohen, K. L., 276n
Coleman, James, 97, 105, 112
Collins, Randall, 30
Cooper, Russell, 73
Cornfield, Jerome, 16
Costner, Herbert L., 24
Cowell, R., 13
Cox, David R., 14, 16
Crane, Jonathan, 51n
Crouchley, R., 274
Crowder, Kyle, 51n
Curran, Sara R., 114

Daniels, Michael J., 21
Danziger, Sheldon, 267
Datta, G. S., 21
Davies, R. B., 274
Dawid, A. Philip, 13
De Graaf, Nan, 8
De Leeuw, Jan, 236, 237, 249
Delfiner, Pierre, 27
Dempster, Arthur P., 21
Denton, Nancy A., 27
Devlin, Susan J., 276n
Diekmann, Andreas, 15
Dijkstra, W., 29
DiPrete, Thomas A., 21, 111, 119
Dirac, Gabriel A., 333n
Dominitz, Jeff, 111
Doreian, Patrick, 306, 327
Du, J. T., 25
Duncan, Beverly, 27
Duncan, Greg, 51n
Duncan, Otis Dudley, 4, 6, 11, 12, 12f, 13, 27
Duneier, Mitchell, 52
Durkheim, Emile, 2
Durlauf, Steven, 50, 51n, 61, 62, 66, 71, 74, 78, 79, 79n, 81, 84, 107, 108n, 113, 116

Earls, Felton, 51n, 83
Eisenberg, Theodore, 2
Eliason, Scott R., 6
Elliott, Michael R., 21
Elster, Jon, 70
Entwisle, Barbara, 21, 114
Erbring, Lutz, 108n, 109, 112

Even, Shimon, 324
Everett, Martin G., 324n, 326, 349

Fahrmeir, Ludwig, 15
Fararo, Thomas, 306, 365
Faust, K., 26, 309, 329, 351
Fay, Robert E., 22
Featherman, David L., 11, 25, 218
Ferguson, Linda R., 15
Festinger, Leon, 310
Fienberg, Stephen E., 2, 9, 374
Fisher, R. A., 92t, 251
Flay, Brian R., 274
Ford, Lester R., 331, 332, 333
Formann, Anton K., 237, 249, 250, 255
Forristal, Jerry D., 21, 111, 119
Foster, Brian L., 328
Fraley, Christina, 30, 224
Frank, Ove, 26, 388
Franzosi, Roberto, 28, 29
Freedman, David A., 12
Freeman, Linton C., 319, 329n, 354n
French, John R. P., Jr., 310n
Fulkerson, David R., 331, 332, 333

Gagnon, J., 26
Ganzeboom, Harry B. G., 7
Gatsonis, Constantine, 21
Gelman, Andrew, 21
Gibbons, Alan, 324
Gilks, Walter R., 14
Gilula, Zvi, 133, 138, 139, 145, 146, 160, 162, 163, 164, 167, 169, 182, 224, 230, 232, 232n, 235, 236, 236n, 237, 249, 251, 257, 261n
Givens, Geof H., 30
Glaeser, Edward, 56n, 59
Glass, David V., 5
Glymour, Clark, 14, 24
Gnanadesikan, Ramanathan, 276n
Godecker, Amy L., 114, 114n
Goldberg, Jack, 274
Goldstein, Harvey, 21
Good, Irving J., 137
Goodman, Leo A., 6, 8, 9, 133, 134, 154, 157, 190, 191, 192, 210n, 215n, 219, 220, 224, 227, 230, 249, 255
Gottschalk, Peter, 267, 270
Govaert, Gérard, 9
Gower, John C., 233n
Grannis, Richard, 315, 350
Granovetter, Mark, 49n, 69, 110, 112, 117, 316
Gray, R., 18
Green, Jerry, 54n, 65
Green, Peter J., 280
Greenacre, Michael J., 133, 233n
Gross, Neal, 310
Grusky, David, 8, 9
Guilkey, David K., 114
Guttman, Louis, 133, 134, 154
Guttorp, Peter, 30

Haberman, Shelby J., 6, 131, 132, 133, 134, 138, 139, 140, 145, 146, 160, 162, 163, 164, 167, 169, 182, 224, 225, 226n, 230, 236, 237, 249, 251, 255, 262
Hagenaars, Jacques A., 9, 224, 227, 230, 246
Haider, Steven, 270
Hand, David J., 233n
Handcock, Mark S., 10, 270, 272, 279, 280, 285, 287, 290, 290n, 300
Hannan, Michael T., 14
Hanneman, R. A., 30
Harary, Frank, 307, 309, 321n, 322, 323, 324, 326n, 327, 328n, 329, 329n, 333n, 336n
Harvey, O., 52
Hauser, Robert M., 9, 11, 12, 13, 25, 112, 119, 218
Heckerman, David, 9
Heckman, James J., 18, 25, 50n, 53n
Hedeker, Donald, 274, 300
Hedges, Larry J., 21

Heimer, Karen, 13f
Heinen, T., 133, 224, 244, 255
Henry, Neal W., 224
Henry, Neil W., 8, 133
Hermalin, A. I., 21
Hill, D. H., 15
Hill, Jennifer L., 25
Hirshleifer, David, 58n
Hoeting, Jennifer A., 300
Hoijtink, H., 14
Holland, Paul, 25, 362, 374
Hood, W., 52
Horowitz, Joel, 78
Hosmer, David W., 17, 18
Hotz, V. Joseph, 25
Hout, Michael, 6, 7, 7t, 8, 9, 17, 190, 191, 192, 196n, 210n, 215n, 219
Hrycak, Alexandra, 29
Hu, Frank B., 274
Hummon, Norman P., 365
Hunt, Lyn, 224

Iacobucci, D., 362
Iversen, G. R., 20, 115, 119

Jackman, Simon, 31
Jain, Pawan K., 280n
Jankowski, Martín, 196n
Jeffreys, Harold, 166
Jencks, Christopher, 113
Jenkins, Gwilym, 275
Jennings, Helen H., 310
Johnson, Joyce S., 245
Jolliffe, Ian T., 276n, 289n
Jones, K. S., 28
Jones, M. C., 275
Jöreskog, Karl G., 12
Jorgensen, Murray, 224

Kadushin, Charles, 329n, 354n
Kagel, John H., 103
Kahneman, Daniel, 96
Kalmijn, M., 8
Kandel, Denise B., 30
Kannel, W., 16
Karlin, S., 364
Kass, Robert E., 9, 17, 26, 31, 166
Katz, Elihu, 112
Katz, Lawrence, 51
Katz, Leo, 362
Kettenring, John R., 276n
Kim, Hyojoung, 30
Kindel, P., 237
Klebanov, P., 51n
Kling, Jeffrey, 51
Knorr-Held, Leo, 15
Kodama, Yuji, 323
Kohlmann, Thomas, 237
Kolchin, Valentin F., 338n
Koput, Kenneth W., 307n
Koster, Jan, 14
Kozol, Jonathan, 50n
Kranton, Rachel, 53n, 103
Krueger, Alan, 50n
Krugman, Paul, 72, 74
Kruskal, J. B., 29
Krzanowski, W. J., 224
Kuo, H. H. D., 13
Kushner, Herbert J., 377, 391

Lahiri, Partha, 21
Laird, Nan M., 21
Lang, Joseph B., 8
Laumann, Edward O., 26
Lauritzen, Steffan, 13
Lawler, Edward J., 341
Lawrence, C. E., 29
Lawrence, C. J., 224
Layne-Farrar, Anne, 50n
Lazarsfeld, Paul F., 8, 133, 224
Leenders, Roger Th. A. J., 362, 364
Leinhardt, Samuel, 362
Lemeshow, Stanley, 17, 18
Lesaffre, Emmanuel, 300
Lesthaeghe, Ron J., 113n
Levy, Frank, 267
Lewis, Steven M., 15

Liang, Kung-Yee, 267, 273
Lieberson, Stanley L., 30
Liebman, Jeffrey, 51
Lindley, Dennis V., 20
Lindstrom, Mary J., 283n, 300
Little, Roderick J. A., 21, 22, 276n, 289n
Liu, J. S., 29
Locantore, N., 276n
Logan, John A., 17
Long, J. Scott, 13, 16
Longford, Nicholas, 21, 274
Louie, Miriam Ching Yoon, 117
Loury, Glenn, 50, 50n
Lu, K. L., 21
Luijkx, Ruud, 7
Lynch, G. S., 9
Lynch, Kevin G., 278, 300

Maddala, G. S., 363, 368
Madigan, David, 300
Magee, W. J., 28
Magidson, J., 224, 233n, 252, 259n, 261, 262
Maiti, T., 21
Manski, Charles C., 25, 51n, 55, 74, 74n, 76, 79n, 83
Manski, Charles F., 25, 108n, 109n, 111, 112n, 119
Mare, Robert D., 18
Markovsky, Barry, 341
Marron, J. S., 276n
Marsden, Peter V., 15
Martin, William E., 310
Marwell, Gerald, 114
Mas-Colell, Andrea, 54n, 65
Mason, William M., 9, 21
Massey, Douglas S., 27
Matheron, Georges, 27
Matsueda, Ross L., 13f
Mattussek, S., 237
Mayer, Karl Ulrich, 14
Mayer, Susan E., 113
Mayer, T. F., 362, 366
McAdam, Doug, 114
McCullagh, Peter, 18
McCulloch, Charles E., 274
McCullouch, Robert, 21
McCutcheon, Allan L., 224, 227, 230, 232n
McLachlan, Geoffrey J., 224
McManus, Douglas, 79
McMurrer, Daniel, 267
Meek, Christopher, 14, 24
Menger, Karl, 329, 353
Menzel, Herbert, 112
Michael, R., 26
Michaels, S., 26
Minick, Susan S., 8
Mizruchi, Mark S., 350
Moffitt, Robert, 74, 270
Mollié, Annie, 27
Monro, S., 363, 377
Moody, James, 305, 309, 319, 320, 325n, 350, 352
Moore, Gwen, 354n
Mordt, Gabriele, 30
Moreno, Jacob L., 310
Morenoff, Jeffrey, 51n, 83
Morowitz, Harold, 307n
Morris, Carl N., 20
Morris, Martina, 10, 27, 30, 270, 272, 290, 290n
Mosteller, Frederich, 137
Moustaki, Irini, 224
Mrvar, Andrej, 342f
Murnane, Robert, 267
Muthén, Bengt, 13, 277n, 278, 300

Nagin, Daniel S., 9, 25, 278, 300
Nakao, Keiko, 11
Nelder, John A., 16, 18
Neuwald, A. F., 29
Newman, Mark, 305, 309, 311, 330, 332n, 345, 349
Nordmoe, Erie D., 179
Norman, Robert, 309, 321n, 329n
Norris, J. R., 364

Ogden, R. Todd, 280
Oliver, Pamela E., 114
Olkin, Ingram, 21
Omar, R., 21
Ostrom, Elinor, 103
Owen-Smith, Jason, 307n

Padgett, John F., 26
Palloni, Alberto, 112n, 113
Palmer, Edgar N., 338n
Pattison, Philippa, 26, 27, 388
Pearl, Judea, 24
Pearlin, Leonard I., 245
Pentz, Mary A., 274
Petersen, Trond, 14
Pflug, Georg Ch., 377, 391
Pinheiro, José, 300
Podolny, Joel, 15
Polyak, B. T., 377, 390
Poole, David, 30
Portes, Alejandro, 115n
Powell, Walter W., 307n
Powers, Daniel, 16
Prahl, Ralph, 114
Prentice, Ross L., 267, 273
Proctor, Charles H., 362

Rabin, Matthew, 98, 103
Raftery, Adrian E., 7, 9, 10, 14, 15, 17, 26, 30, 31, 166, 224, 277n, 300
Ragin, Charles, 30
Ramakrishnan, Viswanathan, 300
Ramsay, James O., 283, 283n
Rao, J. N. K., 22
Rasch, George, 134, 157
Raspe, H. H., 237
Raudenbush, Stephen W., 21, 28
Raudenbush, Steven, 75n
Raykov, Tenko, 275n
Reagan, Patricia, 51n
Reiss, Albert J., Jr., 29
Rice, John A., 276, 280, 282, 286n
Richardson, Sylvia, 14
Richardson, Thomas S., 14, 24
Rindfuss, Ronald R., 114
Robbins, H., 363, 377
Roberts, Carl W., 28, 29
Roeder, Kathryn, 9, 278, 300
Roemer, John, 82
Rogoff, Nathalie, 5
Rosenbaum, James, 51
Rossi, Peter, 21
Roth, Alvin E., 103, 103n
Rubin, Donald B., 21, 22, 25
Rubinowitz, Leonard, 51
Rubinstein, Ariel, 58
Ruppert, David, 377, 390
Ryff, Carol D., 28

Sampson, Robert J., 28, 51n, 83
Sankoff, D., 29
Savage, Leonard J., 133, 136, 138
Savage, M., 29
Sawangdee, Yothin, 114
Sawhill, Isabel, 267
Sayed, H. A. A., 21
Schachter, Stanley, 310
Schaeffer, Nora C., 245
Schafer, Joseph L., 22
Scheines, Richard, 14, 24
Scheinkman, José, 56n, 59
Schelling, Thomas, 71
Schriever, B. F., 133
Schuessler, Karl F., 4
Schwarz, Gideon, 9, 149, 163, 165, 166, 167, 169, 300
Scott, John, 323, 324n, 329n
Scott, Marc, 270, 272, 279, 280, 285, 287, 290, 290n, 300
Sealand, N., 51n
Seidman, Stephen B., 327, 328
Sensenbrenner, Julia, 115n
Shedden, Kerby, 277n, 278, 300
Shenton, L. R., 372, 374
Sheridan, Jennifer T., 11
Sherif, C., 52
Sherif, Muzafer, 52

Shirley, Paul, 326
Sikkel, D., 249
Silverman, Bernard W., 276, 280, 283, 283n, 286n
Siminoff, Jeffrey S., 300
Simmel, Georg, 309, 354n
Simpson, D. G., 276n
Singer, Burton, 28
Smith, Adrian F. M., 20
Snijders, Tom A. B., 21, 362, 363, 372, 374, 377, 378, 383
Sobel, Michael E., 2, 8, 12, 25, 276n, 289n
Soong, Roland, 49n, 110, 112, 117
Sorensen, Ann Marie, 8
South, Scott, 51n
Spiegelhalter, David J., 13, 14
Spirtes, Peter, 14, 24
Stein, Daniel, 71
Stern, Hal S., 21
Stevens, Gillian, 11
Stovel, Katherine, 29
Strang, David, 15, 112, 118
Strauss, David, 26, 388
Sucoff, Clea, 51n

Taris, T., 29
Taylor, H. M., 364
Theil, Henri, 148
Thompson, Elizabeth A., 27
Thompson, S., 21
Thomson, Elizabeth, 114, 114n
Thornton, A., 15
Tobin, James, 18
Todd, Petra, 50n
Tomes, Nigel, 50
Topel, Robert H., 272
Treas, Judith, 11
Treiman, Donald J., 7, 11
Tripoli, N., 276n
Truett, J., 16
Tsai, Chih-Ling, 300
Tuma, Nancy Brandon, 14, 15
Turner, R., 21
Tutte, William T., 322
Tversky, Amos, 96

Udry, J. R., 26
Uebersax, J. S., 224
Upchurch, Dawn, 51n

Van de Bunt, Gerhard G., 363, 378, 384
Van de Geer, John P., 133
Van der Ark, L. Andries, 224, 225, 230, 232, 232n, 235, 236n, 237, 249, 257, 261n
Van der Heijden, Peter G. M., 224, 225, 230, 232, 232n, 235, 236, 236n, 237, 249, 257, 261n
Van Duijn, Marijtje A. J., 363, 374, 377, 378, 383
Verbeke, Geert, 300
Verma, T., 24
Vermunt, Jeroen K., 224, 233n, 252, 259n, 261, 262
Volinsky, Chris T., 300
Vonesh, Edward F., 300

Wahl, R. J., 6
Walden, Andrew T., 30
Walker, James R., 113
Wallace, David L., 137
Wallis, Kenneth, 74
Walters, R., 48n
Walzer, Michael, 82
Ward, Michael P., 272
Warren, John R., 11
Wasmus, A., 237
Wasserman, Larry, 9, 166
Wasserman, Stanley, 26, 27, 309, 329, 351, 362, 364, 383, 388
Watkins, Susan C., 113n
Watts, Duncan J., 320, 338n, 351, 352, 352n
Weakliem, David L., 8, 10
Wedderburn, R. W. M., 16

Weinberg, Bruce, 51n
Welch, Ivo, 58n
Western, Bruce, 31
Whinston, Michael, 54n, 65
White, B., 52
White, Douglas R., 305, 307n, 309, 311, 320, 325n, 330, 332n, 345, 349, 350, 352, 353
White, Harrison C., 26
Whitney, Hassler, 327
Willett, P., 28
Wilson, William Julius, 51
Winship, Christopher, 18
Wolfe, John H., 224
Wong, G. Y., 21
Woodward, Katherine L., 327
Wooton, J. C., 29
Wright, Erik Olin, 196n
Wright, Sewall, 12, 92t

Xie, Yu, 2, 8, 15, 16, 191, 210n, 214
Xu, Weichun, 300

Yamaguchi, Kazuo, 8, 14, 15, 27, 30, 191, 202, 210n, 214
Yang, I., 8
Yang, M., 21
Yankow, Jeffrey, 51n
Yeomans, Julia, 70n
Yin, George, 377, 391
York, Jeremy, 27
Young, Alice A., 108n, 109, 112

Zachary, Wayne W., 317, 333, 341
Zaslavsky, Alan, 21
Zeger, Scott L., 267, 273
Zeggelink, Evelien P. H., 363
Zeh, Judith E., 30
Zhang, J. T., 276n

SUBJECT INDEX

abortion attitudes data, application of categorical profiles to, 166–79
adhesion. *See* social networks, *subheading* cohesion and adhesion
Akaike information criterion, 163–5
asymptotic distribution and relation with the *p* model, 388–9

BIC, use of, 9, 10
binary choice model (social interactions), 78–80
binary decision rules (social interactions), 60–5
  multiple equilibria, 66–8
  properties of, 65–9
  social welfare, 68–9
bi-plots (LC models)
  conditional probabilities, formulation using, 255–7
  1982 General Social Survey data (LC models), 233–7
  restricted two-factor model, 244, 245
  rheumatoid arthritis data, 242
  two-factor model, 251–1, 254
Bowle's commentary re: Durlaf's approach to social interactions, 89–96
  Durlaf's response, 123–4

categorical data analysis, 5–8
  categorical profiles. *See* categorical profiles
  latent class (LC) models. *See* latent class (LC) models
  multiway tables, association in. *See* multiway tables, association in
categorical profiles, 130–4
  abortion attitudes data, application to, 166–79
  conditional independence of response variables given an explanatory variable, 150–2
  Guttman scaling, 154
  models and data summaries, 134–6
    entropy and logarithmic penalty function, 136–8
    estimation, 160–2, 180–2
    examples of, 149–60
    information from summaries, 145–6
    log-linear models, 139–42
    normal approximations, 162, 182–5
    optimal prediction, 143–5, 180
    prediction sets, comparison under sampling, 146–9, 163–6
    probability prediction functions, 138–9
  mutual independence of response variables, 149–50
  prediction sets, comparison under sampling, 146–9
    Akaike information criterion, 163–5

- Bayesian information criterion, 165–6
- hypothesis tests, 163
- saturated model for a categorical explanatory variable, 142–5
- saturated model without explanatory variables, 141
- symmetric interactions associated with category accounts, 155
- symmetric interactions with scored reactions, 155–9
- two-way interactions associated with average responses and explanatory variables, 159–62
- two-way interactions of response variables, 152–4
- two-way interactions of responses and a categorical explanatory variable, 154–5

causality in unit-level survey data, 23–6
cohesion. *See* social networks, *subheading* cohesion and adhesion
conditional density. *See* social networks
counterfactual approach to causality, 24, 25–6
covariance models for latent structure (in longitudinal data), 265–72
- application and comparison, 289–99
- confidence intervals, construction of, 300–1
- general multiple proto-spline model, 282–3
- illustration, 287–9
- individual-specific analysis, 273–5
- latent class (LC) models, 277–8
- latent curve models, 275–7
  - double latent curve model, 293–5
  - single latent curve model, 291–3
- population-average analysis, 273
- proto-spline models
  - general multiple proto-spline model, 282–3
  - mixed effects models, link to, 283–7
  - single proto-spline model, 279–81, 291–3
- random quadratic model, 290–1
- single proto-spline model, 279–81, 291–3
- variance partitions, comparing, 295–8

Cox model, 14–15
cross-tabulations
- categorical data analysis, 5–8
- historical overview, 3–4
- hypothesis testing and model selection, 9–10
- latent class models. *See* latent class (LC) models

Dechter's commentary re: Durlaf's approach to social interactions, 107–20
- Durlaf's response, 127–8

double latent curve model, 293–5

ecometrics, 28–9
economic models of individual choice, 49. *See also* social interactions/ interdependence
entropy and logarithmic penalty function, 136–8
event-history analysis, 14–15, 14–17

fixed effects multilevel model, 19–20
Ford-Fulkerson Corollaries/Theorems
- Global Ford-Fulkerson (Edge-Cut) Theorem, 333
- Global Ford-Fulkerson (Node-Flow-Edge-Cut) Corollary, 332
- Local Ford-Fulkerson (Edge-Cut) Theorem, 333
- Local Ford-Fulkerson (Node-Flow-Edge-Cut) Corollary, 332

future directions, 31–3

general multiple proto-spline model, 282–3
geostatistics models, 27

Global Ford-Fulkerson (Edge-Cut) Theorem, 333
Global Ford-Fulkerson (Node-Flow-Edge-Cut) Corollary, 332
Global Menger's Theorem A, 330
Global Menger's Theorem B, 333
graphical displays/models, 24
  latent class (LC) models
    1982 General Social Survey data (LC models), 232–7
    restricted two-factor model, 247–8
    rheumatoid arthritis data, 240–3
    two-factor model, 251–1, 253
  social networks (cohesion and adhesion), 321–2
    connectivity and multiple independent paths as cohesion, 329–30
    connectivity and resistance to pulling apart by removal of nodes, 322–5
    edge connectivity, and resistance to pulling apart by removal of edges, 325–9
    edge connectivity and edge-independent paths as adhesion, 333–4
    edge-flow connectivity and node-flow connectivity, 330–2
Guttman scaling, 154

historical overview, 1–5

imputation, 21–2
individual choice-based framework, 53–9. *See also* social interactions/interdependence
  binary decision rules, 60–5
  linear decision rules, 59–60
inequality, poverty and, 50–2

job satisfaction and self-employment status, 196–8
  partitioning association, 212–14
  unconstrained intercepts, models with, 210–12
  uniform association, models based on, 198–210

latent class (LC) models, 8–9, 223–5
  1982 General Social Survey data, 230–7
  bi-plots
    conditional probabilities, formulation using, 255–7
    1982 General Social Survey data (LC models), 233–7
    restricted two-factor model, 244, 245
    rheumatoid arthritis data, 242
    two-factor model, 251–1, 254
  class-membership probabilities, functions of, 257–61
  cluster model, 225–7
  covariance models for latent structure (in longitudinal data), 277–8
    single latent curve model, 291–3
  estimation of, 261–2
  factor model, 227–30
    extensions to, 244–9
  graphic displays
    1982 General Social Survey data (LC models), 232–7
    restricted two-factor model, 247–8
    rheumatoid arthritis data, 240–3
    two-factor model, 251–1, 253
  identification issues, 249–52
  rheumatoid arthritis data, 237–43
latent curve models, 275–7
  double latent curve model, 293–5
  single latent curve model, 291–3
LC models. *See* latent class (LC) models
limited dependent variables, 16, 17–19
linear decision rules (social interactions), 59–60
linear-in-means models (social interactions), 74–8

LISREL model, 13, 14
Local Ford-Fulkerson (Edge-Cut) Theorem, 333
Local Ford-Fulkerson (Node-Flow-Edge-Cut) Corollary, 332
Local Menger's Theorem A, 330
Local Menger's Theorem B, 333
logistic regression, 16, 17–18
log-linear models (categorical profiles), 139–42
log-log regression, 17
longitudinal data analysis. *See* covariance models for latent structure (in longitudinal data)

macrosociology, 30–1
MAR (missing at random), 23
Markov chains
  continuous, 362, 364–5. *See also* social networks, *subheading* dynamics, evaluation of
  Markov chain Monte Carlo (MCMC) methods, 363
  with random utility component, 367–8
Markov models, 13, 14
Markov random fields, 27
MCAR (missing completely at random), 22
MCMC (Markov chain Monte Carlo) methods, 363
"memberships theory of inequality," 50
Menger's Theorems
  Global Menger's Theorem A, 330
  Global Menger's Theorem B, 333
  Local Menger's Theorem A, 330
  Local Menger's Theorem B, 333
methodological individualism, 69–70
missing at random (MAR), 23
missing completely at random (MCAR), 22
missing data (unit-level survey data), 21–3
moment estimators (social networks), 373–7
multilevel models (unit-level survey data), 19–21
multiple imputation, 22–3
multiway tables, association in, 190
  job satisfaction and self-employment status, 196–8
    partitioning association, 212–14
    unconstrained intercepts, models with, 210–12
    uniform association, models based on, 198–210
  regression-type approach, 190–1
    layer scores, identification of, 192–5
    special cases of the general model, 192
  social (nonfarm) mobility in three countries, 214–19

narrative and sequence analysis, 29–30
networks. *See* social networks
1982 General Social Survey data (LC models), 230–7
nominal dependent variables, 17–18
nonergodicity, 72–3

occupational status, measurement of, 11
ordinal dependent variables, 18

path adhesion (social networks), 312–13
path cohesion (social networks), 310–11
population-average analysis, 273
poverty and inequality, 50–2
probit regression, 17
proportional hazards model, 14–15
proto-spline models
  general multiple proto-spline model, 282–3
  mixed effects models, link to, 283–7

single proto-spline model, 279–81, 291–3

qualitative data, 28–9
association between two variables across a third. *See* multiway tables, association in

random effects multilevel models, 20–1
random quadratic model, 290–1
regression imputation, 22
rheumatoid arthritis data (LC Models), 237–43

self-employment status, job satisfaction and, 196–8
partitioning association, 212–14
unconstrained intercepts, models with, 210–12
uniform association, models based on, 198–210
simulation models, 30
single imputation, 22
single latent curve model, 291–3
single proto-spline model, 279–81, 291–3
social interactions/interdependence, 47–53
binary choice model, 78–80
binary decision rules, 60–5
multiple equilibria, 66–8
properties of, 65–9
social welfare, 68–9
Bowle's commentary, 89–96
Durlaf's response, 123–4
Dechter's commentary, 107–20
Durlaf's response, 127–8
future research, 82–3
individual choice-based framework, 53–9
linear decision rules, 59–60
linear-in-means models, 74–8
methodological individualism, 69–70
public policy implications, 80–2
statistical implementation, 74–80
statistical mechanics, 70–1
emergent properties, 71–2
nonergodicity, 72–3
phase transition, 73
symmetry breaking, 72
universality, 73–4
Tao and Winship's commentary, 97–105
Durlaf's response, 124–7
social networks, 26–7
asymptotic distribution and relation with the *p* model, 388–9
cohesion and adhesion, 306–8, 351–6
adhesion hypotheses, 316–18
cohesion hypotheses, 313–16
conditional density and other variables, 318–21, 335–6
connectivity and multiple independent paths as cohesion, 329–30
connectivity and resistance to pulling apart by removal of nodes, 322–5
edge connectivity, and resistance to pulling apart by removal of edges, 325–9
edge connectivity and edge-independent paths as adhesion, 333–4
edge-flow connectivity and node-flow connectivity, 330–2
graph theoretic foundations, 321–34
hierarchical properties of adhesive/cohesive blocks, 334
intuitions and concepts, 308–13
measurement of cohesion, 336–40
path adhesion, 312–13
path cohesion, 310–11
structural adhesion, 312
structural cohesion, 309–10
subgroup cohesion, 341
subgroup inhomogeneities, 341

testing predictiveness of cohesion measures on a large scale, 349–51
Zachary's Karate Club, an empirical example, 341–9
dynamics, evaluation of, 361–3
asymptotic distribution and relation with the p model, 388–9
contiunous-time Markov chains, 364–5
extended model specification, 382–7
moment estimators, 373–7
stochastic actor-oriented models, 365–72
stochastic approximation, 377–8, 390–3
university freshmen, 378–81, 387–8
moment estimators, 373–7
path adhesion, 312–13
path cohesion, 310–11
stochastic actor-oriented models for network evolution, 365
basic model ingredients, 365–6
intensity matrix, 368
Markov chain with random utility component, 367–8
objective function, 366–7
specification of model, 369–72
stochastic approximation, 377–8, 390–3
structural adhesion, 312
structural cohesion, 309–10
university freshmen, evolving network of, 378–81, 387–8
social (nonfarm) mobility in three countries, 214–19
solidarity (social networks), 306
spatial data, 27
statistical mechanics (social interactions), 70–1
emergent properties, 71–2
nonergodicity, 72–3
phase transition, 73
symmetry breaking, 72
universality, 73–4
stochastic actor-oriented models for network evolution, 365
basic model ingredients, 365–6
intensity matrix, 368
Markov chain with random utility component, 367–8
objective function, 366–7
specification of model, 369–72
stochastic approximation (social networks), 377–8, 390–3
structural adhesion (social networks), 312
structural cohesion (social networks), 309–10
structural equation models, 24
uses of, 12–14

Tao and Winship's commentary re: Durlaf's approach to social interactions, 97–105
Durlaf's response, 124–7
textual data, 28
Tobit model, 18
two-sided logit models, 17

unit-level survey data, 10
causality, 23–6
event-history analysis, 14–17
historical overview, 3–4
limited dependent variables, 16, 17–19
missing data, 21–3
multilevel models, 19–21
occupational status, measurement of, 11
structured equation models, uses of, 12–14
university freshmen, evolving network of, 378–81, 387–8

Whitney's Theorem, 328–9